CASE CLOSED™

VOLUME 19

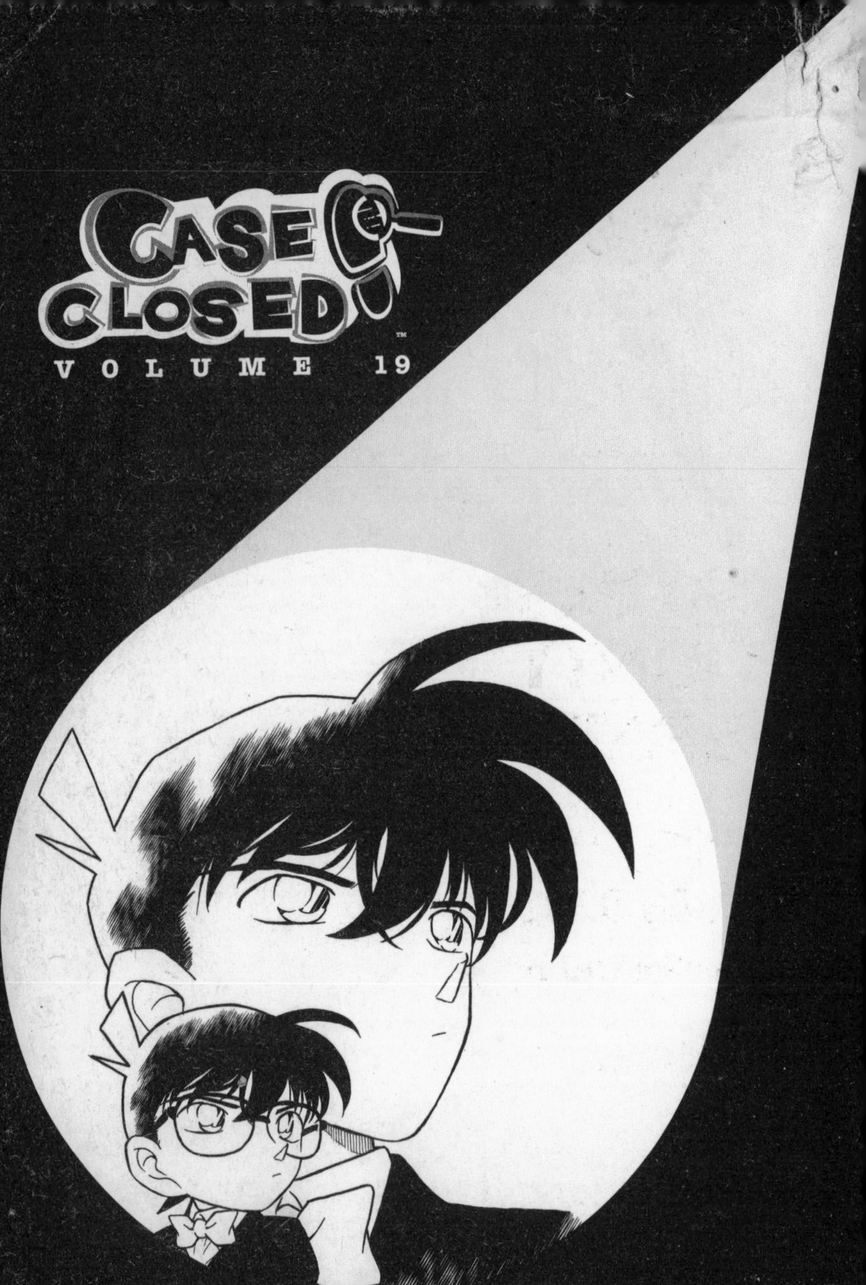

Gosho Aoyama

Case Briefing:

Subject:
Occupation:
Special Skills:
Equipment:

Jimmy Kudo, a.k.a. Conan Edogawa
High School Student/Detective
Analytical thinking and deductive reasoning, Soccer
Bow Tie Voice Transmitter, Super Sneakers,
Homing Glasses, Stretchy Suspenders

The subject is hot on the trail of a pair of suspicious men in black when he is attacked from behind and administered a strange substance which physically transforms him into a first grader. When the subject confides in the eccentric inventor Dr. Agasa, they decide to keep the subject's true identity a secret for the safety of everyone around him. Assuming the new identity of first-grader Conan Edogawa, the subject continues to assist the police force on their most baffling cases. The only problem is that most crime-solving professionals won't take a little kid's advice!

Table of Contents

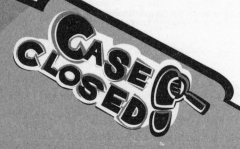

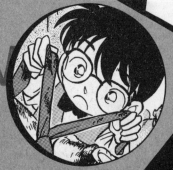

CONFIDEN

CASE CLOSED

Volume 19 • VIZ Media Edition

GOSHO AOYAMA

Translation
Naoko Amemiya

Touch-up & Lettering
Freeman Wong

Cover & Graphics Design
Andrea Rice

Editor
Shaenon K. Garrity

Editor in Chief, Books **Alvin Lu**
Editor in Chief, Magazines **Marc Weidenbaum**
VP of Publishing Licensing **Rika Inouye**
VP of Sales **Gonzalo Ferreyra**
Sr. VP of Marketing **Liza Coppola**
Publisher **Hyoe Narita**

store.viz.com

www.viz.com

Printed in the U.S.A.
Published by VIZ Media, LLC
P.O. Box 77010
San Francisco, CA 94107

10 9 8 7 6 5 4 3 2 1
First printing, September 2007

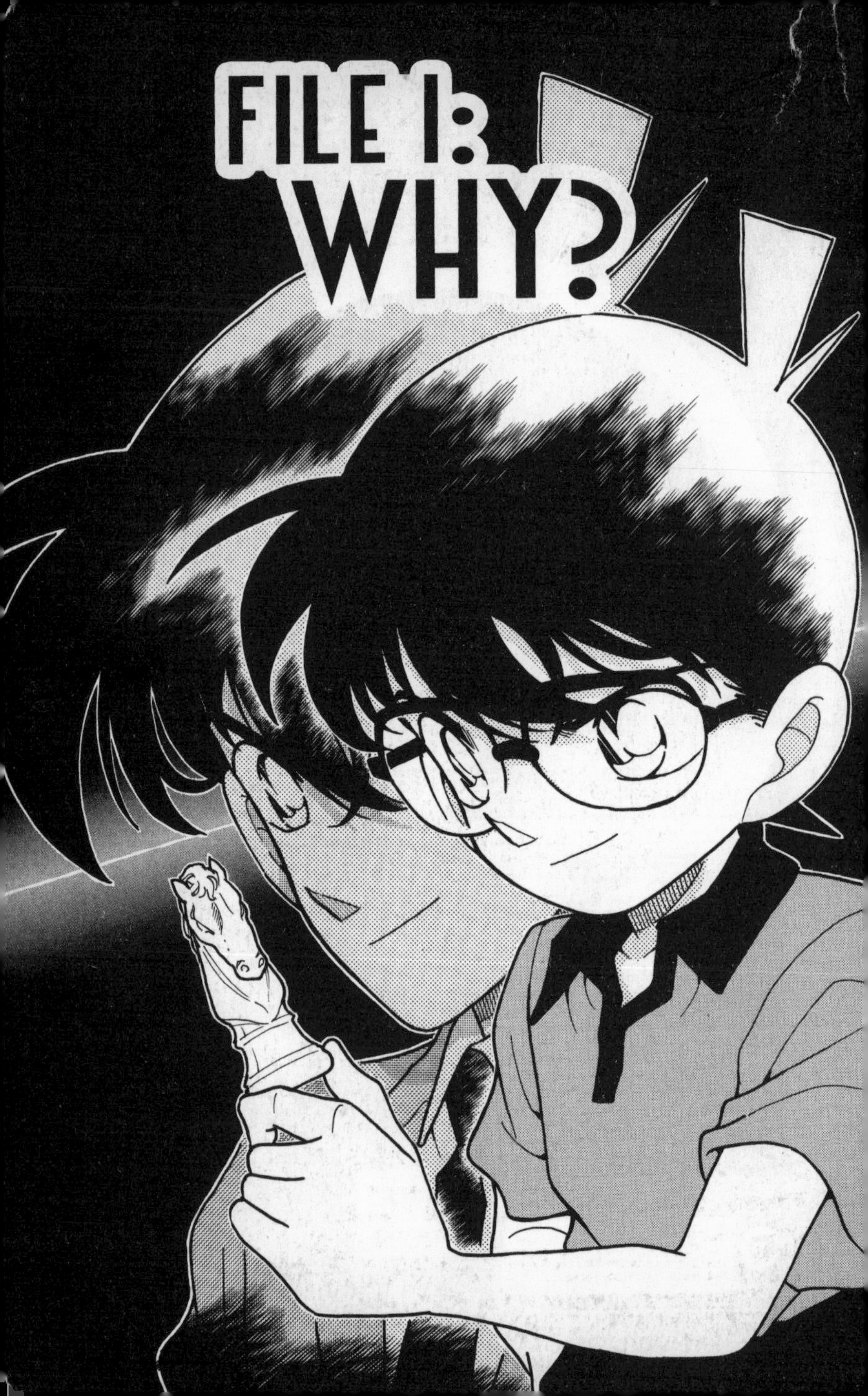
FILE 1:
WHY?

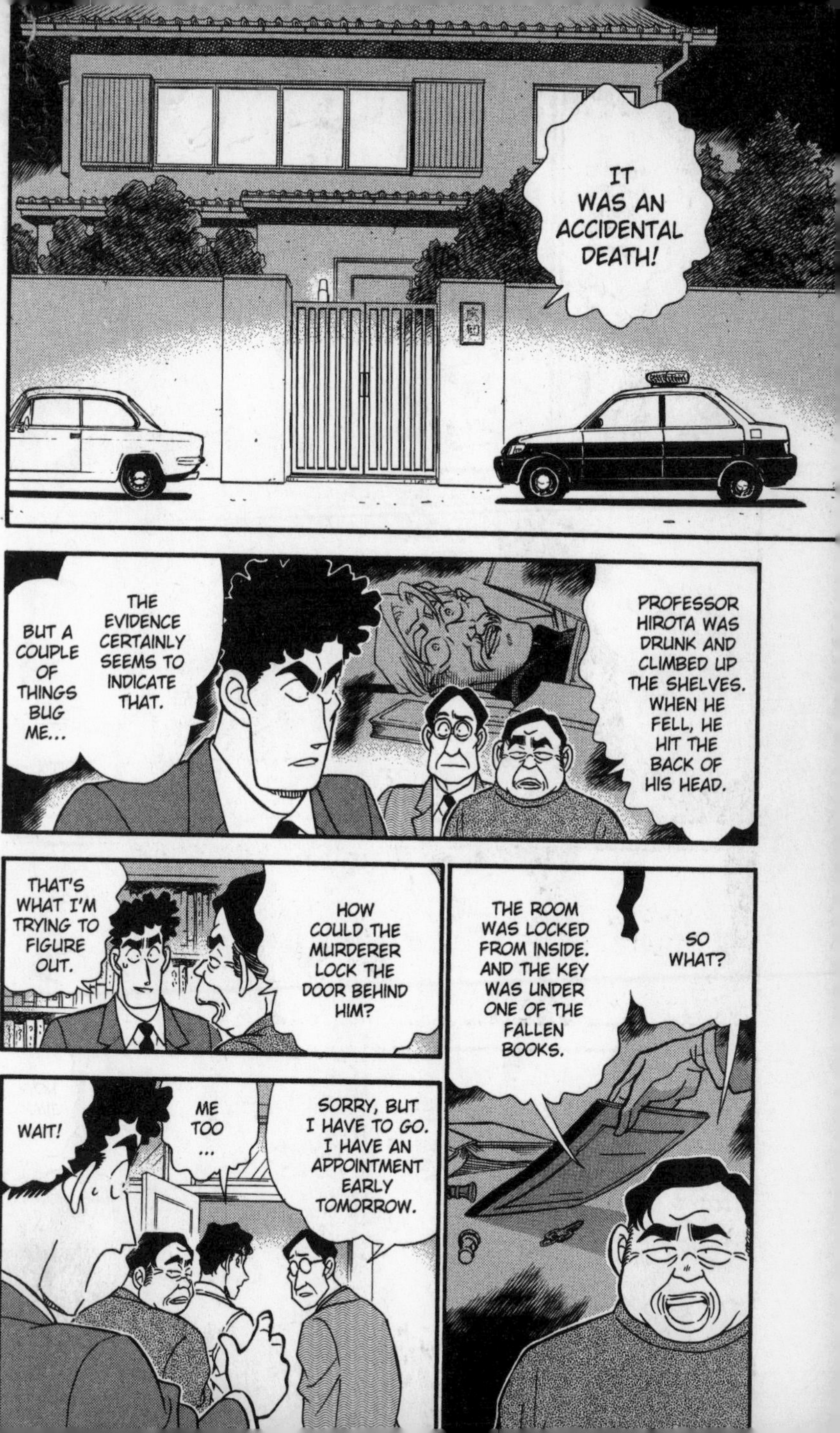
IT WAS AN ACCIDENTAL DEATH!
PROFESSOR HIROTA WAS DRUNK AND CLIMBED UP THE SHELVES. WHEN HE FELL, HE HIT THE BACK OF HIS HEAD.
THE EVIDENCE CERTAINLY SEEMS TO INDICATE THAT.
BUT A COUPLE OF THINGS BUG ME...
SO WHAT?
THE ROOM WAS LOCKED FROM INSIDE. AND THE KEY WAS UNDER ONE OF THE FALLEN BOOKS.
HOW COULD THE MURDERER LOCK THE DOOR BEHIND HIM?
THAT'S WHAT I'M TRYING TO FIGURE OUT.
SORRY, BUT I HAVE TO GO. I HAVE AN APPOINTMENT EARLY TOMORROW.
ME TOO ...
WAIT!

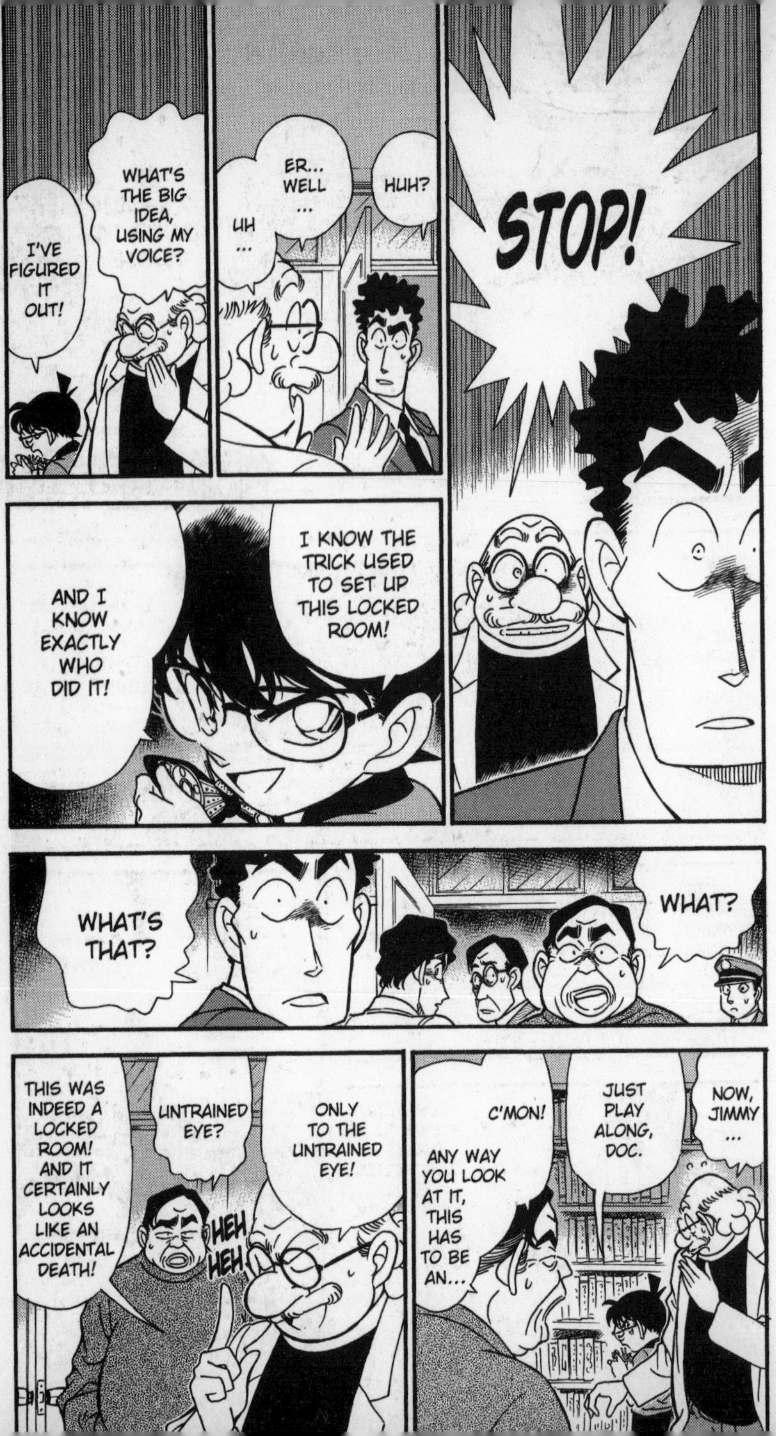
STOP!
HUH?
ER... WELL ...
UH ...
WHAT'S THE BIG IDEA, USING MY VOICE?
I'VE FIGURED IT OUT!
I KNOW THE TRICK USED TO SET UP THIS LOCKED ROOM!
AND I KNOW EXACTLY WHO DID IT!
WHAT?
WHAT'S THAT?
NOW, JIMMY ...
JUST PLAY ALONG, DOC.
C'MON!
ANY WAY YOU LOOK AT IT, THIS HAS TO BE AN...
ONLY TO THE UNTRAINED EYE!
UNTRAINED EYE?
HEH HEH
THIS WAS INDEED A LOCKED ROOM! AND IT CERTAINLY LOOKS LIKE AN ACCIDENTAL DEATH!

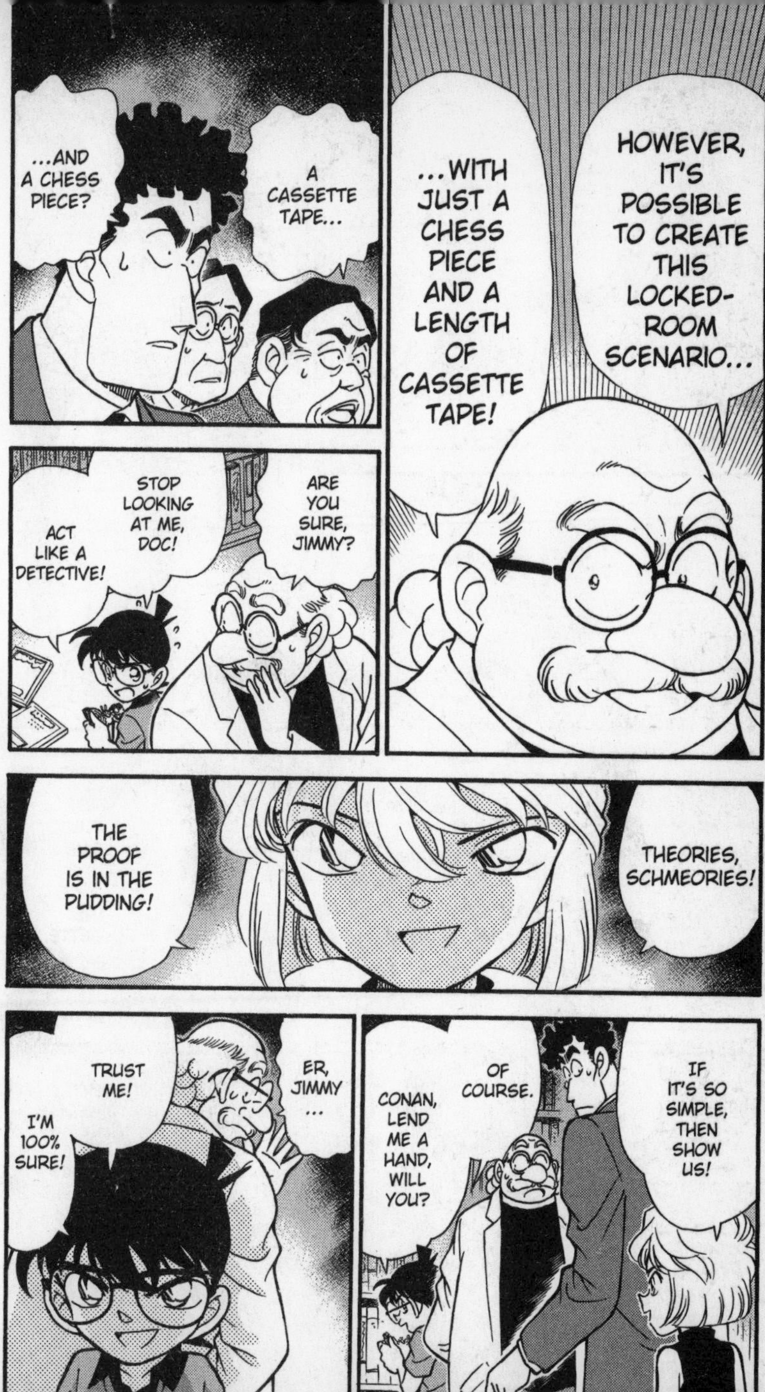
HOWEVER, IT'S POSSIBLE TO CREATE THIS LOCKED-ROOM SCENARIO...
...WITH JUST A CHESS PIECE AND A LENGTH OF CASSETTE TAPE!
A CASSETTE TAPE...
...AND A CHESS PIECE?
ARE YOU SURE, JIMMY?
STOP LOOKING AT ME, DOC!
ACT LIKE A DETECTIVE!
THEORIES, SCHMEORIES!
THE PROOF IS IN THE PUDDING!
IF IT'S SO SIMPLE, THEN SHOW US!
OF COURSE.
CONAN, LEND ME A HAND, WILL YOU?
ER, JIMMY ...
TRUST ME!
I'M 100% SURE!

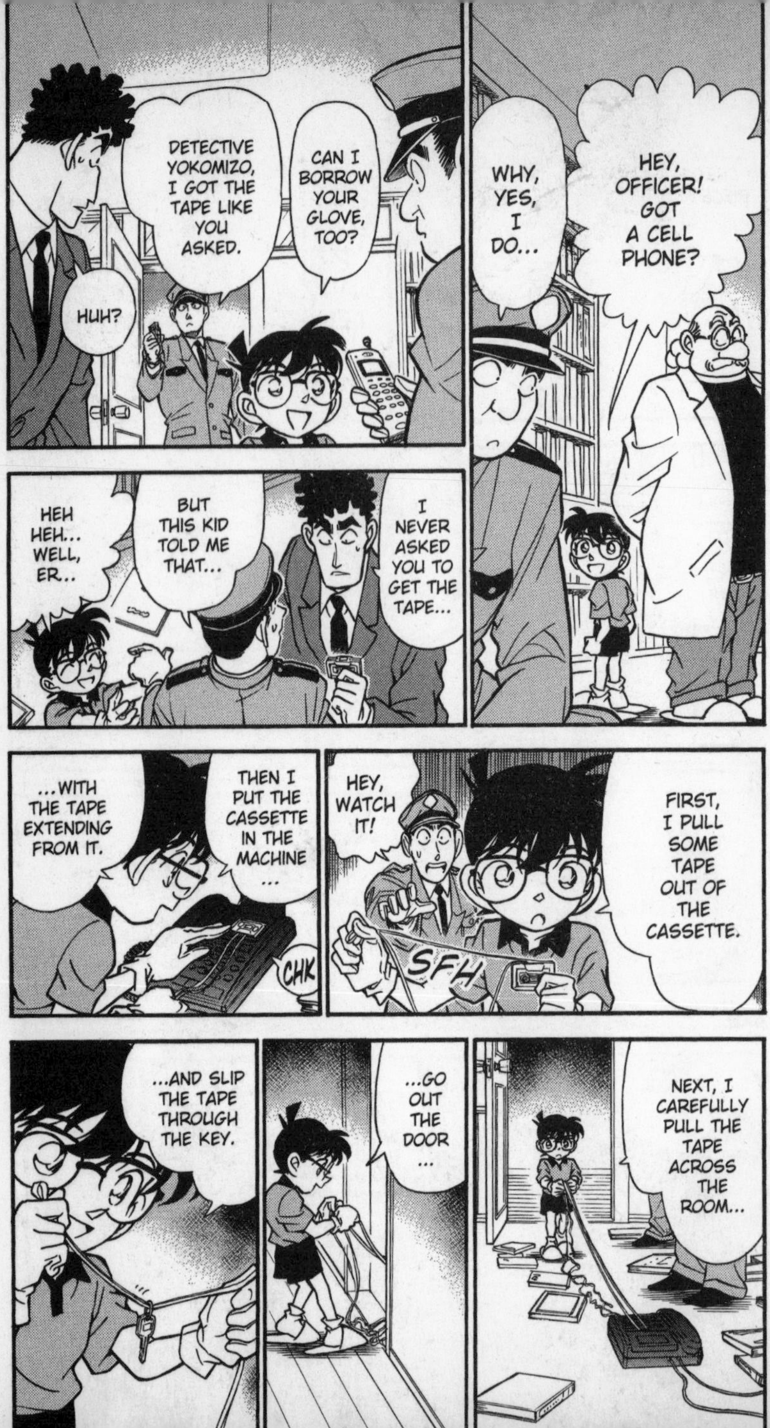
HEY, OFFICER! GOT A CELL PHONE?
WHY, YES, I DO...
CAN I BORROW YOUR GLOVE, TOO?
DETECTIVE YOKOMIZO, I GOT THE TAPE LIKE YOU ASKED.
HUH?
I NEVER ASKED YOU TO GET THE TAPE...
BUT THIS KID TOLD ME THAT...
HEH HEH... WELL, ER...
FIRST, I PULL SOME TAPE OUT OF THE CASSETTE.
HEY, WATCH IT!
SFH
THEN I PUT THE CASSETTE IN THE MACHINE ...
...WITH THE TAPE EXTENDING FROM IT.
CHK
NEXT, I CAREFULLY PULL THE TAPE ACROSS THE ROOM...
...GO OUT THE DOOR ...
...AND SLIP THE TAPE THROUGH THE KEY.

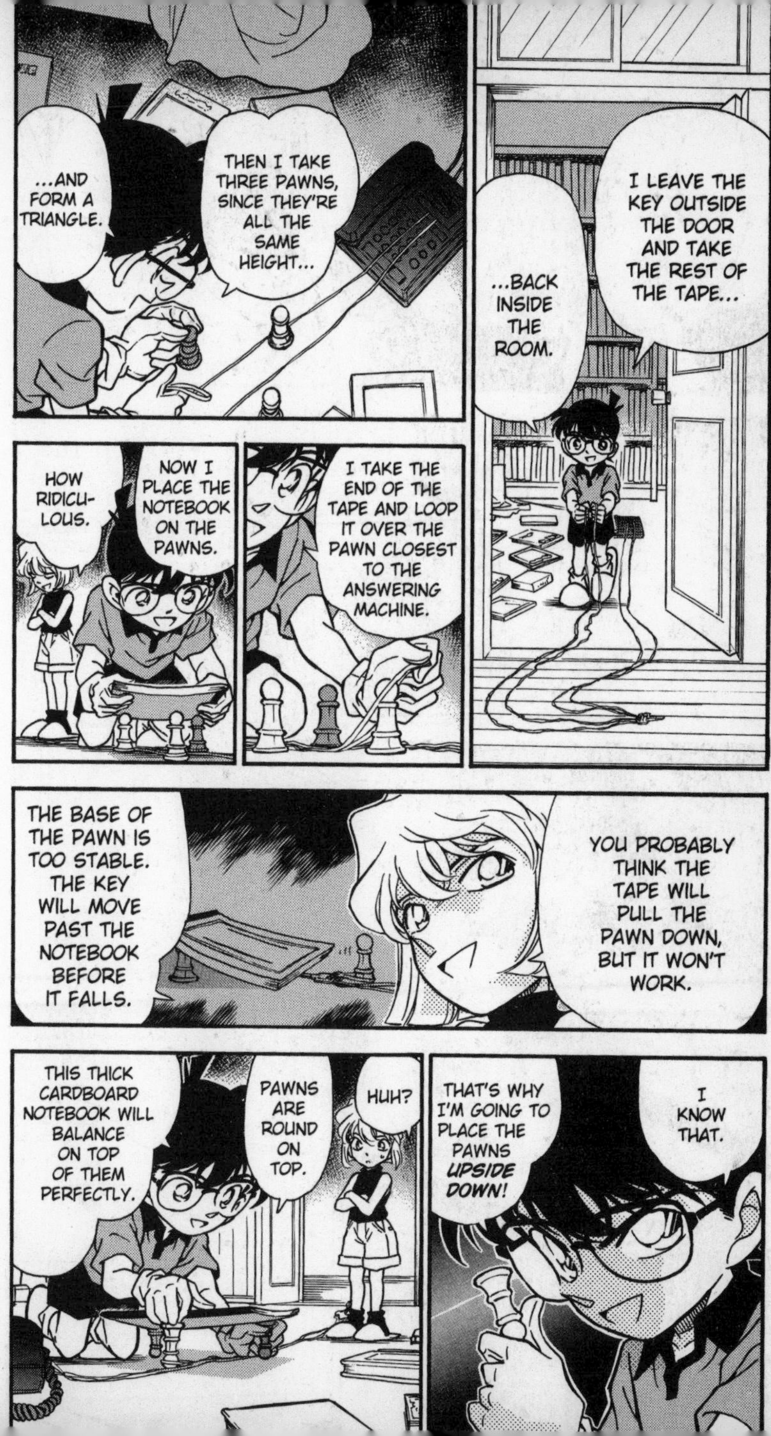
I LEAVE THE KEY OUTSIDE THE DOOR AND TAKE THE REST OF THE TAPE...
...BACK INSIDE THE ROOM.
THEN I TAKE THREE PAWNS, SINCE THEY'RE ALL THE SAME HEIGHT...
...AND FORM A TRIANGLE.
I TAKE THE END OF THE TAPE AND LOOP IT OVER THE PAWN CLOSEST TO THE ANSWERING MACHINE.
NOW I PLACE THE NOTEBOOK ON THE PAWNS.
HOW RIDICULOUS.
YOU PROBABLY THINK THE TAPE WILL PULL THE PAWN DOWN, BUT IT WON'T WORK.
THE BASE OF THE PAWN IS TOO STABLE. THE KEY WILL MOVE PAST THE NOTEBOOK BEFORE IT FALLS.
I KNOW THAT.
THAT'S WHY I'M GOING TO PLACE THE PAWNS *UPSIDE DOWN!*
HUH?
PAWNS ARE ROUND ON TOP.
THIS THICK CARDBOARD NOTEBOOK WILL BALANCE ON TOP OF THEM PERFECTLY.

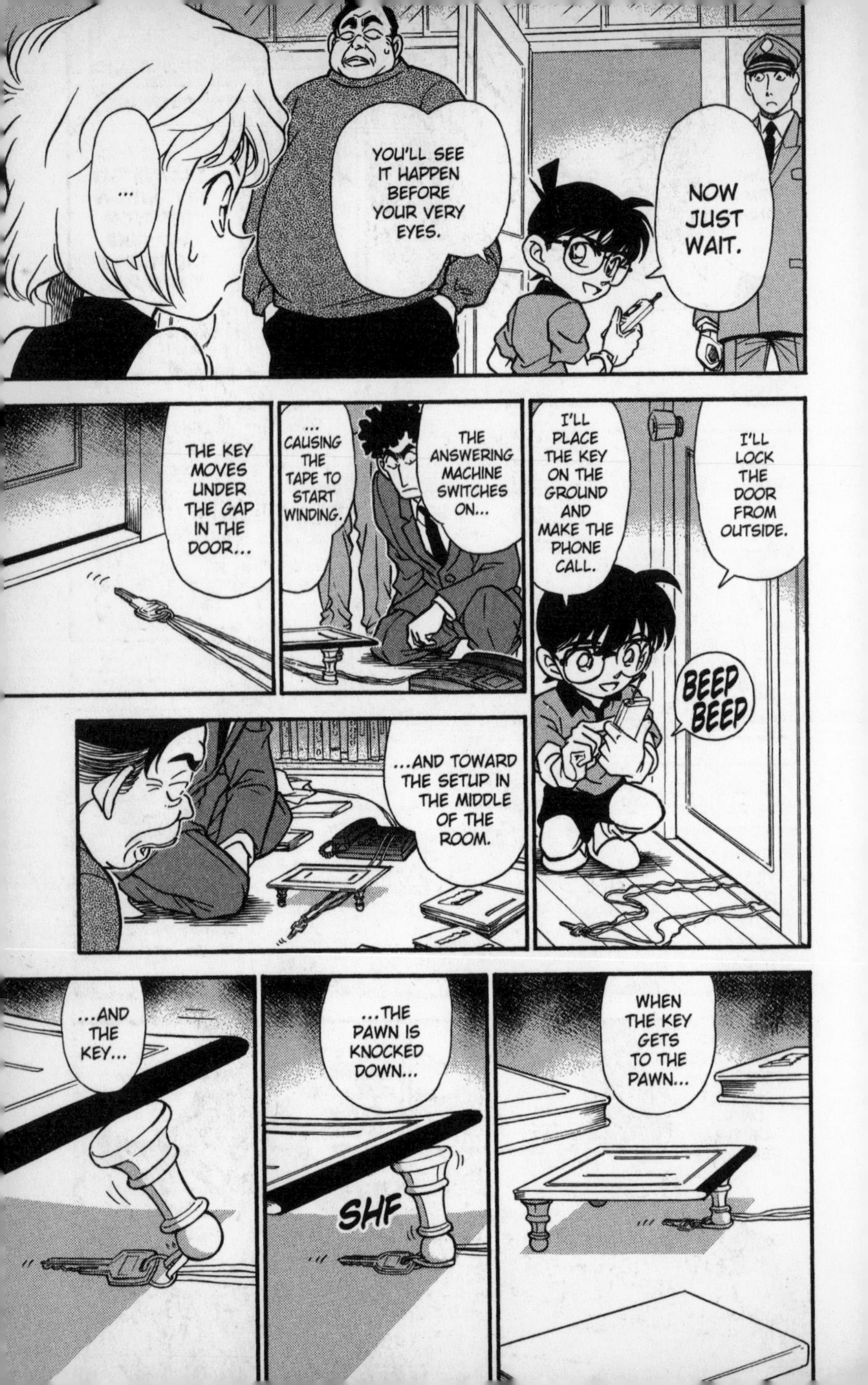
NOW JUST WAIT.
YOU'LL SEE IT HAPPEN BEFORE YOUR VERY EYES.
...
I'LL LOCK THE DOOR FROM OUTSIDE.
I'LL PLACE THE KEY ON THE GROUND AND MAKE THE PHONE CALL.
BEEP BEEP
THE ANSWERING MACHINE SWITCHES ON...
...CAUSING THE TAPE TO START WINDING.
THE KEY MOVES UNDER THE GAP IN THE DOOR...
...AND TOWARD THE SETUP IN THE MIDDLE OF THE ROOM.
WHEN THE KEY GETS TO THE PAWN...
...THE PAWN IS KNOCKED DOWN...
SHF
...AND THE KEY...

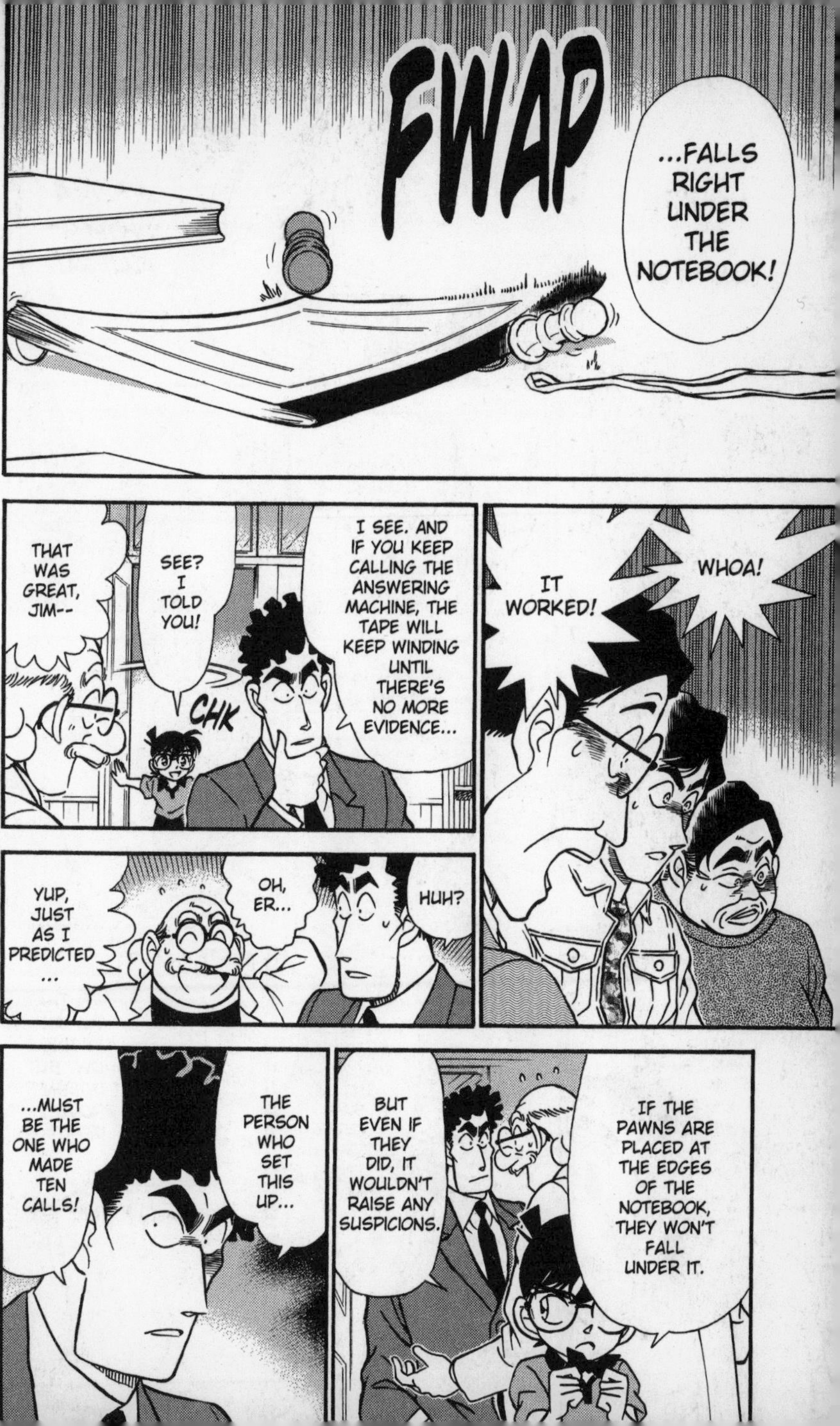
FWAP
...FALLS RIGHT UNDER THE NOTEBOOK!
WHOA!
IT WORKED!
I SEE. AND IF YOU KEEP CALLING THE ANSWERING MACHINE, THE TAPE WILL KEEP WINDING UNTIL THERE'S NO MORE EVIDENCE...
SEE? I TOLD YOU!
CHK
THAT WAS GREAT, JIM--
HUH?
OH, ER...
YUP, JUST AS I PREDICTED...
IF THE PAWNS ARE PLACED AT THE EDGES OF THE NOTEBOOK, THEY WON'T FALL UNDER IT.
BUT EVEN IF THEY DID, IT WOULDN'T RAISE ANY SUSPICIONS.
THE PERSON WHO SET THIS UP...
...MUST BE THE ONE WHO MADE TEN CALLS!

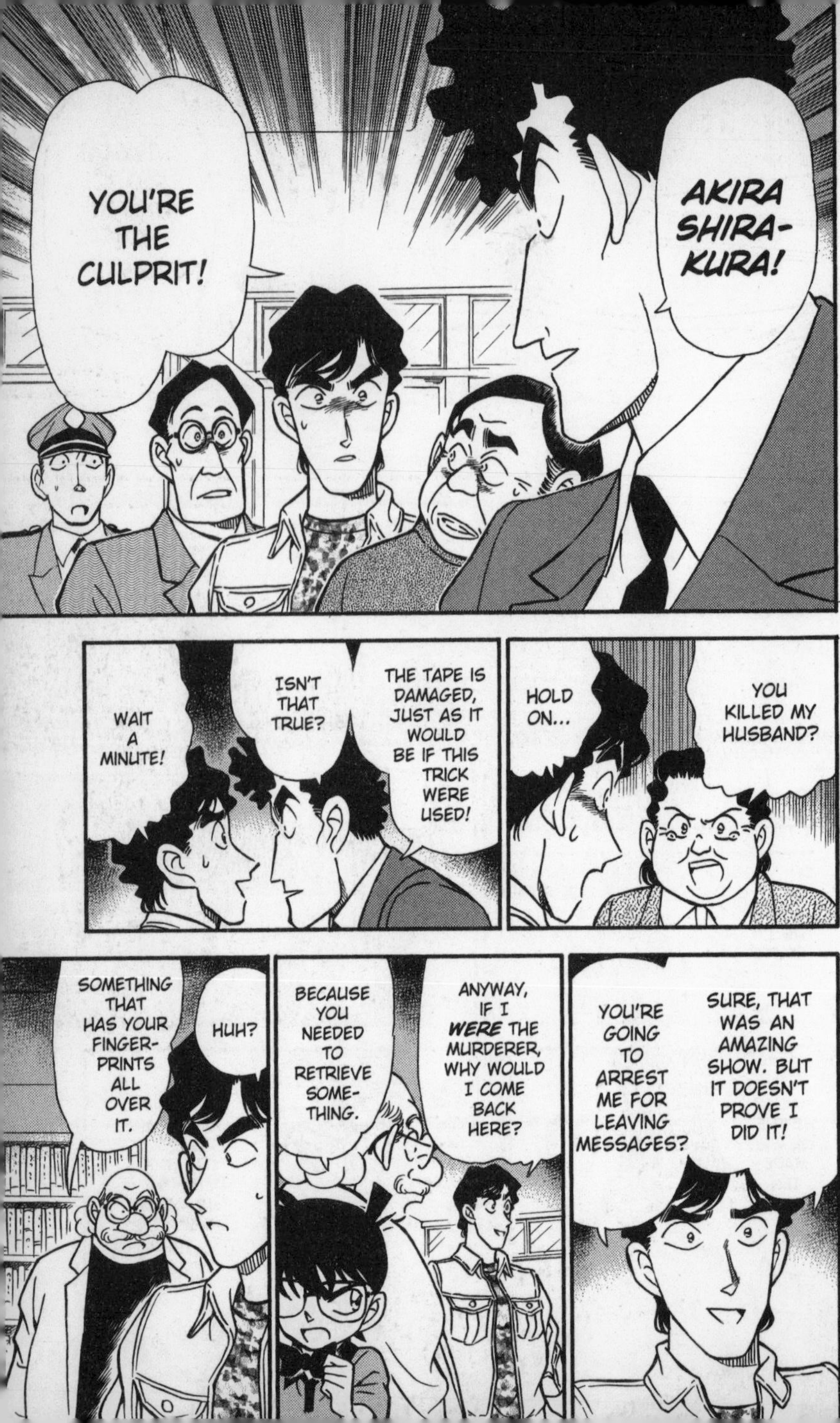
AKIRA SHIRA-KURA!
YOU'RE THE CULPRIT!
YOU KILLED MY HUSBAND?
HOLD ON...
THE TAPE IS DAMAGED, JUST AS IT WOULD BE IF THIS TRICK WERE USED!
ISN'T THAT TRUE?
WAIT A MINUTE!
SURE, THAT WAS AN AMAZING SHOW. BUT IT DOESN'T PROVE I DID IT!
YOU'RE GOING TO ARREST ME FOR LEAVING MESSAGES?
ANYWAY, IF I *WERE* THE MURDERER, WHY WOULD I COME BACK HERE?
BECAUSE YOU NEEDED TO RETRIEVE SOME-THING.
HUH?
SOMETHING THAT HAS YOUR FINGER-PRINTS ALL OVER IT.

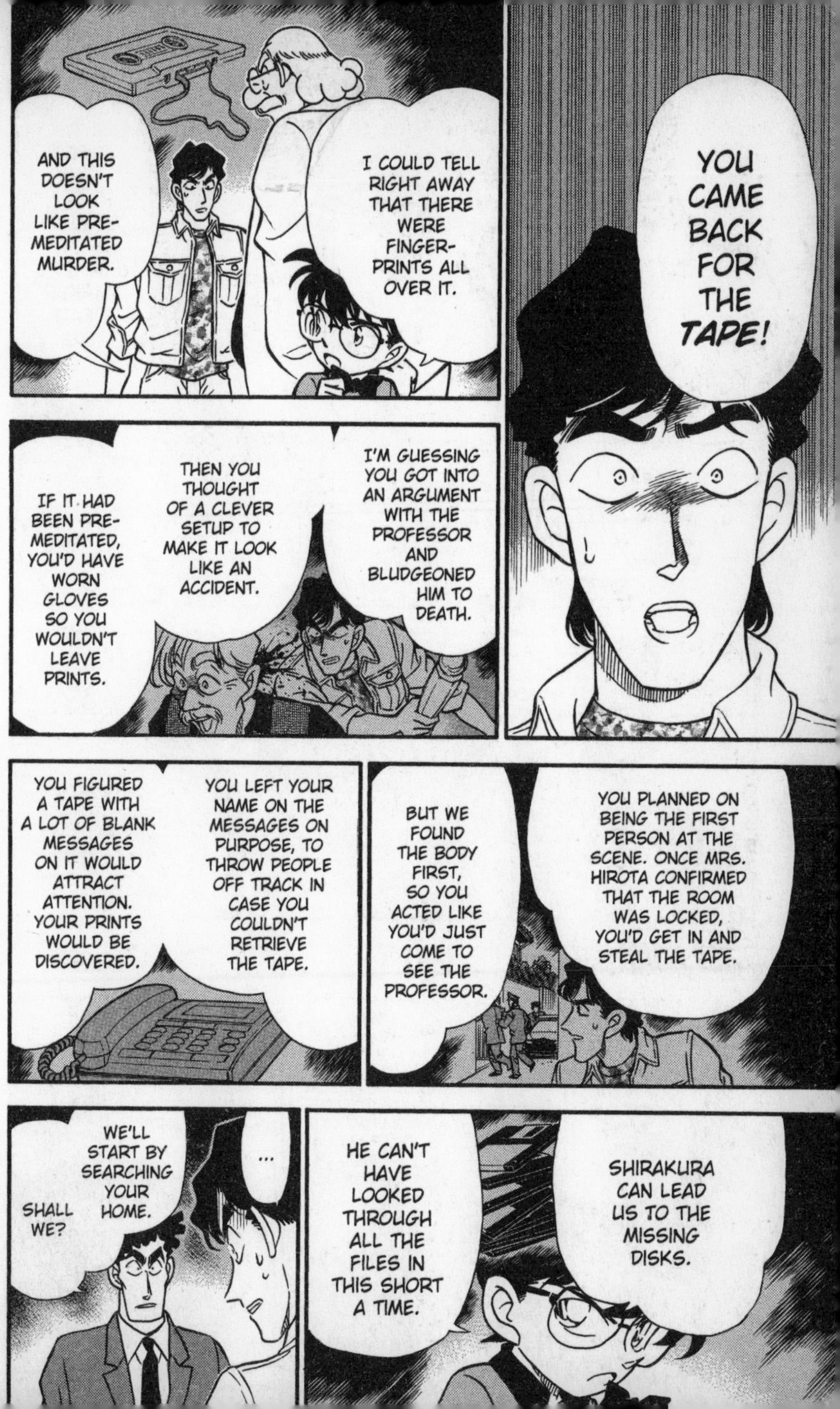
YOU CAME BACK FOR THE *TAPE!*
I COULD TELL RIGHT AWAY THAT THERE WERE FINGER-PRINTS ALL OVER IT.
AND THIS DOESN'T LOOK LIKE PRE-MEDITATED MURDER.
I'M GUESSING YOU GOT INTO AN ARGUMENT WITH THE PROFESSOR AND BLUDGEONED HIM TO DEATH.
THEN YOU THOUGHT OF A CLEVER SETUP TO MAKE IT LOOK LIKE AN ACCIDENT.
IF IT HAD BEEN PRE-MEDITATED, YOU'D HAVE WORN GLOVES SO YOU WOULDN'T LEAVE PRINTS.
YOU PLANNED ON BEING THE FIRST PERSON AT THE SCENE. ONCE MRS. HIROTA CONFIRMED THAT THE ROOM WAS LOCKED, YOU'D GET IN AND STEAL THE TAPE.
BUT WE FOUND THE BODY FIRST, SO YOU ACTED LIKE YOU'D JUST COME TO SEE THE PROFESSOR.
YOU LEFT YOUR NAME ON THE MESSAGES ON PURPOSE, TO THROW PEOPLE OFF TRACK IN CASE YOU COULDN'T RETRIEVE THE TAPE.
YOU FIGURED A TAPE WITH A LOT OF BLANK MESSAGES ON IT WOULD ATTRACT ATTENTION. YOUR PRINTS WOULD BE DISCOVERED.
SHIRAKURA CAN LEAD US TO THE MISSING DISKS.
HE CAN'T HAVE LOOKED THROUGH ALL THE FILES IN THIS SHORT A TIME.
...
WE'LL START BY SEARCHING YOUR HOME.
SHALL WE?

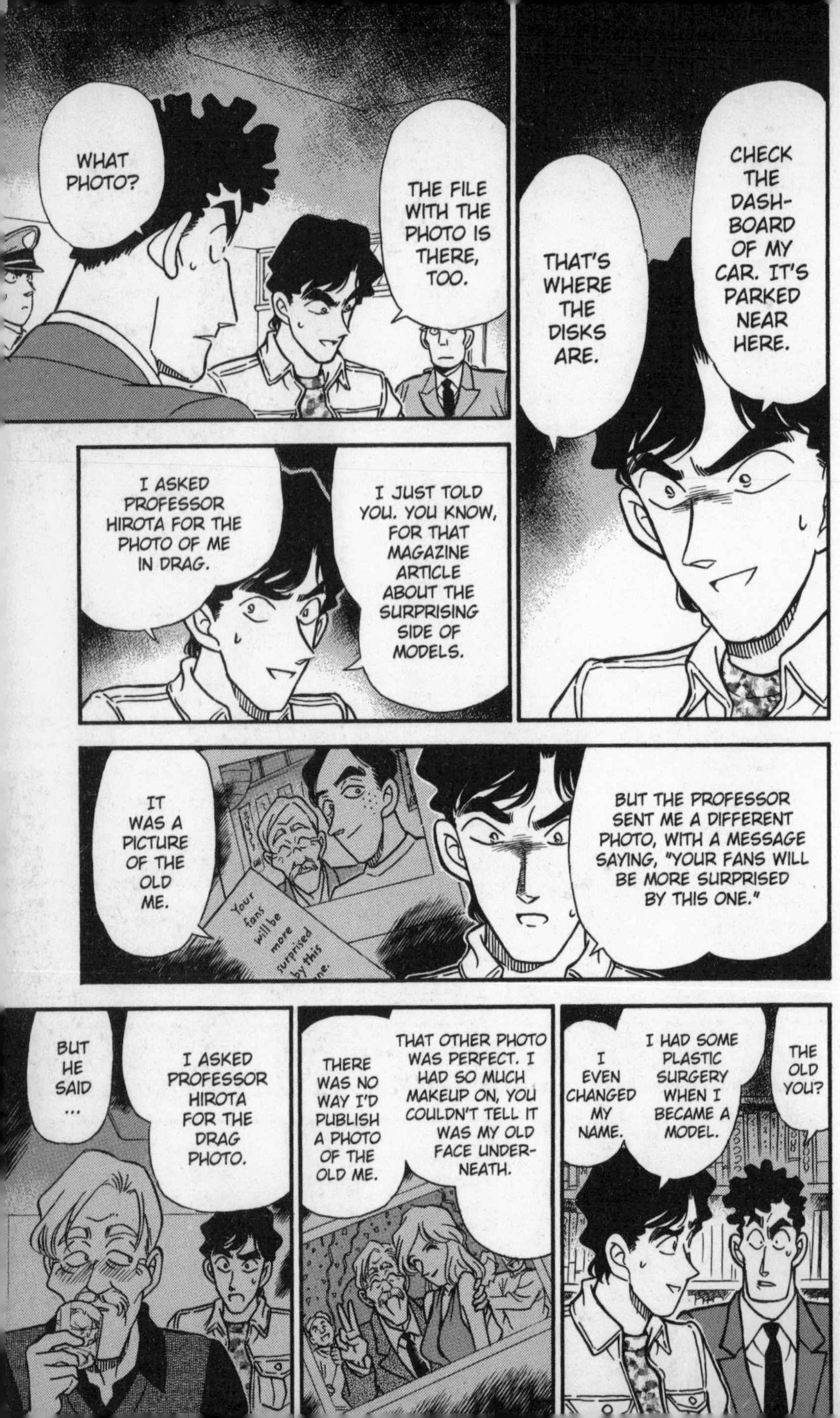
CHECK THE DASH-BOARD OF MY CAR. IT'S PARKED NEAR HERE.
THAT'S WHERE THE DISKS ARE.
THE FILE WITH THE PHOTO IS THERE, TOO.
WHAT PHOTO?
I JUST TOLD YOU. YOU KNOW, FOR THAT MAGAZINE ARTICLE ABOUT THE SURPRISING SIDE OF MODELS.
I ASKED PROFESSOR HIROTA FOR THE PHOTO OF ME IN DRAG.
BUT THE PROFESSOR SENT ME A DIFFERENT PHOTO, WITH A MESSAGE SAYING, "YOUR FANS WILL BE MORE SURPRISED BY THIS ONE."
IT WAS A PICTURE OF THE OLD ME.
Your fans will be more surprised by this
THE OLD YOU?
I HAD SOME PLASTIC SURGERY WHEN I BECAME A MODEL.
I EVEN CHANGED MY NAME.
THAT OTHER PHOTO WAS PERFECT. I HAD SO MUCH MAKEUP ON, YOU COULDN'T TELL IT WAS MY OLD FACE UNDER-NEATH.
THERE WAS NO WAY I'D PUBLISH A PHOTO OF THE OLD ME.
I ASKED PROFESSOR HIROTA FOR THE DRAG PHOTO.
BUT HE SAID ...

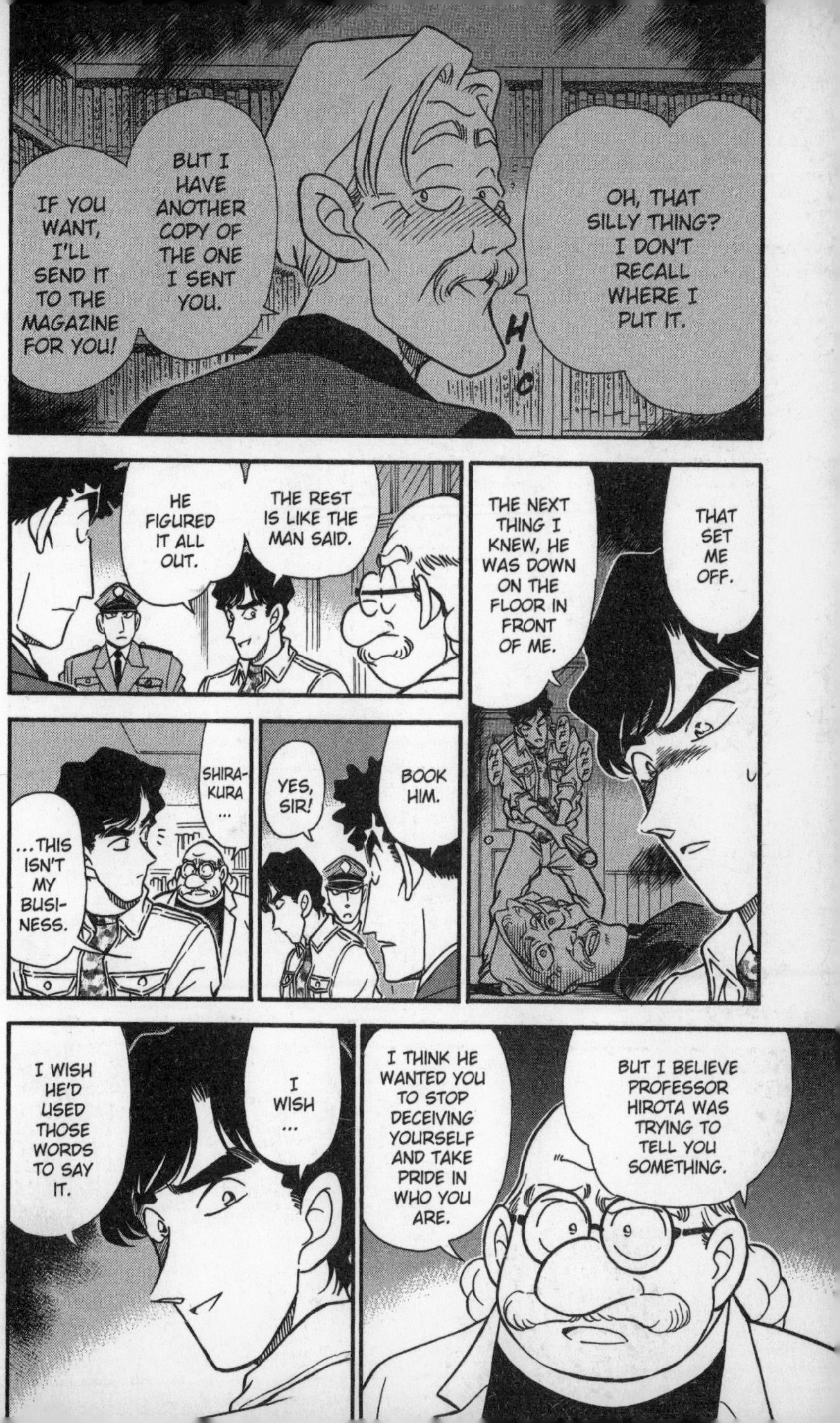
OH, THAT SILLY THING? I DON'T RECALL WHERE I PUT IT.
HIC
BUT I HAVE ANOTHER COPY OF THE ONE I SENT YOU.
IF YOU WANT, I'LL SEND IT TO THE MAGAZINE FOR YOU!
THAT SET ME OFF.
THE NEXT THING I KNEW, HE WAS DOWN ON THE FLOOR IN FRONT OF ME.
THE REST IS LIKE THE MAN SAID.
HE FIGURED IT ALL OUT.
BOOK HIM.
YES, SIR!
SHIRAKURA...
...THIS ISN'T MY BUSINESS.
BUT I BELIEVE PROFESSOR HIROTA WAS TRYING TO TELL YOU SOMETHING.
I THINK HE WANTED YOU TO STOP DECEIVING YOURSELF AND TAKE PRIDE IN WHO YOU ARE.
I WISH...
I WISH HE'D USED THOSE WORDS TO SAY IT.

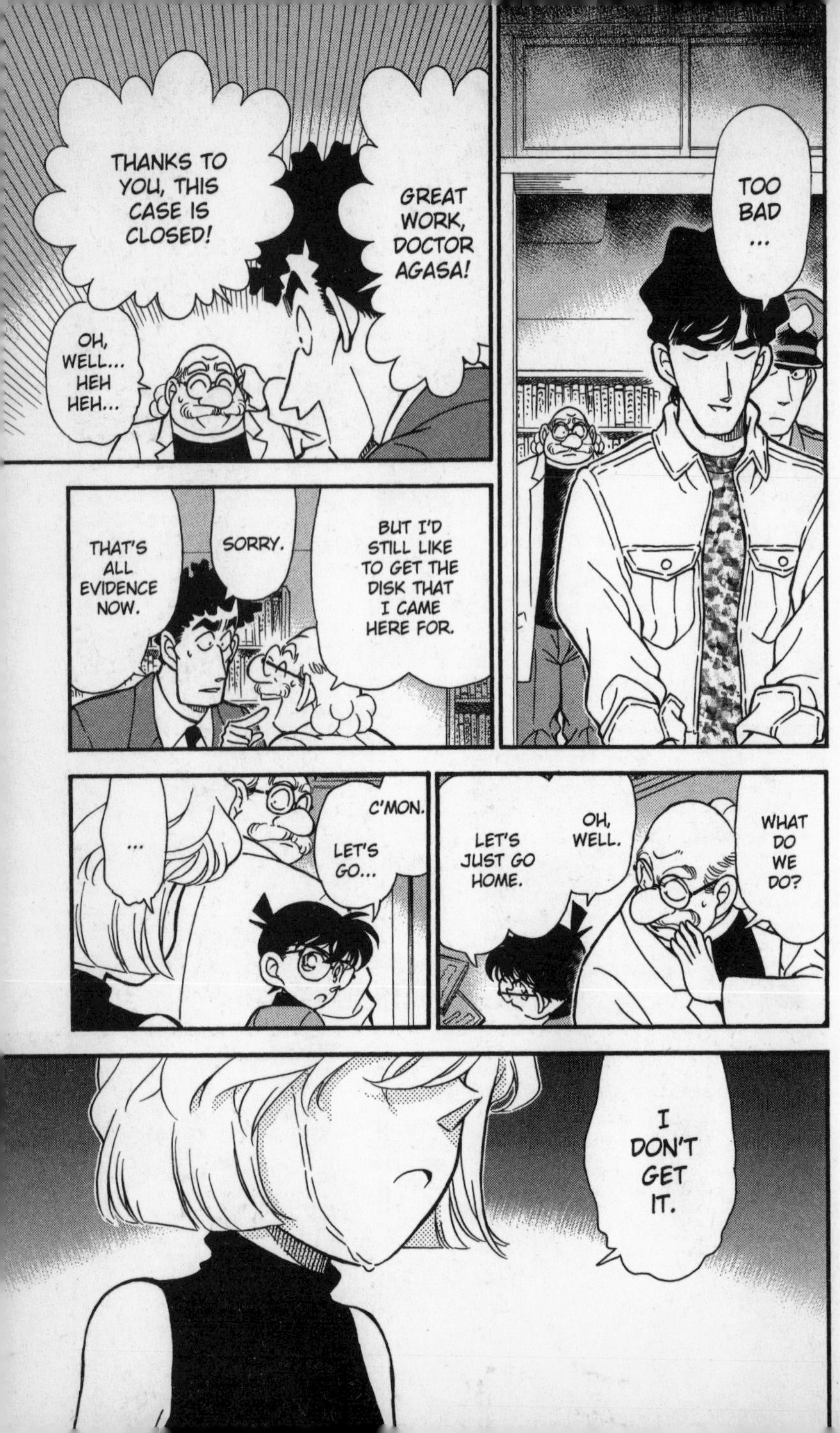
TOO BAD ...
GREAT WORK, DOCTOR AGASA!
THANKS TO YOU, THIS CASE IS CLOSED!
OH, WELL... HEH HEH...
BUT I'D STILL LIKE TO GET THE DISK THAT I CAME HERE FOR.
SORRY.
THAT'S ALL EVIDENCE NOW.
WHAT DO WE DO?
OH, WELL.
LET'S JUST GO HOME.
C'MON.
LET'S GO...
...
I DON'T GET IT.

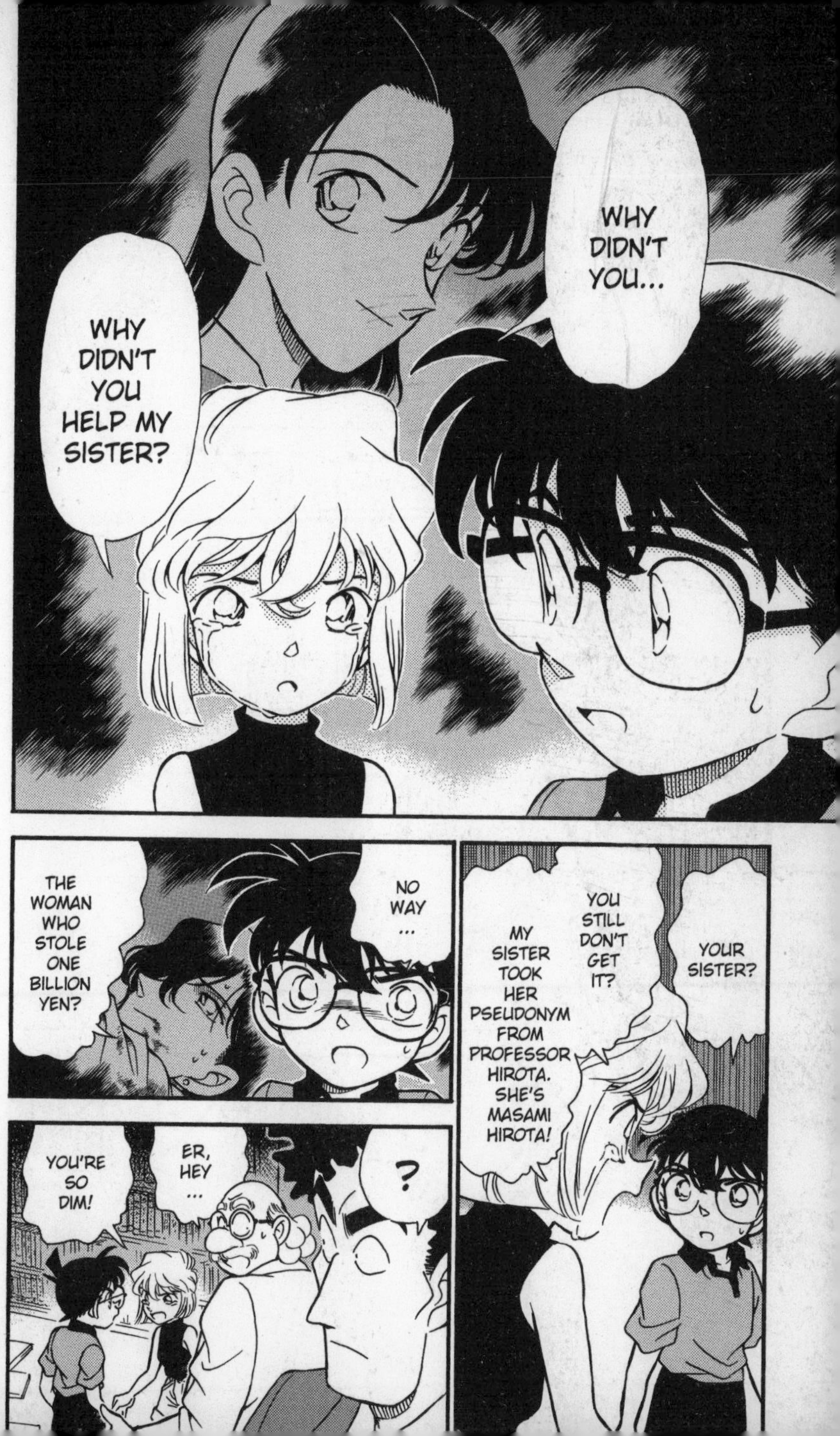
WHY DIDN'T YOU...
WHY DIDN'T YOU HELP MY SISTER?
YOUR SISTER?
YOU STILL DON'T GET IT?
MY SISTER TOOK HER PSEUDONYM FROM PROFESSOR HIROTA. SHE'S MASAMI HIROTA!
NO WAY ...
THE WOMAN WHO STOLE ONE BILLION YEN?
?
ER, HEY ...
YOU'RE SO DIM!

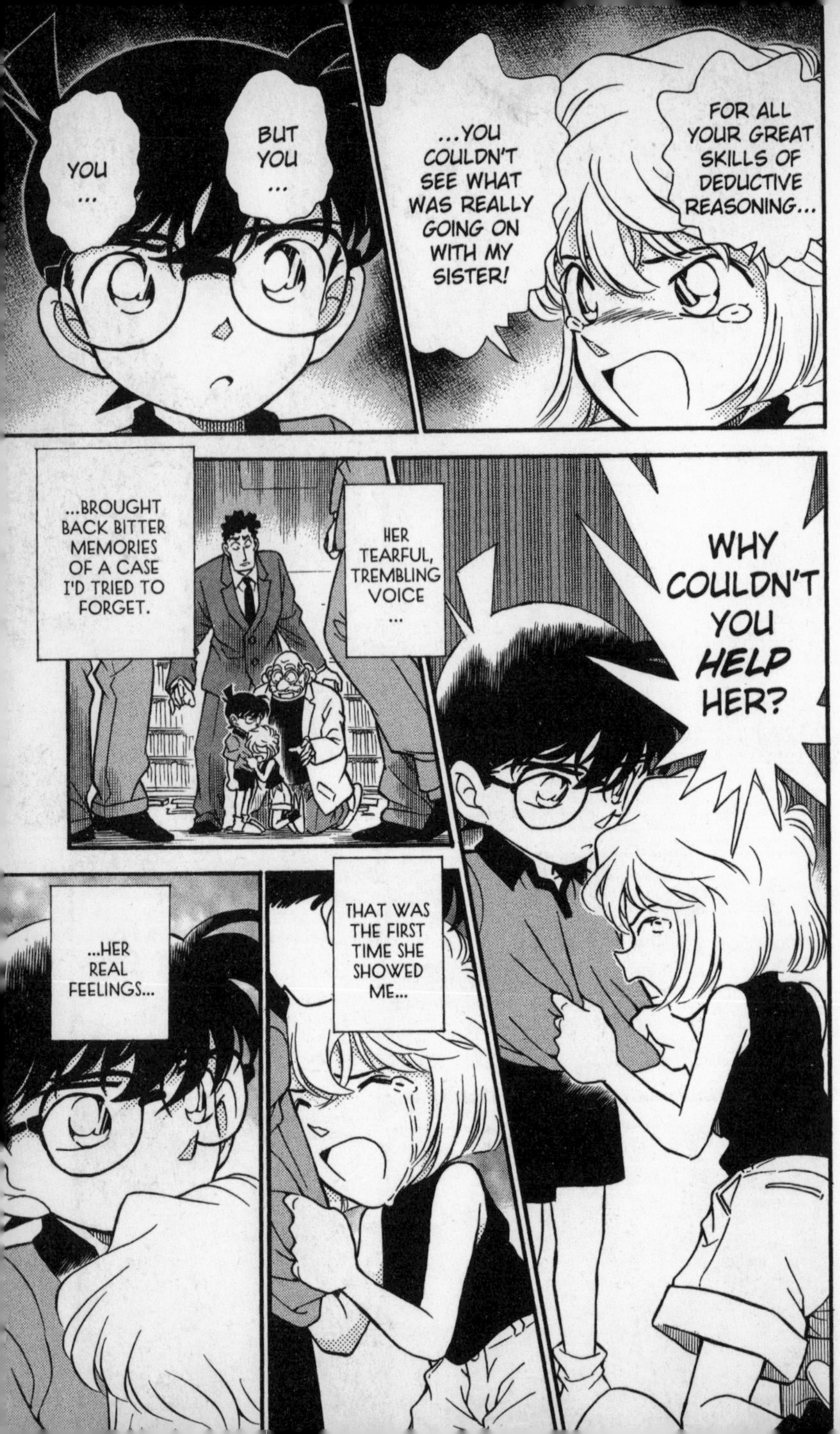
FOR ALL YOUR GREAT SKILLS OF DEDUCTIVE REASONING...
...YOU COULDN'T SEE WHAT WAS REALLY GOING ON WITH MY SISTER!
BUT YOU ...
YOU ...
WHY COULDN'T YOU *HELP* HER?
HER TEARFUL, TREMBLING VOICE ...
...BROUGHT BACK BITTER MEMORIES OF A CASE I'D TRIED TO FORGET.
THAT WAS THE FIRST TIME SHE SHOWED ME...
...HER REAL FEELINGS...

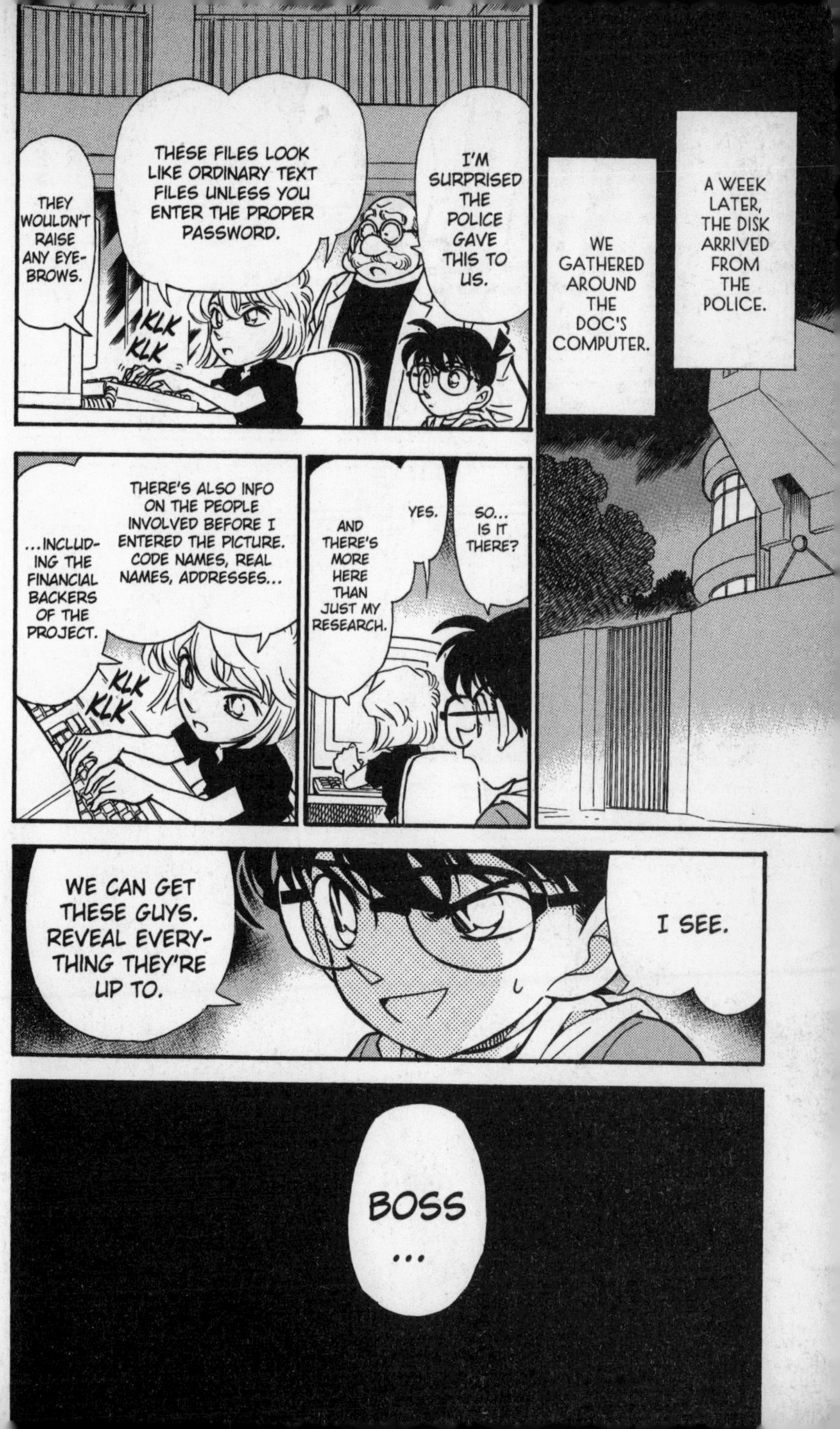
A WEEK LATER, THE DISK ARRIVED FROM THE POLICE.
WE GATHERED AROUND THE DOC'S COMPUTER.
I'M SURPRISED THE POLICE GAVE THIS TO US.
THESE FILES LOOK LIKE ORDINARY TEXT FILES UNLESS YOU ENTER THE PROPER PASSWORD.
THEY WOULDN'T RAISE ANY EYE-BROWS.
KLK KLK
SO... IS IT THERE?
YES.
AND THERE'S MORE HERE THAN JUST MY RESEARCH.
THERE'S ALSO INFO ON THE PEOPLE INVOLVED BEFORE I ENTERED THE PICTURE. CODE NAMES, REAL NAMES, ADDRESSES...
...INCLUD-ING THE FINANCIAL BACKERS OF THE PROJECT.
KLK KLK
I SEE.
WE CAN GET THESE GUYS. REVEAL EVERY-THING THEY'RE UP TO.
BOSS ...

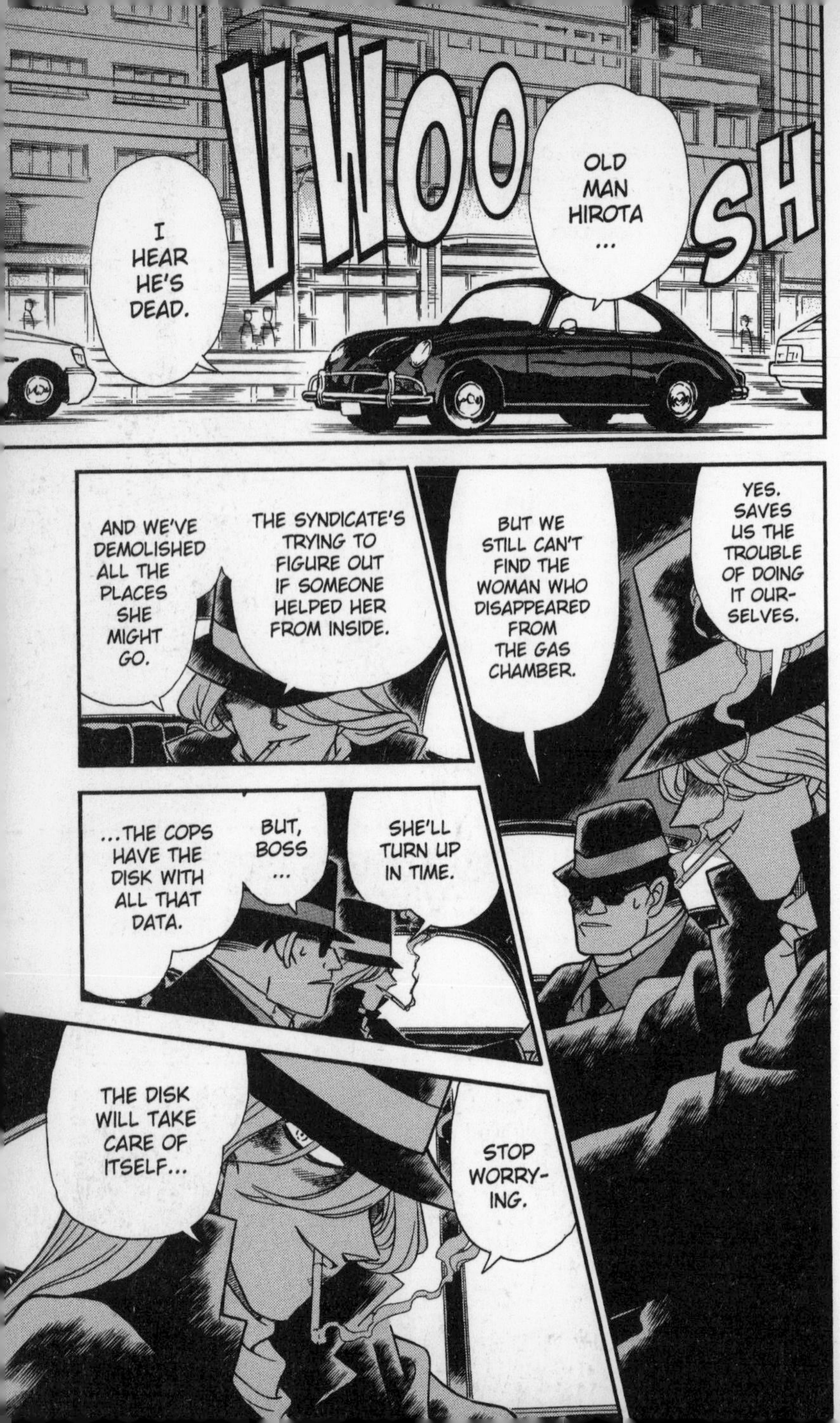
VWOOSH
OLD MAN HIROTA ...
I HEAR HE'S DEAD.
YES. SAVES US THE TROUBLE OF DOING IT OUR-SELVES.
BUT WE STILL CAN'T FIND THE WOMAN WHO DISAPPEARED FROM THE GAS CHAMBER.
THE SYNDICATE'S TRYING TO FIGURE OUT IF SOMEONE HELPED HER FROM INSIDE.
AND WE'VE DEMOLISHED ALL THE PLACES SHE MIGHT GO.
SHE'LL TURN UP IN TIME.
BUT, BOSS ...
...THE COPS HAVE THE DISK WITH ALL THAT DATA.
STOP WORRY-ING.
THE DISK WILL TAKE CARE OF ITSELF...

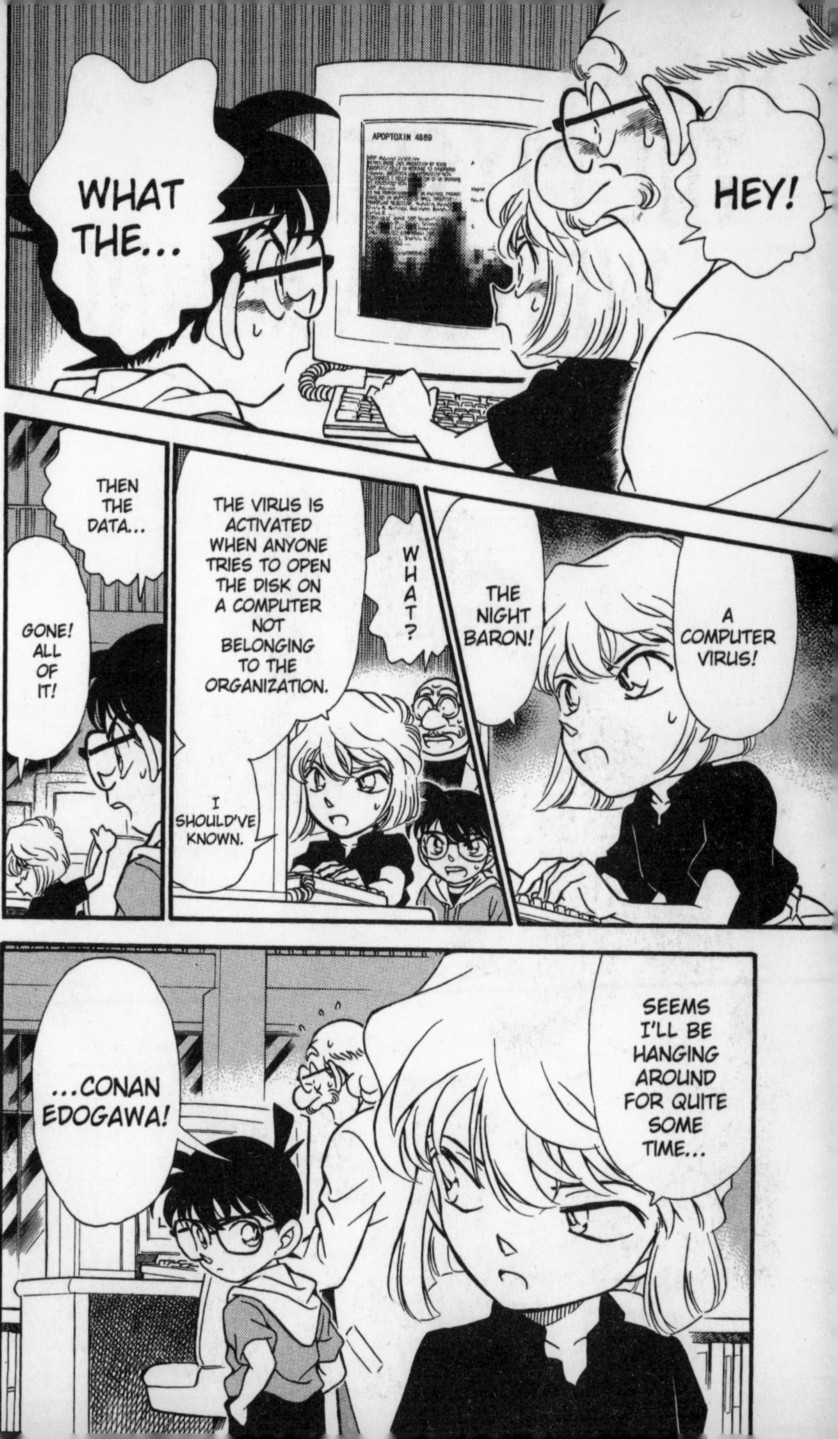
APOPTOXIN 4869
HEY!
WHAT THE...
A COMPUTER VIRUS!
THE NIGHT BARON!
WHAT?
THE VIRUS IS ACTIVATED WHEN ANYONE TRIES TO OPEN THE DISK ON A COMPUTER NOT BELONGING TO THE ORGANIZATION.
I SHOULD'VE KNOWN.
THEN THE DATA...
GONE! ALL OF IT!
SEEMS I'LL BE HANGING AROUND FOR QUITE SOME TIME...
...CONAN EDOGAWA!

FILE 2: THE MYSTERY WRITER VANISHES

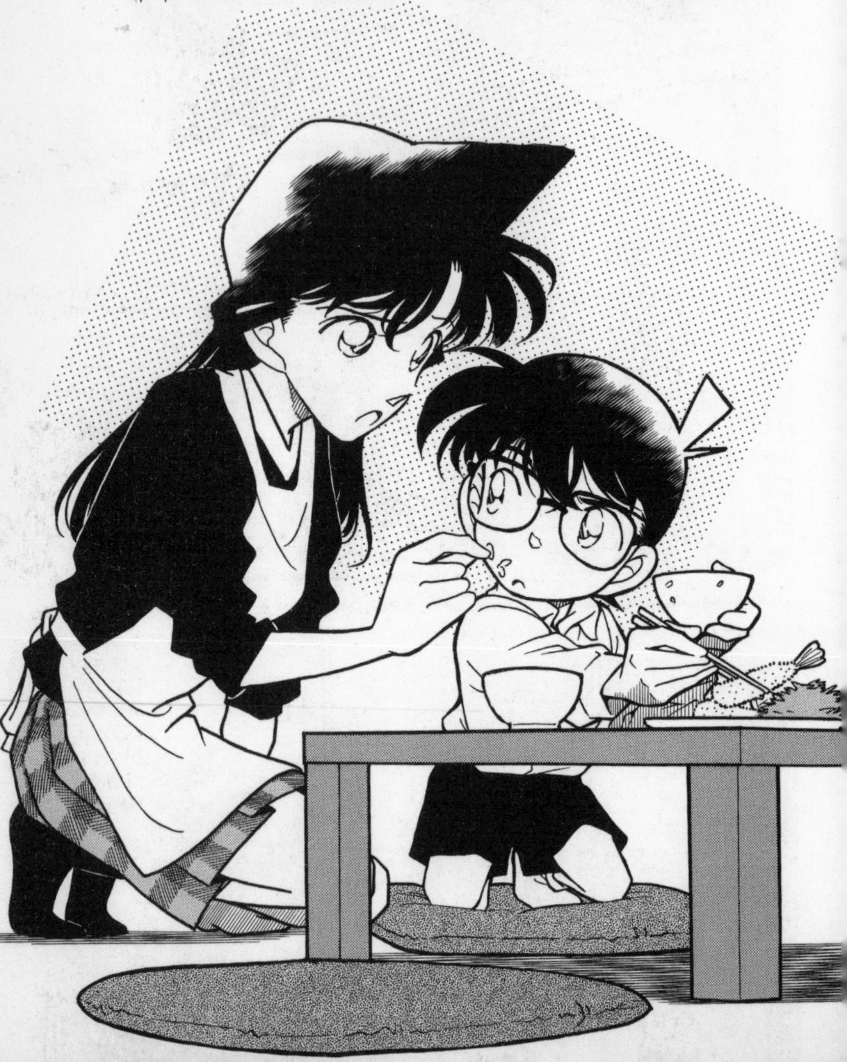

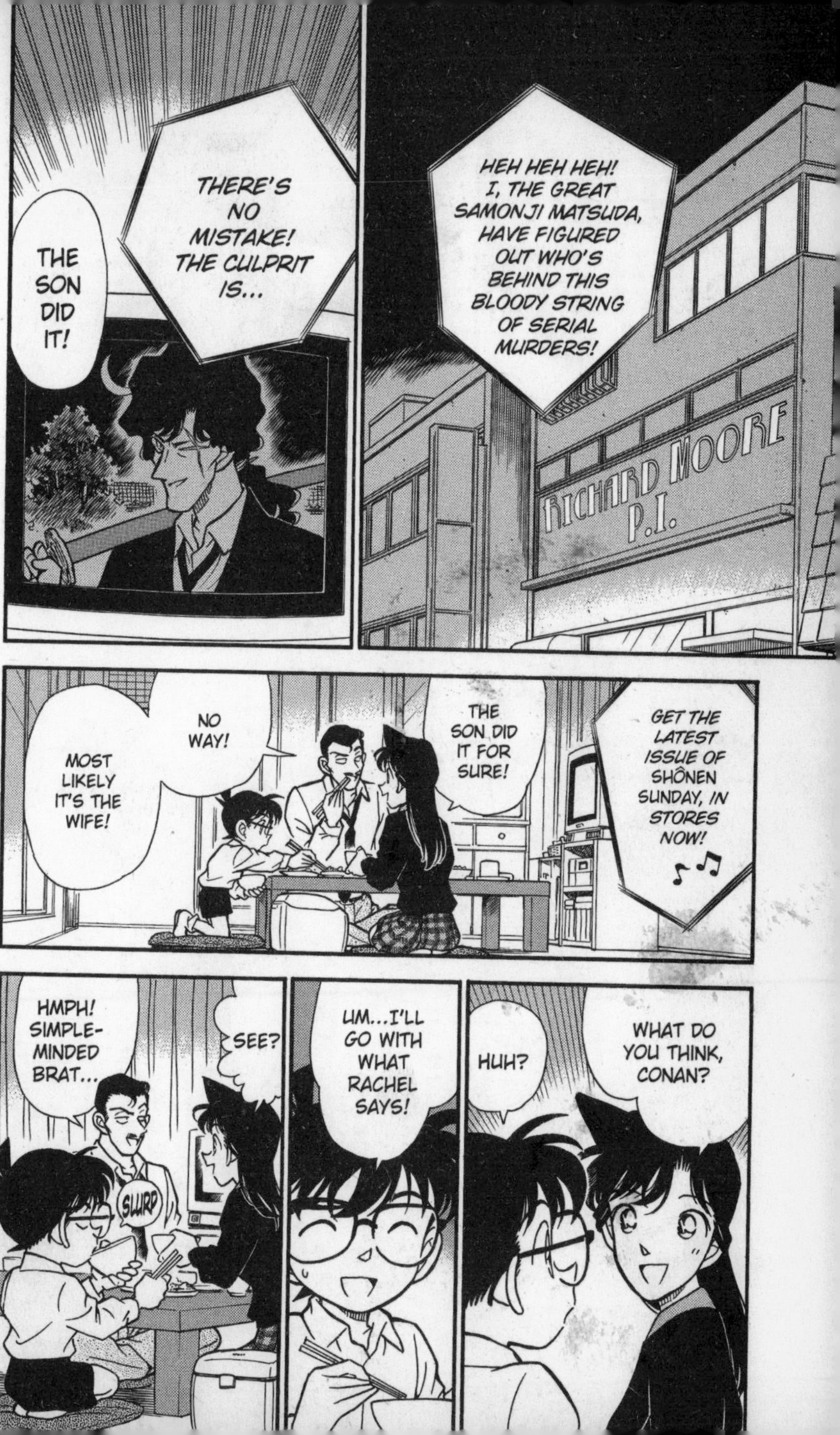
HEH HEH HEH! I, THE GREAT SAMONJI MATSUDA, HAVE FIGURED OUT WHO'S BEHIND THIS BLOODY STRING OF SERIAL MURDERS!
RICHARD MOORE P.I.
THERE'S NO MISTAKE! THE CULPRIT IS...
THE SON DID IT!
GET THE LATEST ISSUE OF SHÔNEN SUNDAY, IN STORES NOW!
THE SON DID IT FOR SURE!
NO WAY!
MOST LIKELY IT'S THE WIFE!
WHAT DO YOU THINK, CONAN?
HUH?
UM...I'LL GO WITH WHAT RACHEL SAYS!
SEE?
HMPH! SIMPLE-MINDED BRAT...
SLURP

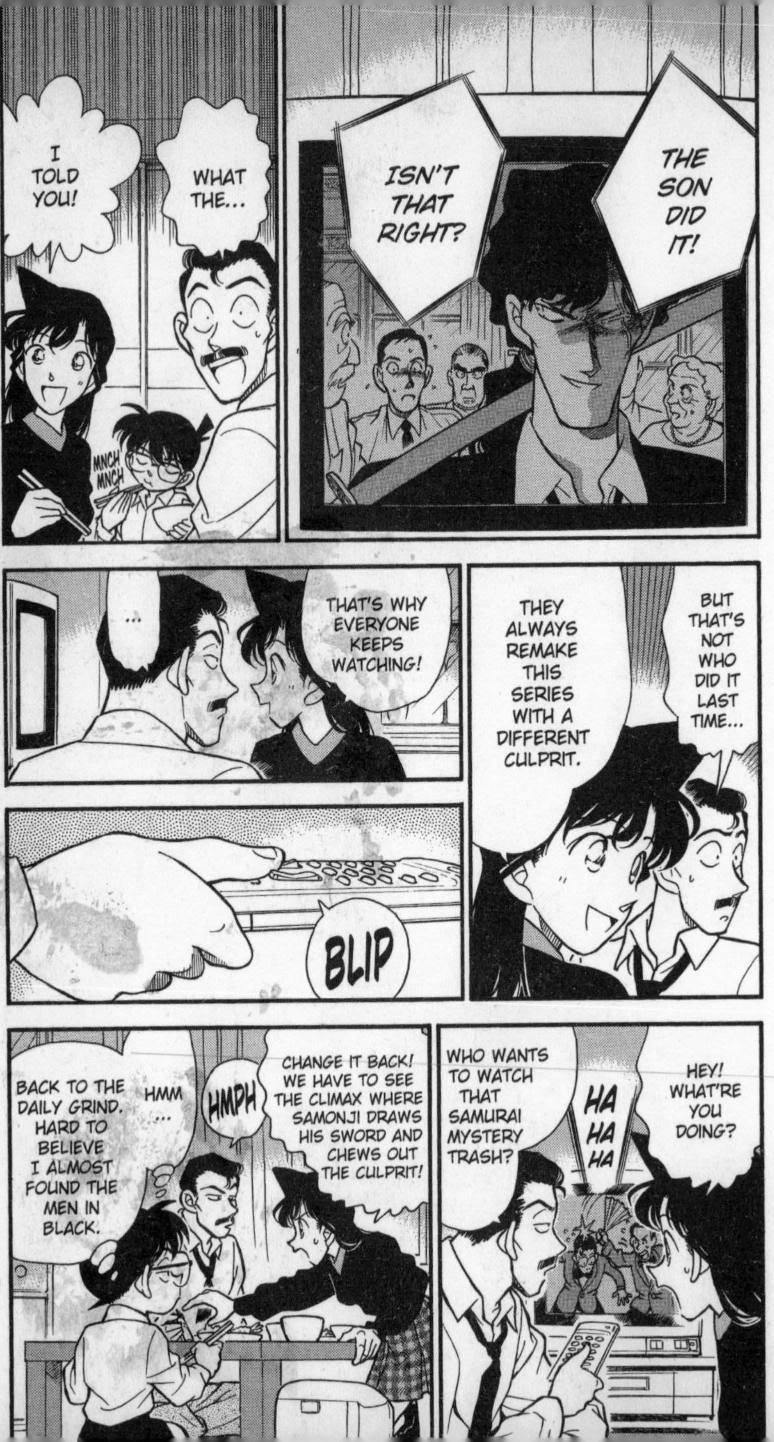
THE SON DID IT!
ISN'T THAT RIGHT?
WHAT THE...
I TOLD YOU!
MNCH MNCH
BUT THAT'S NOT WHO DID IT LAST TIME...
THEY ALWAYS REMAKE THIS SERIES WITH A DIFFERENT CULPRIT.
THAT'S WHY EVERYONE KEEPS WATCHING!
...
BLIP
HEY! WHAT'RE YOU DOING?
HA HA HA
WHO WANTS TO WATCH THAT SAMURAI MYSTERY TRASH?
CHANGE IT BACK! WE HAVE TO SEE THE CLIMAX WHERE SAMONJI DRAWS HIS SWORD AND CHEWS OUT THE CULPRIT!
HMPH
HMM...
BACK TO THE DAILY GRIND. HARD TO BELIEVE I ALMOST FOUND THE MEN IN BLACK.

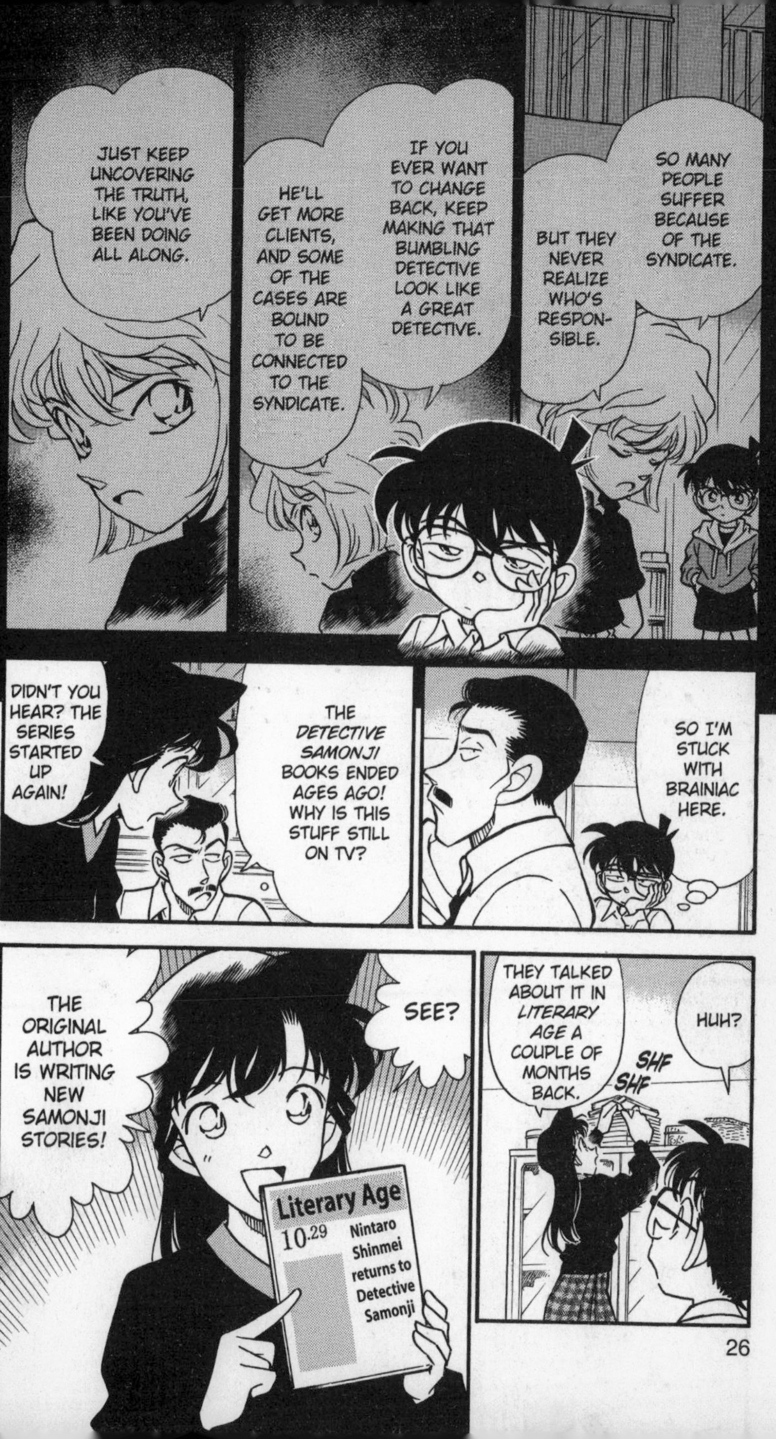
SO MANY PEOPLE SUFFER BECAUSE OF THE SYNDICATE.
BUT THEY NEVER REALIZE WHO'S RESPON-SIBLE.
IF YOU EVER WANT TO CHANGE BACK, KEEP MAKING THAT BUMBLING DETECTIVE LOOK LIKE A GREAT DETECTIVE.
HE'LL GET MORE CLIENTS, AND SOME OF THE CASES ARE BOUND TO BE CONNECTED TO THE SYNDICATE.
JUST KEEP UNCOVERING THE TRUTH, LIKE YOU'VE BEEN DOING ALL ALONG.
SO I'M STUCK WITH BRAINIAC HERE.
THE *DETECTIVE SAMONJI* BOOKS ENDED AGES AGO! WHY IS THIS STUFF STILL ON TV?
DIDN'T YOU HEAR? THE SERIES STARTED UP AGAIN!
HUH?
SHF SHF
THEY TALKED ABOUT IT IN *LITERARY AGE* A COUPLE OF MONTHS BACK.
SEE?
THE ORIGINAL AUTHOR IS WRITING NEW SAMONJI STORIES!
Literary Age
10.29
Nintaro Shinmei returns to Detective Samonji

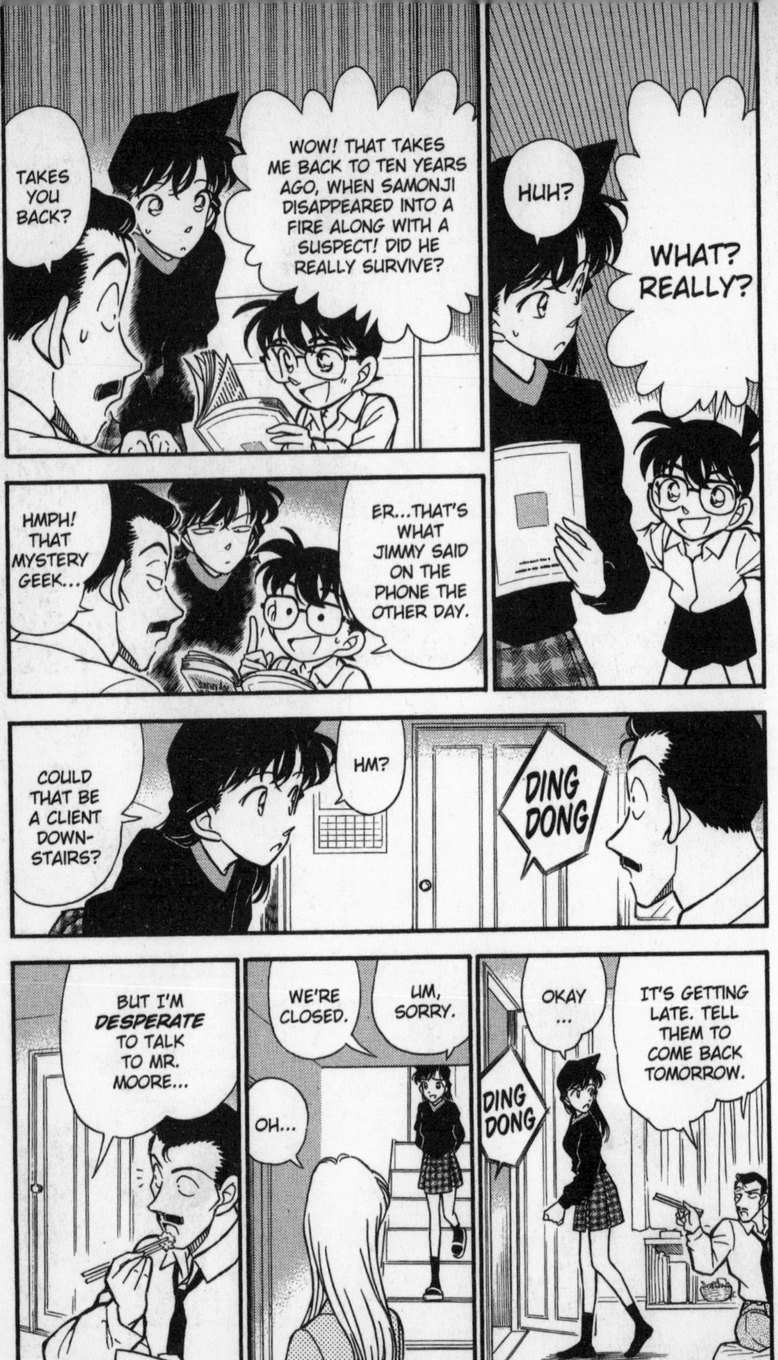

HUH?
WHAT? REALLY?
WOW! THAT TAKES ME BACK TO TEN YEARS AGO, WHEN SAMONJI DISAPPEARED INTO A FIRE ALONG WITH A SUSPECT! DID HE REALLY SURVIVE?
TAKES YOU BACK?
ER...THAT'S WHAT JIMMY SAID ON THE PHONE THE OTHER DAY.
HMPH! THAT MYSTERY GEEK...
DING DONG
HM?
COULD THAT BE A CLIENT DOWN-STAIRS?
IT'S GETTING LATE. TELL THEM TO COME BACK TOMORROW.
OKAY ...
DING DONG
UM, SORRY.
WE'RE CLOSED.
OH...
BUT I'M *DESPERATE* TO TALK TO MR. MOORE...

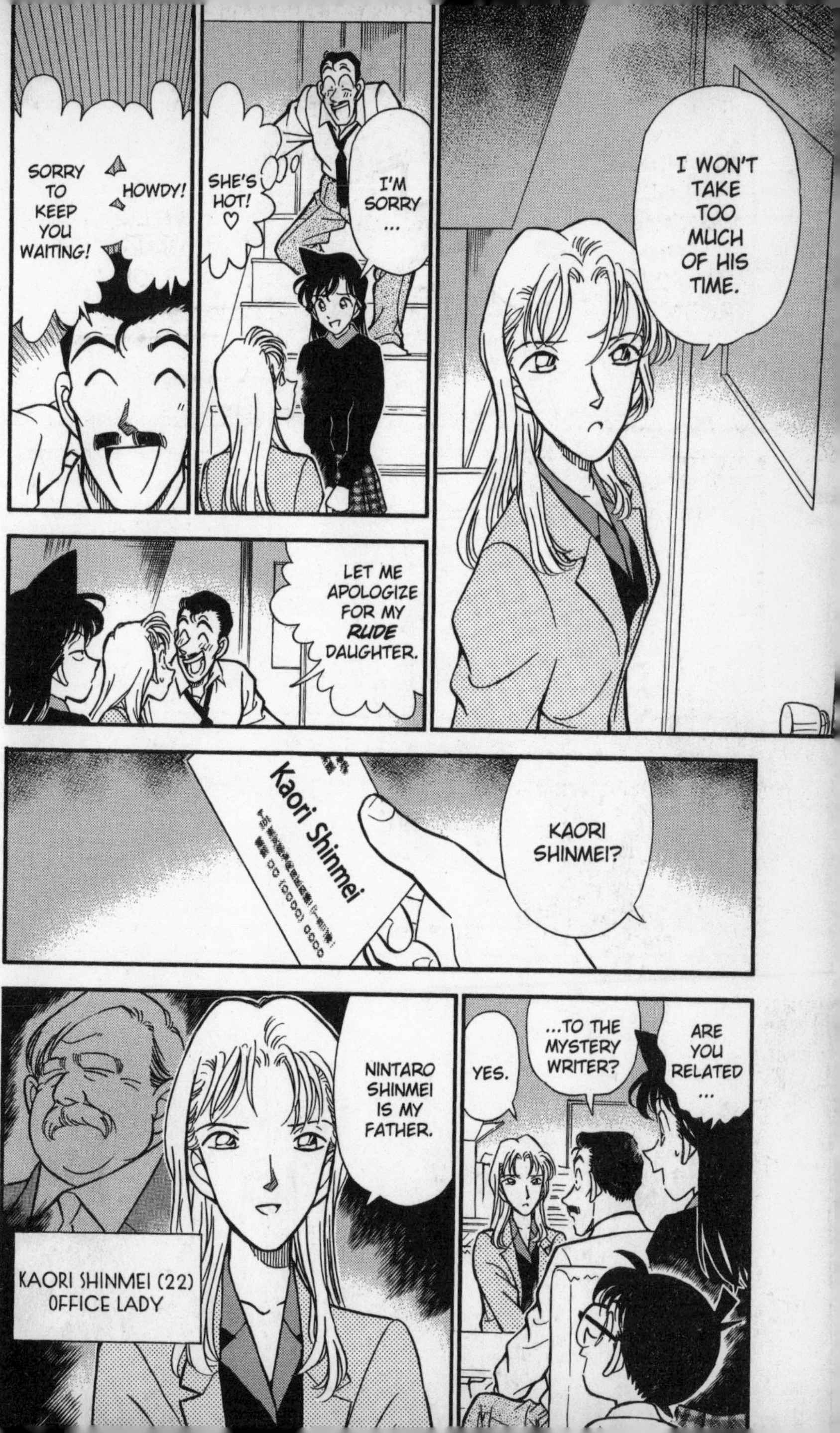
I WON'T TAKE TOO MUCH OF HIS TIME.
I'M SORRY ...
SHE'S HOT! ♡
HOWDY!
SORRY TO KEEP YOU WAITING!
LET ME APOLOGIZE FOR MY *RUDE* DAUGHTER.
KAORI SHINMEI?
Kaori Shinmei
ARE YOU RELATED ...
...TO THE MYSTERY WRITER?
YES.
NINTARO SHINMEI IS MY FATHER.
KAORI SHINMEI (22) OFFICE LADY

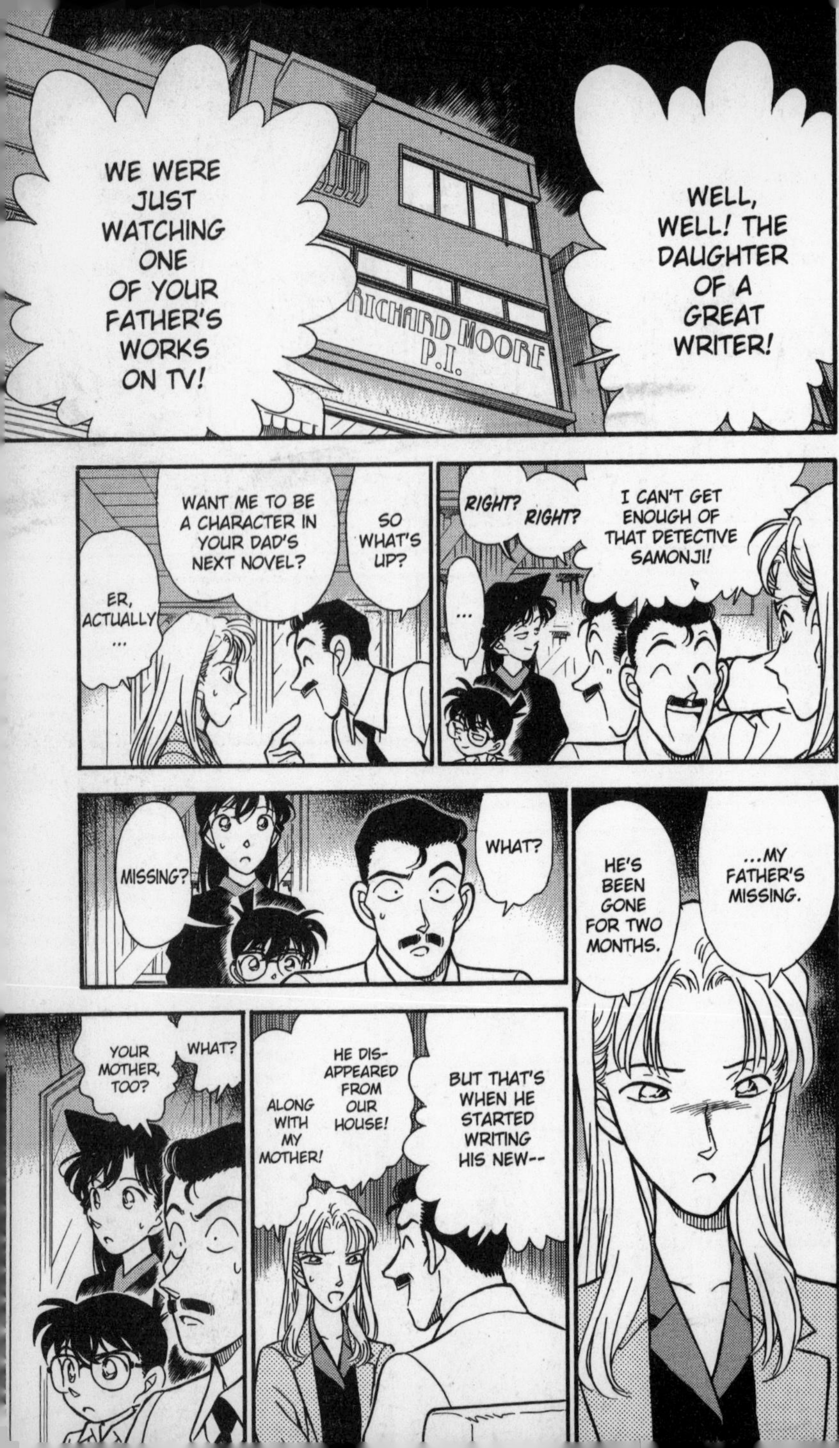
WELL, WELL! THE DAUGHTER OF A GREAT WRITER!
RICHARD MOORE P.I.
WE WERE JUST WATCHING ONE OF YOUR FATHER'S WORKS ON TV!
I CAN'T GET ENOUGH OF THAT DETECTIVE SAMONJI!
RIGHT? RIGHT?
...
SO WHAT'S UP?
WANT ME TO BE A CHARACTER IN YOUR DAD'S NEXT NOVEL?
ER, ACTUALLY ...
...MY FATHER'S MISSING.
HE'S BEEN GONE FOR TWO MONTHS.
WHAT?
MISSING?
BUT THAT'S WHEN HE STARTED WRITING HIS NEW--
HE DIS-APPEARED FROM OUR HOUSE!
ALONG WITH MY MOTHER!
WHAT?
YOUR MOTHER, TOO?

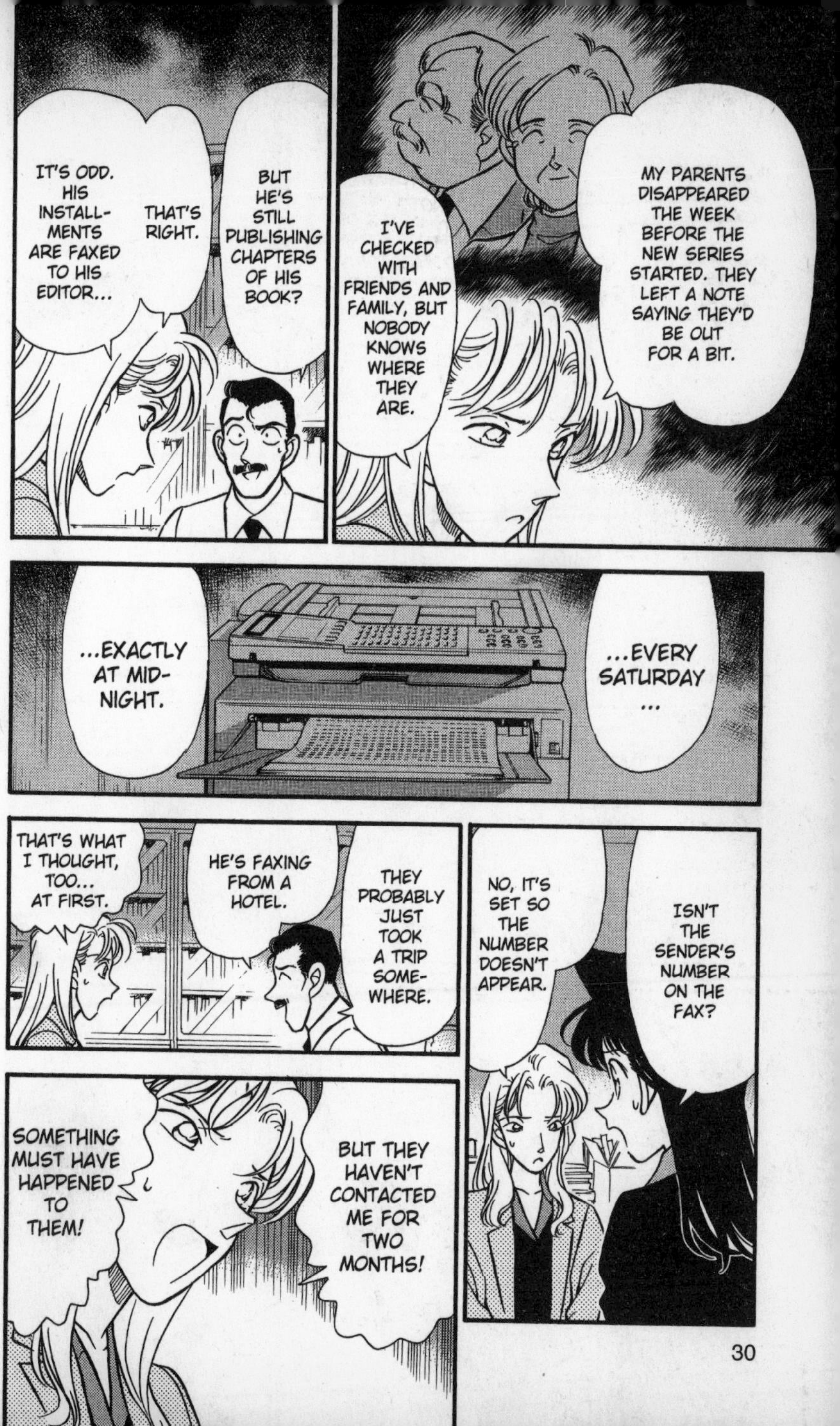
MY PARENTS DISAPPEARED THE WEEK BEFORE THE NEW SERIES STARTED. THEY LEFT A NOTE SAYING THEY'D BE OUT FOR A BIT.
I'VE CHECKED WITH FRIENDS AND FAMILY, BUT NOBODY KNOWS WHERE THEY ARE.
BUT HE'S STILL PUBLISHING CHAPTERS OF HIS BOOK?
THAT'S RIGHT.
IT'S ODD. HIS INSTALL-MENTS ARE FAXED TO HIS EDITOR...
...EVERY SATURDAY ...
...EXACTLY AT MID-NIGHT.
ISN'T THE SENDER'S NUMBER ON THE FAX?
NO, IT'S SET SO THE NUMBER DOESN'T APPEAR.
THEY PROBABLY JUST TOOK A TRIP SOME-WHERE.
HE'S FAXING FROM A HOTEL.
THAT'S WHAT I THOUGHT, TOO... AT FIRST.
BUT THEY HAVEN'T CONTACTED ME FOR TWO MONTHS!
SOMETHING MUST HAVE HAPPENED TO THEM!

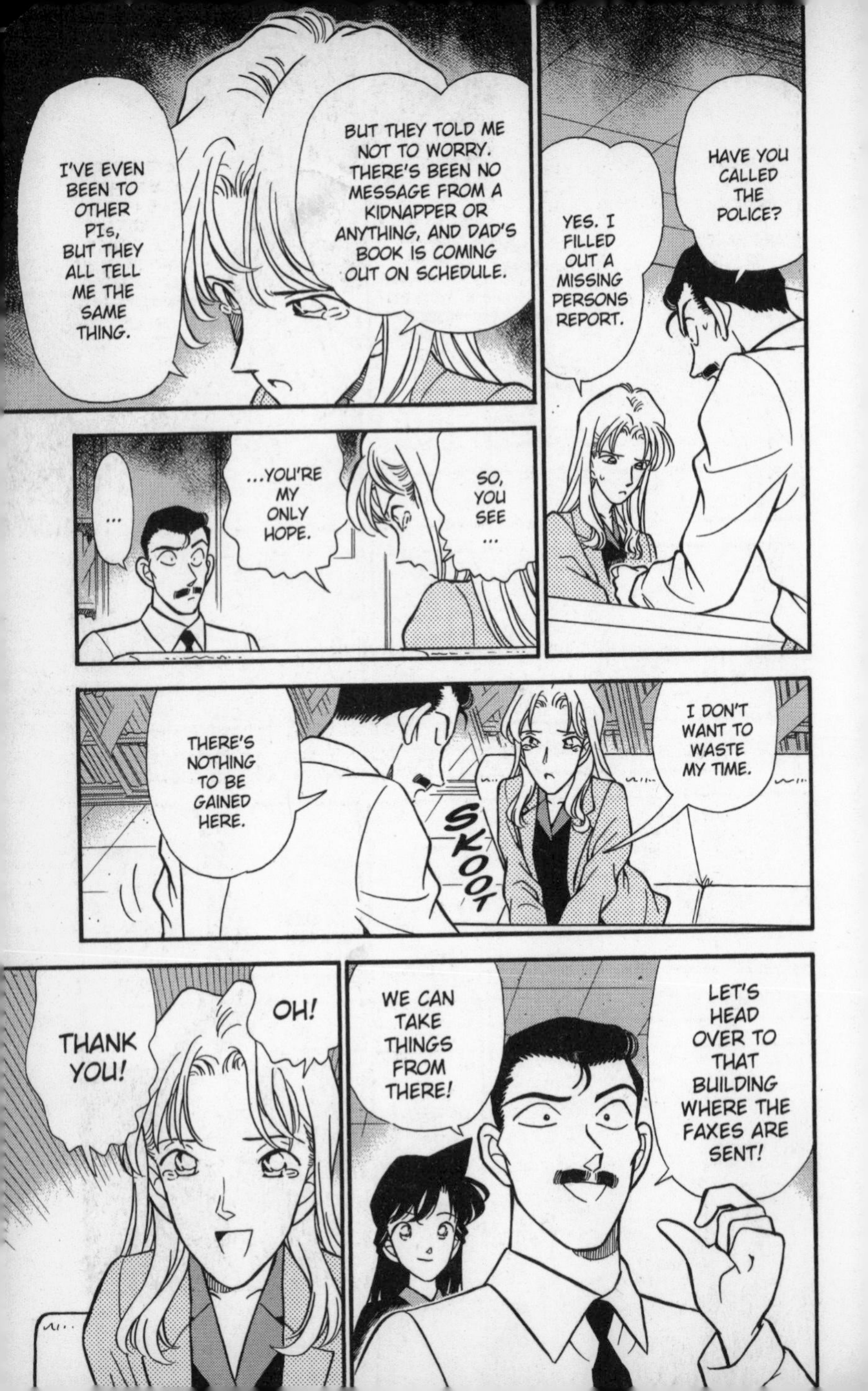
HAVE YOU CALLED THE POLICE?
YES. I FILLED OUT A MISSING PERSONS REPORT.
BUT THEY TOLD ME NOT TO WORRY. THERE'S BEEN NO MESSAGE FROM A KIDNAPPER OR ANYTHING, AND DAD'S BOOK IS COMING OUT ON SCHEDULE.
I'VE EVEN BEEN TO OTHER PIs, BUT THEY ALL TELL ME THE SAME THING.
SO, YOU SEE ...
...YOU'RE MY ONLY HOPE.
...
I DON'T WANT TO WASTE MY TIME.
SKOOT
THERE'S NOTHING TO BE GAINED HERE.
LET'S HEAD OVER TO THAT BUILDING WHERE THE FAXES ARE SENT!
WE CAN TAKE THINGS FROM THERE!
OH!
THANK YOU!

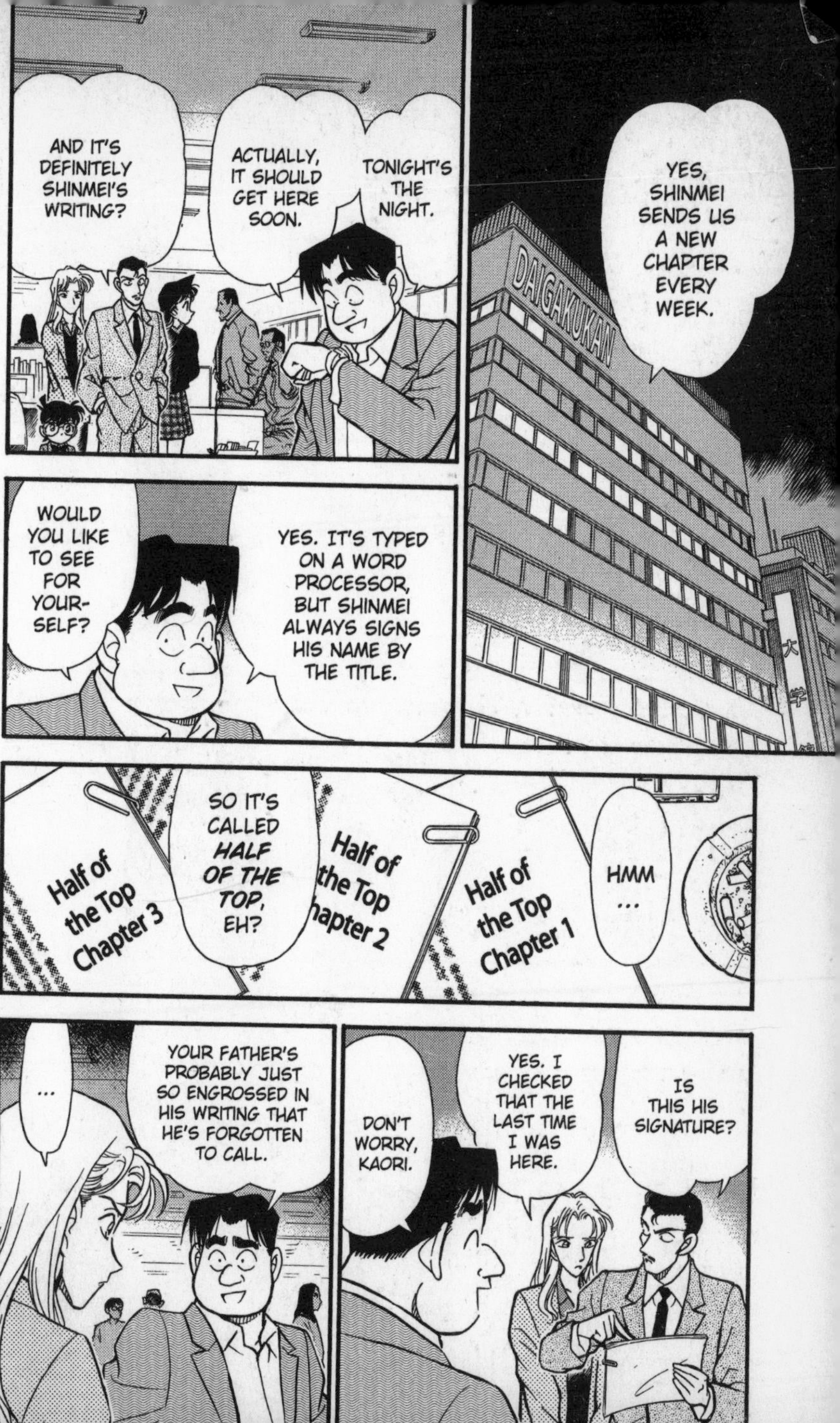
YES, SHINMEI SENDS US A NEW CHAPTER EVERY WEEK.
DAIGAKUKAN
TONIGHT'S THE NIGHT.
ACTUALLY, IT SHOULD GET HERE SOON.
AND IT'S DEFINITELY SHINMEI'S WRITING?
YES. IT'S TYPED ON A WORD PROCESSOR, BUT SHINMEI ALWAYS SIGNS HIS NAME BY THE TITLE.
WOULD YOU LIKE TO SEE FOR YOURSELF?
HMM ...
Half of the Top Chapter 1
Half of the Top hapter 2
SO IT'S CALLED *HALF OF THE TOP*, EH?
Half of the Top Chapter 3
IS THIS HIS SIGNATURE?
YES. I CHECKED THAT THE LAST TIME I WAS HERE.
DON'T WORRY, KAORI.
YOUR FATHER'S PROBABLY JUST SO ENGROSSED IN HIS WRITING THAT HE'S FORGOTTEN TO CALL.
...

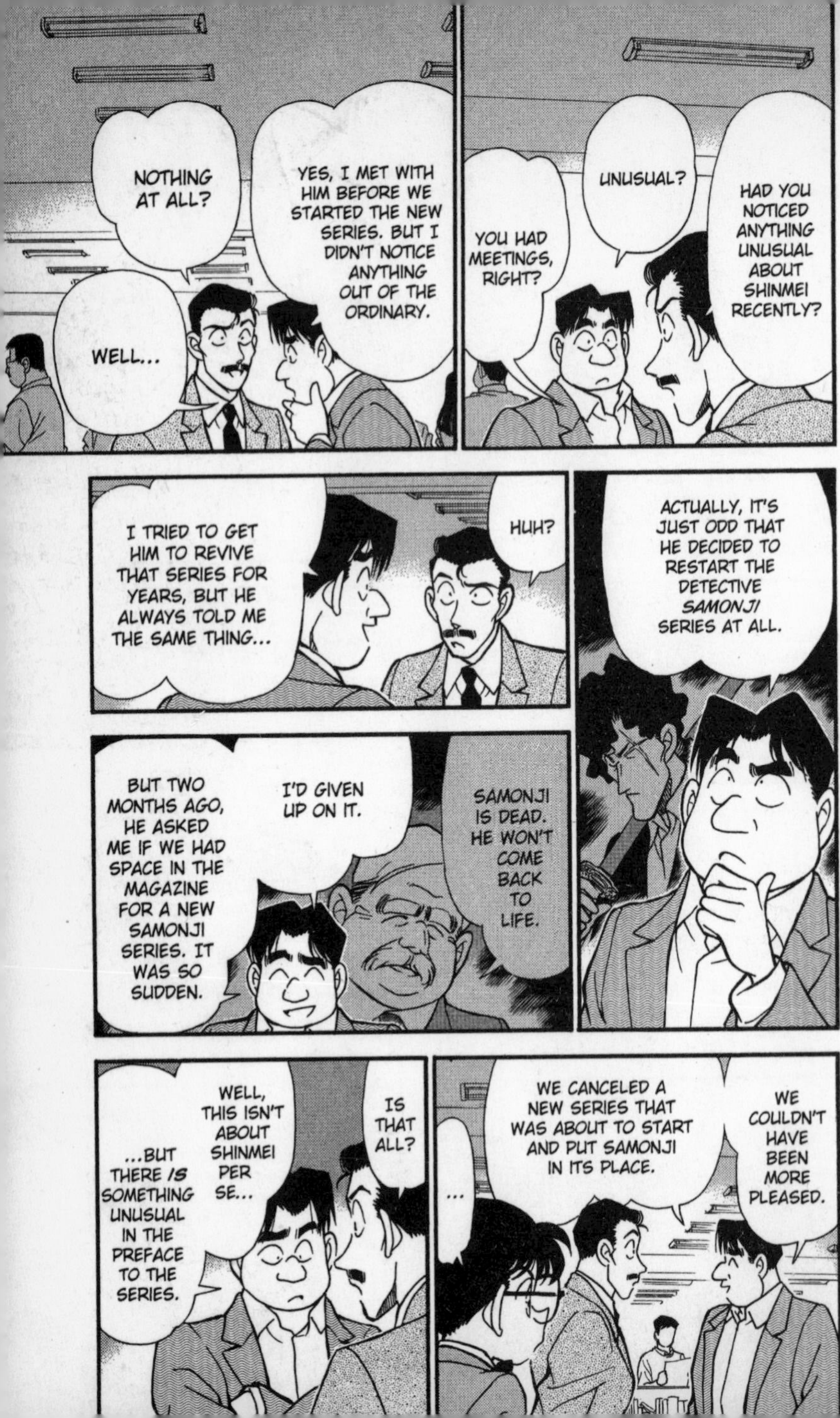
HAD YOU NOTICED ANYTHING UNUSUAL ABOUT SHINMEI RECENTLY?
UNUSUAL?
YOU HAD MEETINGS, RIGHT?
YES, I MET WITH HIM BEFORE WE STARTED THE NEW SERIES. BUT I DIDN'T NOTICE ANYTHING OUT OF THE ORDINARY.
NOTHING AT ALL?
WELL...
ACTUALLY, IT'S JUST ODD THAT HE DECIDED TO RESTART THE DETECTIVE *SAMONJI* SERIES AT ALL.
HUH?
I TRIED TO GET HIM TO REVIVE THAT SERIES FOR YEARS, BUT HE ALWAYS TOLD ME THE SAME THING...
SAMONJI IS DEAD. HE WON'T COME BACK TO LIFE.
I'D GIVEN UP ON IT.
BUT TWO MONTHS AGO, HE ASKED ME IF WE HAD SPACE IN THE MAGAZINE FOR A NEW SAMONJI SERIES. IT WAS SO SUDDEN.
WE COULDN'T HAVE BEEN MORE PLEASED.
WE CANCELED A NEW SERIES THAT WAS ABOUT TO START AND PUT SAMONJI IN ITS PLACE.
...
IS THAT ALL?
WELL, THIS ISN'T ABOUT SHINMEI PER SE...
...BUT THERE *IS* SOMETHING UNUSUAL IN THE PREFACE TO THE SERIES.

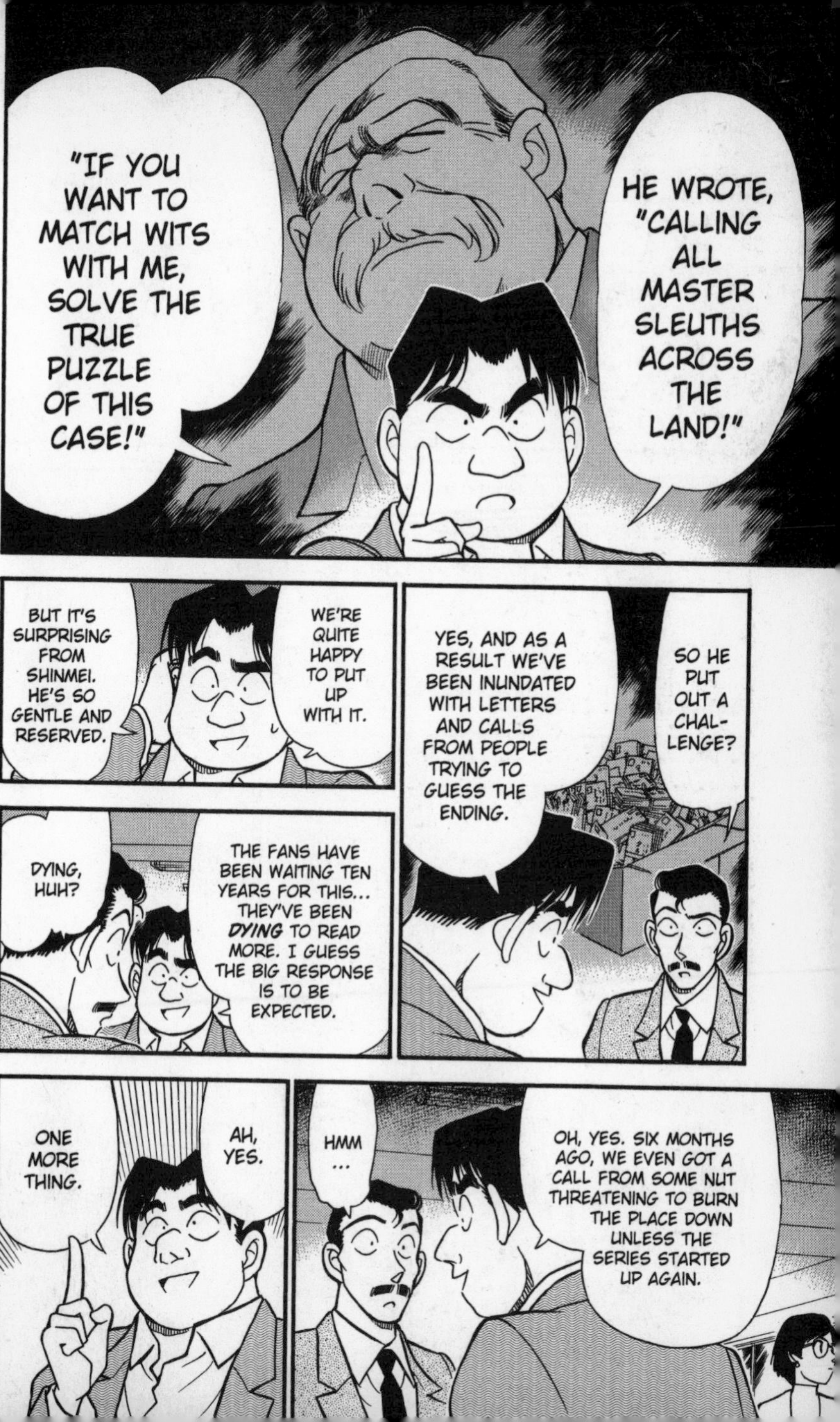
HE WROTE, "CALLING ALL MASTER SLEUTHS ACROSS THE LAND!"
"IF YOU WANT TO MATCH WITS WITH ME, SOLVE THE TRUE PUZZLE OF THIS CASE!"
SO HE PUT OUT A CHAL-LENGE?
YES, AND AS A RESULT WE'VE BEEN INUNDATED WITH LETTERS AND CALLS FROM PEOPLE TRYING TO GUESS THE ENDING.
WE'RE QUITE HAPPY TO PUT UP WITH IT.
BUT IT'S SURPRISING FROM SHINMEI. HE'S SO GENTLE AND RESERVED.
THE FANS HAVE BEEN WAITING TEN YEARS FOR THIS... THEY'VE BEEN *DYING* TO READ MORE. I GUESS THE BIG RESPONSE IS TO BE EXPECTED.
DYING, HUH?
OH, YES. SIX MONTHS AGO, WE EVEN GOT A CALL FROM SOME NUT THREATENING TO BURN THE PLACE DOWN UNLESS THE SERIES STARTED UP AGAIN.
HMM ...
AH, YES.
ONE MORE THING.

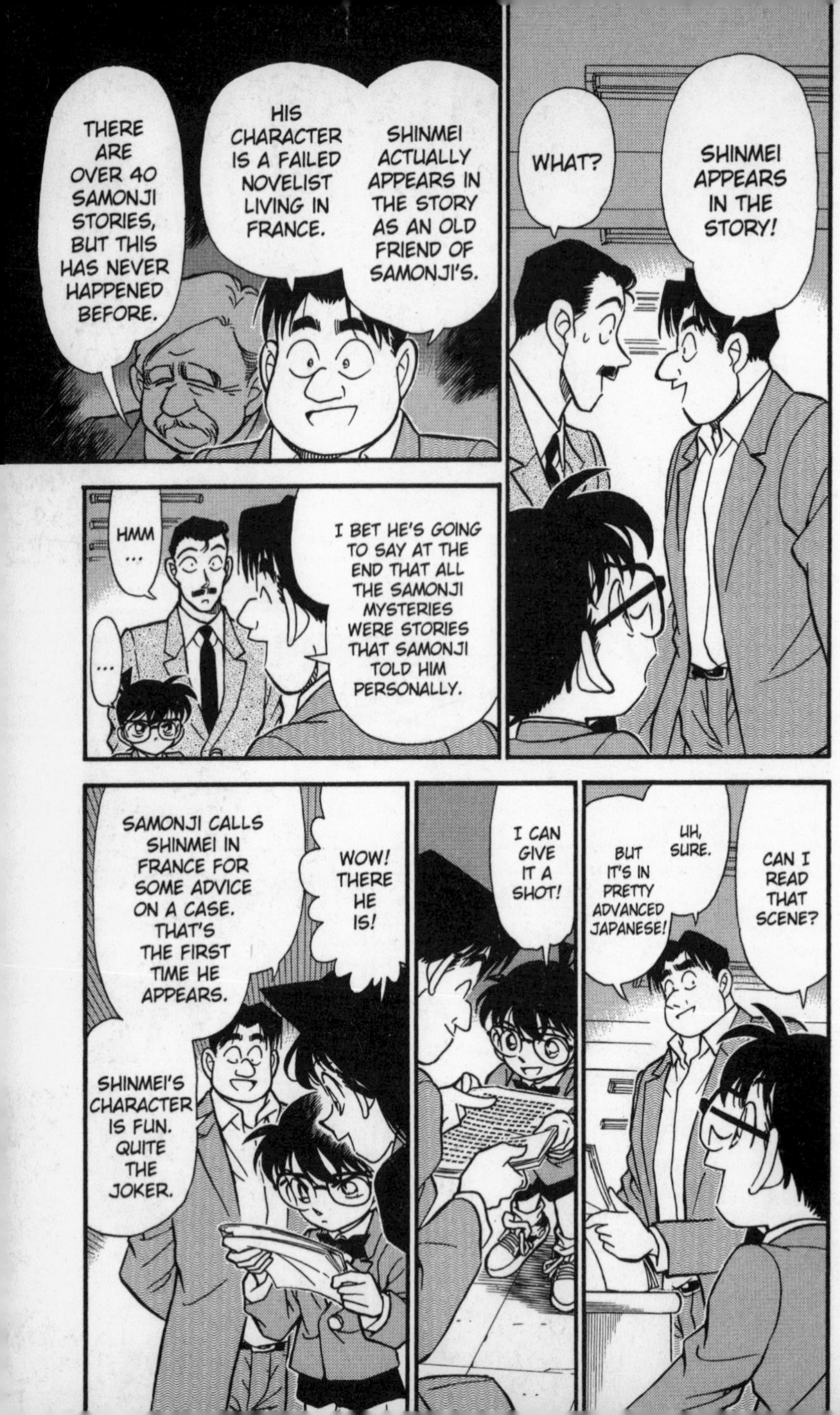
SHINMEI APPEARS IN THE STORY!
WHAT?
SHINMEI ACTUALLY APPEARS IN THE STORY AS AN OLD FRIEND OF SAMONJI'S.
HIS CHARACTER IS A FAILED NOVELIST LIVING IN FRANCE.
THERE ARE OVER 40 SAMONJI STORIES, BUT THIS HAS NEVER HAPPENED BEFORE.
I BET HE'S GOING TO SAY AT THE END THAT ALL THE SAMONJI MYSTERIES WERE STORIES THAT SAMONJI TOLD HIM PERSONALLY.
HMM ...
...
CAN I READ THAT SCENE?
UH, SURE.
BUT IT'S IN PRETTY ADVANCED JAPANESE!
I CAN GIVE IT A SHOT!
WOW! THERE HE IS!
SAMONJI CALLS SHINMEI IN FRANCE FOR SOME ADVICE ON A CASE. THAT'S THE FIRST TIME HE APPEARS.
SHINMEI'S CHARACTER IS FUN. QUITE THE JOKER.

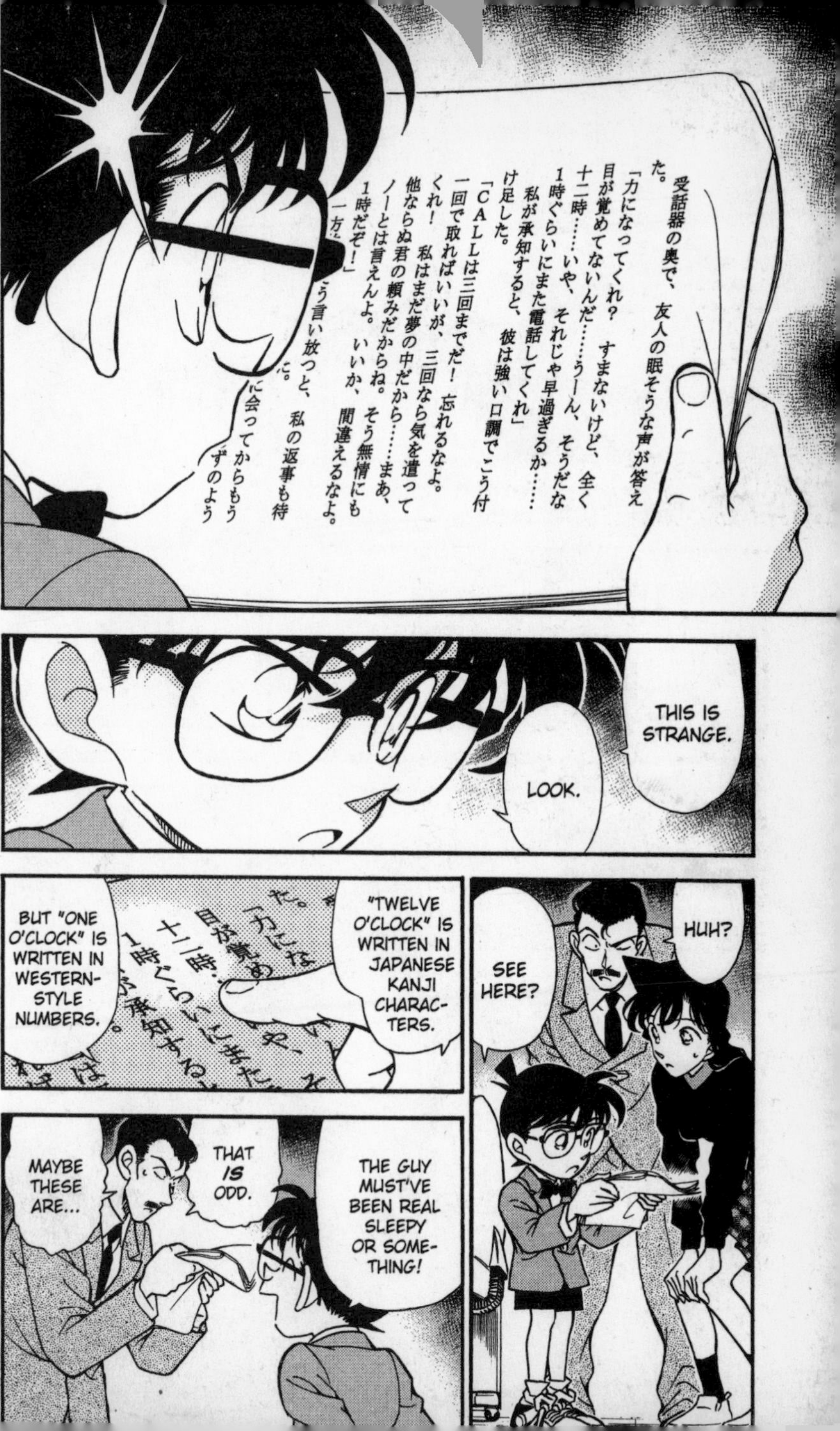
受話器の奥で、友人の眠そうな声が答え
た。
「力になってくれ？　すまないけど、全く
目が覚めてないんだ……うーん、そうだな
十二時……いや、それじゃ早過ぎるか……
1時ぐらいにまた電話してくれ」
私が承知すると、彼は強い口調でこう付
け足した。
「CALLは三回までだ！　忘れるなよ。
一回で取ればいいが、三回なら気を遣って
くれ！　私はまだ夢の中だから……まあ、
他ならぬ君の頼みだからね。そう無情にも
ノーとは言えんよ。いいか、間違えるなよ。
1時だぞ！」
こう言い放つと、私の返事も待
に会ってからもう
ずのよう
THIS IS STRANGE.
LOOK.
HUH?
SEE HERE?
"TWELVE O'CLOCK" IS WRITTEN IN JAPANESE KANJI CHARACTERS.
BUT "ONE O'CLOCK" IS WRITTEN IN WESTERN-STYLE NUMBERS.
THE GUY MUST'VE BEEN REAL SLEEPY OR SOMETHING!
THAT IS ODD.
MAYBE THESE ARE...

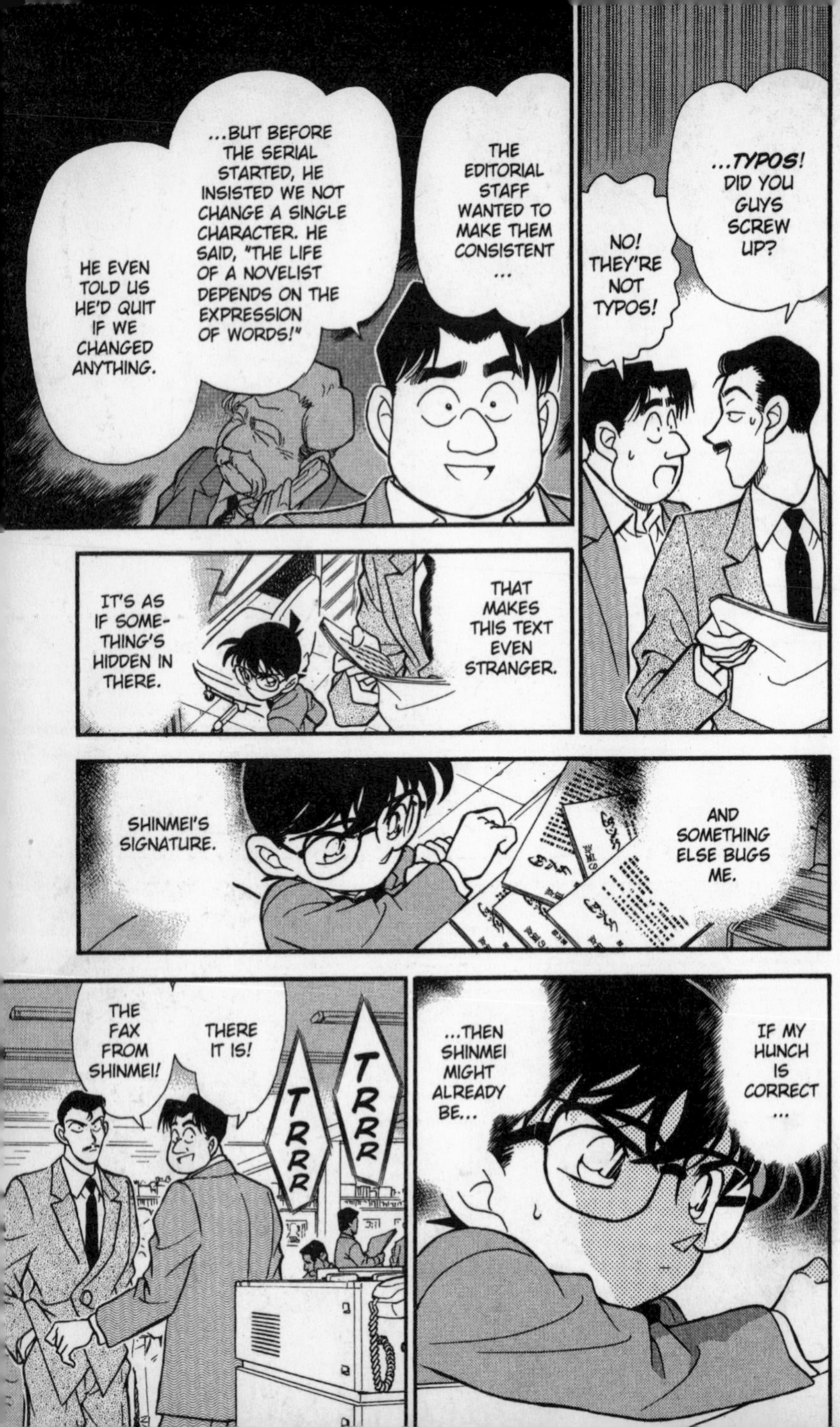
...TYPOS! DID YOU GUYS SCREW UP?
NO! THEY'RE NOT TYPOS!
THE EDITORIAL STAFF WANTED TO MAKE THEM CONSISTENT...
...BUT BEFORE THE SERIAL STARTED, HE INSISTED WE NOT CHANGE A SINGLE CHARACTER. HE SAID, "THE LIFE OF A NOVELIST DEPENDS ON THE EXPRESSION OF WORDS!"
HE EVEN TOLD US HE'D QUIT IF WE CHANGED ANYTHING.
THAT MAKES THIS TEXT EVEN STRANGER.
IT'S AS IF SOME-THING'S HIDDEN IN THERE.
AND SOMETHING ELSE BUGS ME.
SHINMEI'S SIGNATURE.
IF MY HUNCH IS CORRECT...
...THEN SHINMEI MIGHT ALREADY BE...
TRRR
TRRR
THERE IT IS!
THE FAX FROM SHINMEI!

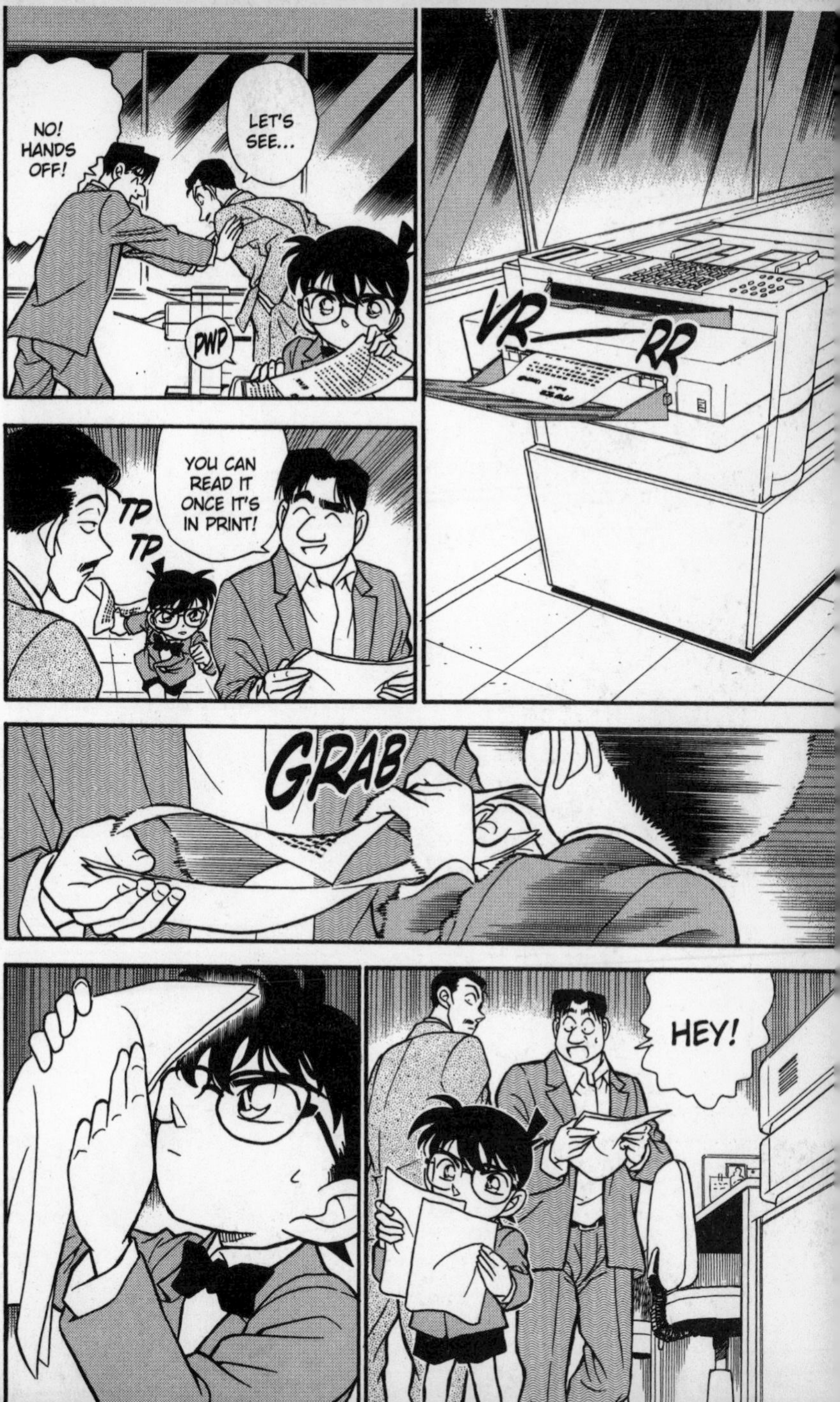
VR—RR
LET'S SEE...
NO! HANDS OFF!
PWP
YOU CAN READ IT ONCE IT'S IN PRINT!
TP TP
GRAB
HEY!

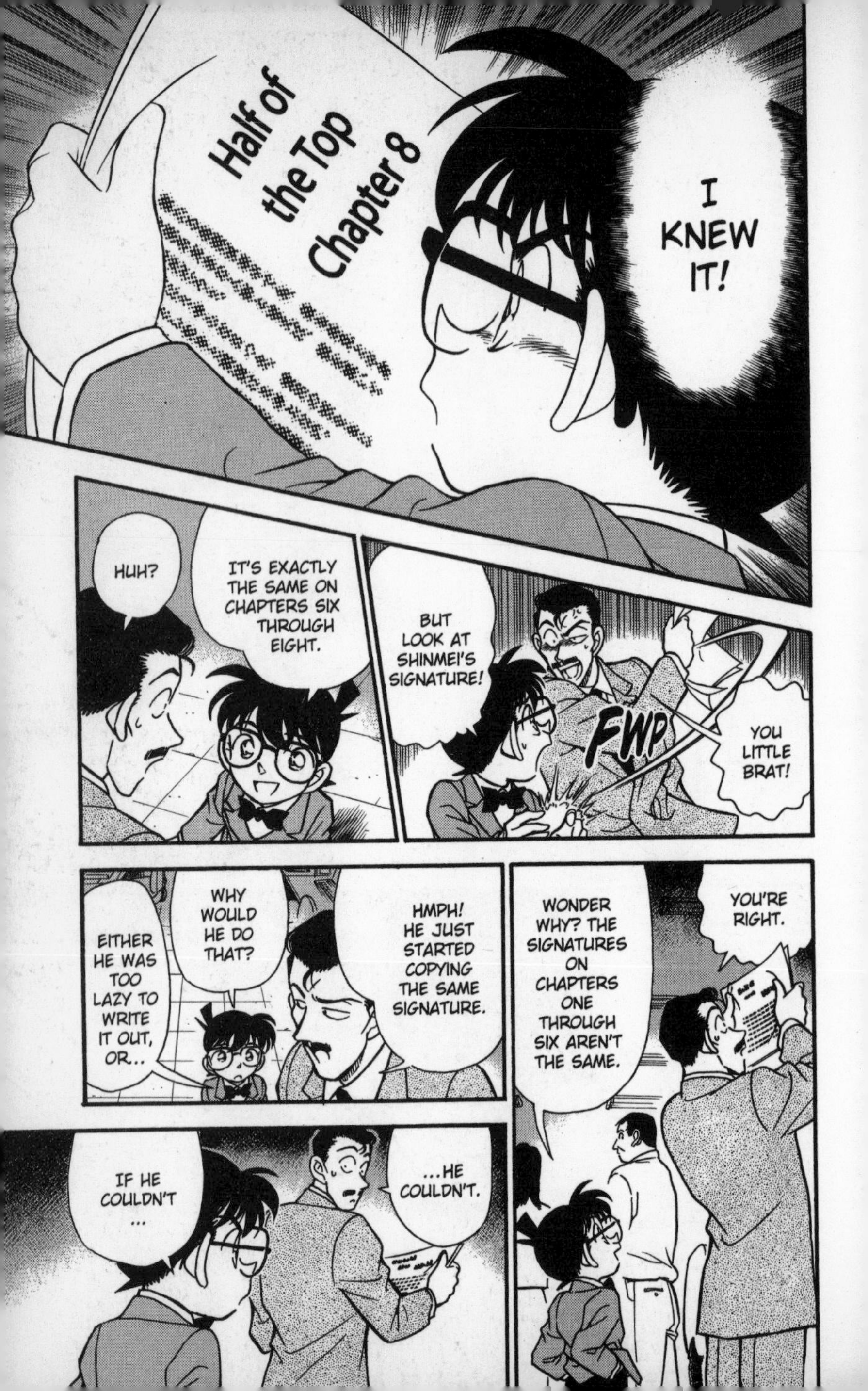
Half of the Top
Chapter 8
I KNEW IT!
BUT LOOK AT SHINMEI'S SIGNATURE!
FWP
YOU LITTLE BRAT!
IT'S EXACTLY THE SAME ON CHAPTERS SIX THROUGH EIGHT.
HUH?
YOU'RE RIGHT.
WONDER WHY? THE SIGNATURES ON CHAPTERS ONE THROUGH SIX AREN'T THE SAME.
HMPH! HE JUST STARTED COPYING THE SAME SIGNATURE.
WHY WOULD HE DO THAT?
EITHER HE WAS TOO LAZY TO WRITE IT OUT, OR...
...HE COULDN'T.
IF HE COULDN'T ...

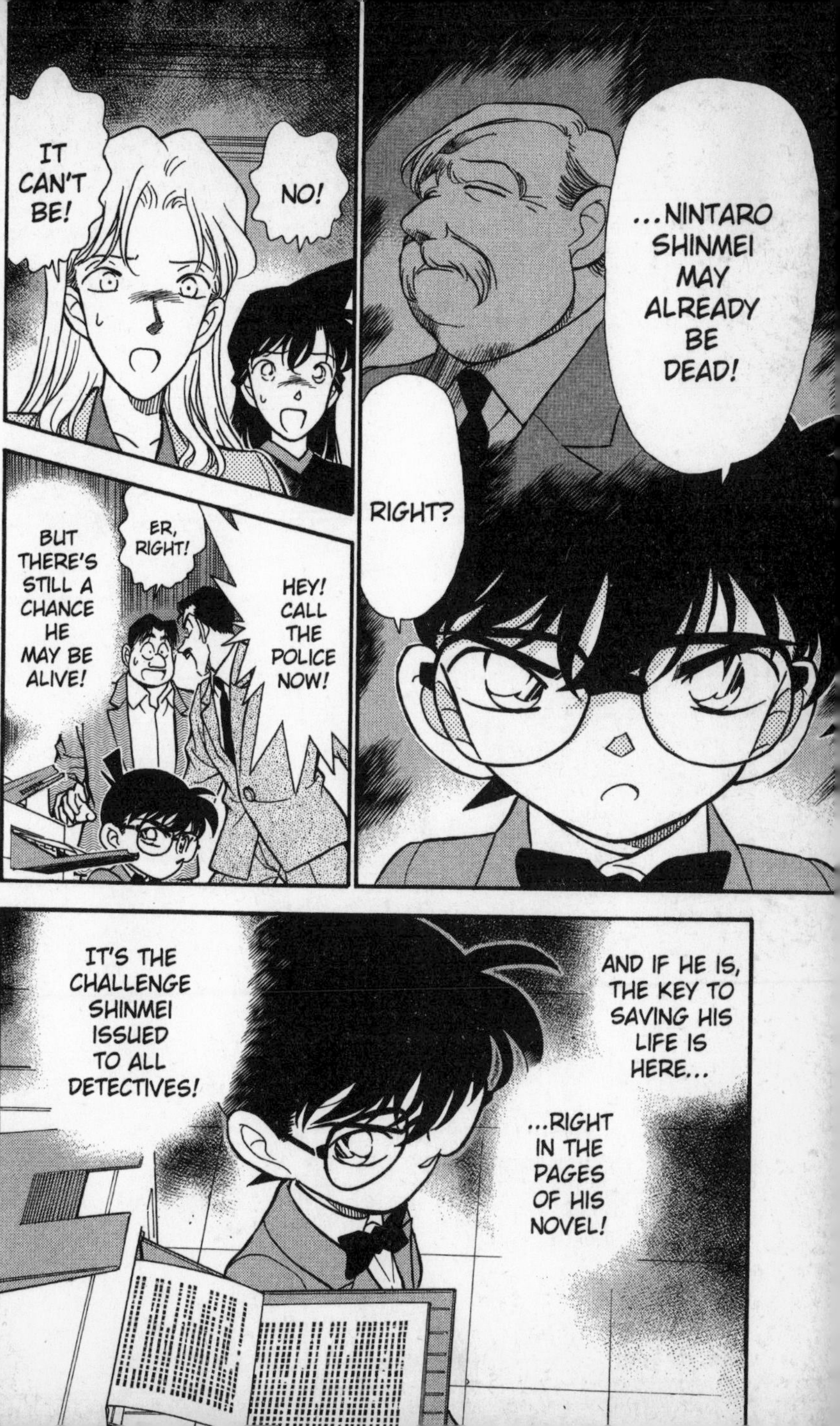
...NINTARO SHINMEI MAY ALREADY BE DEAD!
RIGHT?
NO!
IT CAN'T BE!
HEY! CALL THE POLICE NOW!
ER, RIGHT!
BUT THERE'S STILL A CHANCE HE MAY BE ALIVE!
AND IF HE IS, THE KEY TO SAVING HIS LIFE IS HERE...
...RIGHT IN THE PAGES OF HIS NOVEL!
IT'S THE CHALLENGE SHINMEI ISSUED TO ALL DETECTIVES!

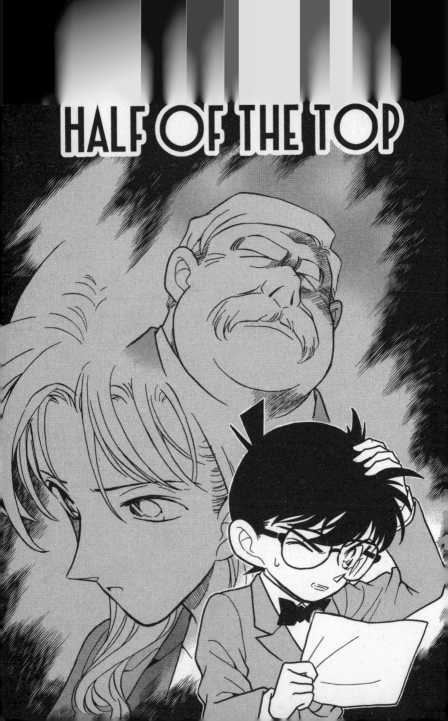

HALF OF THE TOP

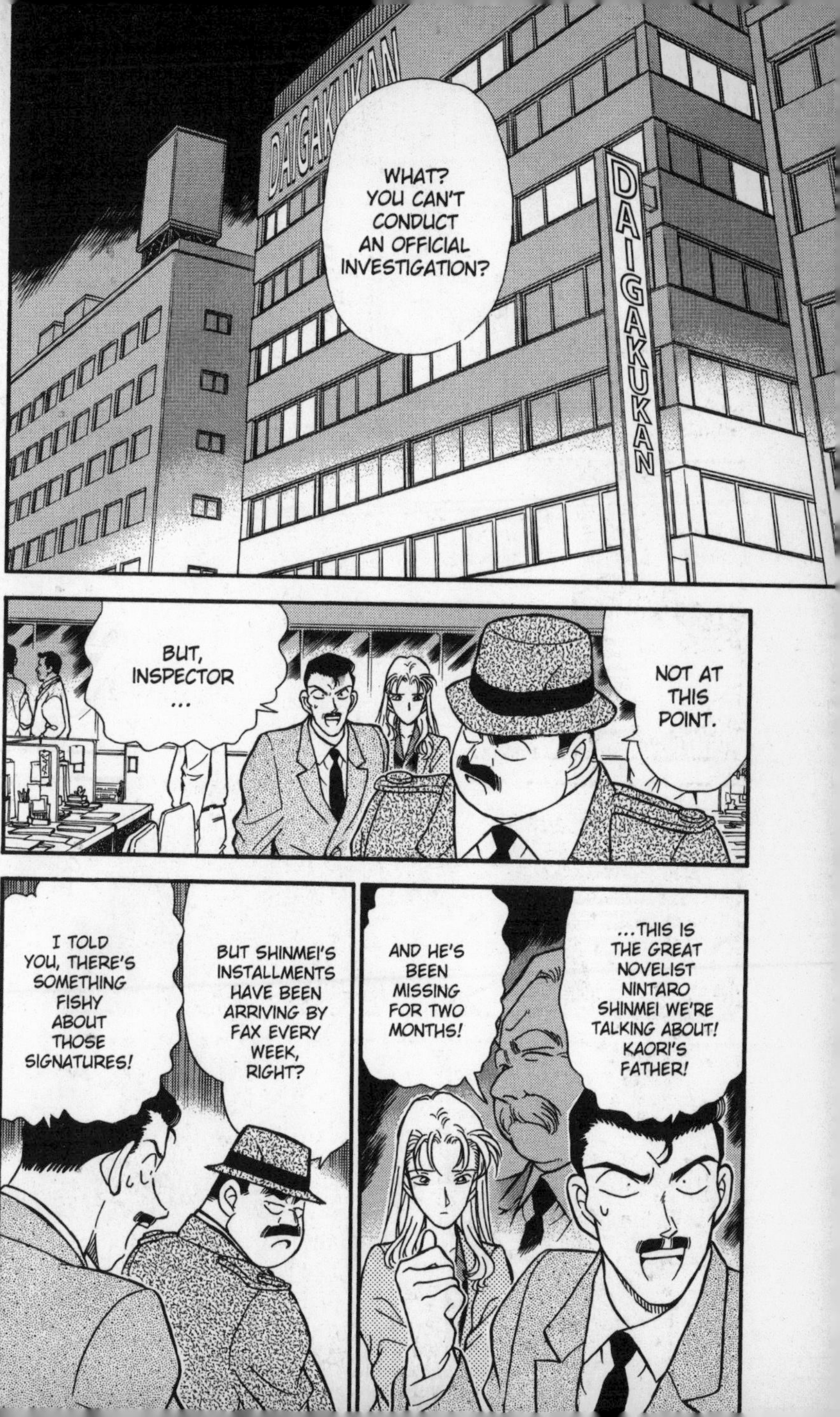
DAIGAKUKAN
DAIGAKUKAN
WHAT? YOU CAN'T CONDUCT AN OFFICIAL INVESTIGATION?
NOT AT THIS POINT.
BUT, INSPECTOR ...
...THIS IS THE GREAT NOVELIST NINTARO SHINMEI WE'RE TALKING ABOUT! KAORI'S FATHER!
AND HE'S BEEN MISSING FOR TWO MONTHS!
BUT SHINMEI'S INSTALLMENTS HAVE BEEN ARRIVING BY FAX EVERY WEEK, RIGHT?
I TOLD YOU, THERE'S SOMETHING FISHY ABOUT THOSE SIGNATURES!

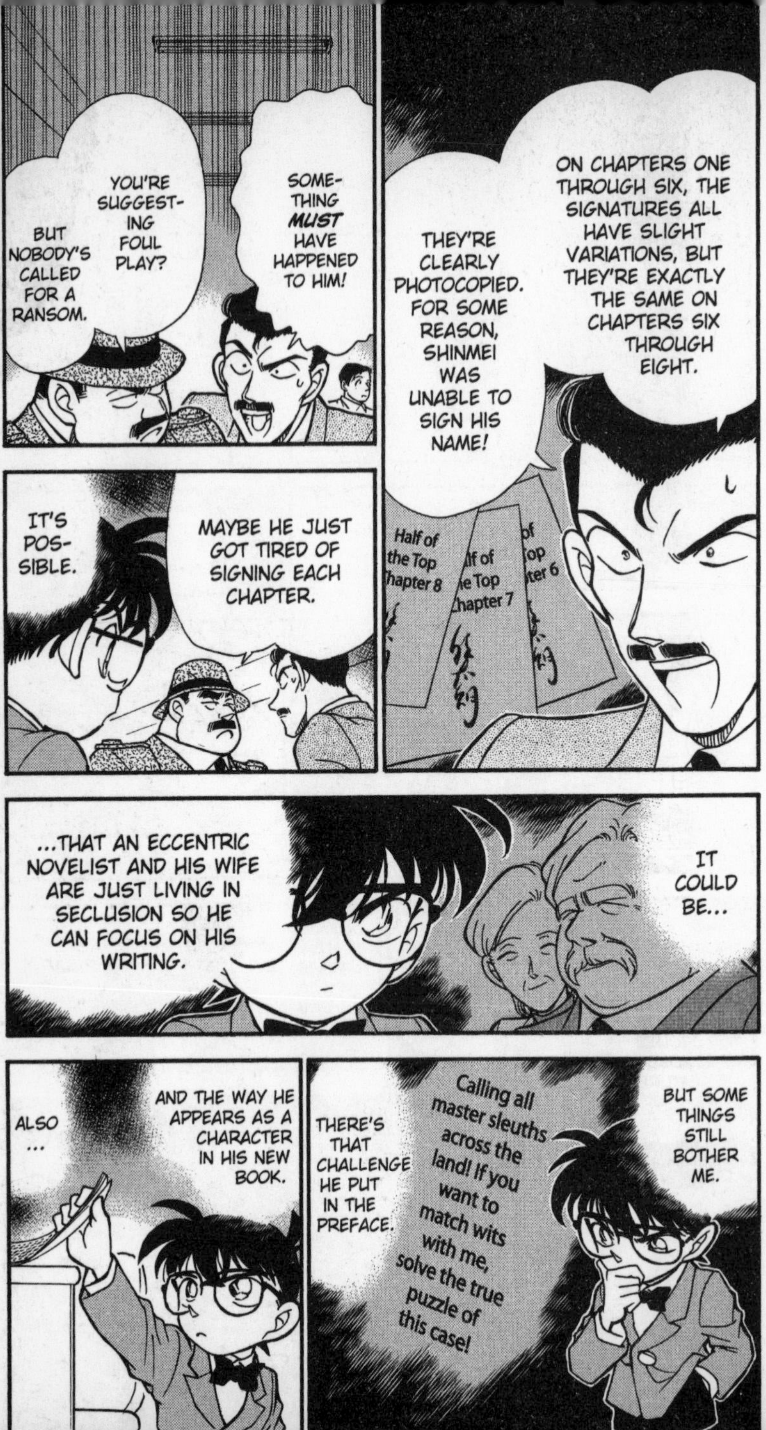
ON CHAPTERS ONE THROUGH SIX, THE SIGNATURES ALL HAVE SLIGHT VARIATIONS, BUT THEY'RE EXACTLY THE SAME ON CHAPTERS SIX THROUGH EIGHT.
THEY'RE CLEARLY PHOTOCOPIED. FOR SOME REASON, SHINMEI WAS UNABLE TO SIGN HIS NAME!
Half of the Top Chapter 8
SOMETHING *MUST* HAVE HAPPENED TO HIM!
YOU'RE SUGGESTING FOUL PLAY?
BUT NOBODY'S CALLED FOR A RANSOM.
MAYBE HE JUST GOT TIRED OF SIGNING EACH CHAPTER.
IT'S POSSIBLE.
IT COULD BE...
...THAT AN ECCENTRIC NOVELIST AND HIS WIFE ARE JUST LIVING IN SECLUSION SO HE CAN FOCUS ON HIS WRITING.
BUT SOME THINGS STILL BOTHER ME.
Calling all master sleuths across the land! If you want to match wits with me, solve the true puzzle of this case!
THERE'S THAT CHALLENGE HE PUT IN THE PREFACE.
AND THE WAY HE APPEARS AS A CHARACTER IN HIS NEW BOOK.
ALSO...

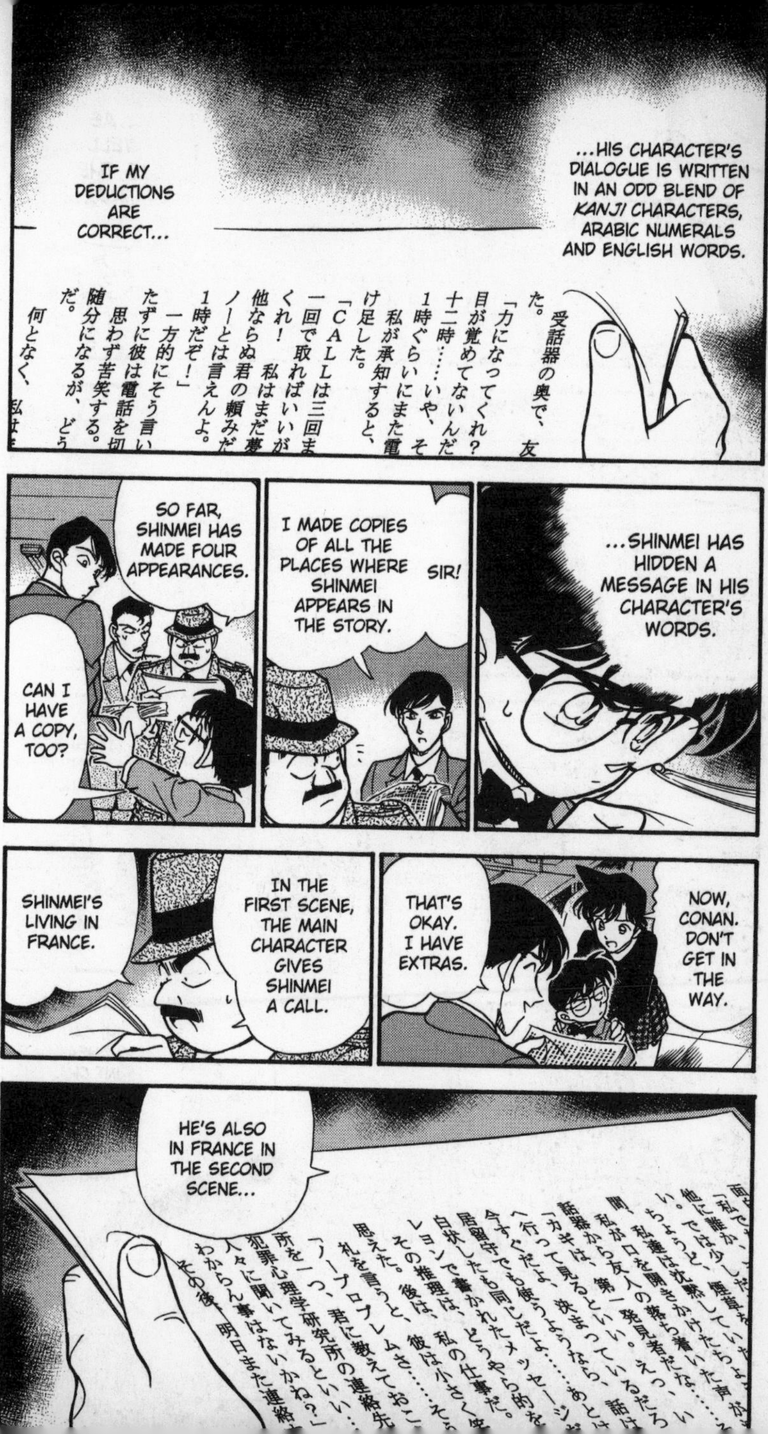
...HIS CHARACTER'S DIALOGUE IS WRITTEN IN AN ODD BLEND OF *KANJI* CHARACTERS, ARABIC NUMERALS AND ENGLISH WORDS.
IF MY DEDUCTIONS ARE CORRECT...
受話器の奥で、友
た。
「力になってくれ？
目が覚めてないんだ
十二時……いや、そ
１時ぐらいにまた電
私が承知すると、
け足した。
「ＣＡＬＬは三回ま
一回で取ればいいが
くれ！　私はまだ夢
他ならぬ君の頼みだ
ノーとは言えんよ。
１時だぞ！」
一方的にそう言い
たずに彼は電話を切
思わず苦笑する。
随分になるが、どう
だ。
何となく、私は
...SHINMEI HAS HIDDEN A MESSAGE IN HIS CHARACTER'S WORDS.
SIR!
I MADE COPIES OF ALL THE PLACES WHERE SHINMEI APPEARS IN THE STORY.
SO FAR, SHINMEI HAS MADE FOUR APPEARANCES.
CAN I HAVE A COPY, TOO?
NOW, CONAN. DON'T GET IN THE WAY.
THAT'S OKAY. I HAVE EXTRAS.
IN THE FIRST SCENE, THE MAIN CHARACTER GIVES SHINMEI A CALL.
SHINMEI'S LIVING IN FRANCE.
HE'S ALSO IN FRANCE IN THE SECOND SCENE...

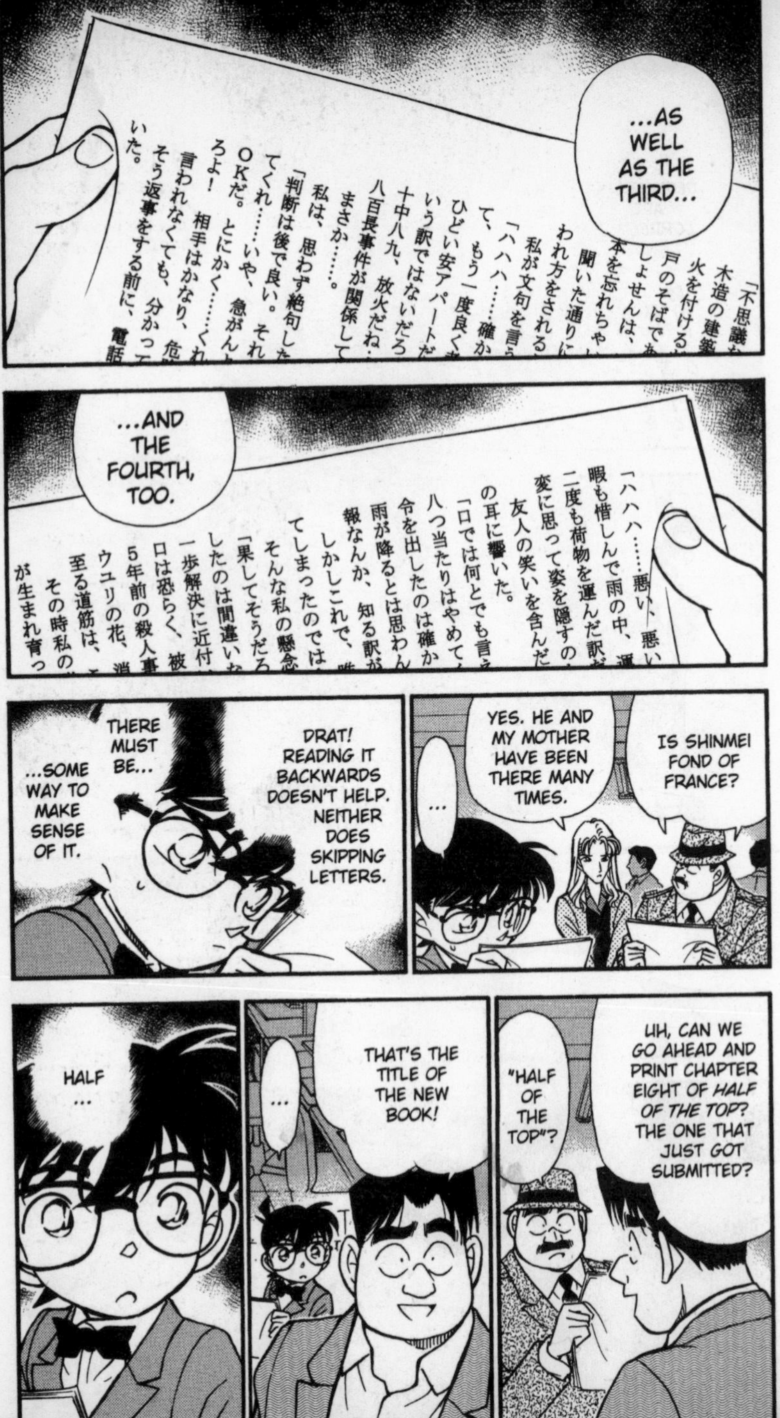
...AS WELL AS THE THIRD...
...AND THE FOURTH, TOO.
IS SHINMEI FOND OF FRANCE?
YES. HE AND MY MOTHER HAVE BEEN THERE MANY TIMES.
...
DRAT! READING IT BACKWARDS DOESN'T HELP. NEITHER DOES SKIPPING LETTERS.
THERE MUST BE...
...SOME WAY TO MAKE SENSE OF IT.
UH, CAN WE GO AHEAD AND PRINT CHAPTER EIGHT OF *HALF OF THE TOP*? THE ONE THAT JUST GOT SUBMITTED?
"HALF OF THE TOP"?
THAT'S THE TITLE OF THE NEW BOOK!
...
HALF ...

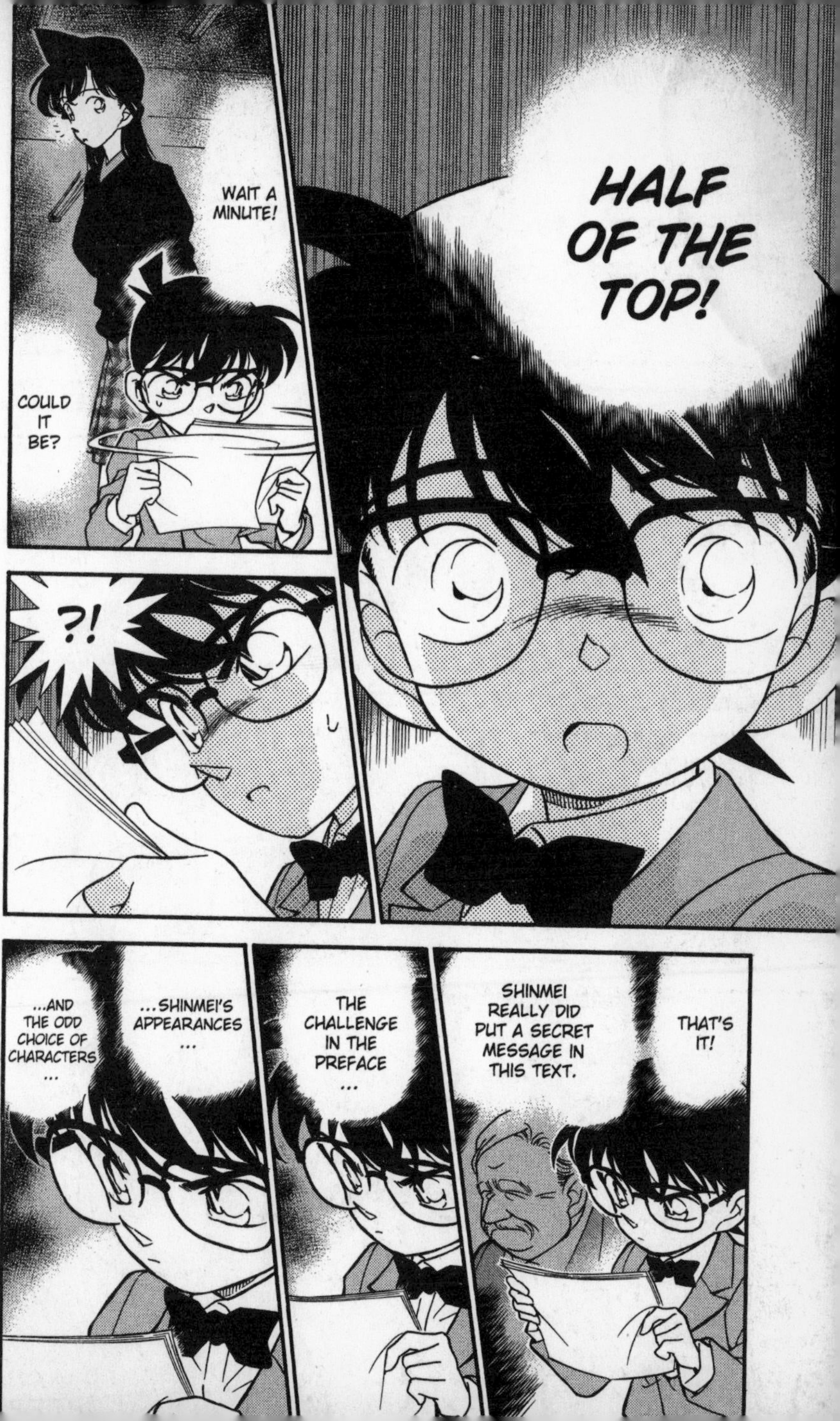
HALF OF THE TOP!
WAIT A MINUTE!
COULD IT BE?
?!
THAT'S IT!
SHINMEI REALLY DID PUT A SECRET MESSAGE IN THIS TEXT.
THE CHALLENGE IN THE PREFACE ...
...SHINMEI'S APPEARANCES ...
...AND THE ODD CHOICE OF CHARACTERS ...

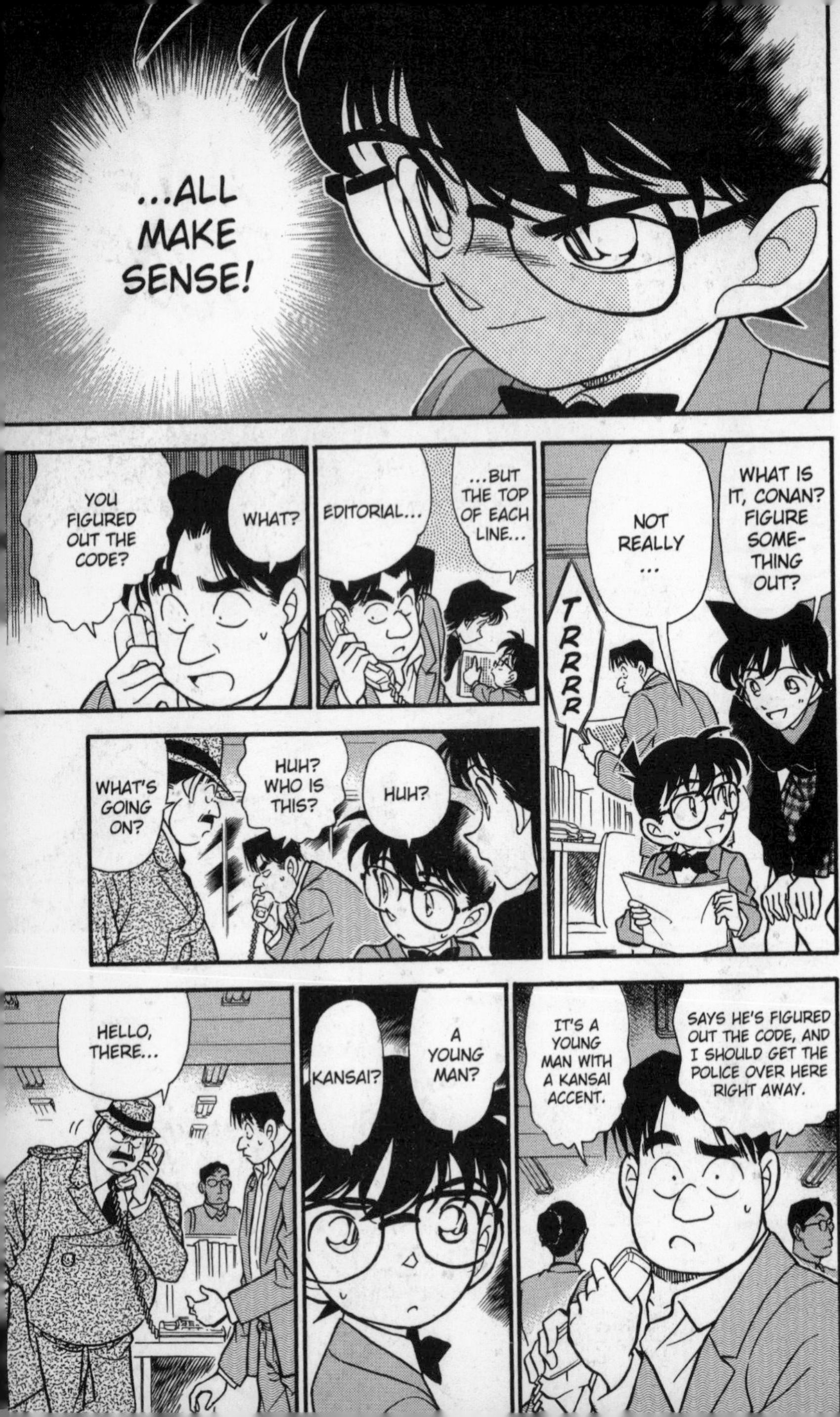
...ALL MAKE SENSE!
WHAT IS IT, CONAN? FIGURE SOME-THING OUT?
NOT REALLY ...
TRRRR
...BUT THE TOP OF EACH LINE...
EDITORIAL...
WHAT?
YOU FIGURED OUT THE CODE?
HUH?
HUH? WHO IS THIS?
WHAT'S GOING ON?
SAYS HE'S FIGURED OUT THE CODE, AND I SHOULD GET THE POLICE OVER HERE RIGHT AWAY.
IT'S A YOUNG MAN WITH A KANSAI ACCENT.
A YOUNG MAN?
KANSAI?
HELLO, THERE...

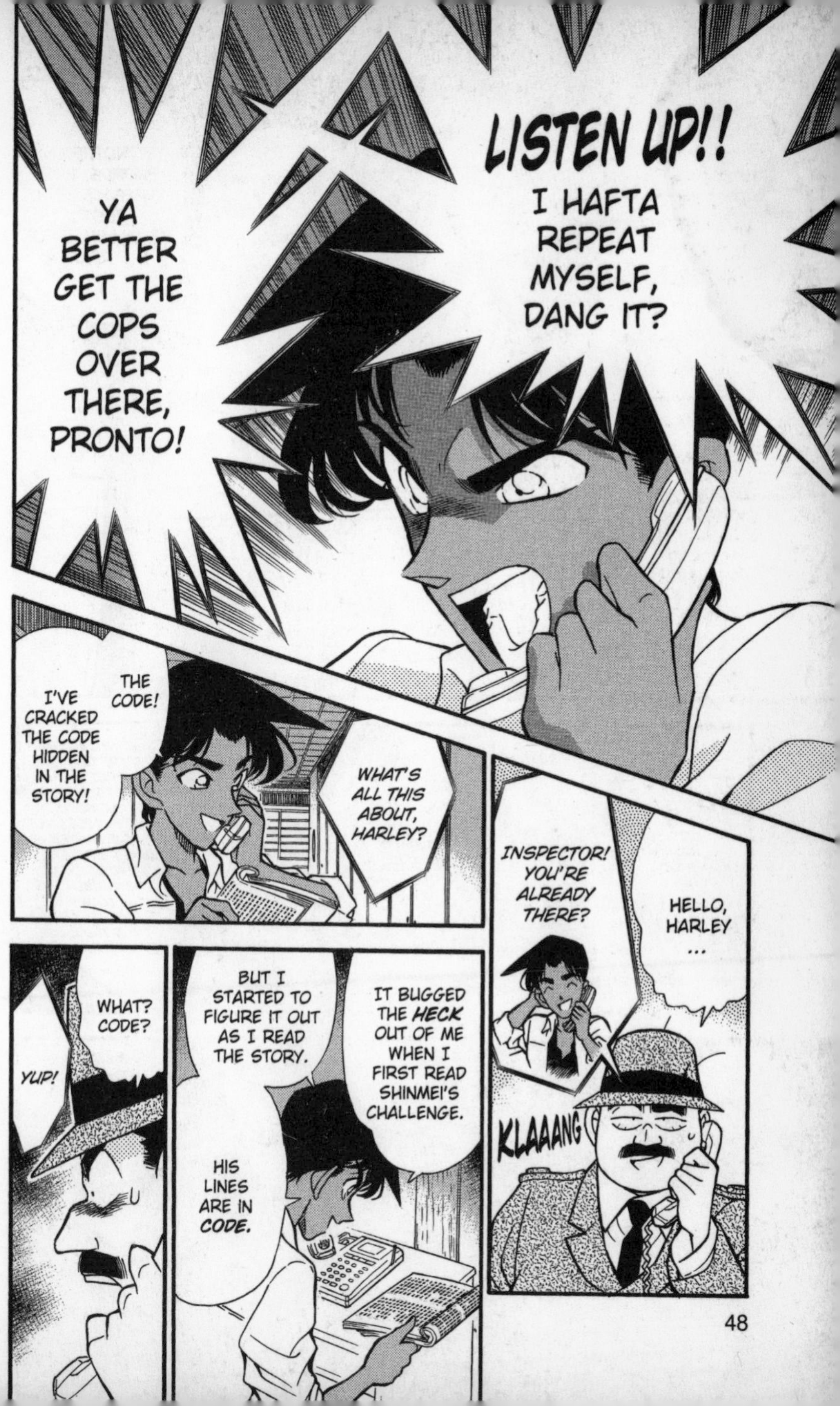
LISTEN UP!!
I HAFTA REPEAT MYSELF, DANG IT?
YA BETTER GET THE COPS OVER THERE, PRONTO!
HELLO, HARLEY...
INSPECTOR! YOU'RE ALREADY THERE?
KLAAANG
WHAT'S ALL THIS ABOUT, HARLEY?
THE CODE!
I'VE CRACKED THE CODE HIDDEN IN THE STORY!
IT BUGGED THE HECK OUT OF ME WHEN I FIRST READ SHINMEI'S CHALLENGE.
BUT I STARTED TO FIGURE IT OUT AS I READ THE STORY.
HIS LINES ARE IN CODE.
WHAT? CODE?
YUP!

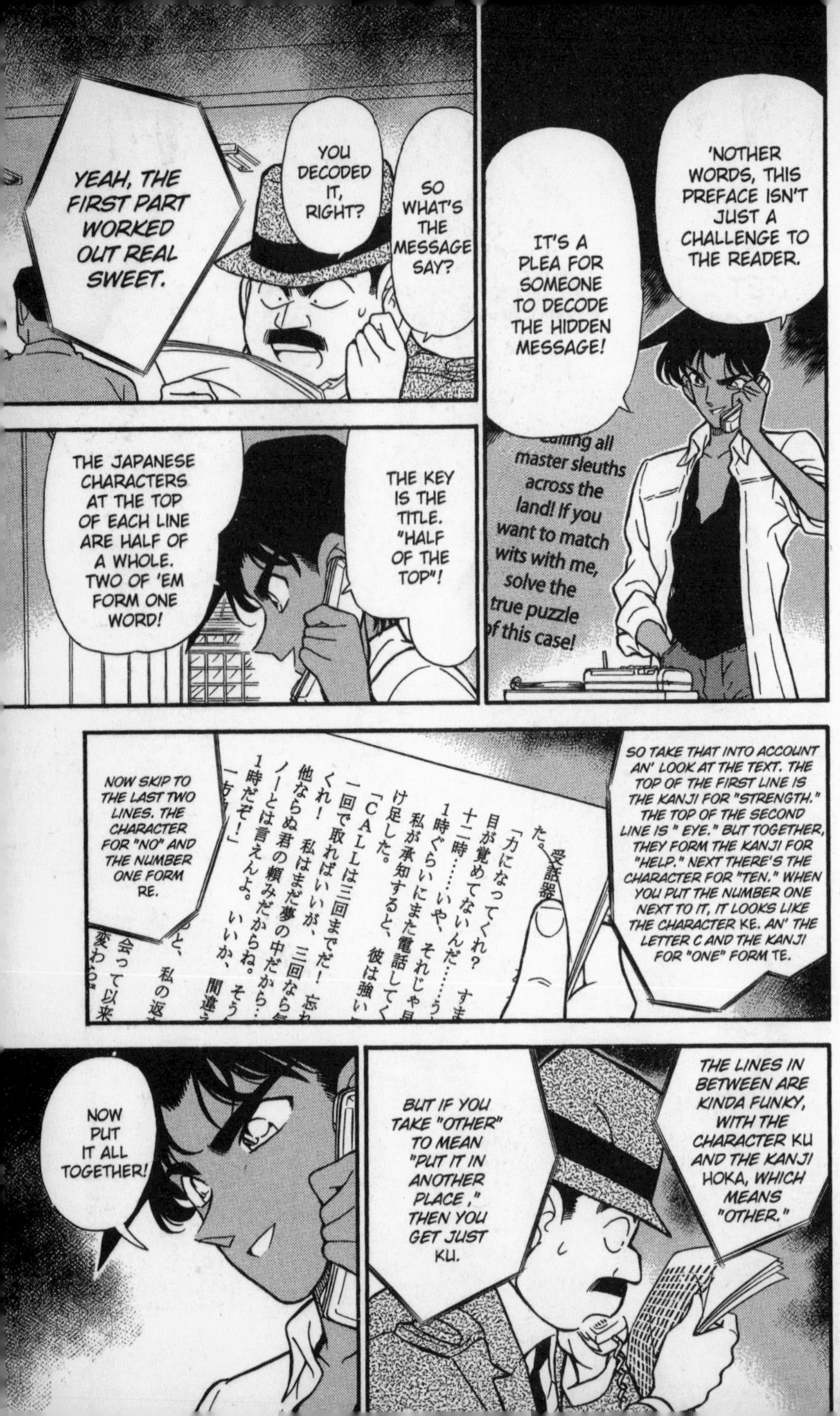
'NOTHER WORDS, THIS PREFACE ISN'T JUST A CHALLENGE TO THE READER.
IT'S A PLEA FOR SOMEONE TO DECODE THE HIDDEN MESSAGE!
calling all master sleuths across the land! If you want to match wits with me, solve the true puzzle of this case!
YOU DECODED IT, RIGHT?
SO WHAT'S THE MESSAGE SAY?
YEAH, THE FIRST PART WORKED OUT REAL SWEET.
THE KEY IS THE TITLE. "HALF OF THE TOP"!
THE JAPANESE CHARACTERS AT THE TOP OF EACH LINE ARE HALF OF A WHOLE. TWO OF 'EM FORM ONE WORD!
SO TAKE THAT INTO ACCOUNT AN' LOOK AT THE TEXT. THE TOP OF THE FIRST LINE IS THE KANJI FOR "STRENGTH." THE TOP OF THE SECOND LINE IS " EYE." BUT TOGETHER, THEY FORM THE KANJI FOR "HELP." NEXT THERE'S THE CHARACTER FOR "TEN." WHEN YOU PUT THE NUMBER ONE NEXT TO IT, IT LOOKS LIKE THE CHARACTER KE. AN' THE LETTER C AND THE KANJI FOR "ONE" FORM TE.
受話器
た。
「力になってくれ？
目が覚めてないんだ……
十二時……いや、それじゃ
1時ぐらいにまた電話して
私が承知すると、彼は強い
け足した。
「CALLは三回までだ！
一回で取ればいいが、三回なら
くれ！ 私はまだ夢の中だから…
他ならぬ君の頼みだからね。
ノーとは言えんよ。 いいか、
1時だぞ！」
NOW SKIP TO THE LAST TWO LINES. THE CHARACTER FOR "NO" AND THE NUMBER ONE FORM RE.
THE LINES IN BETWEEN ARE KINDA FUNKY, WITH THE CHARACTER KU AND THE KANJI HOKA, WHICH MEANS "OTHER."
BUT IF YOU TAKE "OTHER" TO MEAN "PUT IT IN ANOTHER PLACE," THEN YOU GET JUST KU.
NOW PUT IT ALL TOGETHER!

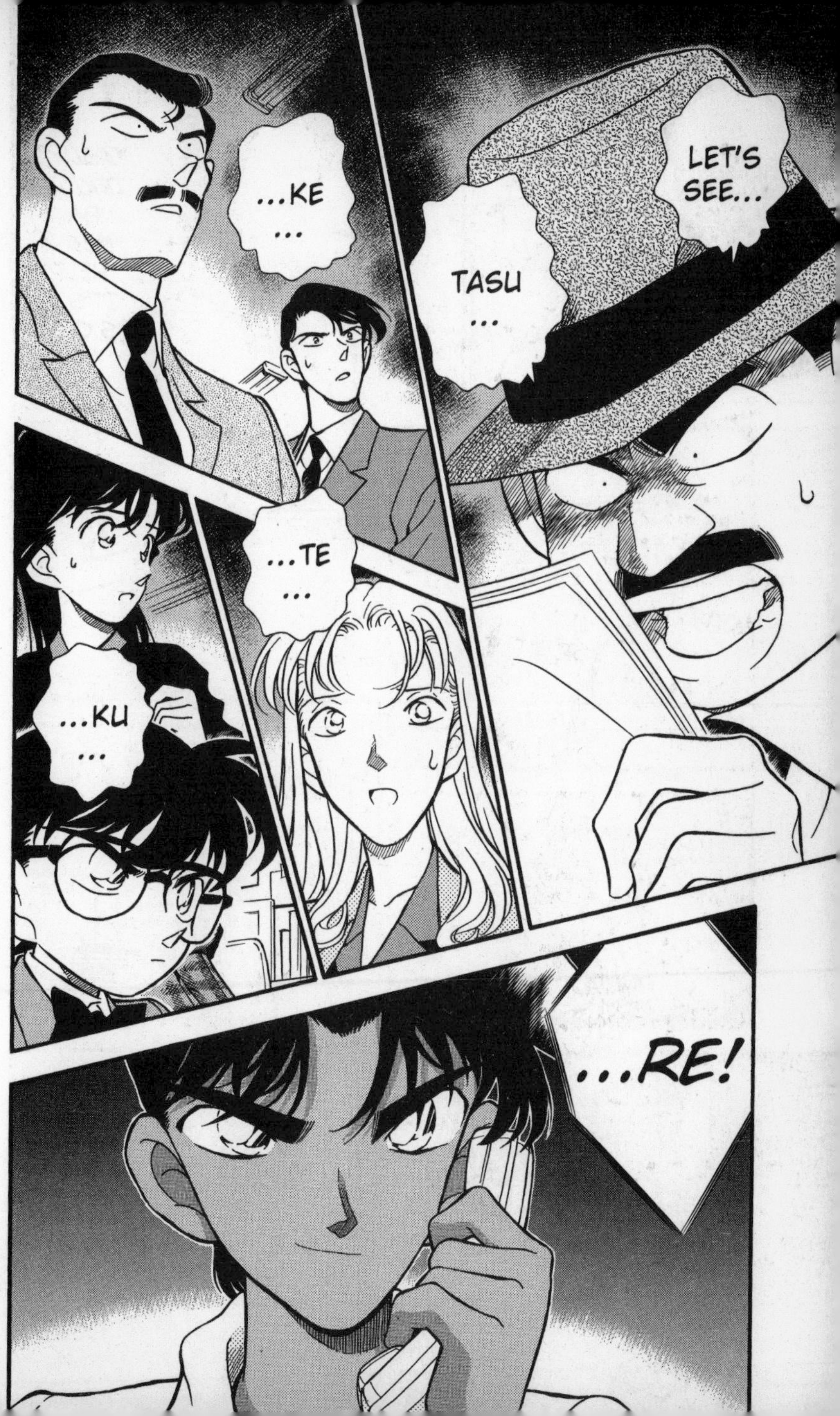
LET'S SEE...
TASU ...
...KE ...
...TE ...
...KU ...
...RE!

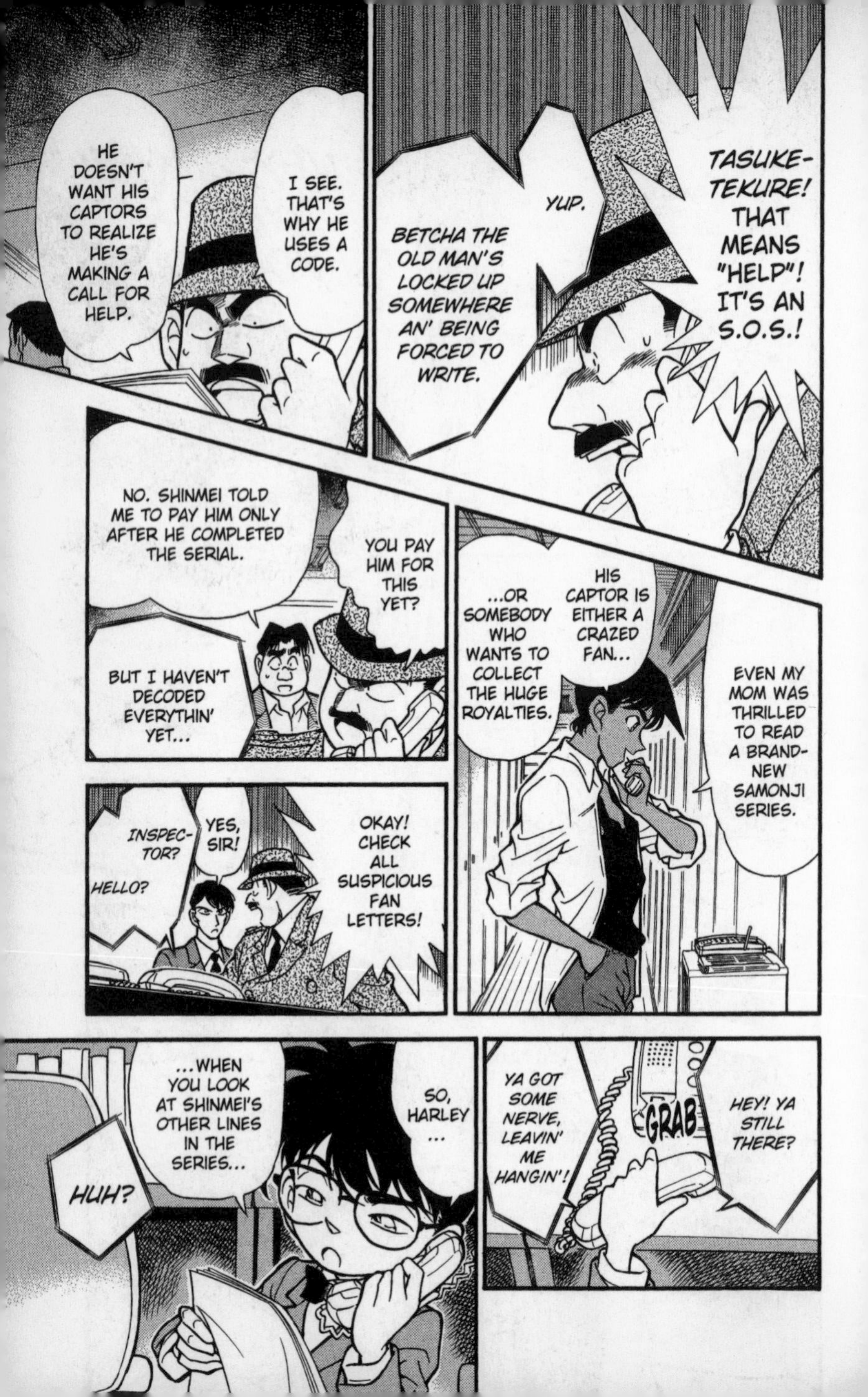
TASUKE-TEKURE! THAT MEANS "HELP"! IT'S AN S.O.S.!
YUP.
BETCHA THE OLD MAN'S LOCKED UP SOMEWHERE AN' BEING FORCED TO WRITE.
I SEE. THAT'S WHY HE USES A CODE.
HE DOESN'T WANT HIS CAPTORS TO REALIZE HE'S MAKING A CALL FOR HELP.
YOU PAY HIM FOR THIS YET?
NO. SHINMEI TOLD ME TO PAY HIM ONLY AFTER HE COMPLETED THE SERIAL.
BUT I HAVEN'T DECODED EVERYTHIN' YET...
EVEN MY MOM WAS THRILLED TO READ A BRAND-NEW SAMONJI SERIES.
HIS CAPTOR IS EITHER A CRAZED FAN...
...OR SOMEBODY WHO WANTS TO COLLECT THE HUGE ROYALTIES.
OKAY! CHECK ALL SUSPICIOUS FAN LETTERS!
YES, SIR!
INSPECTOR?
HELLO?
HEY! YA STILL THERE?
GRAB
YA GOT SOME NERVE, LEAVIN' ME HANGIN'!
SO, HARLEY...
...WHEN YOU LOOK AT SHINMEI'S OTHER LINES IN THE SERIES...
HUH?

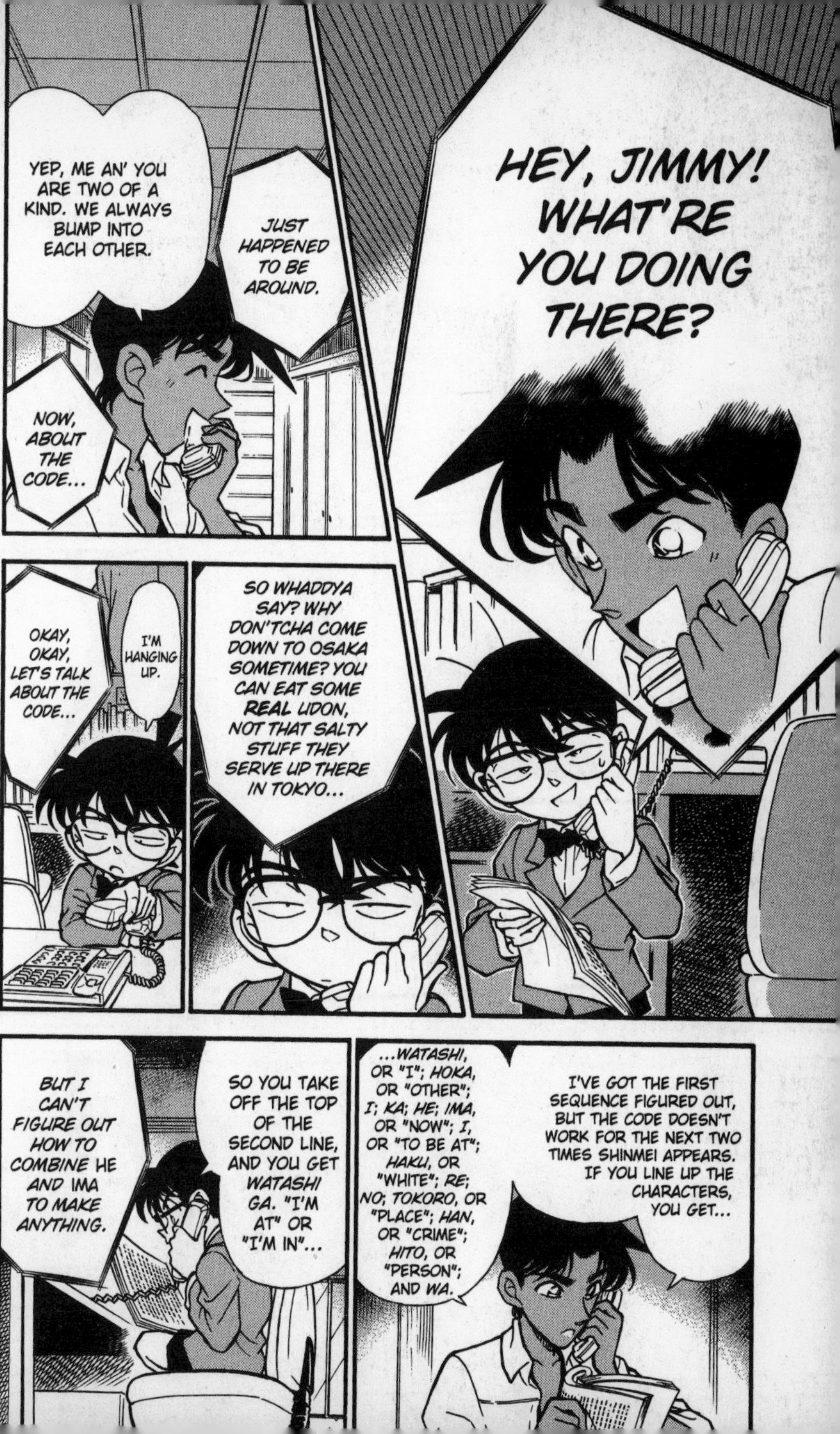
HEY, JIMMY! WHAT'RE YOU DOING THERE?
JUST HAPPENED TO BE AROUND.
YEP, ME AN' YOU ARE TWO OF A KIND. WE ALWAYS BUMP INTO EACH OTHER.
NOW, ABOUT THE CODE...
SO WHADDYA SAY? WHY DON'TCHA COME DOWN TO OSAKA SOMETIME? YOU CAN EAT SOME REAL UDON, NOT THAT SALTY STUFF THEY SERVE UP THERE IN TOKYO...
I'M HANGING UP.
OKAY, OKAY, LET'S TALK ABOUT THE CODE...
I'VE GOT THE FIRST SEQUENCE FIGURED OUT, BUT THE CODE DOESN'T WORK FOR THE NEXT TWO TIMES SHINMEI APPEARS. IF YOU LINE UP THE CHARACTERS, YOU GET...
...WATASHI, OR "I"; HOKA, OR "OTHER"; I; KA; HE; IMA, OR "NOW"; I, OR "TO BE AT"; HAKU, OR "WHITE"; RE; NO; TOKORO, OR "PLACE"; HAN, OR "CRIME"; HITO, OR "PERSON"; AND WA.
SO YOU TAKE OFF THE TOP OF THE SECOND LINE, AND YOU GET WATASHI GA. "I'M AT" OR "I'M IN"...
BUT I CAN'T FIGURE OUT HOW TO COMBINE HE AND IMA TO MAKE ANYTHING.

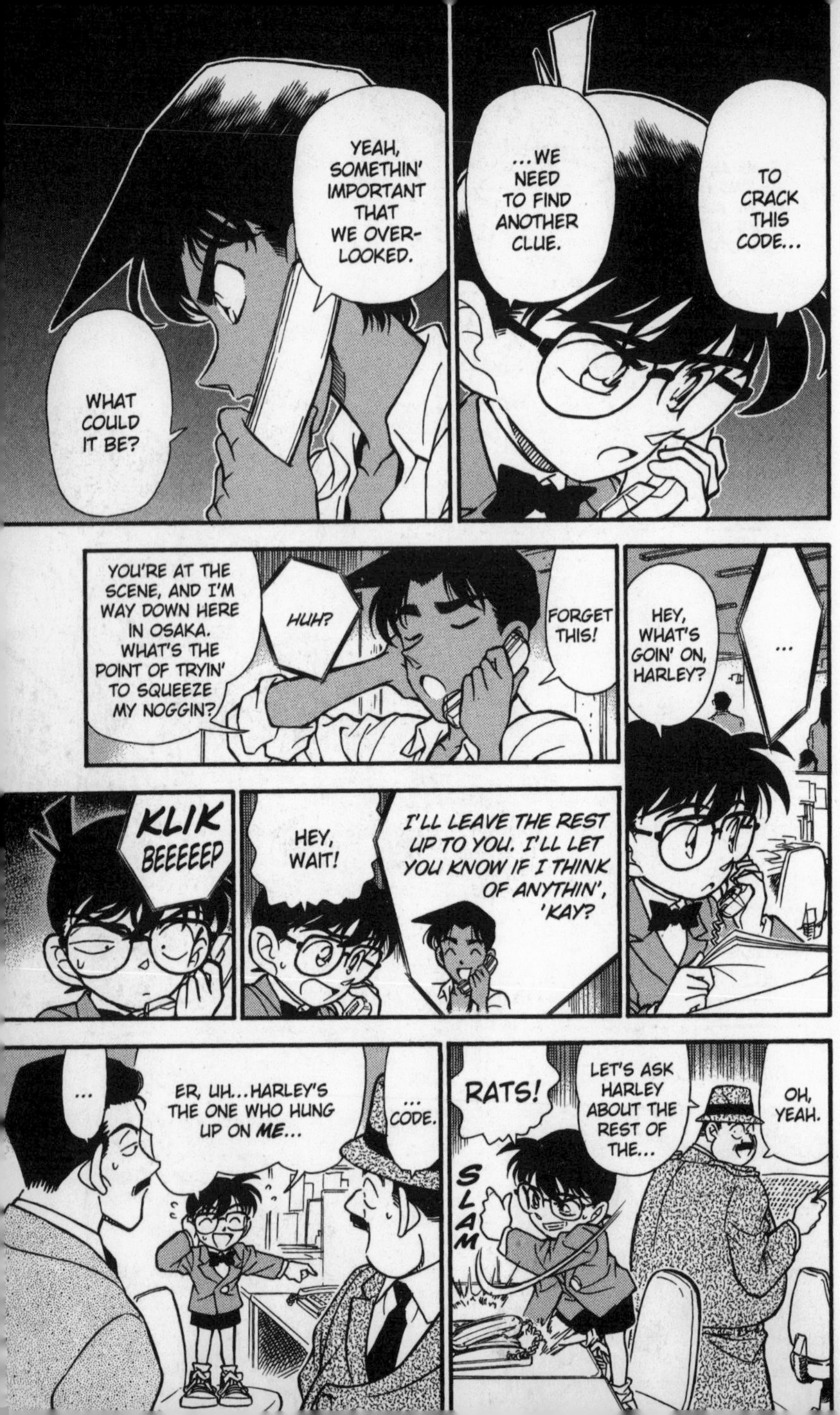
TO CRACK THIS CODE...
...WE NEED TO FIND ANOTHER CLUE.
YEAH, SOMETHIN' IMPORTANT THAT WE OVER-LOOKED.
WHAT COULD IT BE?
...
HEY, WHAT'S GOIN' ON, HARLEY?
FORGET THIS!
HUH?
YOU'RE AT THE SCENE, AND I'M WAY DOWN HERE IN OSAKA. WHAT'S THE POINT OF TRYIN' TO SQUEEZE MY NOGGIN?
I'LL LEAVE THE REST UP TO YOU. I'LL LET YOU KNOW IF I THINK OF ANYTHIN', 'KAY?
HEY, WAIT!
KLIK BEEEEEP
OH, YEAH.
LET'S ASK HARLEY ABOUT THE REST OF THE...
RATS!
SLAM
...CODE.
ER, UH...HARLEY'S THE ONE WHO HUNG UP ON **ME**...
...

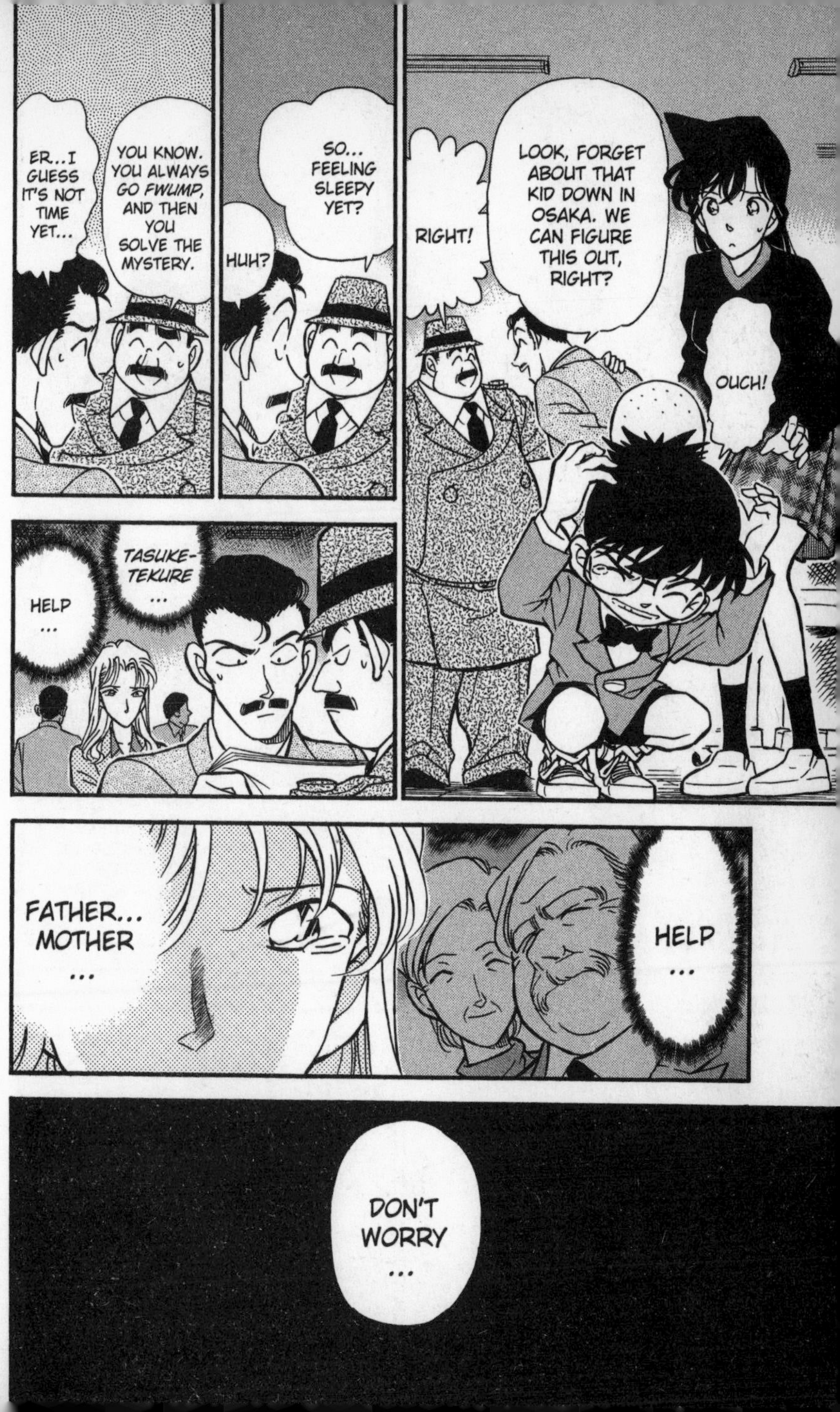
LOOK, FORGET ABOUT THAT KID DOWN IN OSAKA. WE CAN FIGURE THIS OUT, RIGHT?
RIGHT!
OUCH!
SO... FEELING SLEEPY YET?
HUH?
YOU KNOW. YOU ALWAYS GO *FWUMP*, AND THEN YOU SOLVE THE MYSTERY.
ER...I GUESS IT'S NOT TIME YET...
TASUKE-TEKURE ...
HELP ...
HELP ...
FATHER... MOTHER ...
DON'T WORRY ...

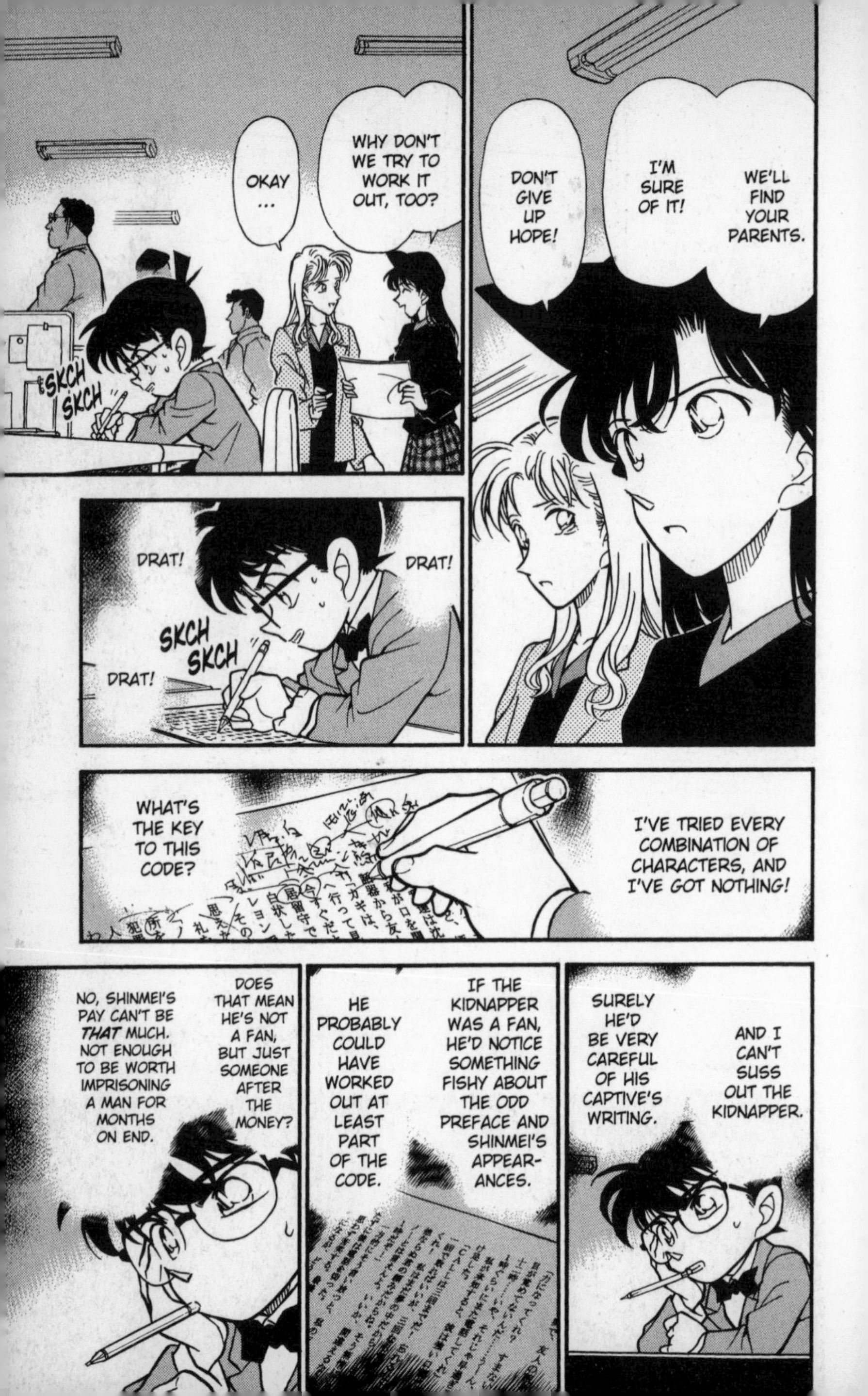
WE'LL FIND YOUR PARENTS.
I'M SURE OF IT!
DON'T GIVE UP HOPE!
WHY DON'T WE TRY TO WORK IT OUT, TOO?
OKAY ...
SKCH SKCH
DRAT!
DRAT!
SKCH SKCH
DRAT!
I'VE TRIED EVERY COMBINATION OF CHARACTERS, AND I'VE GOT NOTHING!
WHAT'S THE KEY TO THIS CODE?
AND I CAN'T SUSS OUT THE KIDNAPPER.
SURELY HE'D BE VERY CAREFUL OF HIS CAPTIVE'S WRITING.
IF THE KIDNAPPER WAS A FAN, HE'D NOTICE SOMETHING FISHY ABOUT THE ODD PREFACE AND SHINMEI'S APPEAR-ANCES.
HE PROBABLY COULD HAVE WORKED OUT AT LEAST PART OF THE CODE.
DOES THAT MEAN HE'S NOT A FAN, BUT JUST SOMEONE AFTER THE MONEY?
NO, SHINMEI'S PAY CAN'T BE *THAT* MUCH. NOT ENOUGH TO BE WORTH IMPRISONING A MAN FOR MONTHS ON END.

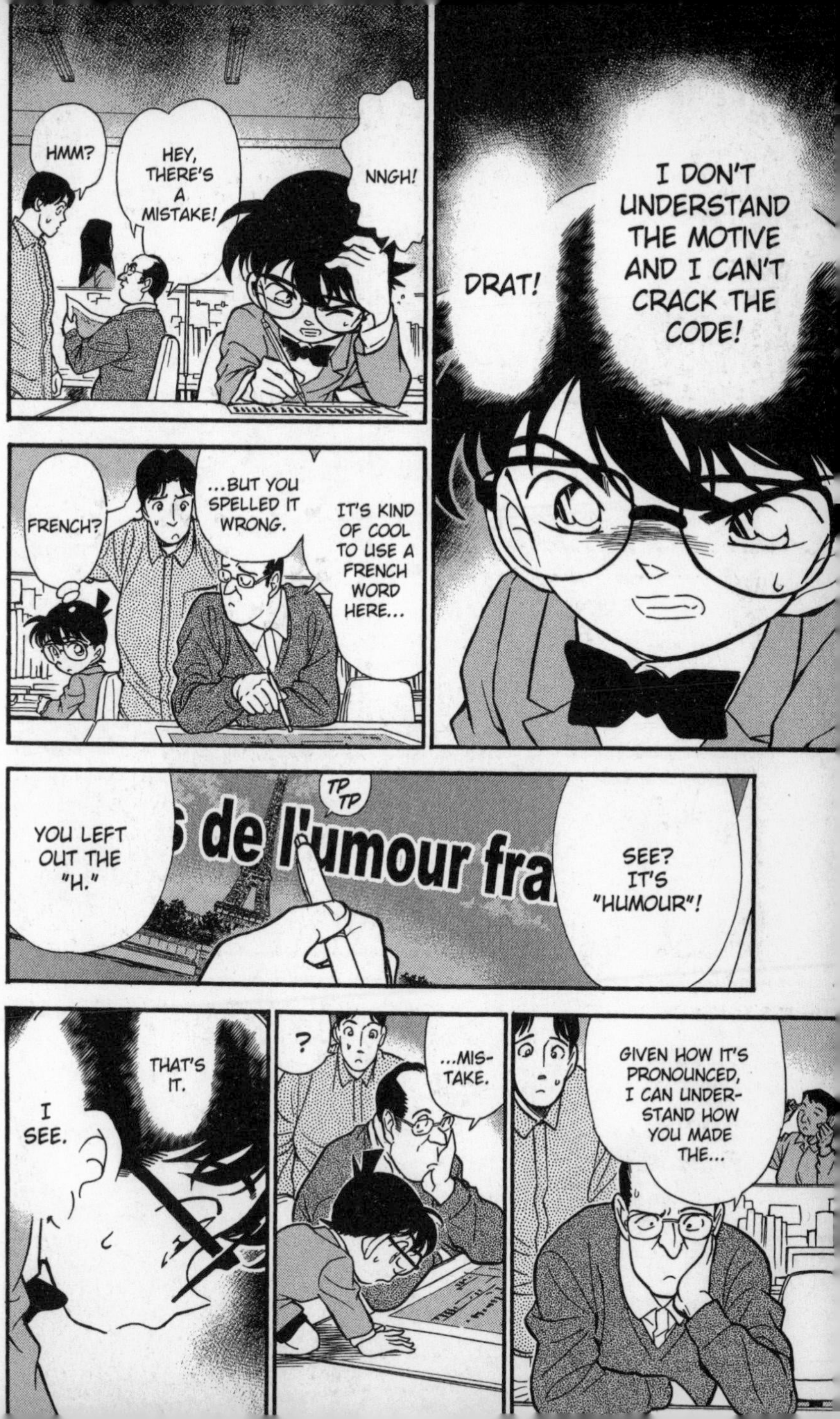

I DON'T UNDERSTAND THE MOTIVE AND I CAN'T CRACK THE CODE!
DRAT!
NNGH!
HEY, THERE'S A MISTAKE!
HMM?
IT'S KIND OF COOL TO USE A FRENCH WORD HERE...
...BUT YOU SPELLED IT WRONG.
FRENCH?
SEE? IT'S "HUMOUR"!
TP TP
s de l'umour fra
YOU LEFT OUT THE "H."
GIVEN HOW IT'S PRONOUNCED, I CAN UNDER-STAND HOW YOU MADE THE...
...MIS-TAKE.
?
THAT'S IT.
I SEE.

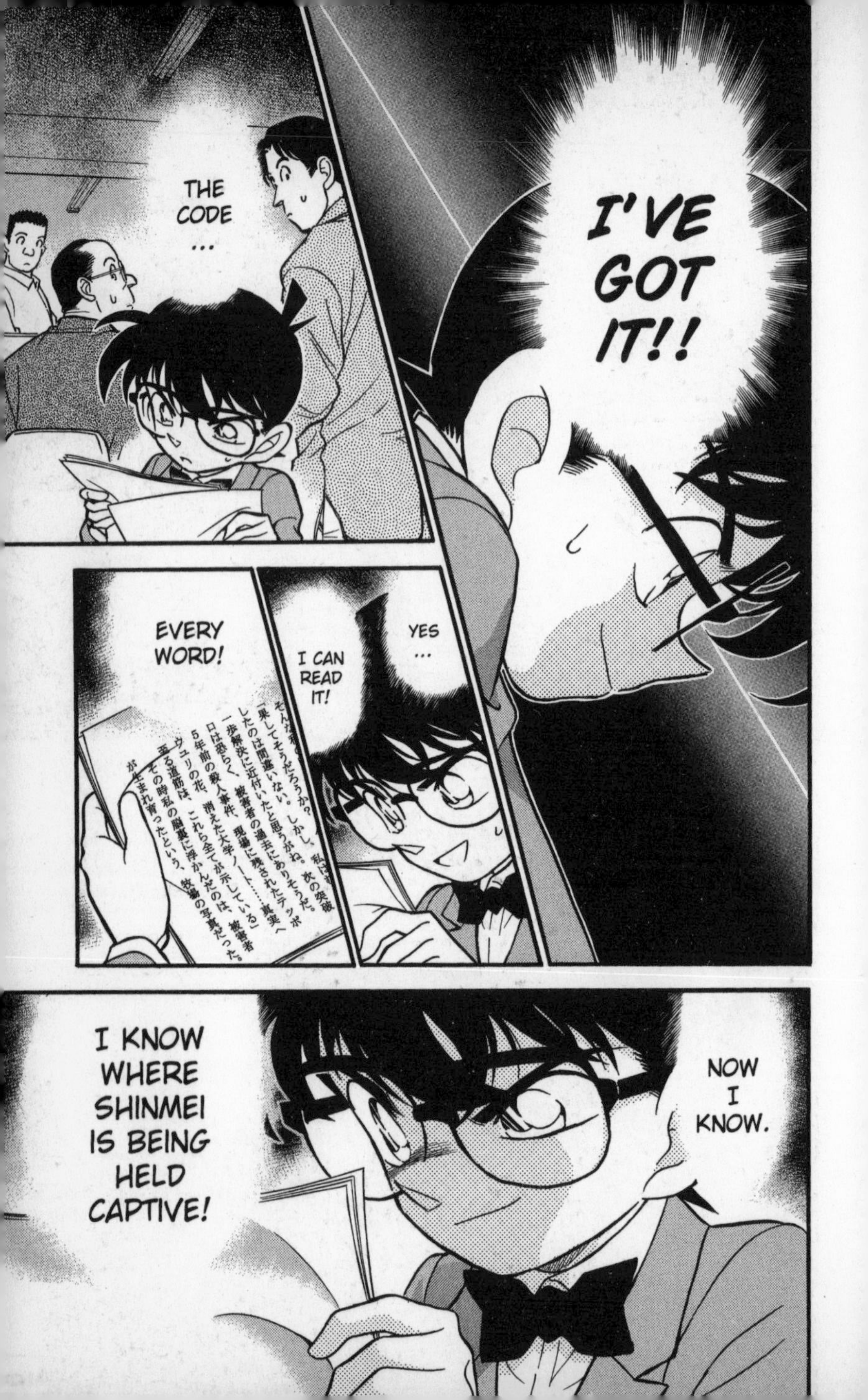
I'VE GOT IT!!
THE CODE ...
YES ...
I CAN READ IT!
EVERY WORD!
「果してそうだろうか？ 私は
したのは間違いない。しかし、
一歩解決に近付いたと思うがね。次の突破
口は恐らく、被害者の過去にありそうだ。
5年前の殺人事件、現場に残されたテッポ
ウユリの花、消えた大学ノート……真実へ
至る道筋は、これら全てが示している」
その時私の脳裏に浮かんだのは、被害者
が生まれ育ったという、牧場の写真だった。
NOW I KNOW.
I KNOW WHERE SHINMEI IS BEING HELD CAPTIVE!

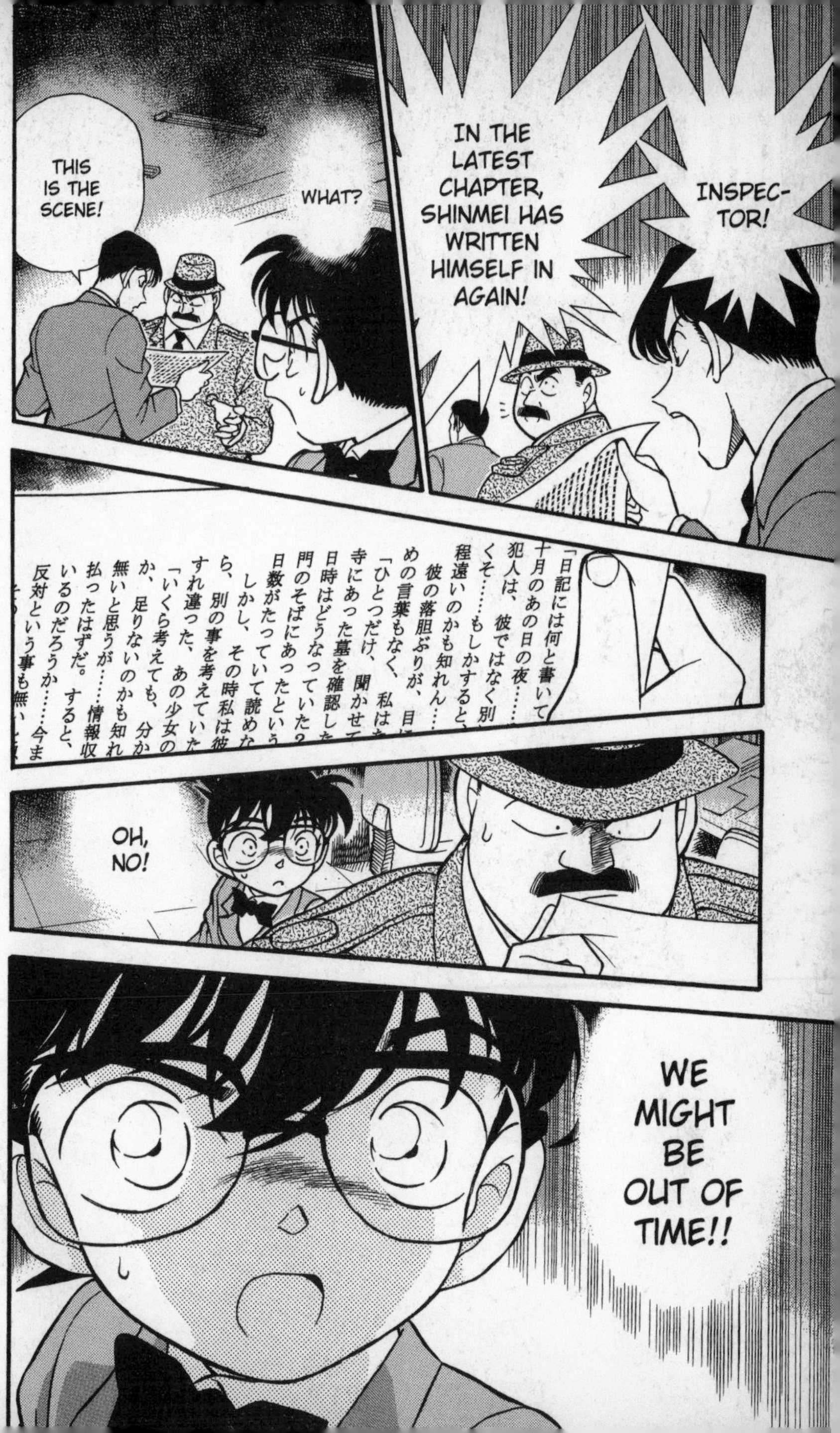
INSPECTOR!
IN THE LATEST CHAPTER, SHINMEI HAS WRITTEN HIMSELF IN AGAIN!
WHAT?
THIS IS THE SCENE!
「日記には何と書いて
十月のあの日の夜……
犯人は、彼ではなく別
くそ……もしかすると、
程遠いのかも知れん……
彼の落胆ぶりが、目
めの言葉もなく、私は
「ひとつだけ、聞かせて
寺にあった墓を確認した
日時はどうなっていた
門のそばにあったとい
日数がたっていて読めな
しかし、その時私は彼
ら、別の事を考えていた
すれ違った、あの少女の
「いくら考えても、分か
か、足りないのかも知れ
無いと思うが……情報収
払ったはずだ。すると、
いるのだろうか……今ま
反対という事も無
OH, NO!
WE MIGHT BE OUT OF TIME!!

WHEN IN FRANCE...

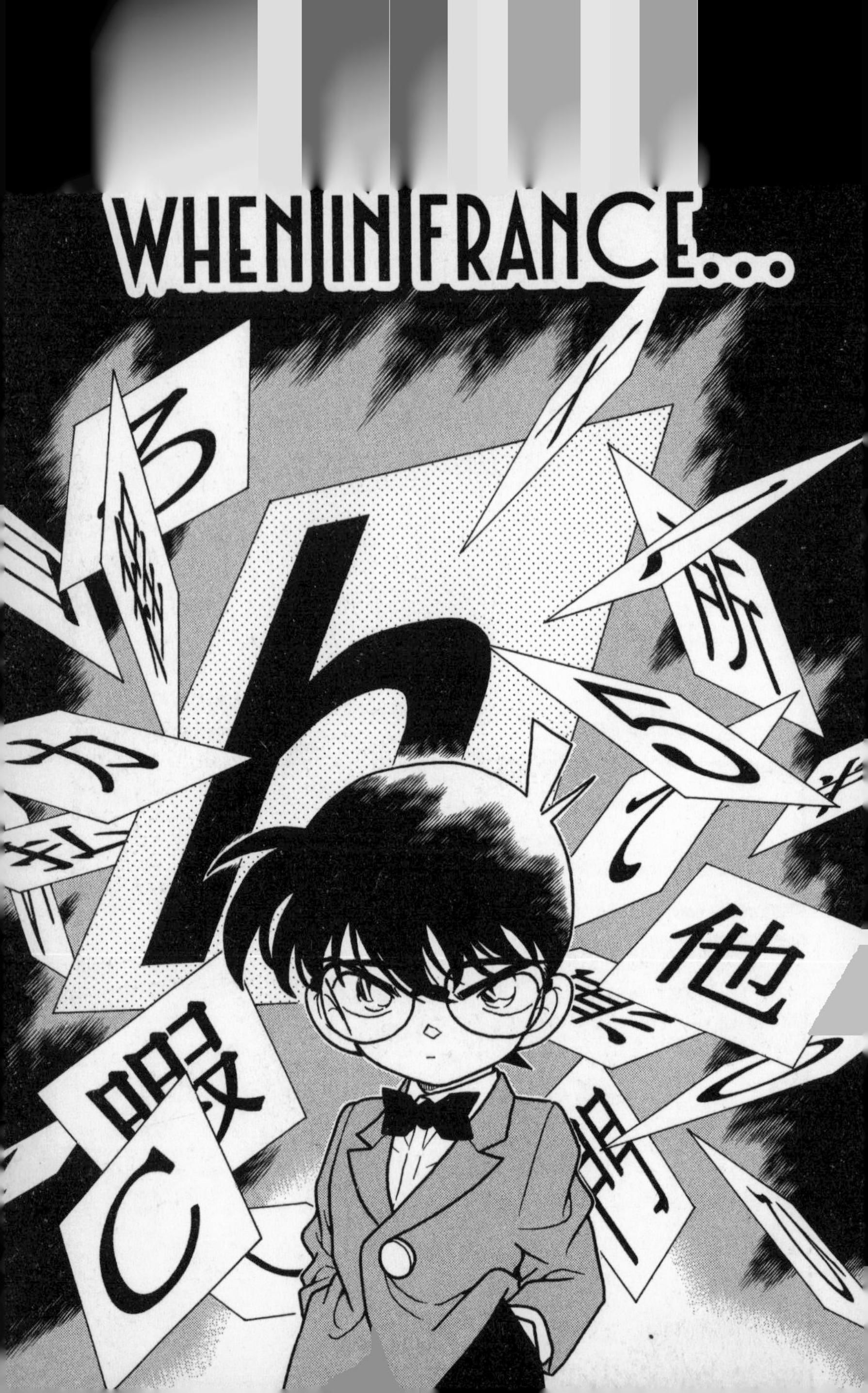

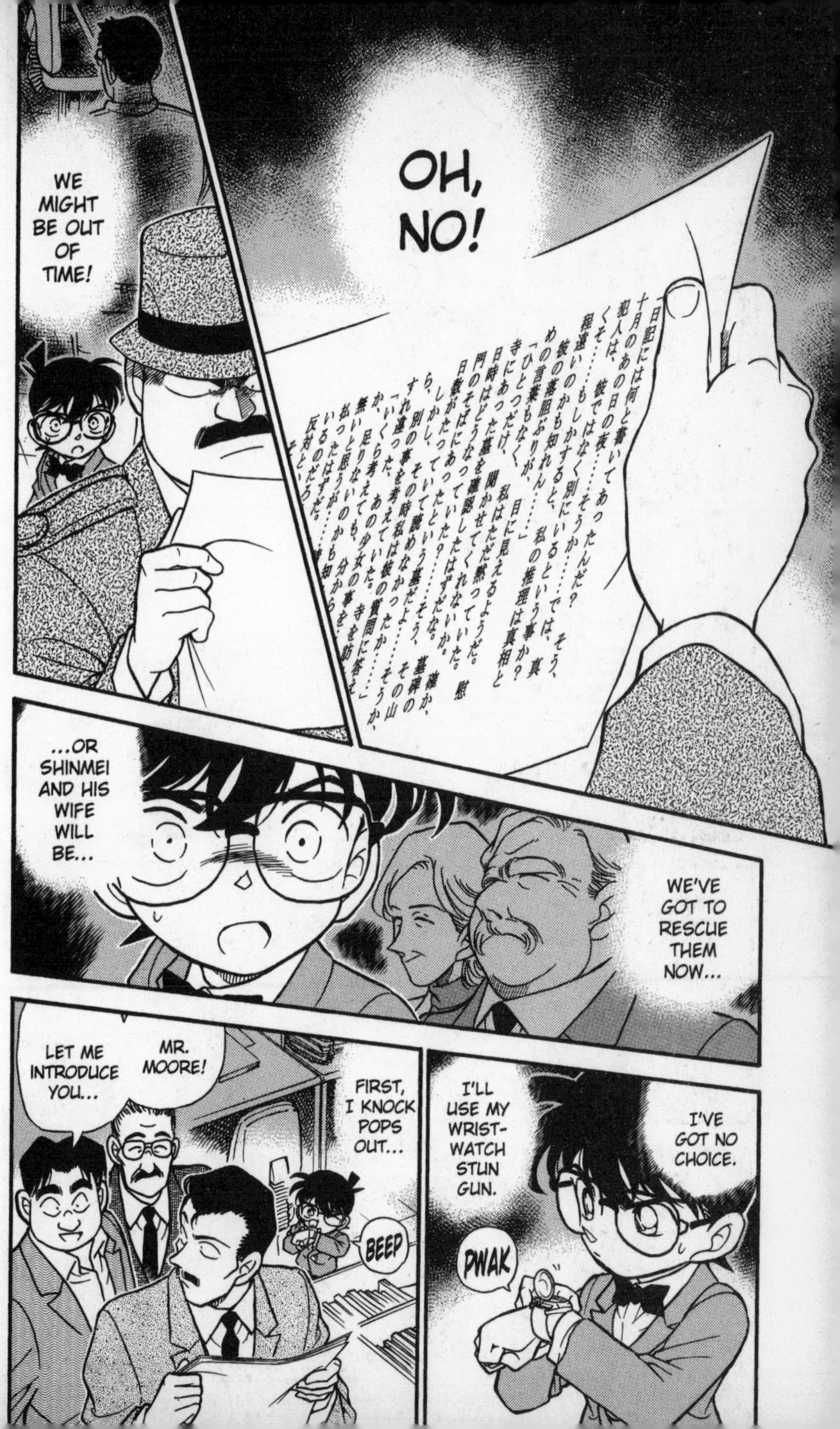
OH, NO!
WE MIGHT BE OUT OF TIME!
...OR SHINMEI AND HIS WIFE WILL BE...
WE'VE GOT TO RESCUE THEM NOW...
I'VE GOT NO CHOICE.
I'LL USE MY WRIST-WATCH STUN GUN.
PWAK
FIRST, I KNOCK POPS OUT...
BEEP
MR. MOORE!
LET ME INTRODUCE YOU...

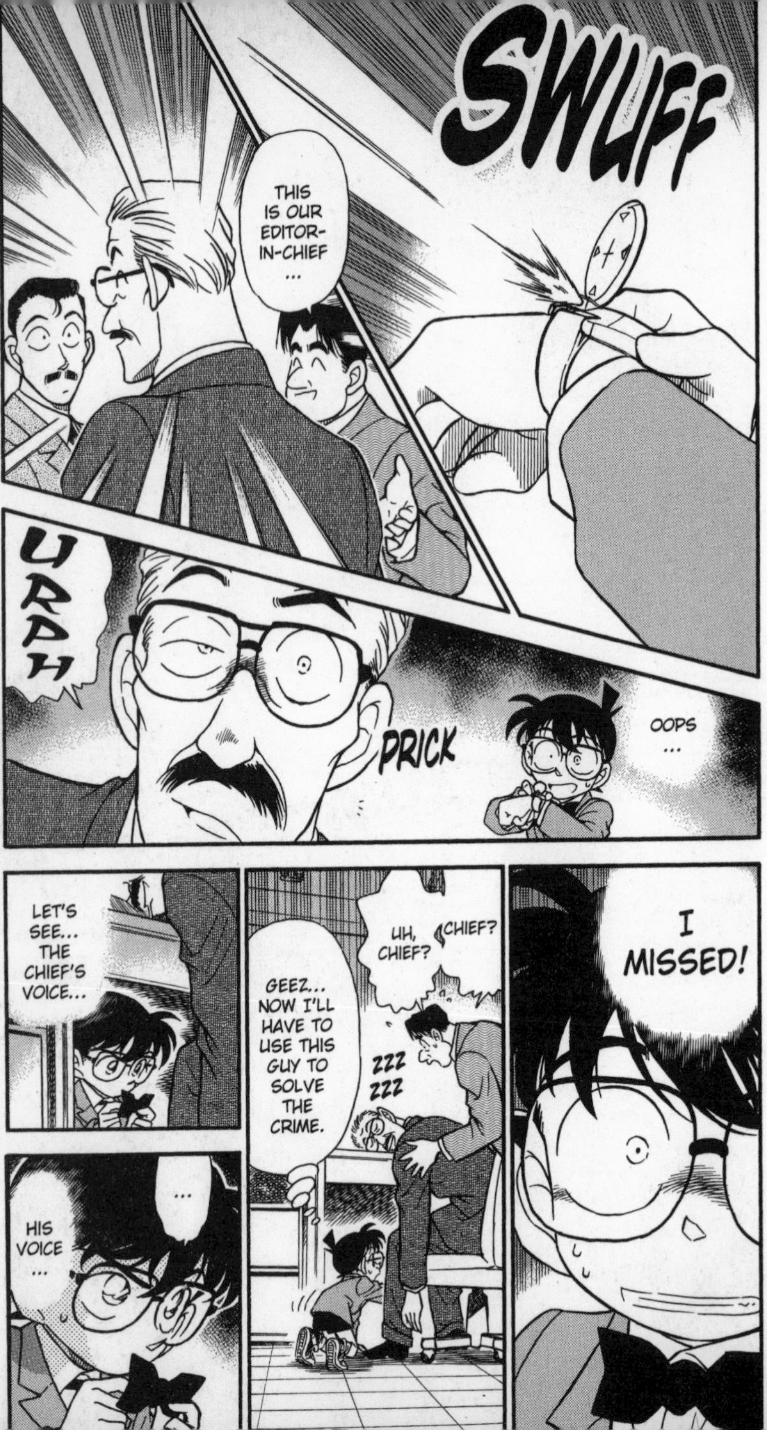
SWUFF
THIS IS OUR EDITOR-IN-CHIEF ...
OOPS ...
PRICK
URPH
I MISSED!
CHIEF?
UH, CHIEF?
ZZZ ZZZ
GEEZ... NOW I'LL HAVE TO USE THIS GUY TO SOLVE THE CRIME.
LET'S SEE... THE CHIEF'S VOICE...
...
HIS VOICE ...

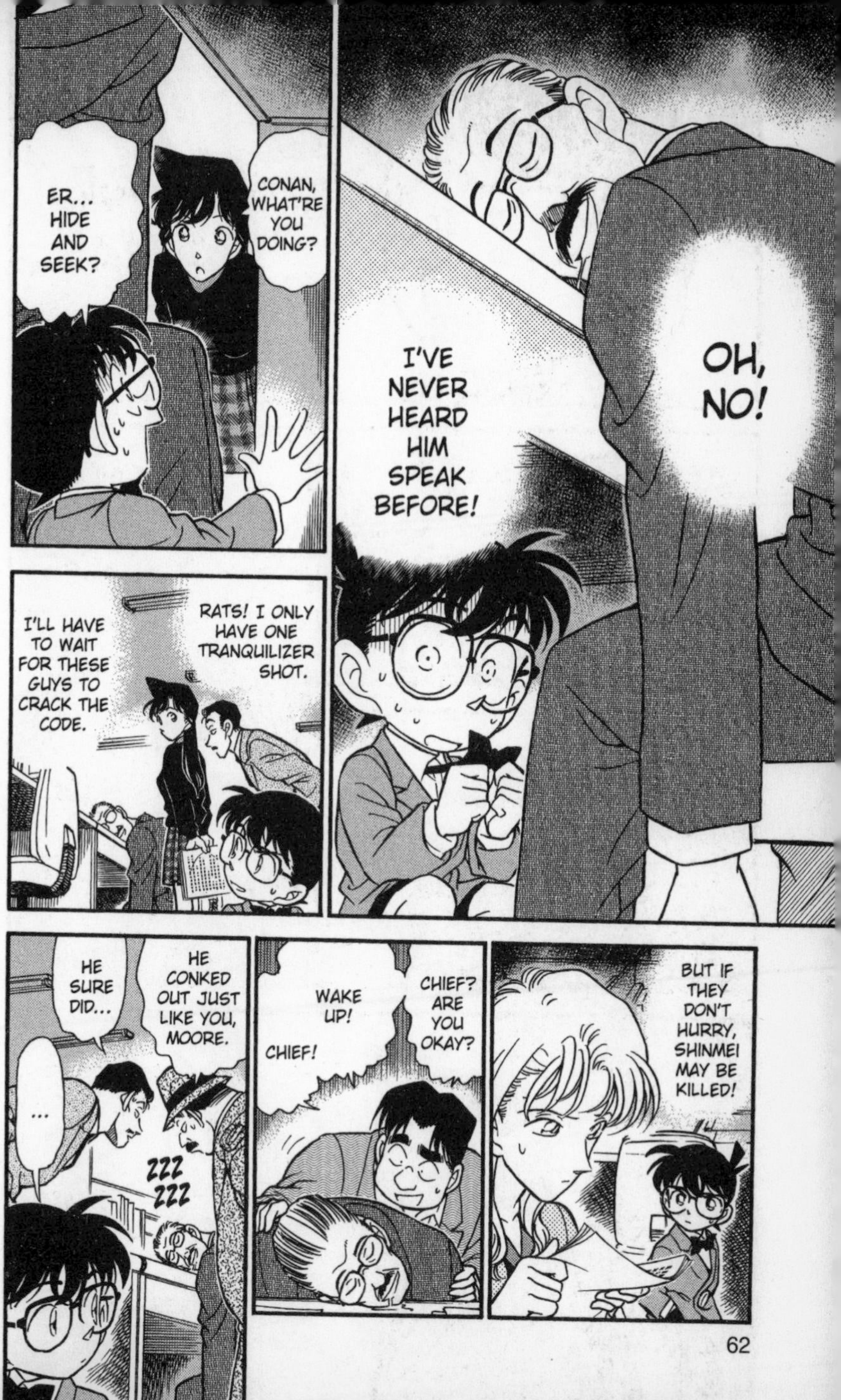
OH, NO!
I'VE NEVER HEARD HIM SPEAK BEFORE!
CONAN, WHAT'RE YOU DOING?
ER... HIDE AND SEEK?
RATS! I ONLY HAVE ONE TRANQUILIZER SHOT.
I'LL HAVE TO WAIT FOR THESE GUYS TO CRACK THE CODE.
BUT IF THEY DON'T HURRY, SHINMEI MAY BE KILLED!
CHIEF? ARE YOU OKAY?
WAKE UP!
CHIEF!
HE CONKED OUT JUST LIKE YOU, MOORE.
HE SURE DID...
...
ZZZ
ZZZ

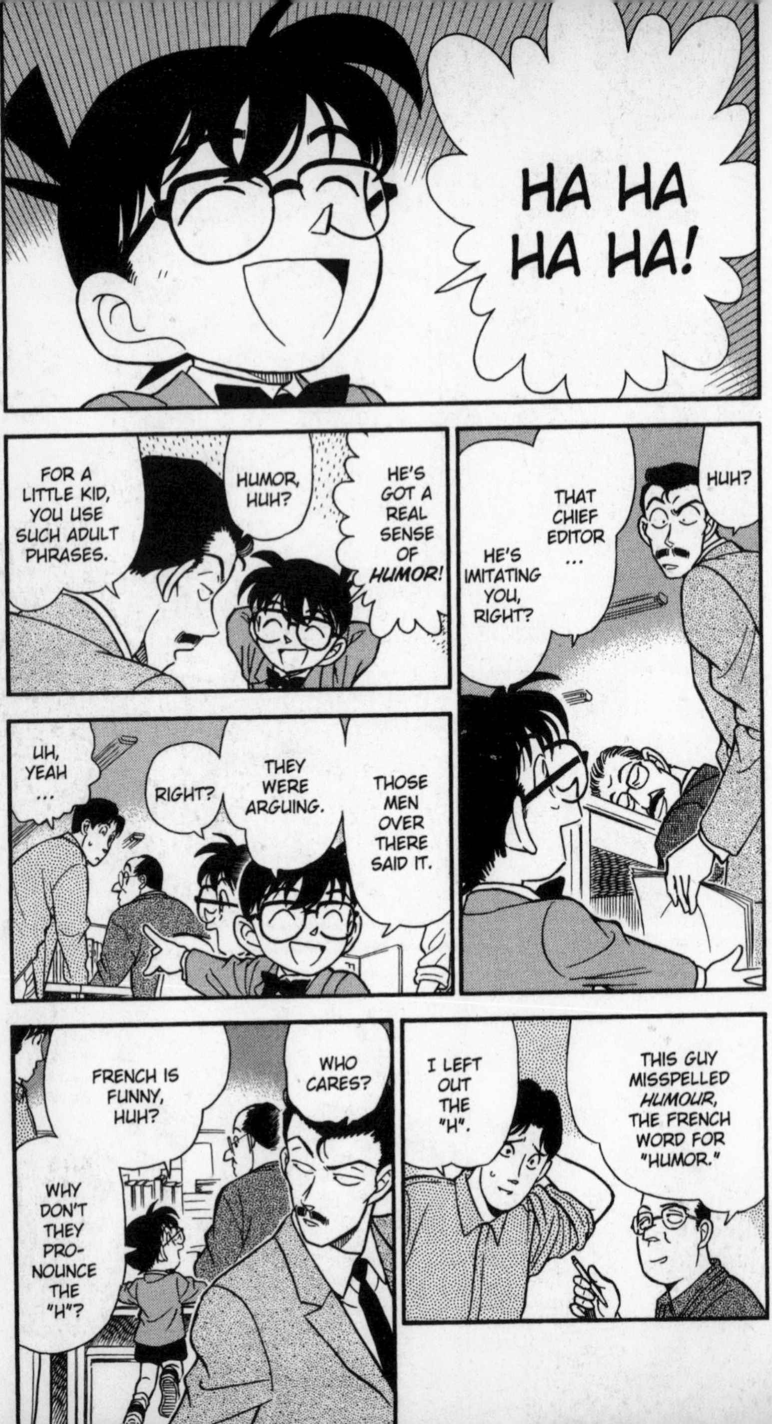
HA HA HA HA!
HUH?
THAT CHIEF EDITOR ...
HE'S IMITATING YOU, RIGHT?
HE'S GOT A REAL SENSE OF *HUMOR*!
HUMOR, HUH?
FOR A LITTLE KID, YOU USE SUCH ADULT PHRASES.
THOSE MEN OVER THERE SAID IT.
THEY WERE ARGUING.
RIGHT?
UH, YEAH ...
THIS GUY MISSPELLED *HUMOUR*, THE FRENCH WORD FOR "HUMOR."
I LEFT OUT THE "H".
WHO CARES?
FRENCH IS FUNNY, HUH?
WHY DON'T THEY PRO-NOUNCE THE "H"?

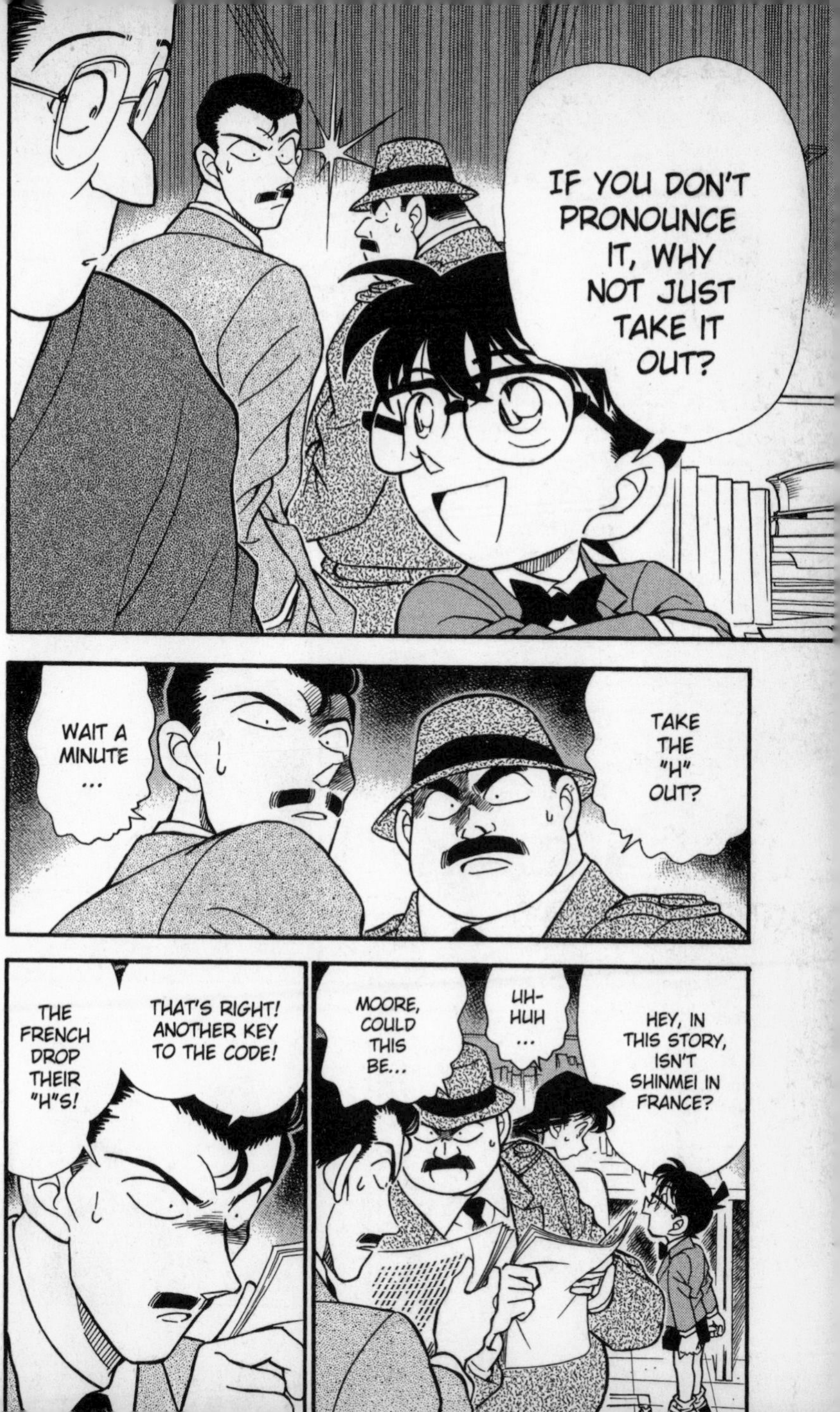
IF YOU DON'T PRONOUNCE IT, WHY NOT JUST TAKE IT OUT?
TAKE THE "H" OUT?
WAIT A MINUTE ...
HEY, IN THIS STORY, ISN'T SHINMEI IN FRANCE?
UH-HUH ...
MOORE, COULD THIS BE...
THAT'S RIGHT! ANOTHER KEY TO THE CODE!
THE FRENCH DROP THEIR "H"S!

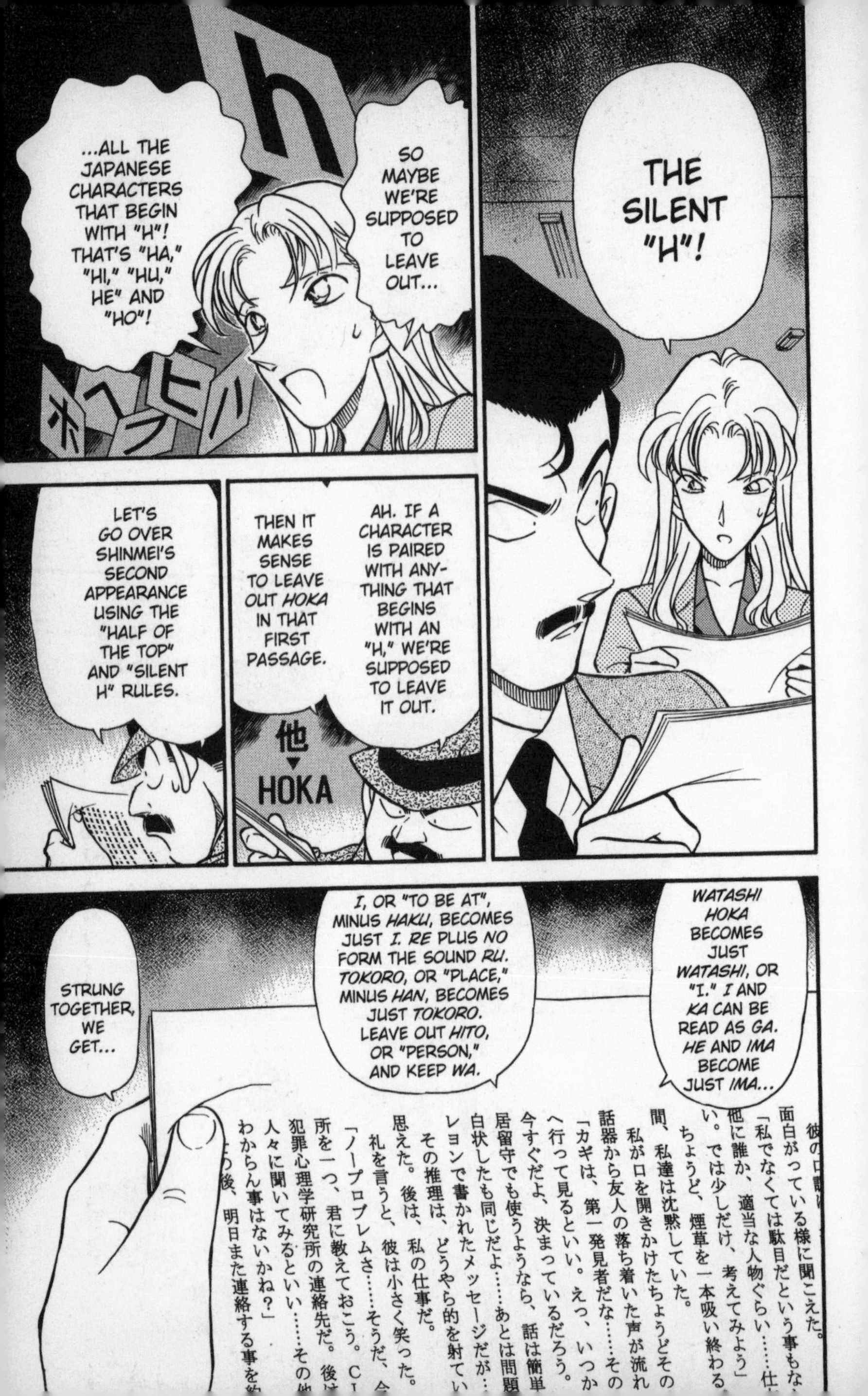
THE SILENT "H"!
SO MAYBE WE'RE SUPPOSED TO LEAVE OUT...
...ALL THE JAPANESE CHARACTERS THAT BEGIN WITH "H"! THAT'S "HA," "HI," "HU," HE" AND "HO"!
ハ ヒ フ ヘ ホ
AH. IF A CHARACTER IS PAIRED WITH ANY-THING THAT BEGINS WITH AN "H," WE'RE SUPPOSED TO LEAVE IT OUT.
THEN IT MAKES SENSE TO LEAVE OUT *HOKA* IN THAT FIRST PASSAGE.
他 ▼ HOKA
LET'S GO OVER SHINMEI'S SECOND APPEARANCE USING THE "HALF OF THE TOP" AND "SILENT H" RULES.
WATASHI HOKA BECOMES JUST *WATASHI*, OR "I." *I* AND *KA* CAN BE READ AS *GA*. *HE* AND *IMA* BECOME JUST *IMA*...
I, OR "TO BE AT", MINUS *HAKU*, BECOMES JUST *I*. *RE* PLUS *NO* FORM THE SOUND *RU*. *TOKORO*, OR "PLACE," MINUS *HAN*, BECOMES JUST *TOKORO*. LEAVE OUT *HITO*, OR "PERSON," AND KEEP *WA*.
STRUNG TOGETHER, WE GET...
面白がっている様に聞こえた。
「私でなくては駄目だという事もな
他に誰か、適当な人物ぐらい……
い。では少しだけ、考えてみよう」
ちょうど、煙草を一本吸い終わる
間、私達は沈黙していた。
私が口を開きかけたちょうどその
話器から友人の落ち着いた声が流れ
「カギは、第一発見者だな……その
へ行って見るといい。えっ、いつか
今すぐだよ、決まっているだろう。
居留守でも使うようなら、話は簡単
白状したも同じだよ……あとは問題
レヨンで書かれたメッセージだが…
その推理は、どうやら的を射てい
思えた。後は、私の仕事だ。
礼を言うと、彼は小さく笑った。
「ノープロブレムさ……そうだ、
所を一つ、君に教えておこう。
犯罪心理学研究所の連絡先だ。後
人々に聞いてみるといい……その
わからん事はないかね？」
の後、明日また連絡する事を

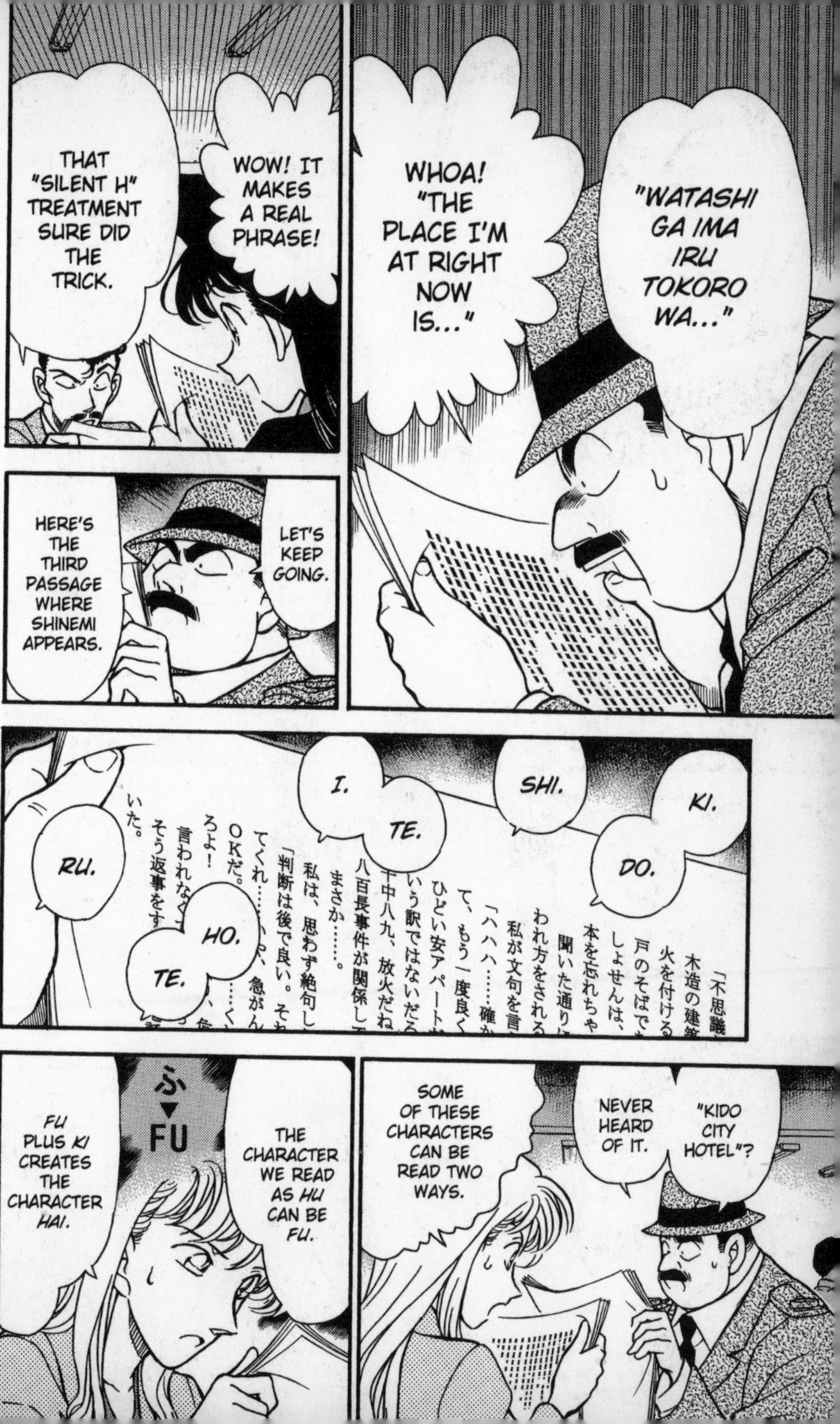

"WATASHI GA IMA IRU TOKORO WA..."
WHOA! "THE PLACE I'M AT RIGHT NOW IS..."
WOW! IT MAKES A REAL PHRASE!
THAT "SILENT H" TREATMENT SURE DID THE TRICK.
LET'S KEEP GOING.
HERE'S THE THIRD PASSAGE WHERE SHINEMI APPEARS.
KI.
DO.
SHI.
TE.
I.
HO.
TE.
RU.
まさか……。
しょせんは、
OKだ。
ろよ！
いた。
"KIDO CITY HOTEL"?
NEVER HEARD OF IT.
SOME OF THESE CHARACTERS CAN BE READ TWO WAYS.
THE CHARACTER WE READ AS HU CAN BE FU.
ふ ▼ FU
FU PLUS KI CREATES THE CHARACTER HAI.

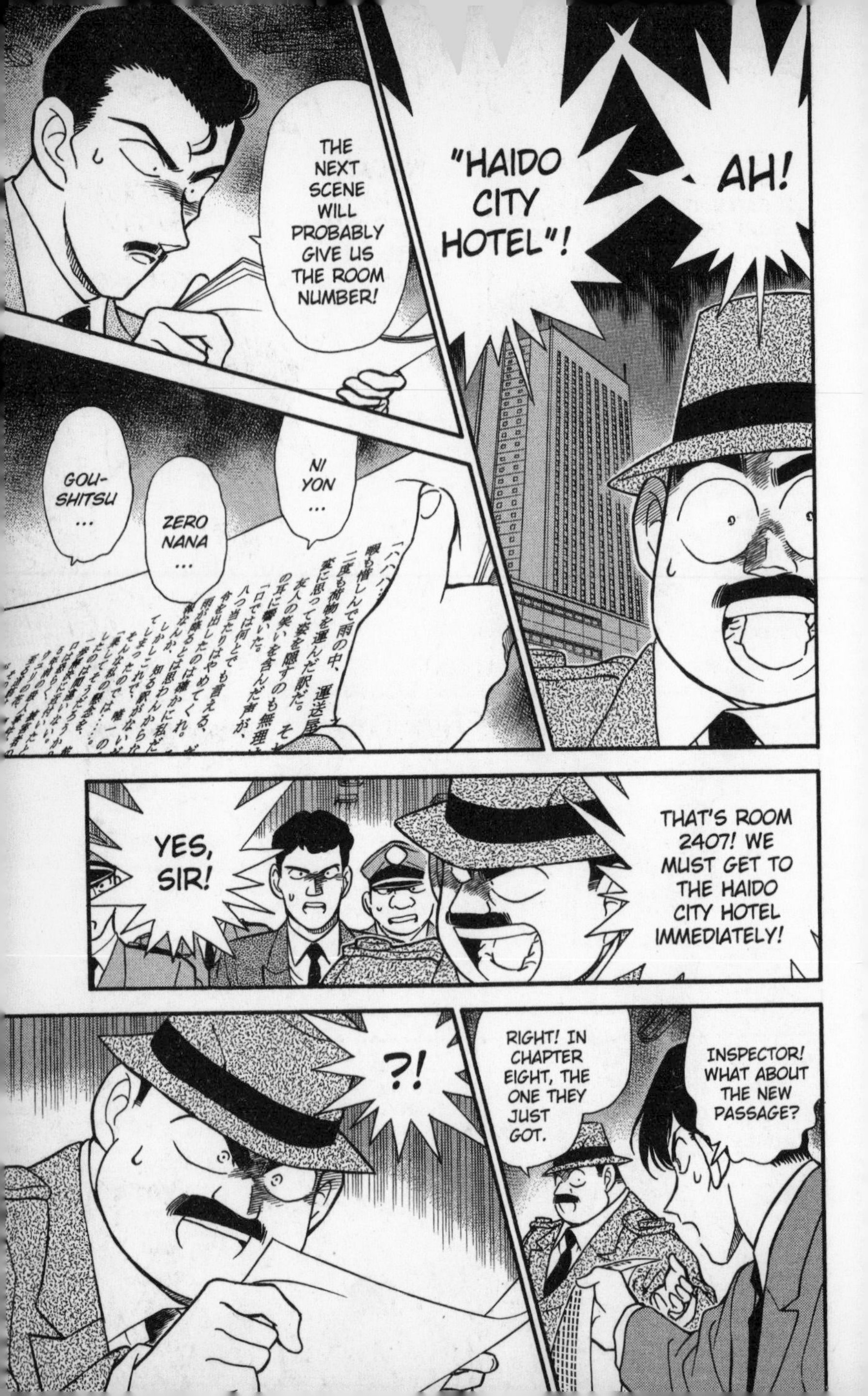
AH!
"HAIDO CITY HOTEL"!
THE NEXT SCENE WILL PROBABLY GIVE US THE ROOM NUMBER!
NI YON ...
ZERO NANA ...
GOU-SHITSU ...
THAT'S ROOM 2407! WE MUST GET TO THE HAIDO CITY HOTEL IMMEDIATELY!
YES, SIR!
INSPECTOR! WHAT ABOUT THE NEW PASSAGE?
RIGHT! IN CHAPTER EIGHT, THE ONE THEY JUST GOT.
?!

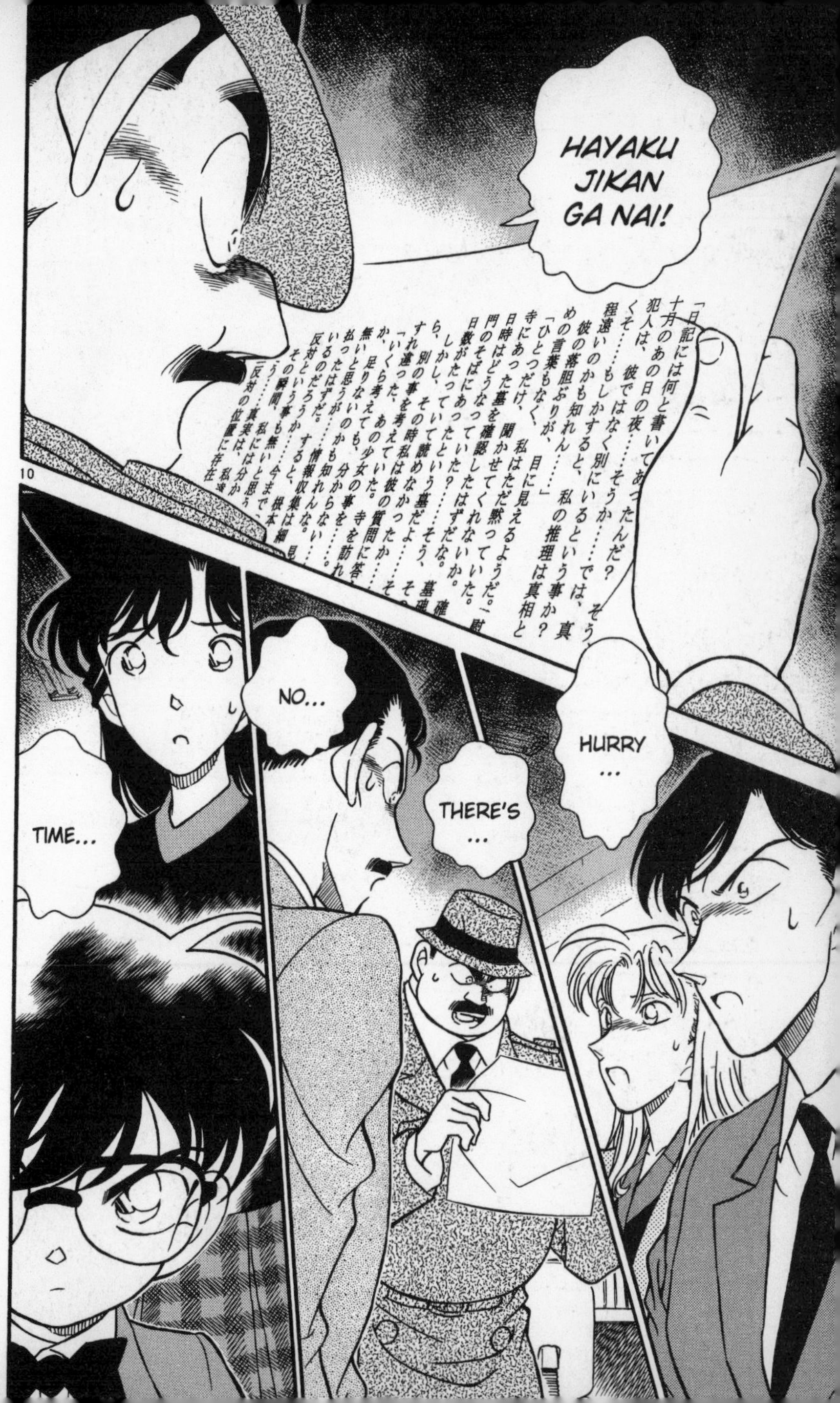
HAYAKU JIKAN GA NAI!
HURRY...
THERE'S...
NO...
TIME...

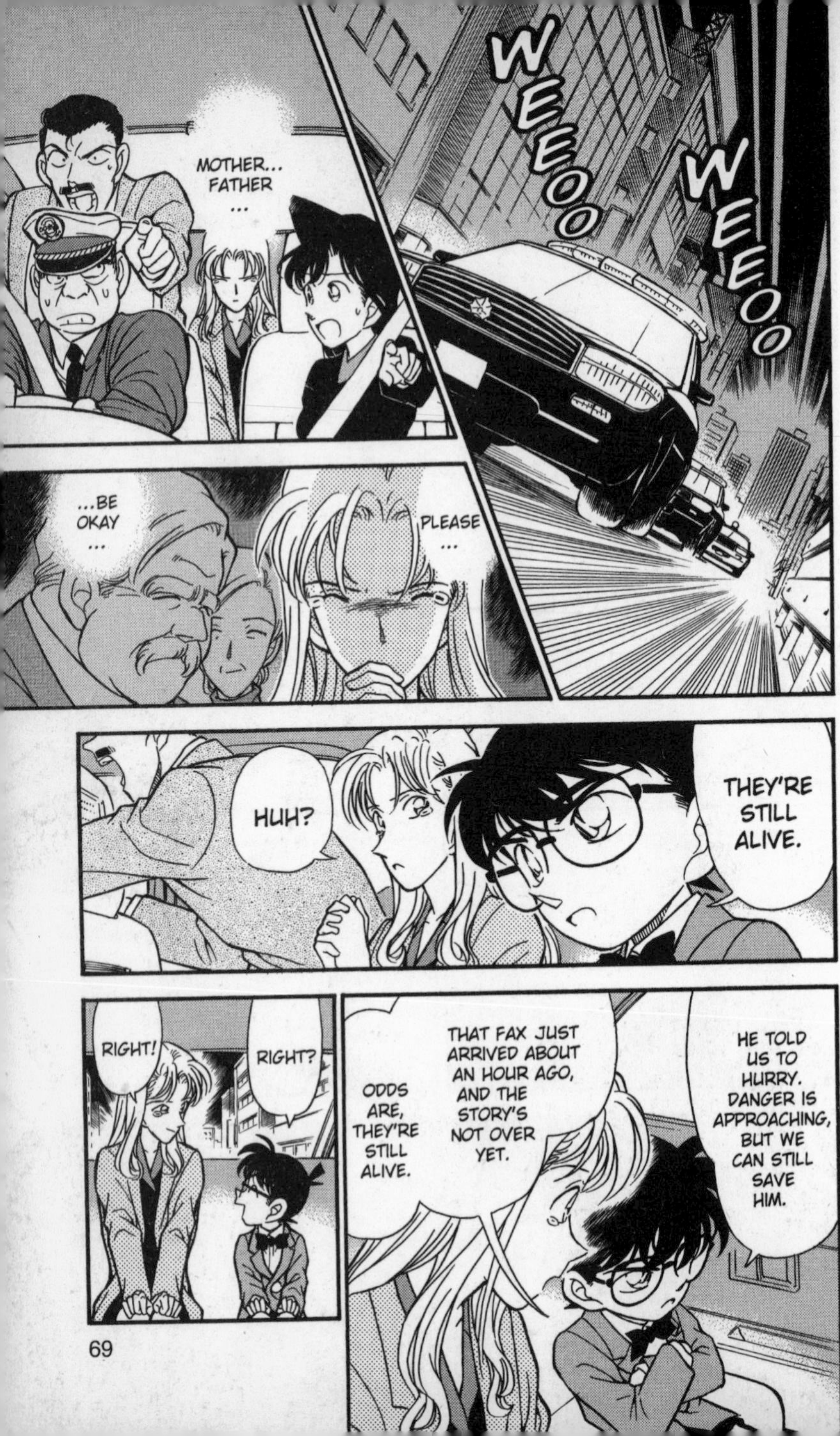
WEEOO
WEEOO
MOTHER... FATHER ...
PLEASE ...
...BE OKAY ...
THEY'RE STILL ALIVE.
HUH?
HE TOLD US TO HURRY. DANGER IS APPROACHING, BUT WE CAN STILL SAVE HIM.
THAT FAX JUST ARRIVED ABOUT AN HOUR AGO, AND THE STORY'S NOT OVER YET.
ODDS ARE, THEY'RE STILL ALIVE.
RIGHT?
RIGHT!

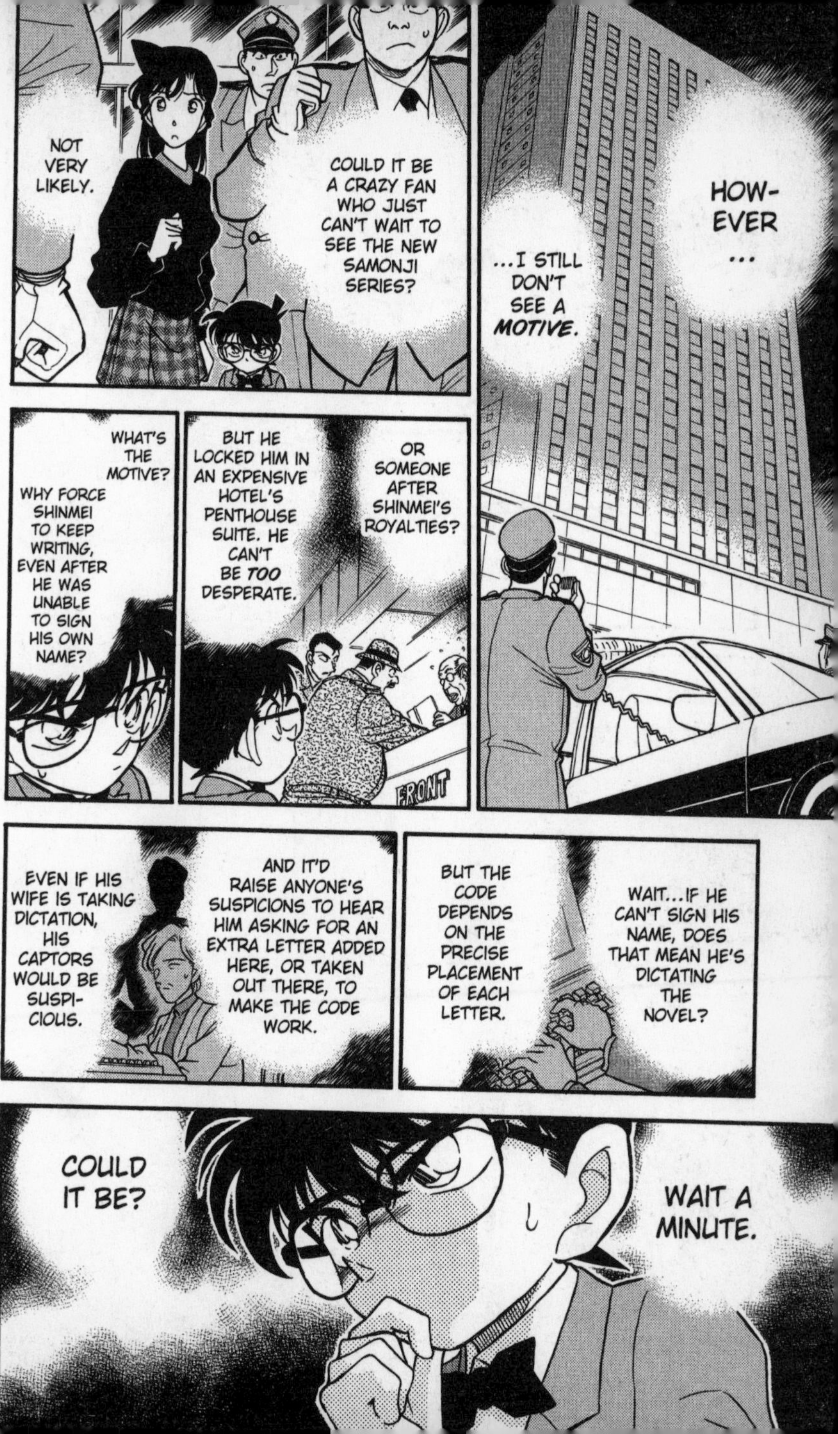
HOW-EVER...
...I STILL DON'T SEE A *MOTIVE*.
COULD IT BE A CRAZY FAN WHO JUST CAN'T WAIT TO SEE THE NEW SAMONJI SERIES?
NOT VERY LIKELY.
OR SOMEONE AFTER SHINMEI'S ROYALTIES?
BUT HE LOCKED HIM IN AN EXPENSIVE HOTEL'S PENTHOUSE SUITE. HE CAN'T BE *TOO* DESPERATE.
FRONT
WHAT'S THE MOTIVE?
WHY FORCE SHINMEI TO KEEP WRITING, EVEN AFTER HE WAS UNABLE TO SIGN HIS OWN NAME?
WAIT...IF HE CAN'T SIGN HIS NAME, DOES THAT MEAN HE'S DICTATING THE NOVEL?
BUT THE CODE DEPENDS ON THE PRECISE PLACEMENT OF EACH LETTER.
AND IT'D RAISE ANYONE'S SUSPICIONS TO HEAR HIM ASKING FOR AN EXTRA LETTER ADDED HERE, OR TAKEN OUT THERE, TO MAKE THE CODE WORK.
EVEN IF HIS WIFE IS TAKING DICTATION, HIS CAPTORS WOULD BE SUSPI-CIOUS.
WAIT A MINUTE.
COULD IT BE?

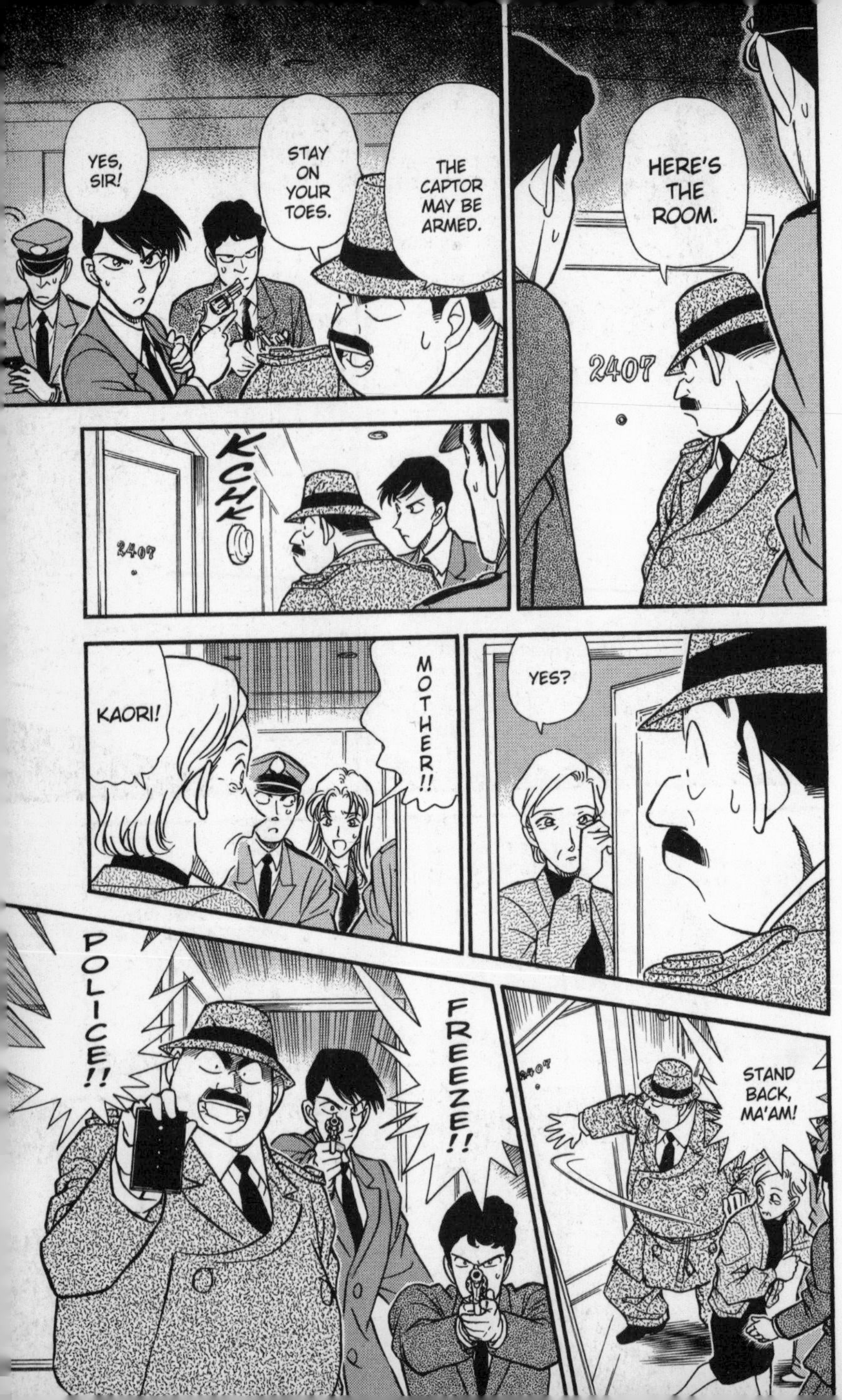
HERE'S THE ROOM.
2407
THE CAPTOR MAY BE ARMED.
STAY ON YOUR TOES.
YES, SIR!
KCHK
2407
YES?
MOTHER!!
KAORI!
STAND BACK, MA'AM!
FREEZE!!
POLICE!!

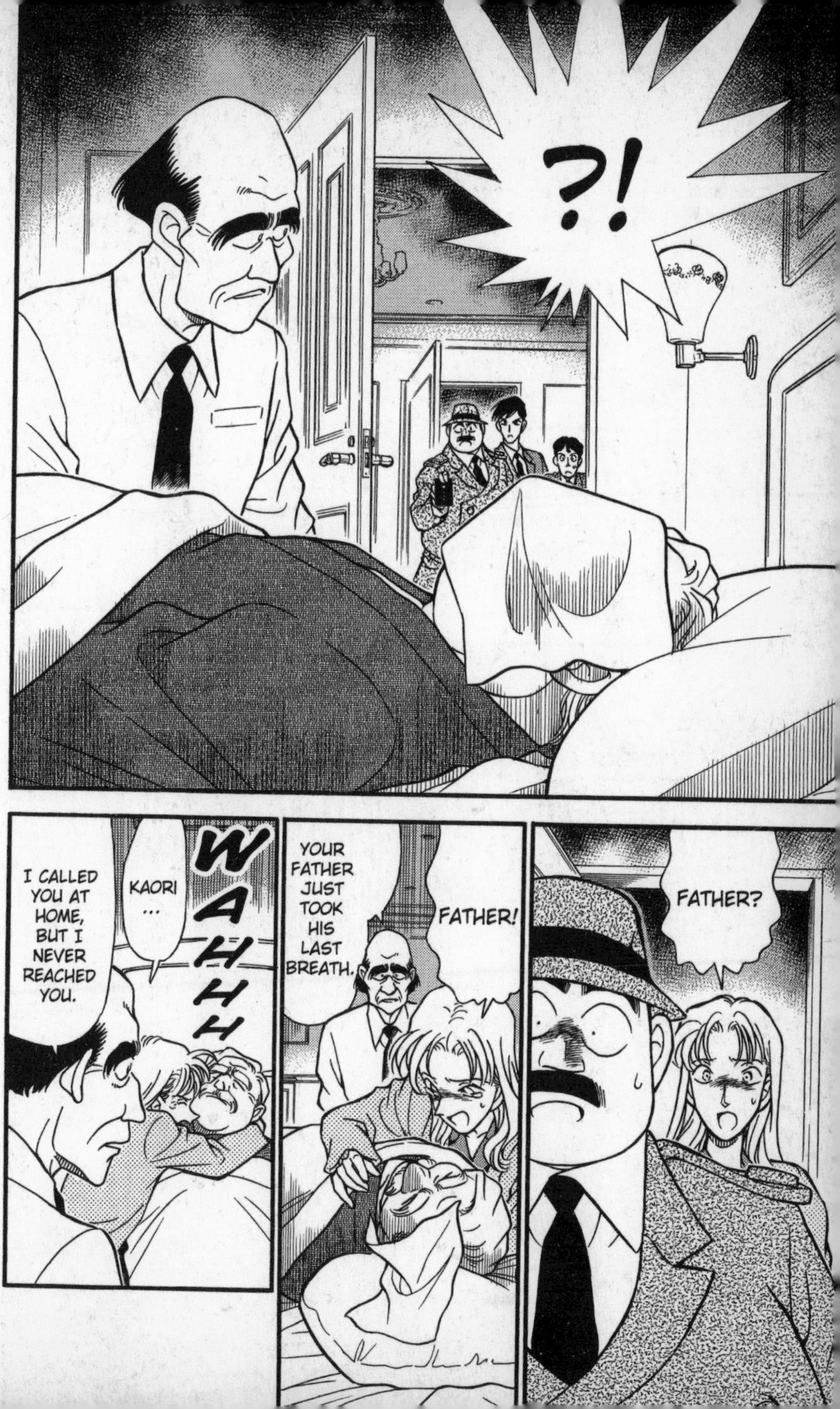
?!
FATHER?
FATHER!
YOUR FATHER JUST TOOK HIS LAST BREATH.
WAHHHH
KAORI ...
I CALLED YOU AT HOME, BUT I NEVER REACHED YOU.

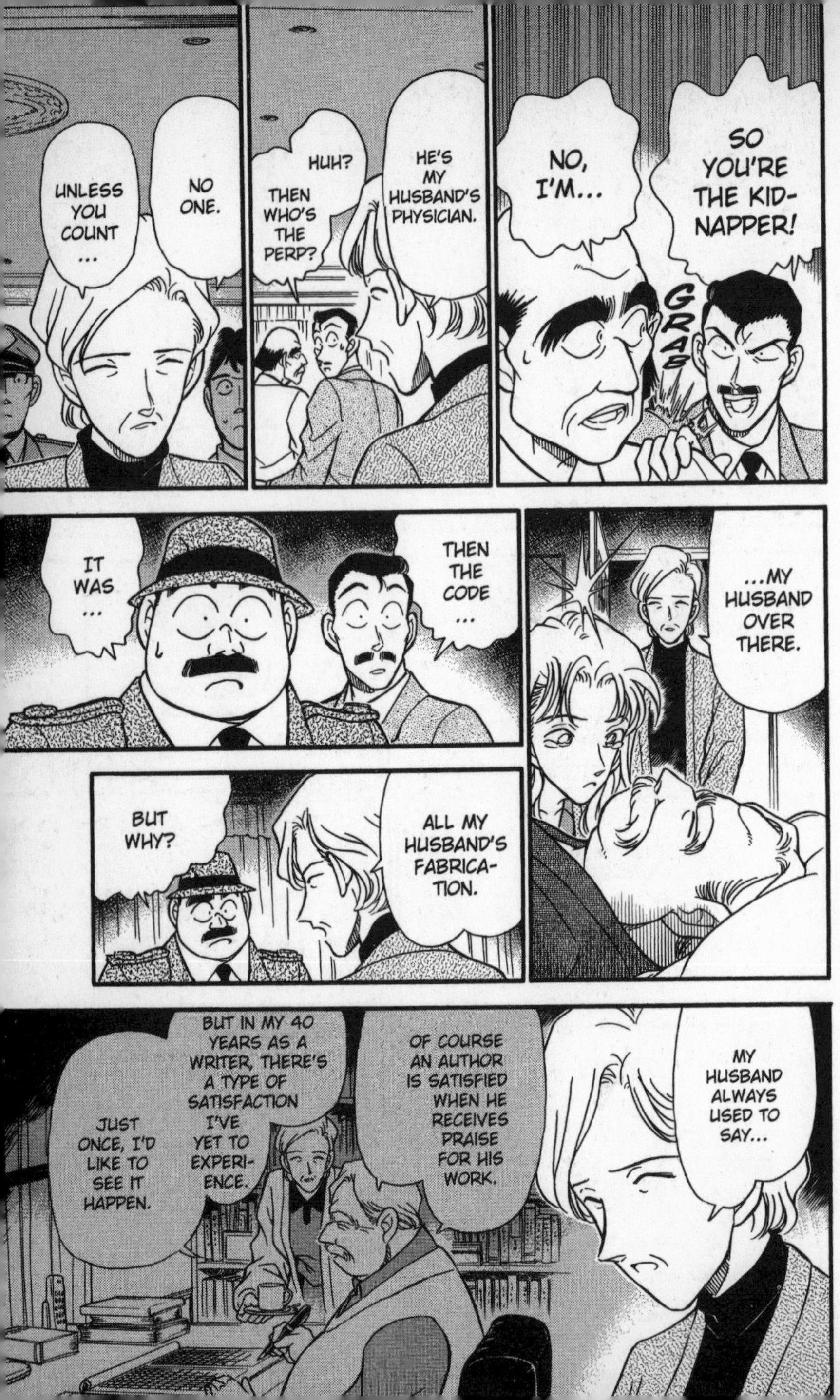
SO YOU'RE THE KID-NAPPER!
GRAB
NO, I'M...
HE'S MY HUSBAND'S PHYSICIAN.
HUH?
THEN WHO'S THE PERP?
NO ONE.
UNLESS YOU COUNT ...
...MY HUSBAND OVER THERE.
THEN THE CODE ...
IT WAS ...
ALL MY HUSBAND'S FABRICA-TION.
BUT WHY?
MY HUSBAND ALWAYS USED TO SAY...
OF COURSE AN AUTHOR IS SATISFIED WHEN HE RECEIVES PRAISE FOR HIS WORK.
BUT IN MY 40 YEARS AS A WRITER, THERE'S A TYPE OF SATISFACTION I'VE YET TO EXPERI-ENCE.
JUST ONCE, I'D LIKE TO SEE IT HAPPEN.

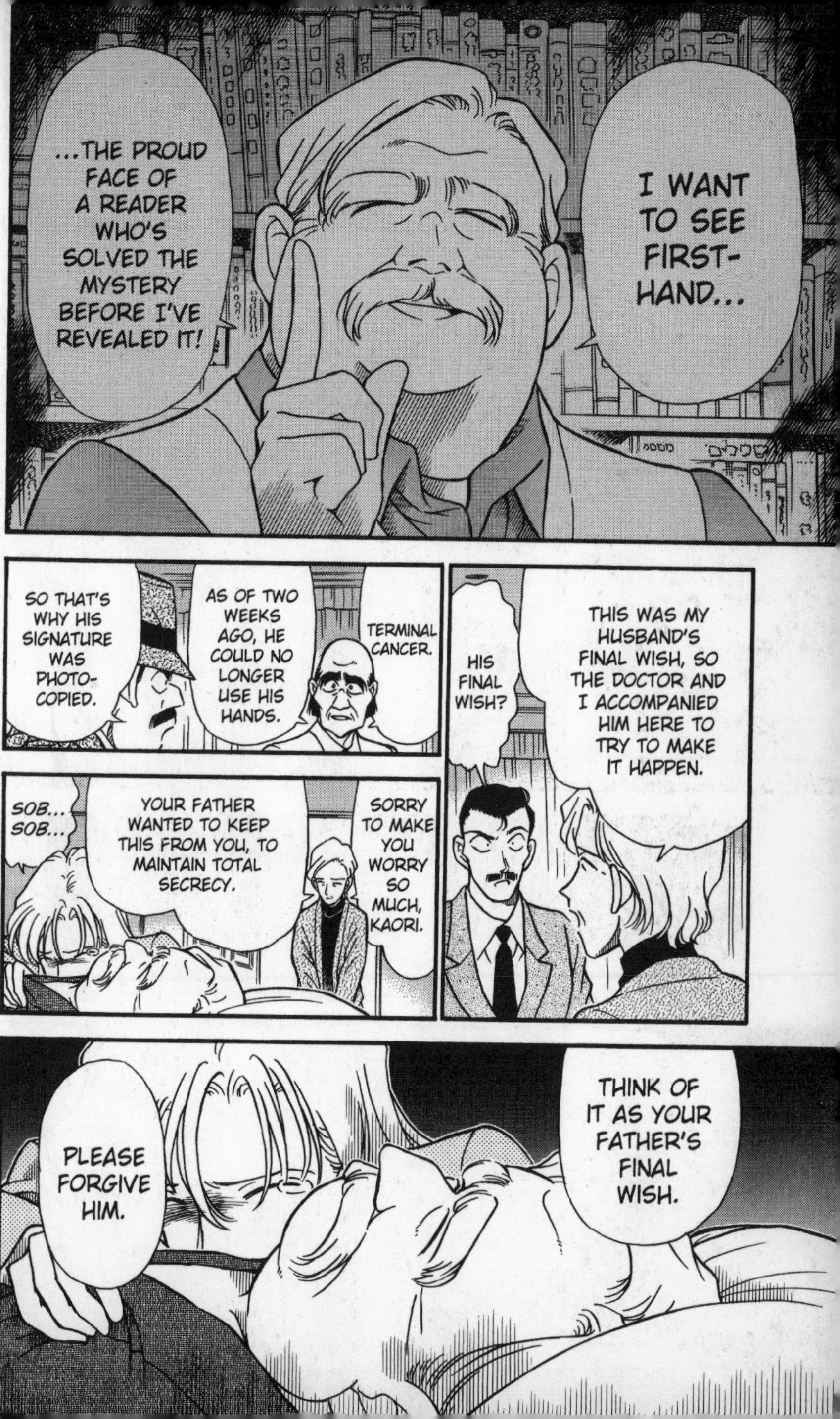
I WANT TO SEE FIRST-HAND...
...THE PROUD FACE OF A READER WHO'S SOLVED THE MYSTERY BEFORE I'VE REVEALED IT!
THIS WAS MY HUSBAND'S FINAL WISH, SO THE DOCTOR AND I ACCOMPANIED HIM HERE TO TRY TO MAKE IT HAPPEN.
HIS FINAL WISH?
TERMINAL CANCER.
AS OF TWO WEEKS AGO, HE COULD NO LONGER USE HIS HANDS.
SO THAT'S WHY HIS SIGNATURE WAS PHOTO-COPIED.
SORRY TO MAKE YOU WORRY SO MUCH, KAORI.
YOUR FATHER WANTED TO KEEP THIS FROM YOU, TO MAINTAIN TOTAL SECRECY.
SOB... SOB...
THINK OF IT AS YOUR FATHER'S FINAL WISH.
PLEASE FORGIVE HIM.

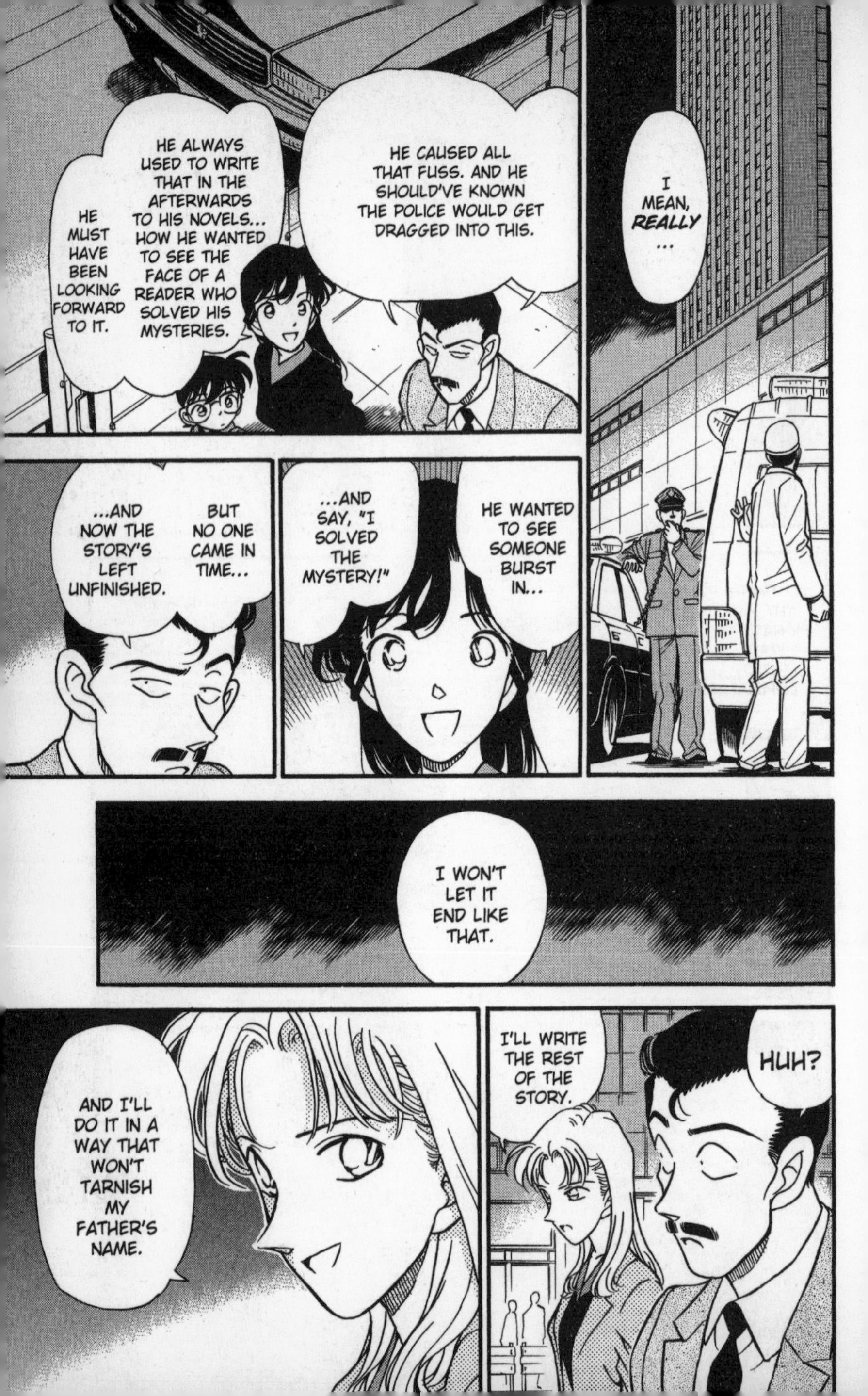

I MEAN, *REALLY*...
HE CAUSED ALL THAT FUSS. AND HE SHOULD'VE KNOWN THE POLICE WOULD GET DRAGGED INTO THIS.
HE ALWAYS USED TO WRITE THAT IN THE AFTERWARDS TO HIS NOVELS... HOW HE WANTED TO SEE THE FACE OF A READER WHO SOLVED HIS MYSTERIES.
HE MUST HAVE BEEN LOOKING FORWARD TO IT.
HE WANTED TO SEE SOMEONE BURST IN...
...AND SAY, "I SOLVED THE MYSTERY!"
BUT NO ONE CAME IN TIME...
...AND NOW THE STORY'S LEFT UNFINISHED.
I WON'T LET IT END LIKE THAT.
HUH?
I'LL WRITE THE REST OF THE STORY.
AND I'LL DO IT IN A WAY THAT WON'T TARNISH MY FATHER'S NAME.

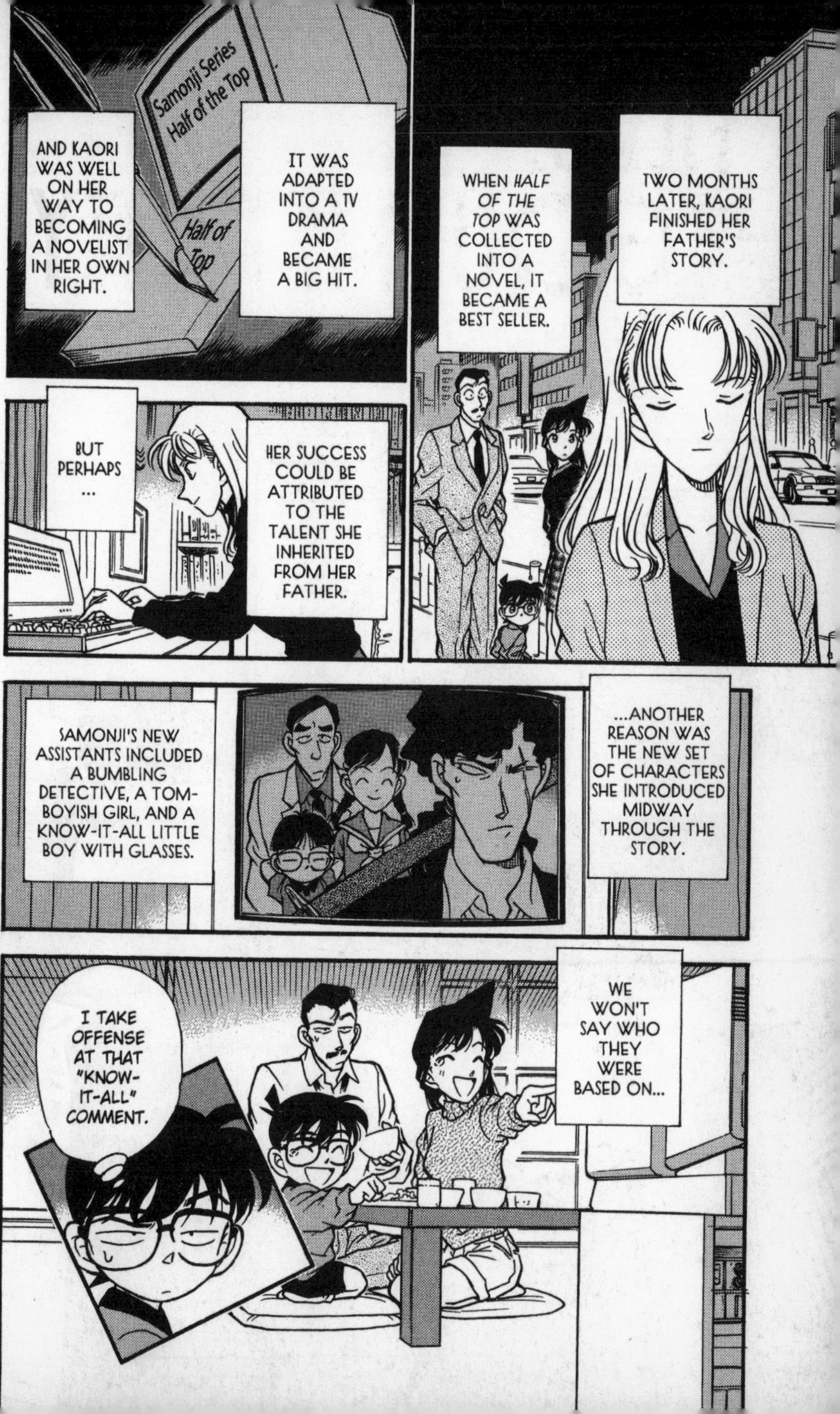
TWO MONTHS LATER, KAORI FINISHED HER FATHER'S STORY.
WHEN *HALF OF THE TOP* WAS COLLECTED INTO A NOVEL, IT BECAME A BEST SELLER.
Samonji Series Half of the Top
IT WAS ADAPTED INTO A TV DRAMA AND BECAME A BIG HIT.
Half of Top
AND KAORI WAS WELL ON HER WAY TO BECOMING A NOVELIST IN HER OWN RIGHT.
HER SUCCESS COULD BE ATTRIBUTED TO THE TALENT SHE INHERITED FROM HER FATHER.
BUT PERHAPS ...
...ANOTHER REASON WAS THE NEW SET OF CHARACTERS SHE INTRODUCED MIDWAY THROUGH THE STORY.
SAMONJI'S NEW ASSISTANTS INCLUDED A BUMBLING DETECTIVE, A TOM-BOYISH GIRL, AND A KNOW-IT-ALL LITTLE BOY WITH GLASSES.
WE WON'T SAY WHO THEY WERE BASED ON...
I TAKE OFFENSE AT THAT "KNOW-IT-ALL" COMMENT.

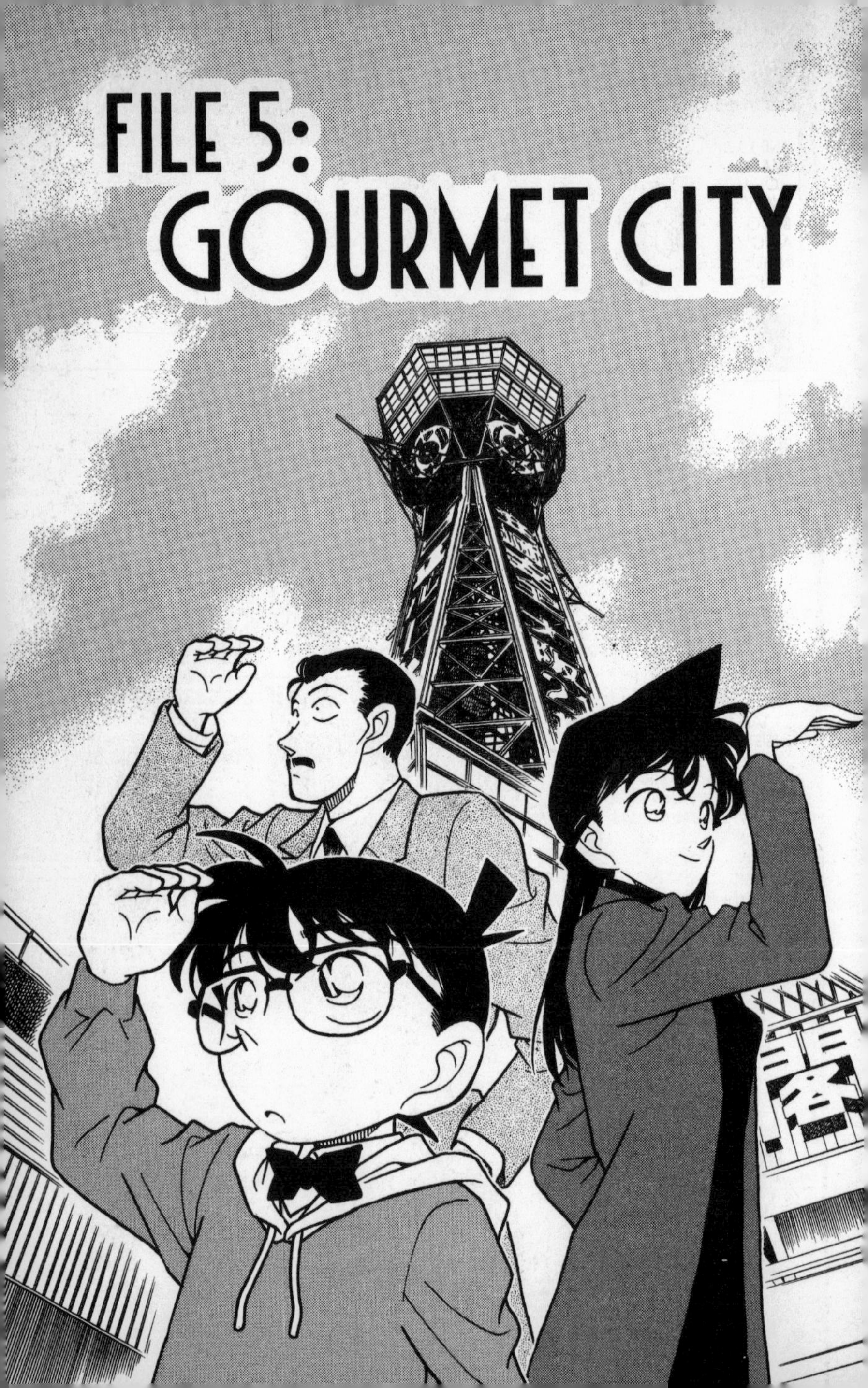
FILE 5:
GOURMET CITY

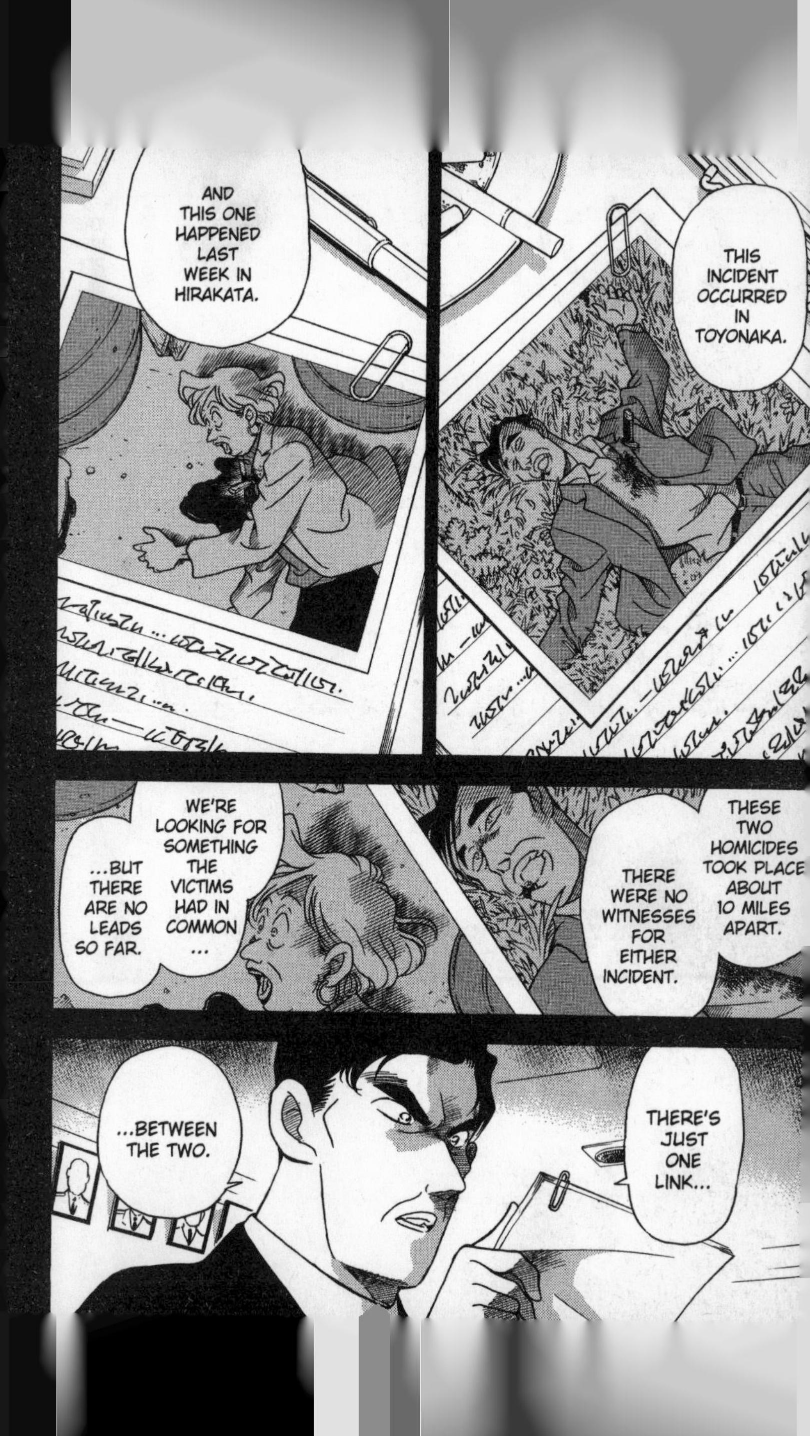
THIS INCIDENT OCCURRED IN TOYONAKA.
AND THIS ONE HAPPENED LAST WEEK IN HIRAKATA.
THESE TWO HOMICIDES TOOK PLACE ABOUT 10 MILES APART.
THERE WERE NO WITNESSES FOR EITHER INCIDENT.
WE'RE LOOKING FOR SOMETHING THE VICTIMS HAD IN COMMON ...
...BUT THERE ARE NO LEADS SO FAR.
THERE'S JUST ONE LINK...
...BETWEEN THE TWO.

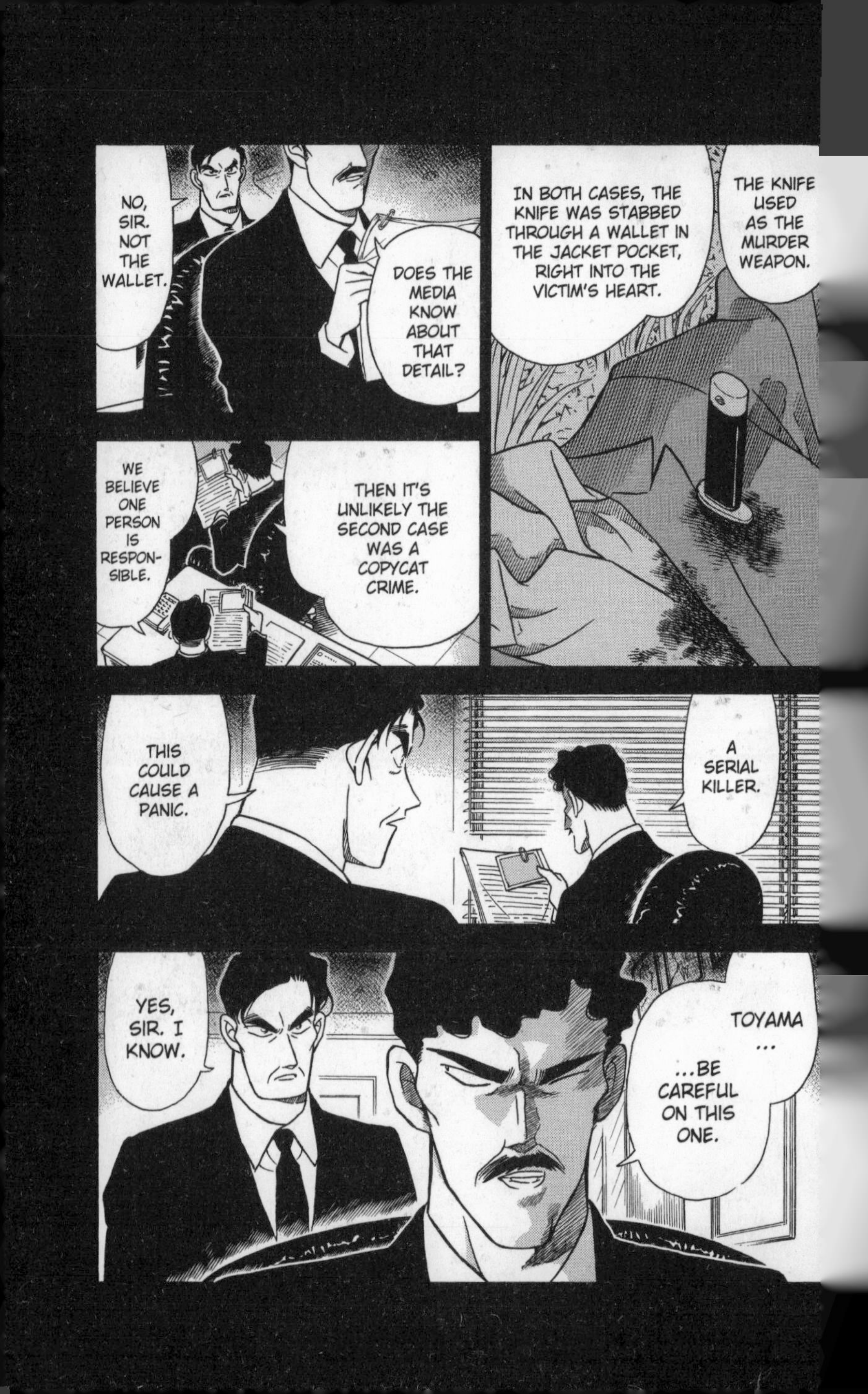
THE KNIFE USED AS THE MURDER WEAPON.
IN BOTH CASES, THE KNIFE WAS STABBED THROUGH A WALLET IN THE JACKET POCKET, RIGHT INTO THE VICTIM'S HEART.
DOES THE MEDIA KNOW ABOUT THAT DETAIL?
NO, SIR. NOT THE WALLET.
THEN IT'S UNLIKELY THE SECOND CASE WAS A COPYCAT CRIME.
WE BELIEVE ONE PERSON IS RESPON-SIBLE.
A SERIAL KILLER.
THIS COULD CAUSE A PANIC.
TOYAMA ...
...BE CAREFUL ON THIS ONE.
YES, SIR. I KNOW.

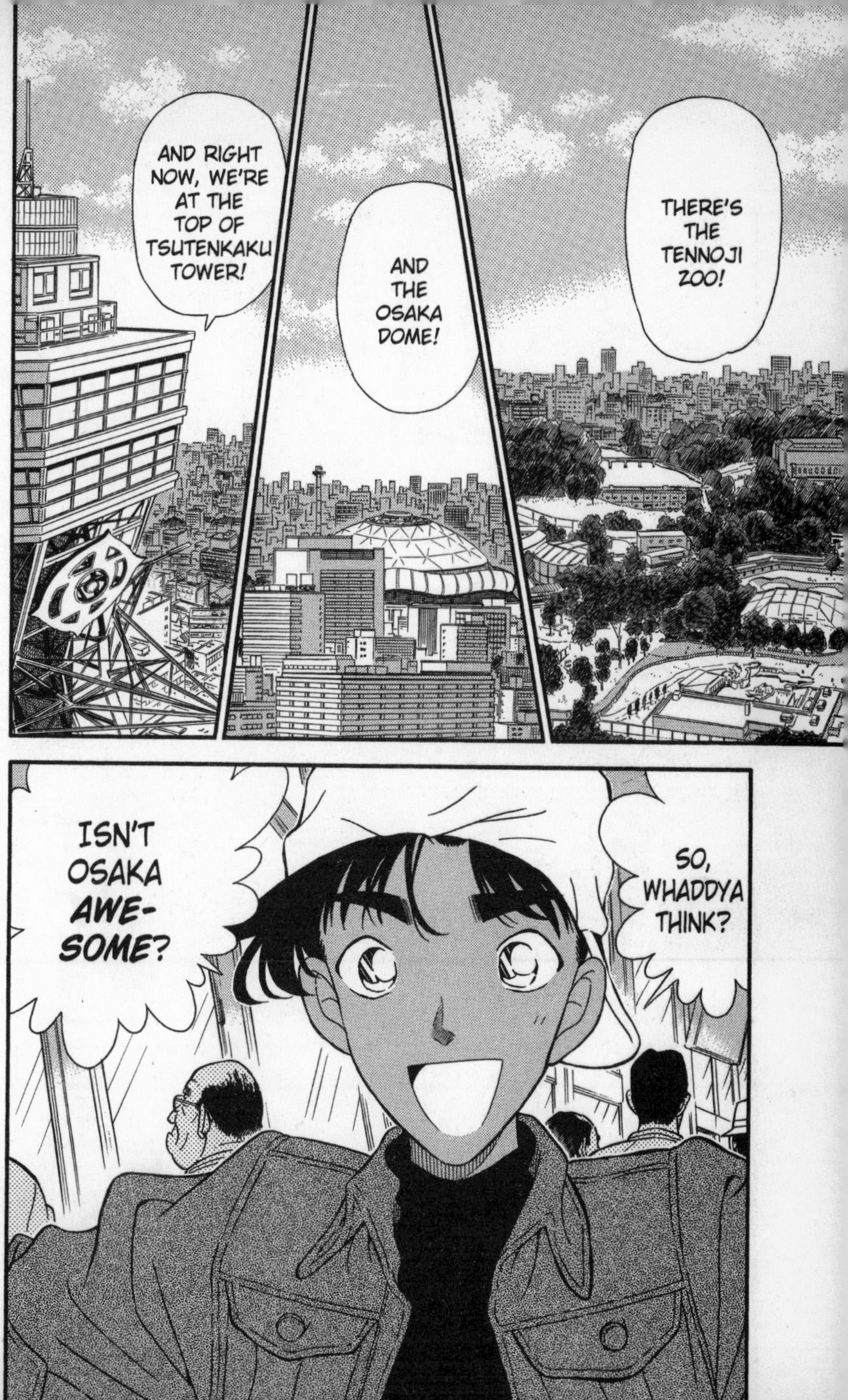
THERE'S THE TENNOJI ZOO!
AND THE OSAKA DOME!
AND RIGHT NOW, WE'RE AT THE TOP OF TSUTENKAKU TOWER!
SO, WHADDYA THINK?
ISN'T OSAKA AWE-SOME?

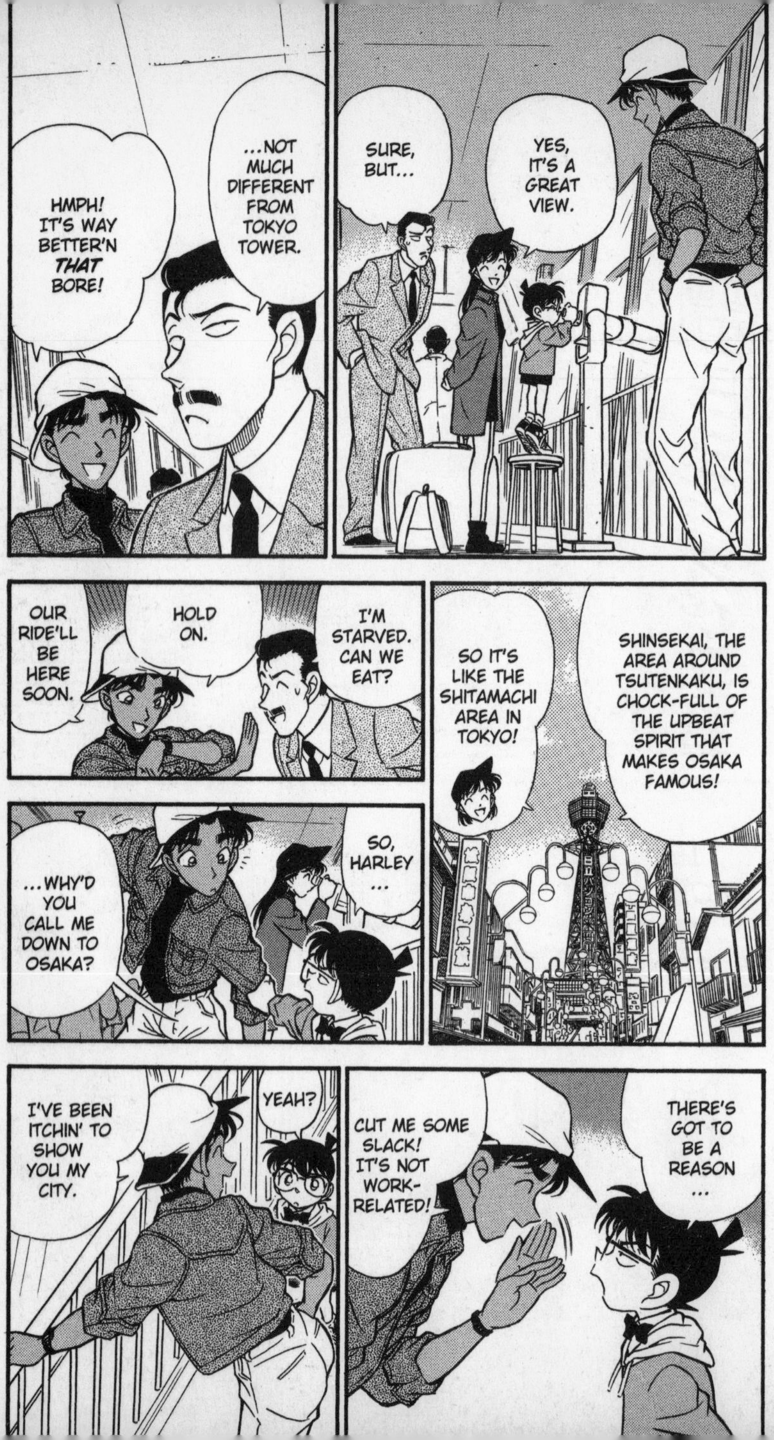
YES, IT'S A GREAT VIEW.
SURE, BUT...
...NOT MUCH DIFFERENT FROM TOKYO TOWER.
HMPH! IT'S WAY BETTER'N *THAT* BORE!
SHINSEKAI, THE AREA AROUND TSUTENKAKU, IS CHOCK-FULL OF THE UPBEAT SPIRIT THAT MAKES OSAKA FAMOUS!
SO IT'S LIKE THE SHITAMACHI AREA IN TOKYO!
I'M STARVED. CAN WE EAT?
HOLD ON.
OUR RIDE'LL BE HERE SOON.
SO, HARLEY...
...WHY'D YOU CALL ME DOWN TO OSAKA?
THERE'S GOT TO BE A REASON...
CUT ME SOME SLACK! IT'S NOT WORK-RELATED!
YEAH?
I'VE BEEN ITCHIN' TO SHOW YOU MY CITY.

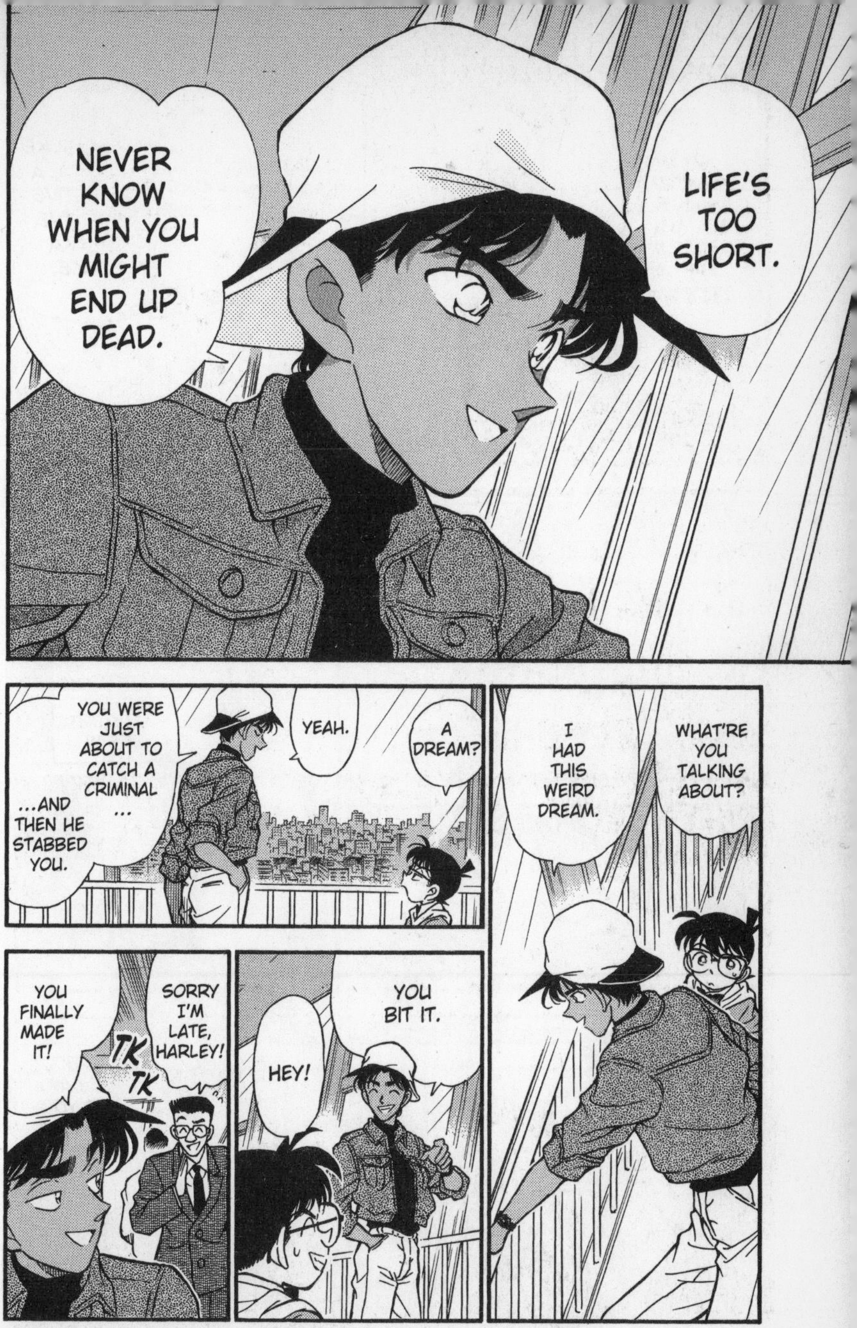
LIFE'S TOO SHORT.
NEVER KNOW WHEN YOU MIGHT END UP DEAD.
WHAT'RE YOU TALKING ABOUT?
I HAD THIS WEIRD DREAM.
A DREAM?
YEAH.
YOU WERE JUST ABOUT TO CATCH A CRIMINAL ...
...AND THEN HE STABBED YOU.
YOU BIT IT.
HEY!
SORRY I'M LATE, HARLEY!
TK TK
YOU FINALLY MADE IT!

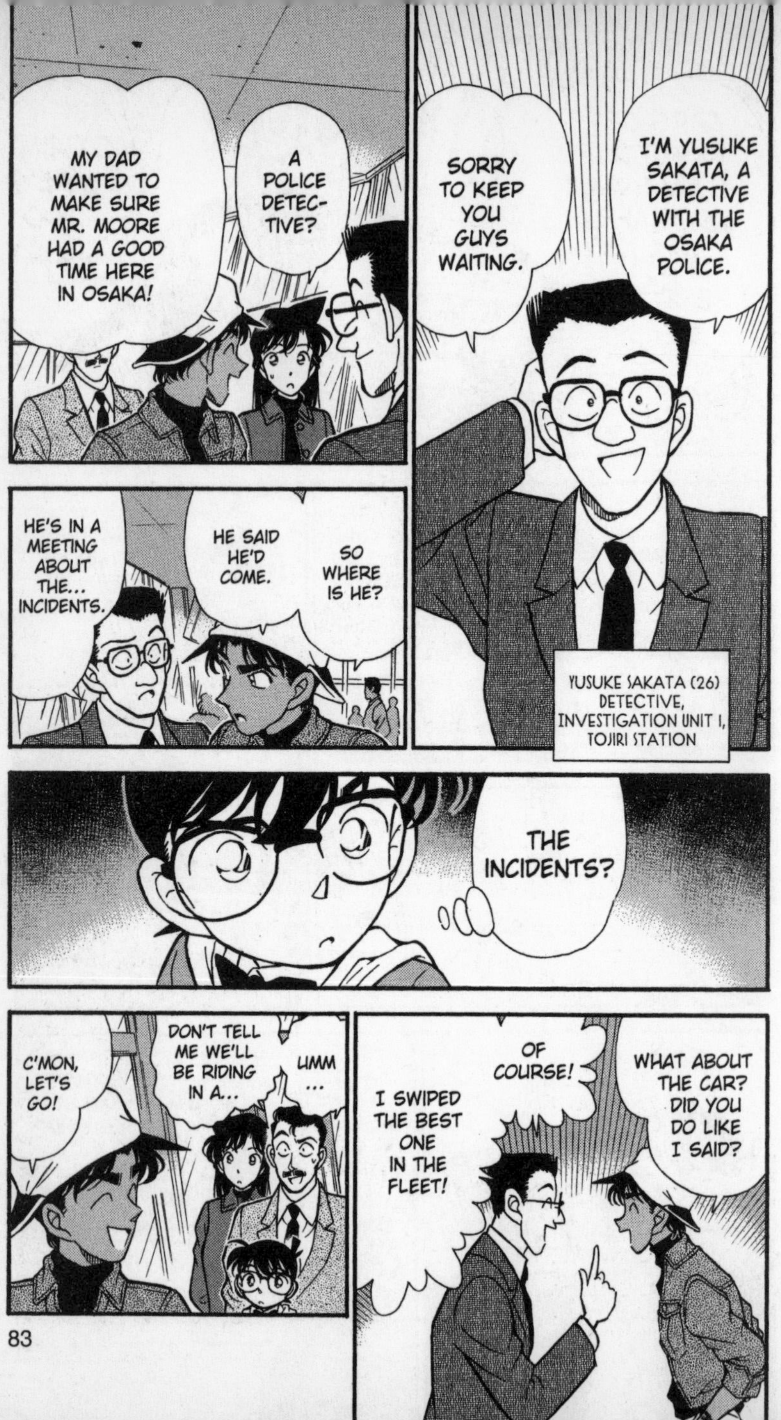
I'M YUSUKE SAKATA, A DETECTIVE WITH THE OSAKA POLICE.
SORRY TO KEEP YOU GUYS WAITING.
YUSUKE SAKATA (26) DETECTIVE, INVESTIGATION UNIT 1, TOJIRI STATION
A POLICE DETEC-TIVE?
MY DAD WANTED TO MAKE SURE MR. MOORE HAD A GOOD TIME HERE IN OSAKA!
HE SAID HE'D COME.
SO WHERE IS HE?
HE'S IN A MEETING ABOUT THE... INCIDENTS.
THE INCIDENTS?
WHAT ABOUT THE CAR? DID YOU DO LIKE I SAID?
OF COURSE!
I SWIPED THE BEST ONE IN THE FLEET!
UMM ...
DON'T TELL ME WE'LL BE RIDING IN A...
C'MON, LET'S GO!

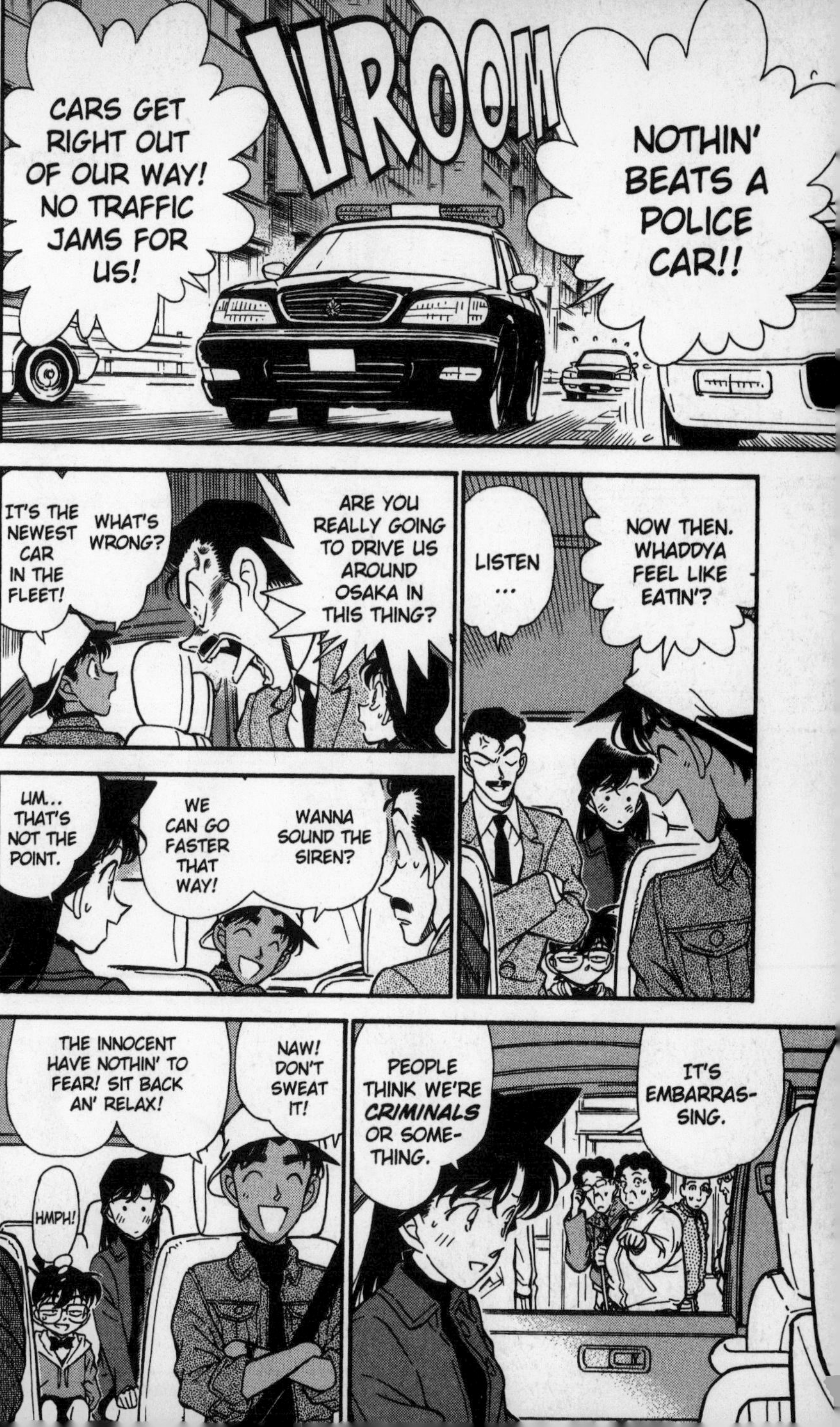
NOTHIN' BEATS A POLICE CAR!!
VROOM
CARS GET RIGHT OUT OF OUR WAY! NO TRAFFIC JAMS FOR US!
NOW THEN. WHADDYA FEEL LIKE EATIN'?
LISTEN ...
ARE YOU REALLY GOING TO DRIVE US AROUND OSAKA IN THIS THING?
WHAT'S WRONG?
IT'S THE NEWEST CAR IN THE FLEET!
WANNA SOUND THE SIREN?
WE CAN GO FASTER THAT WAY!
UM.. THAT'S NOT THE POINT.
IT'S EMBARRAS-SING.
PEOPLE THINK WE'RE *CRIMINALS* OR SOME-THING.
NAW! DON'T SWEAT IT!
THE INNOCENT HAVE NOTHIN' TO FEAR! SIT BACK AN' RELAX!
HMPH!

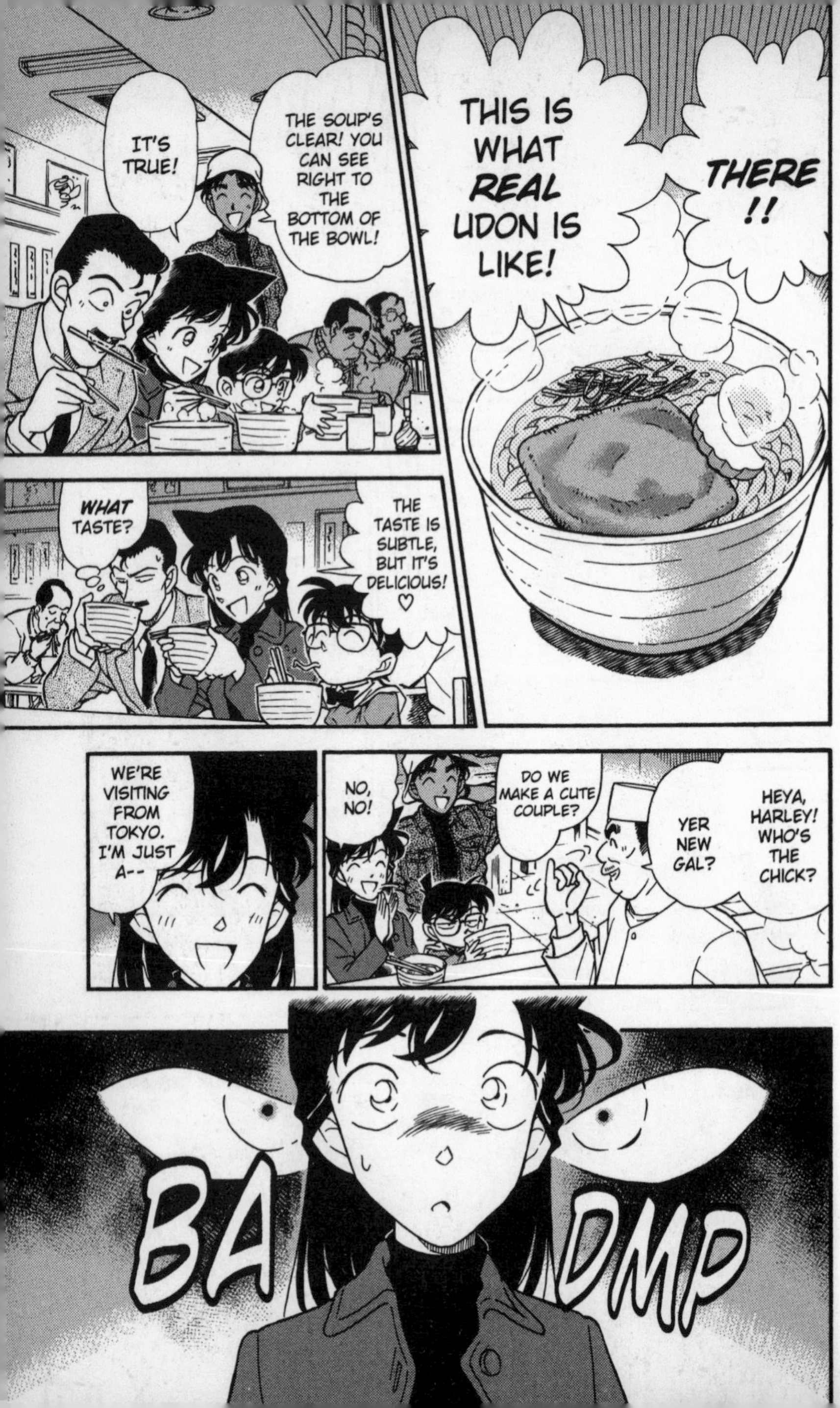
THERE !!
THIS IS WHAT *REAL* UDON IS LIKE!
THE SOUP'S CLEAR! YOU CAN SEE RIGHT TO THE BOTTOM OF THE BOWL!
IT'S TRUE!
THE TASTE IS SUBTLE, BUT IT'S DELICIOUS! ♡
WHAT TASTE?
HEYA, HARLEY! WHO'S THE CHICK?
YER NEW GAL?
DO WE MAKE A CUTE COUPLE?
NO, NO!
WE'RE VISITING FROM TOKYO. I'M JUST A--
BA DMP

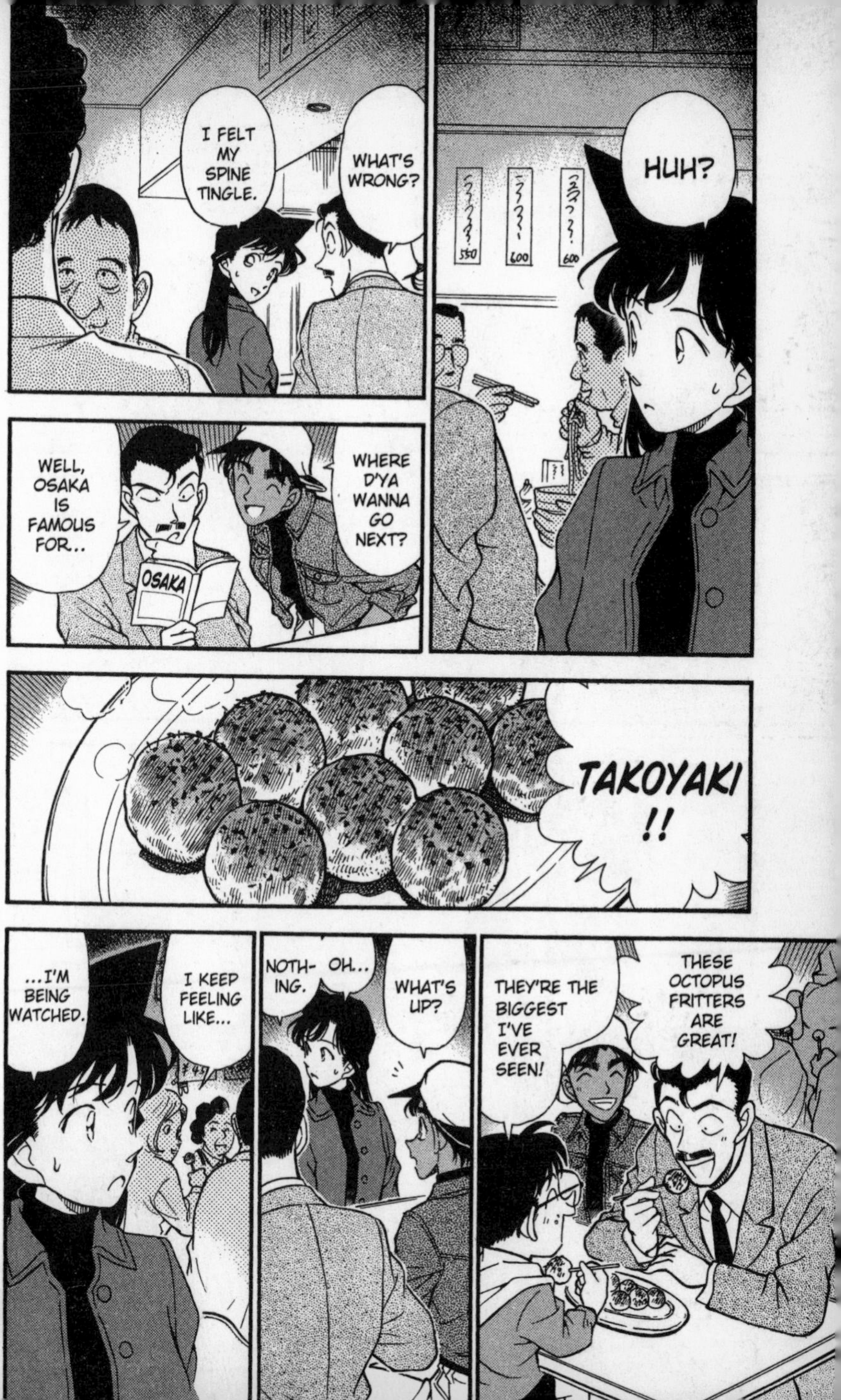

HUH?
WHAT'S WRONG?
I FELT MY SPINE TINGLE.
WHERE D'YA WANNA GO NEXT?
WELL, OSAKA IS FAMOUS FOR...
OSAKA
TAKOYAKI !!
THESE OCTOPUS FRITTERS ARE GREAT!
THEY'RE THE BIGGEST I'VE EVER SEEN!
WHAT'S UP?
OH... NOTH-ING.
I KEEP FEELING LIKE...
...I'M BEING WATCHED.

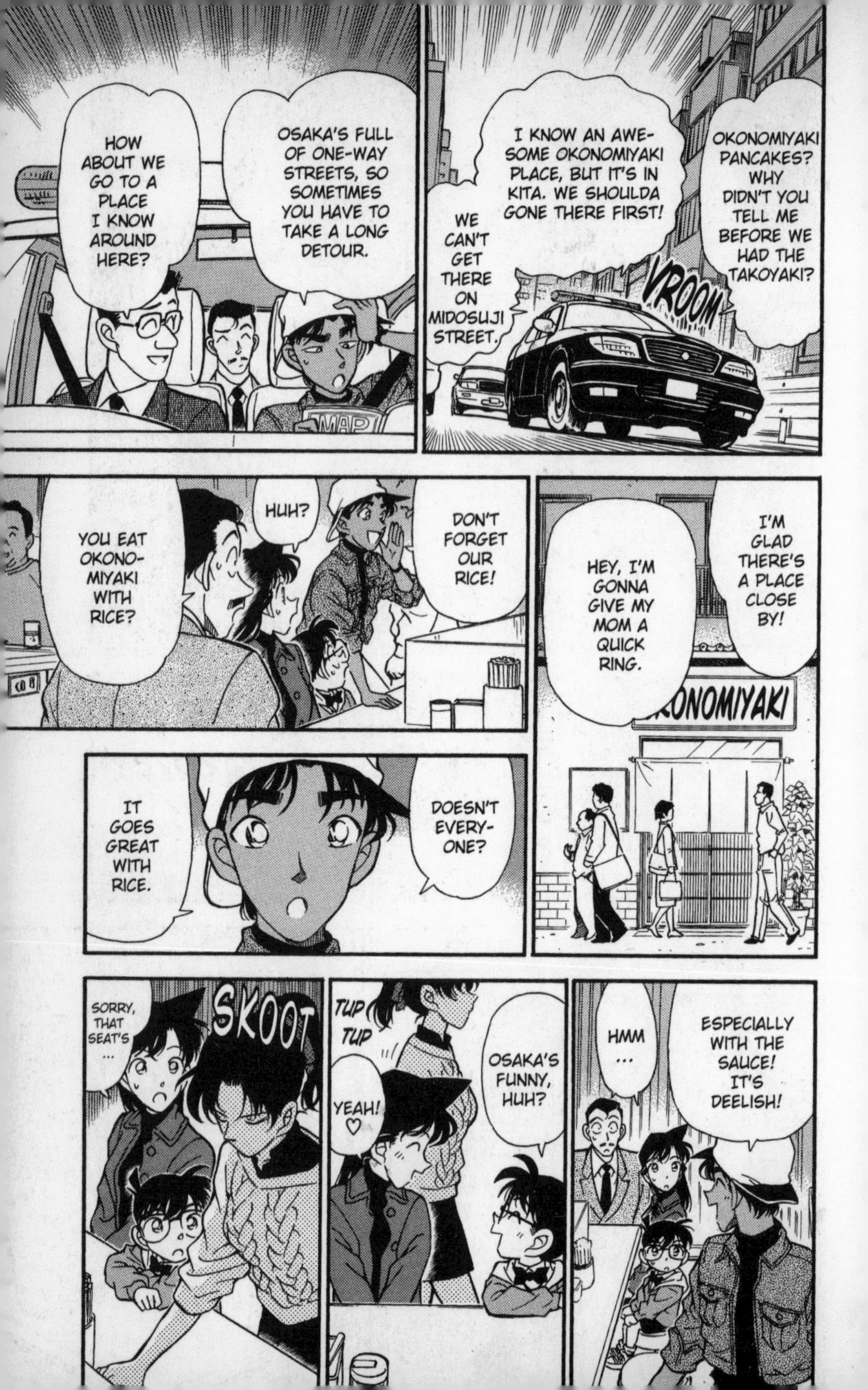
OKONOMIYAKI PANCAKES? WHY DIDN'T YOU TELL ME BEFORE WE HAD THE TAKOYAKI?
VROOM
I KNOW AN AWESOME OKONOMIYAKI PLACE, BUT IT'S IN KITA. WE SHOULDA GONE THERE FIRST!
WE CAN'T GET THERE ON MIDOSUJI STREET.
OSAKA'S FULL OF ONE-WAY STREETS, SO SOMETIMES YOU HAVE TO TAKE A LONG DETOUR.
HOW ABOUT WE GO TO A PLACE I KNOW AROUND HERE?
MAP
I'M GLAD THERE'S A PLACE CLOSE BY!
HEY, I'M GONNA GIVE MY MOM A QUICK RING.
OKONOMIYAKI
DON'T FORGET OUR RICE!
HUH?
YOU EAT OKONOMIYAKI WITH RICE?
DOESN'T EVERYONE?
IT GOES GREAT WITH RICE.
ESPECIALLY WITH THE SAUCE! IT'S DEELISH!
HMM ...
OSAKA'S FUNNY, HUH?
TUP TUP
YEAH! ♡
SKOOT
SORRY, THAT SEAT'S ...

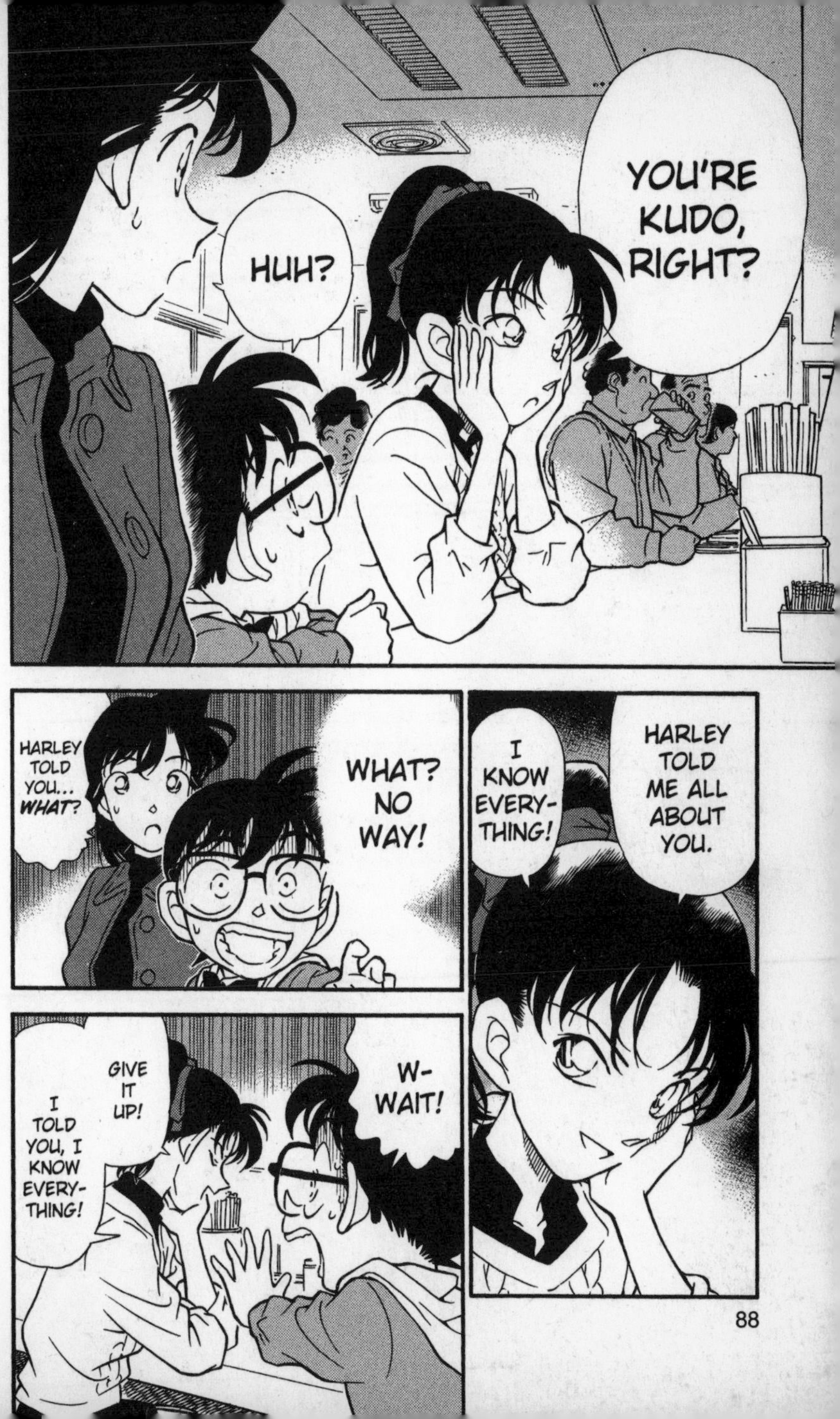
YOU'RE KUDO, RIGHT?
HUH?
HARLEY TOLD ME ALL ABOUT YOU.
I KNOW EVERYTHING!
WHAT? NO WAY!
HARLEY TOLD YOU... *WHAT*?
W-WAIT!
GIVE IT UP!
I TOLD YOU, I KNOW EVERYTHING!

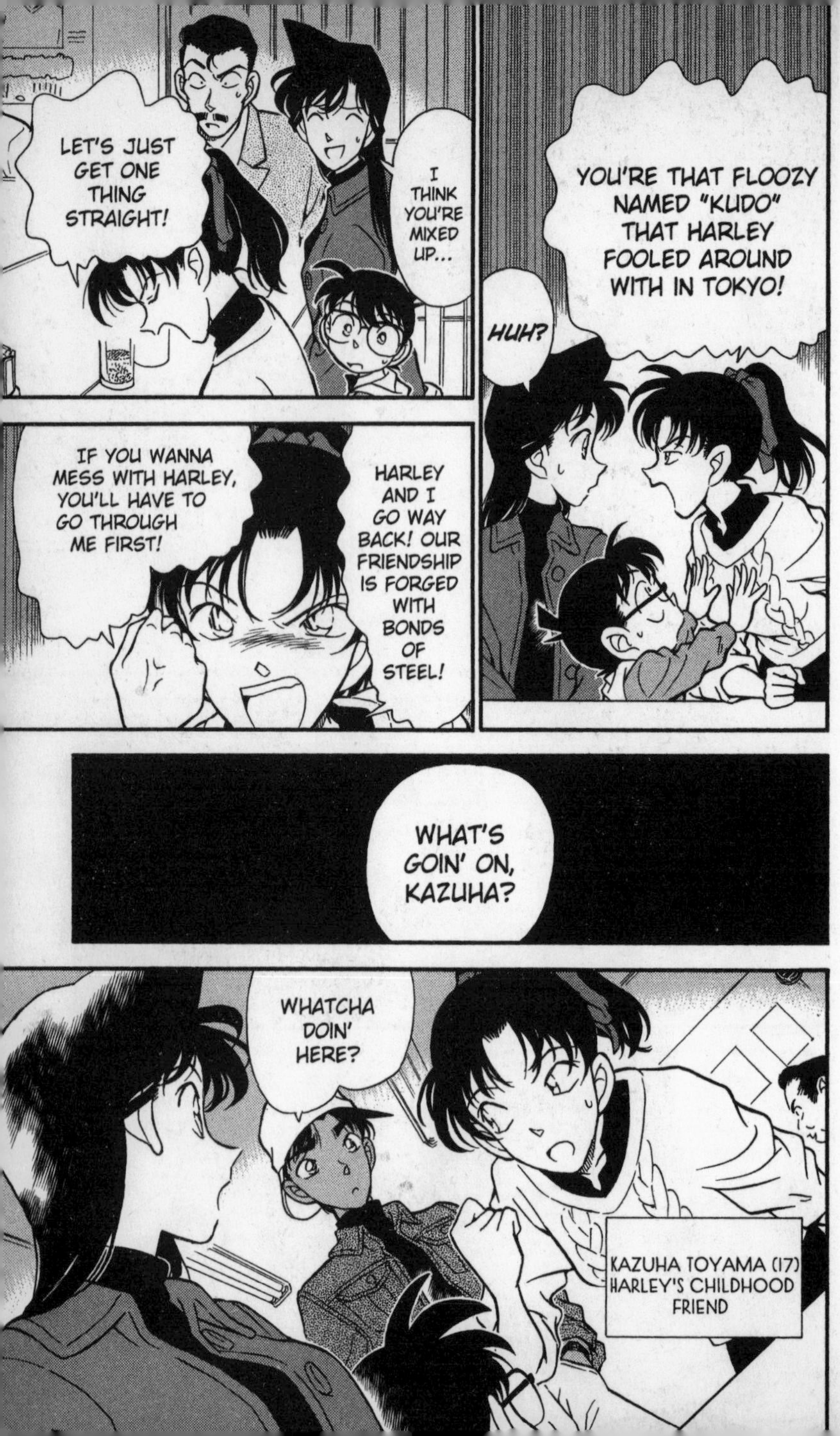
YOU'RE THAT FLOOZY NAMED "KUDO" THAT HARLEY FOOLED AROUND WITH IN TOKYO!
HUH?
I THINK YOU'RE MIXED UP...
LET'S JUST GET ONE THING STRAIGHT!
HARLEY AND I GO WAY BACK! OUR FRIENDSHIP IS FORGED WITH BONDS OF STEEL!
IF YOU WANNA MESS WITH HARLEY, YOU'LL HAVE TO GO THROUGH ME FIRST!
WHAT'S GOIN' ON, KAZUHA?
WHATCHA DOIN' HERE?
KAZUHA TOYAMA (17) HARLEY'S CHILDHOOD FRIEND

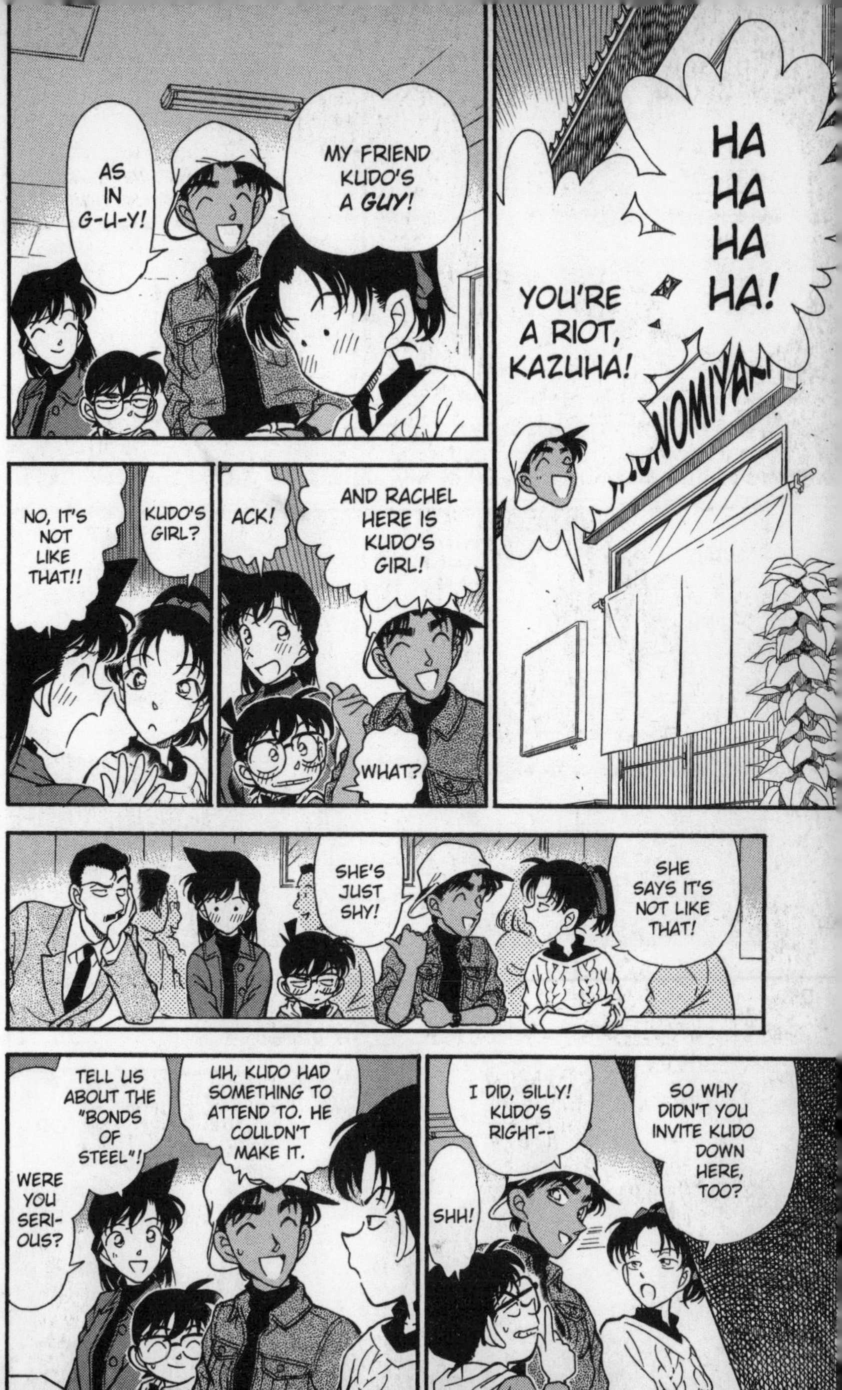
HA HA HA HA!
YOU'RE A RIOT, KAZUHA!
MY FRIEND KUDO'S A GUY!
AS IN G-U-Y!
AND RACHEL HERE IS KUDO'S GIRL!
ACK!
WHAT?
KUDO'S GIRL?
NO, IT'S NOT LIKE THAT!!
SHE SAYS IT'S NOT LIKE THAT!
SHE'S JUST SHY!
SO WHY DIDN'T YOU INVITE KUDO DOWN HERE, TOO?
I DID, SILLY! KUDO'S RIGHT--
SHH!
UH, KUDO HAD SOMETHING TO ATTEND TO. HE COULDN'T MAKE IT.
TELL US ABOUT THE "BONDS OF STEEL"!
WERE YOU SERIOUS?

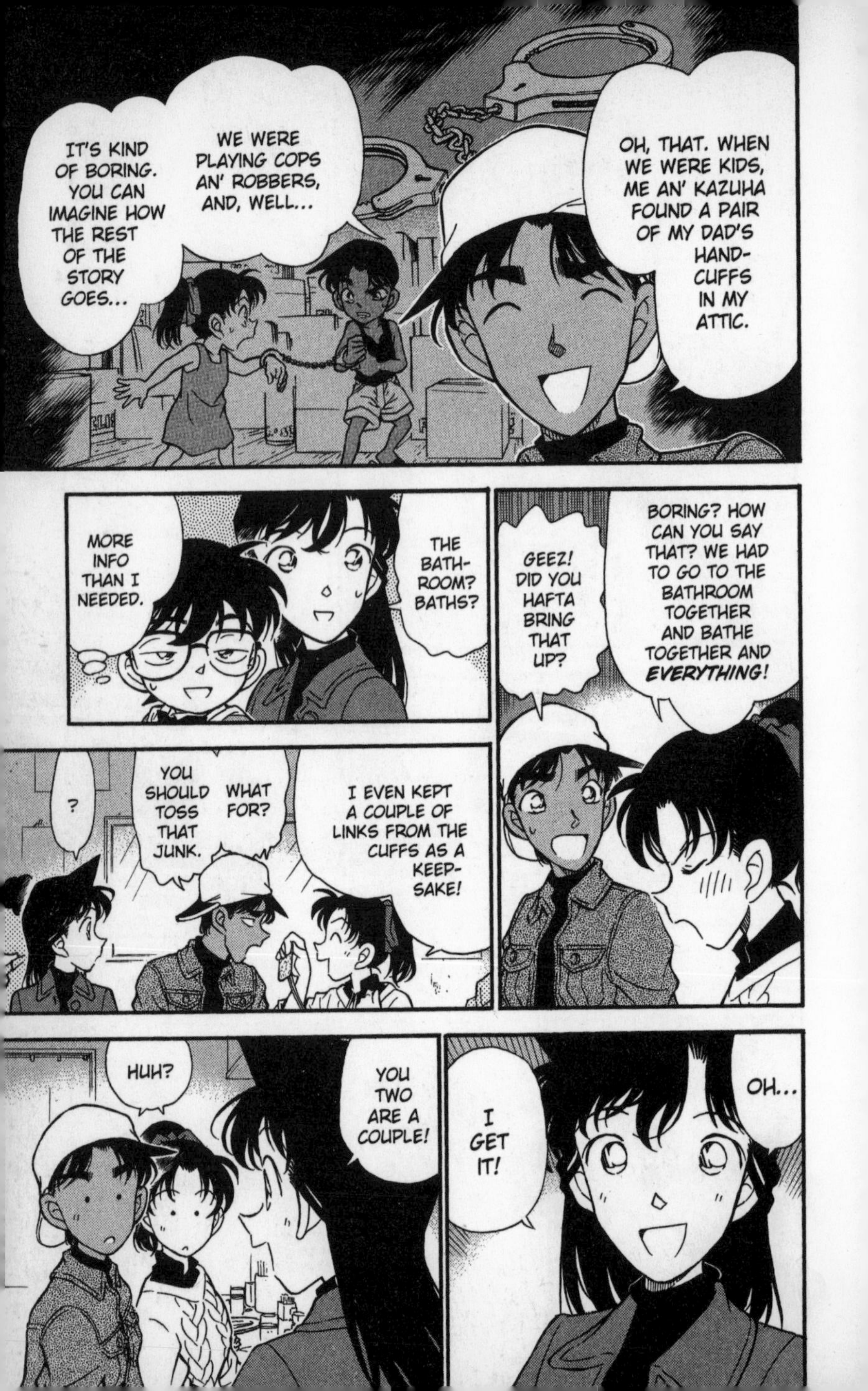

OH, THAT. WHEN WE WERE KIDS, ME AN' KAZUHA FOUND A PAIR OF MY DAD'S HAND-CUFFS IN MY ATTIC.
WE WERE PLAYING COPS AN' ROBBERS, AND, WELL...
IT'S KIND OF BORING. YOU CAN IMAGINE HOW THE REST OF THE STORY GOES...
BORING? HOW CAN YOU SAY THAT? WE HAD TO GO TO THE BATHROOM TOGETHER AND BATHE TOGETHER AND ***EVERYTHING***!
GEEZ! DID YOU HAFTA BRING THAT UP?
THE BATH-ROOM? BATHS?
MORE INFO THAN I NEEDED.
I EVEN KEPT A COUPLE OF LINKS FROM THE CUFFS AS A KEEP-SAKE!
WHAT FOR?
YOU SHOULD TOSS THAT JUNK.
?
OH...
I GET IT!
YOU TWO ARE A COUPLE!
HUH?

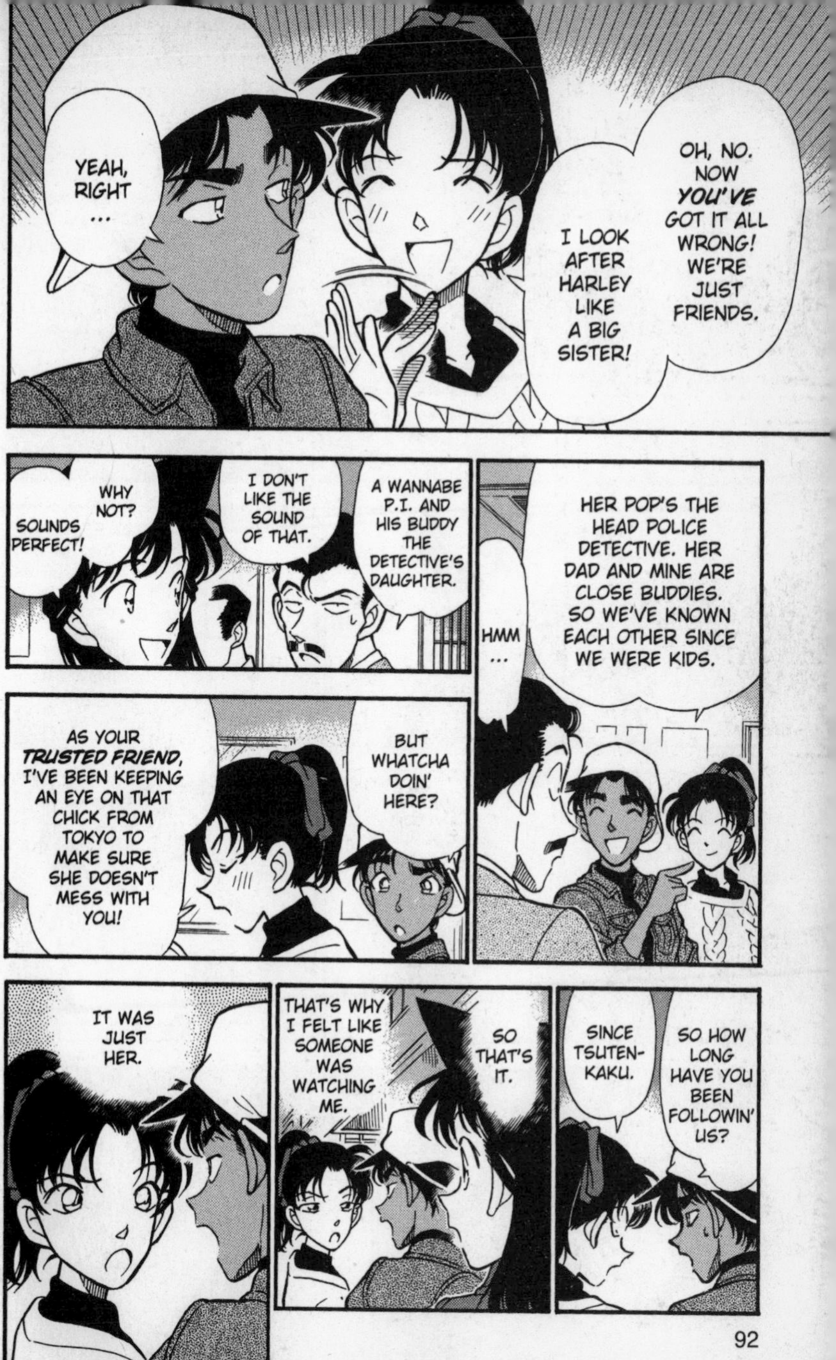
OH, NO. NOW YOU'VE GOT IT ALL WRONG! WE'RE JUST FRIENDS.
I LOOK AFTER HARLEY LIKE A BIG SISTER!
YEAH, RIGHT ...
HER POP'S THE HEAD POLICE DETECTIVE. HER DAD AND MINE ARE CLOSE BUDDIES. SO WE'VE KNOWN EACH OTHER SINCE WE WERE KIDS.
HMM ...
A WANNABE P.I. AND HIS BUDDY THE DETECTIVE'S DAUGHTER.
I DON'T LIKE THE SOUND OF THAT.
WHY NOT? SOUNDS PERFECT!
BUT WHATCHA DOIN' HERE?
AS YOUR TRUSTED FRIEND, I'VE BEEN KEEPING AN EYE ON THAT CHICK FROM TOKYO TO MAKE SURE SHE DOESN'T MESS WITH YOU!
SO HOW LONG HAVE YOU BEEN FOLLOWIN' US?
SINCE TSUTEN-KAKU.
SO THAT'S IT.
THAT'S WHY I FELT LIKE SOMEONE WAS WATCHING ME.
IT WAS JUST HER.

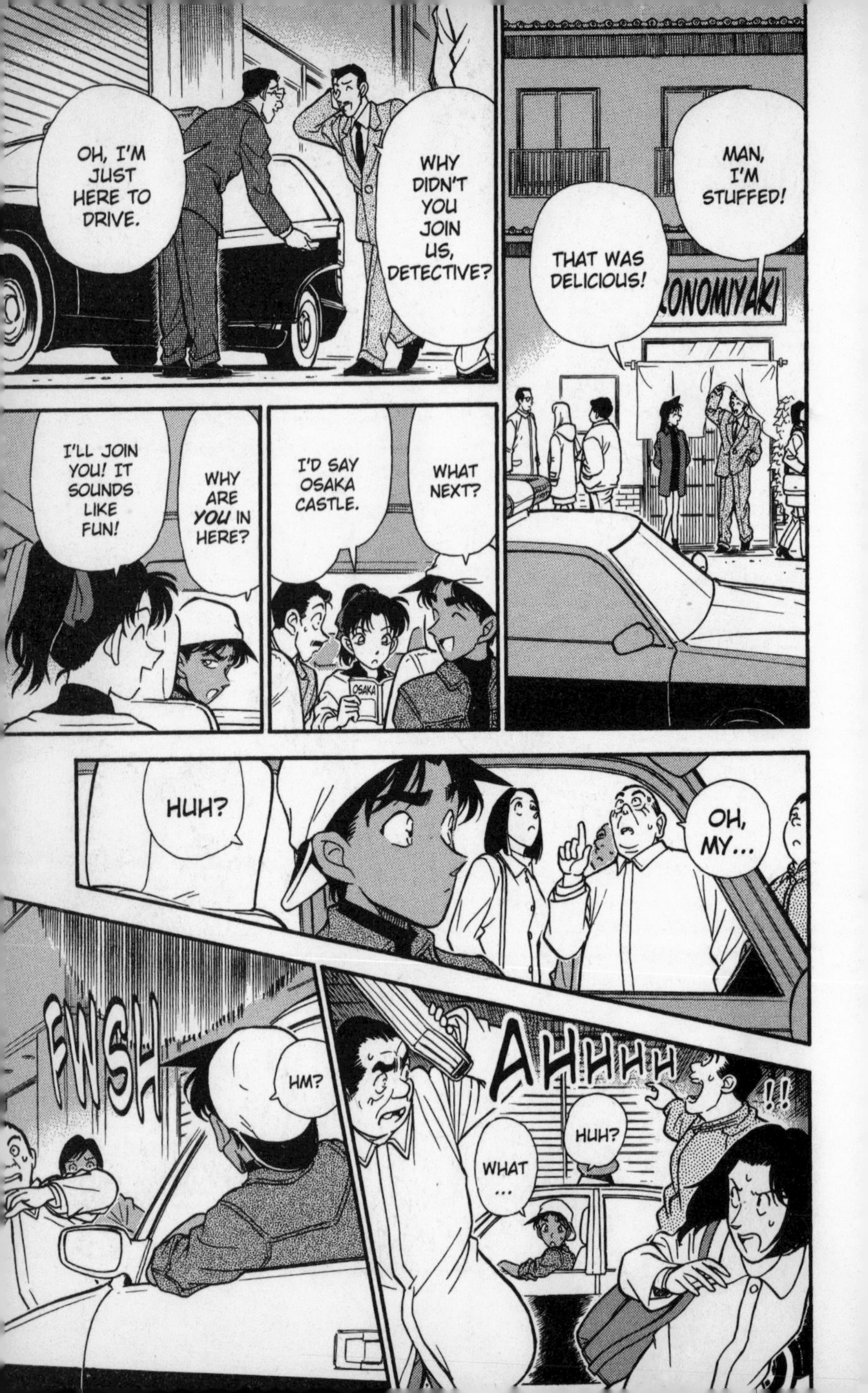
MAN, I'M STUFFED!
THAT WAS DELICIOUS!
ONOMIYAKI
WHY DIDN'T YOU JOIN US, DETECTIVE?
OH, I'M JUST HERE TO DRIVE.
WHAT NEXT?
I'D SAY OSAKA CASTLE.
OSAKA
WHY ARE *YOU* IN HERE?
I'LL JOIN YOU! IT SOUNDS LIKE FUN!
OH, MY...
HUH?
AHHHH!!
HUH?
WHAT...
FWSH
HM?

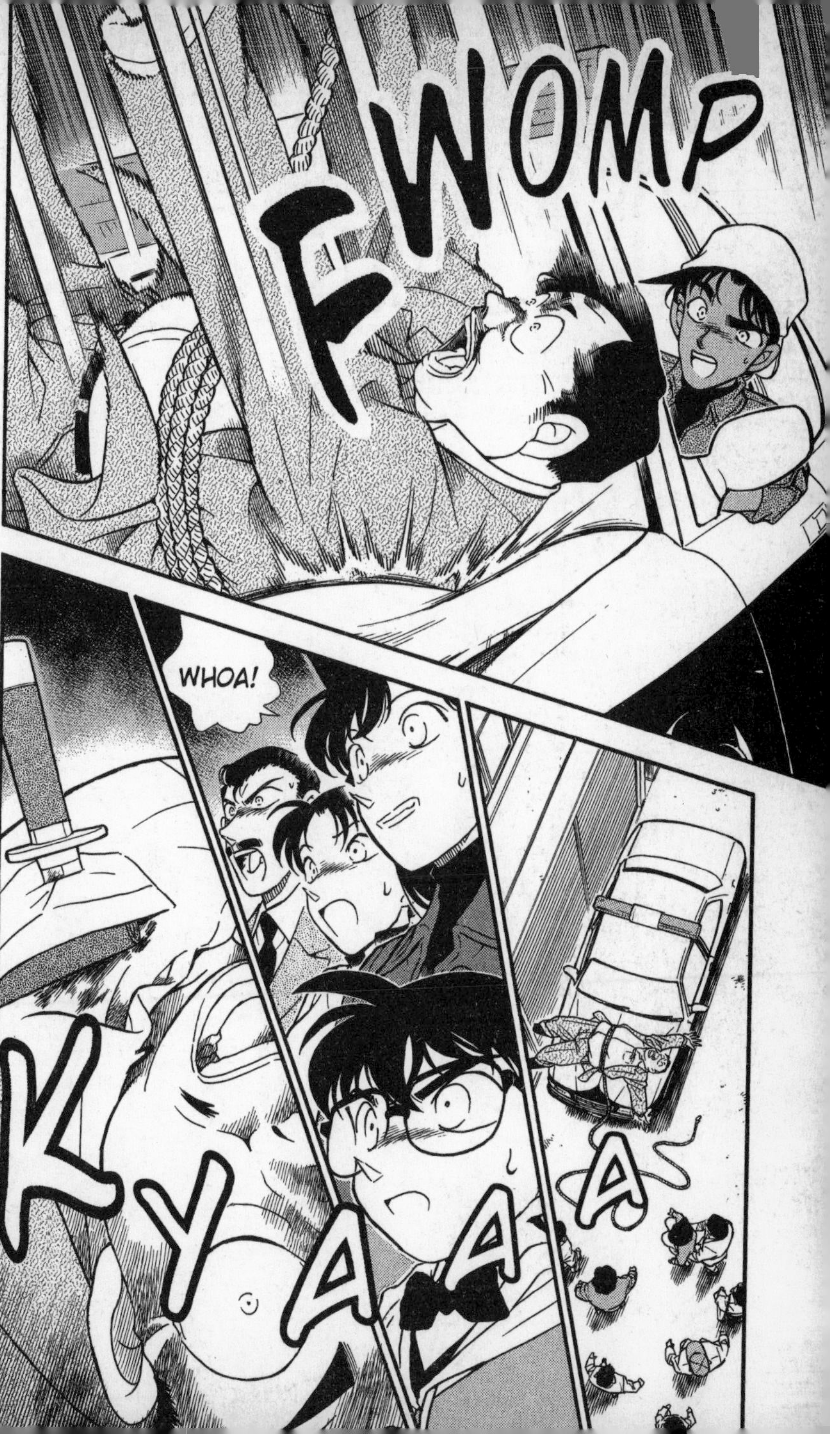
FWOMP
WHOA!
KYAAA

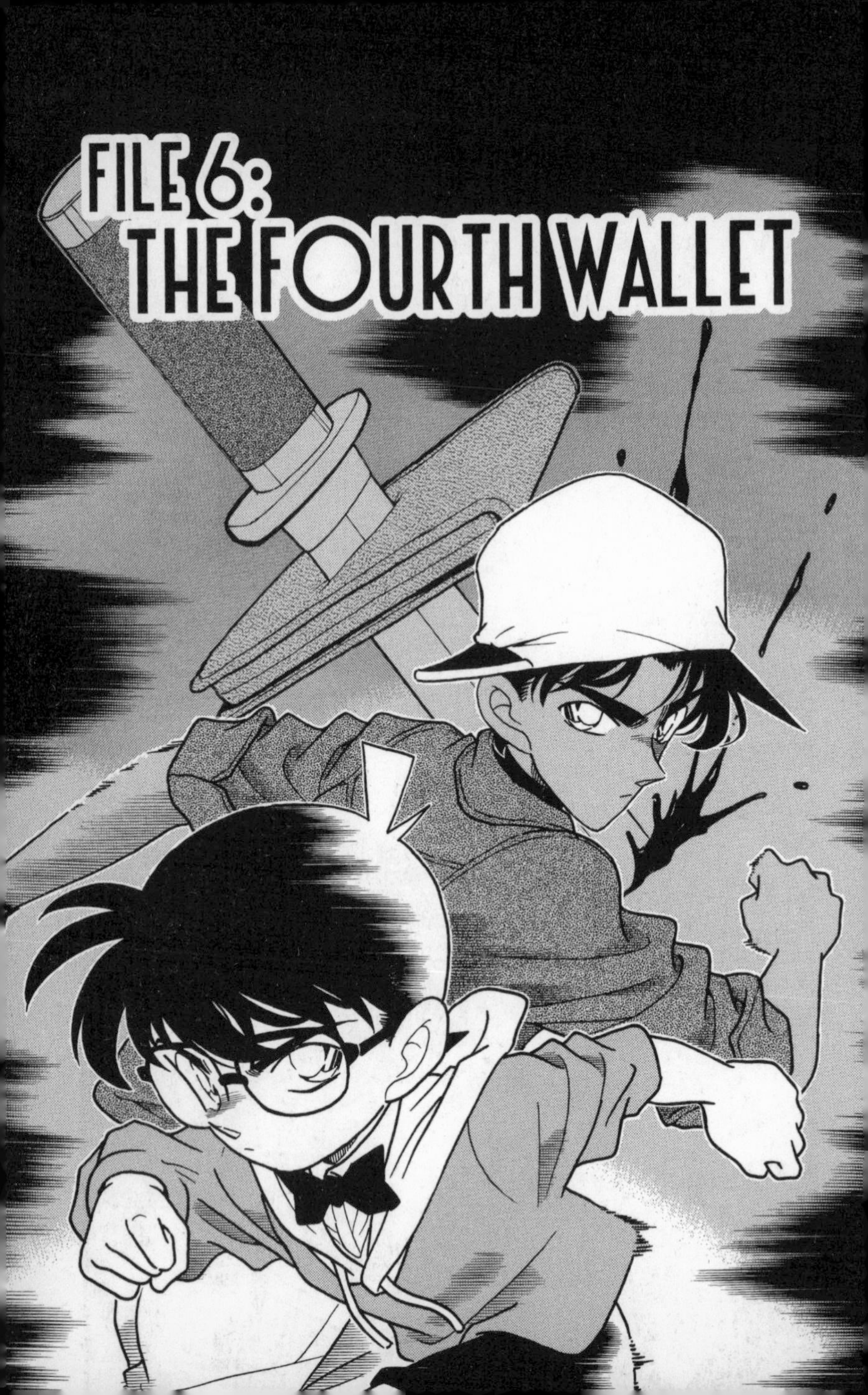
FILE 6:
THE FOURTH WALLET

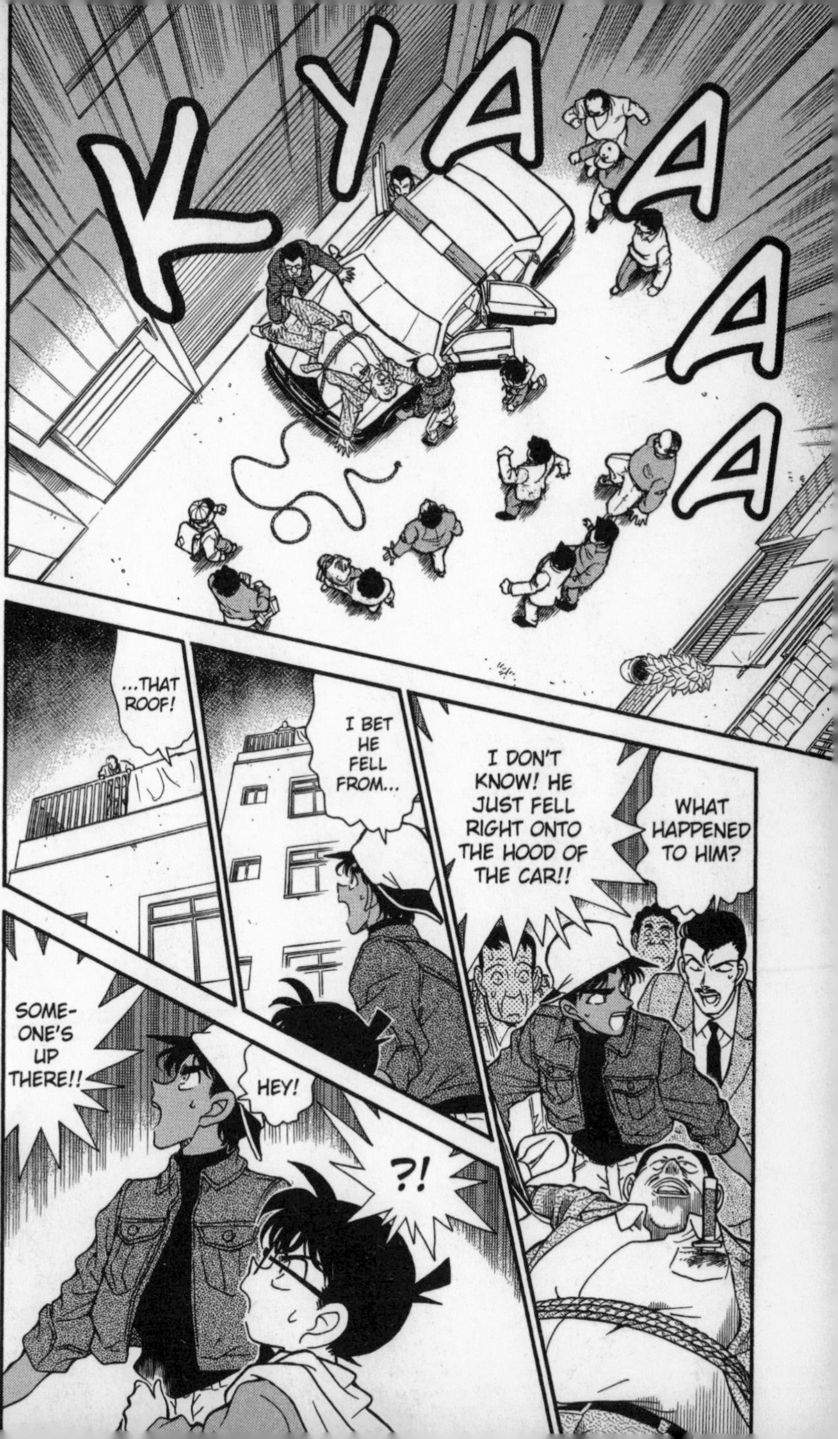
KYAAAA
WHAT HAPPENED TO HIM?
I DON'T KNOW! HE JUST FELL RIGHT ONTO THE HOOD OF THE CAR!!
I BET HE FELL FROM...
...THAT ROOF!
HEY!
SOME-ONE'S UP THERE!!
?!

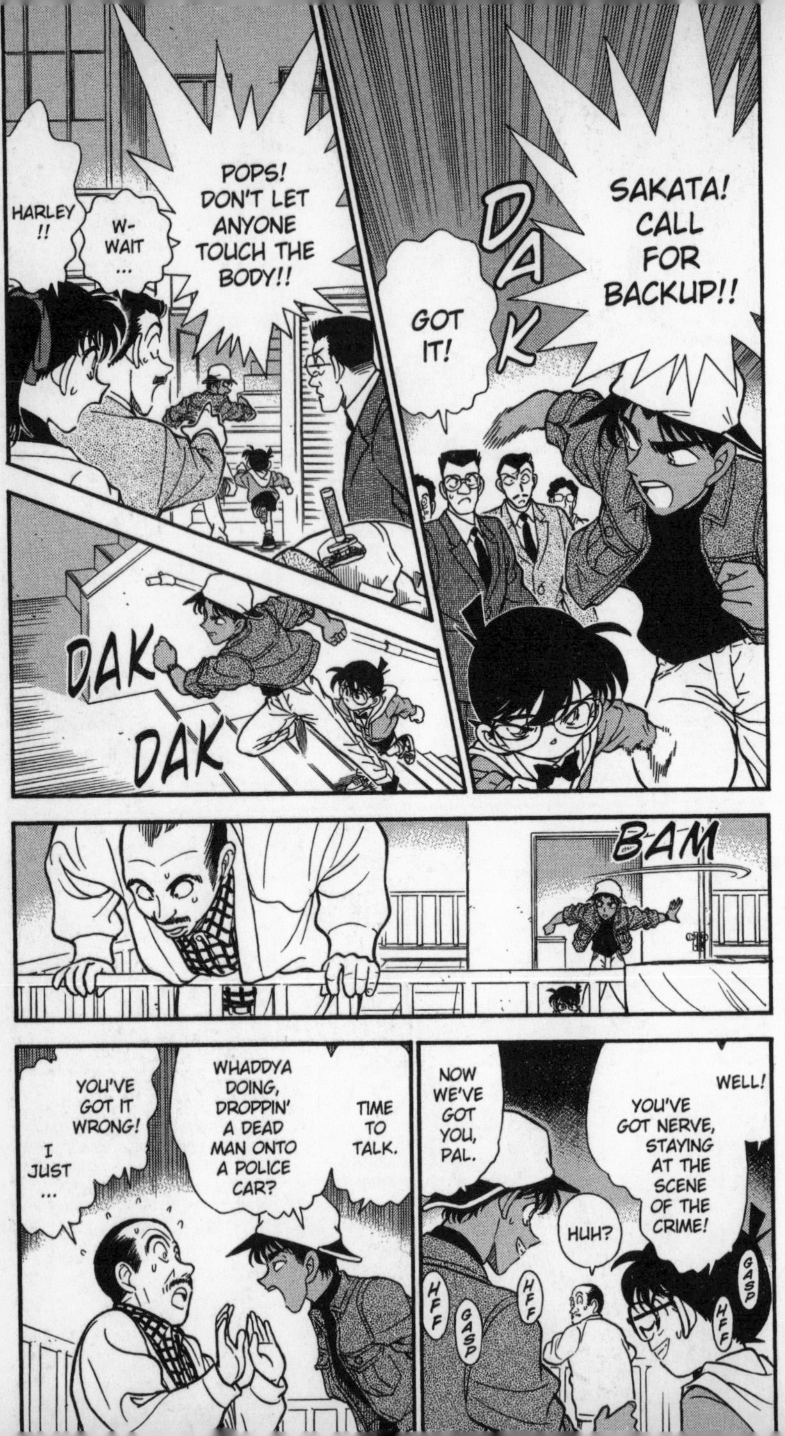
SAKATA! CALL FOR BACKUP!!
DAK
GOT IT!
POPS! DON'T LET ANYONE TOUCH THE BODY!!
W-WAIT...
HARLEY!!
DAK
DAK
BAM
WELL!
YOU'VE GOT NERVE, STAYING AT THE SCENE OF THE CRIME!
NOW WE'VE GOT YOU, PAL.
HUH?
GASP
HFF
HFF
GASP
HFF
TIME TO TALK.
WHADDYA DOING, DROPPIN' A DEAD MAN ONTO A POLICE CAR?
YOU'VE GOT IT WRONG!
I JUST ...

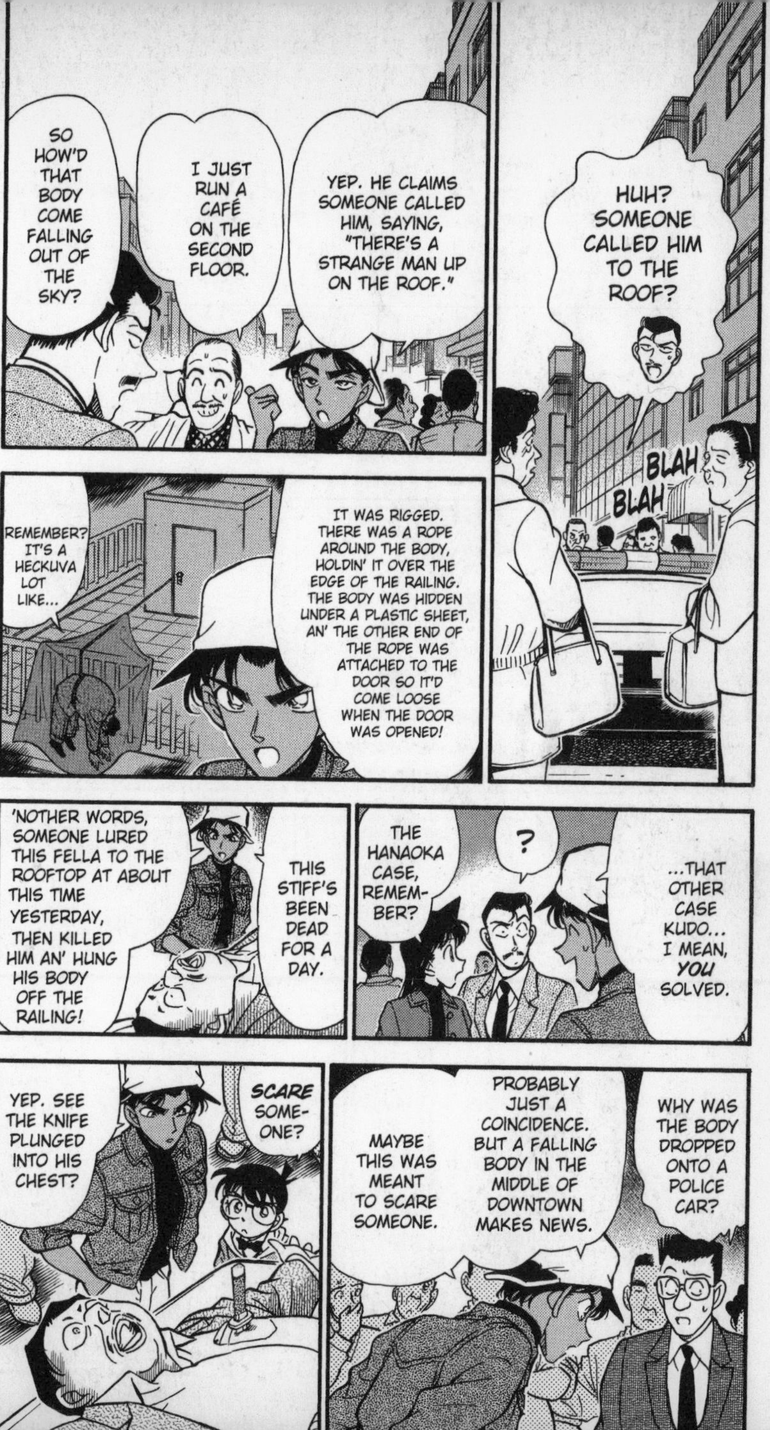
HUH? SOMEONE CALLED HIM TO THE ROOF?
BLAH
BLAH
YEP. HE CLAIMS SOMEONE CALLED HIM, SAYING, "THERE'S A STRANGE MAN UP ON THE ROOF."
I JUST RUN A CAFÉ ON THE SECOND FLOOR.
SO HOW'D THAT BODY COME FALLING OUT OF THE SKY?
IT WAS RIGGED. THERE WAS A ROPE AROUND THE BODY, HOLDIN' IT OVER THE EDGE OF THE RAILING. THE BODY WAS HIDDEN UNDER A PLASTIC SHEET, AN' THE OTHER END OF THE ROPE WAS ATTACHED TO THE DOOR SO IT'D COME LOOSE WHEN THE DOOR WAS OPENED!
REMEMBER? IT'S A HECKUVA LOT LIKE...
...THAT OTHER CASE KUDO... I MEAN, *YOU* SOLVED.
?
THE HANAOKA CASE, REMEMBER?
THIS STIFF'S BEEN DEAD FOR A DAY.
'NOTHER WORDS, SOMEONE LURED THIS FELLA TO THE ROOFTOP AT ABOUT THIS TIME YESTERDAY, THEN KILLED HIM AN' HUNG HIS BODY OFF THE RAILING!
WHY WAS THE BODY DROPPED ONTO A POLICE CAR?
PROBABLY JUST A COINCIDENCE. BUT A FALLING BODY IN THE MIDDLE OF DOWNTOWN MAKES NEWS.
MAYBE THIS WAS MEANT TO SCARE SOMEONE.
SCARE SOME-ONE?
YEP. SEE THE KNIFE PLUNGED INTO HIS CHEST?

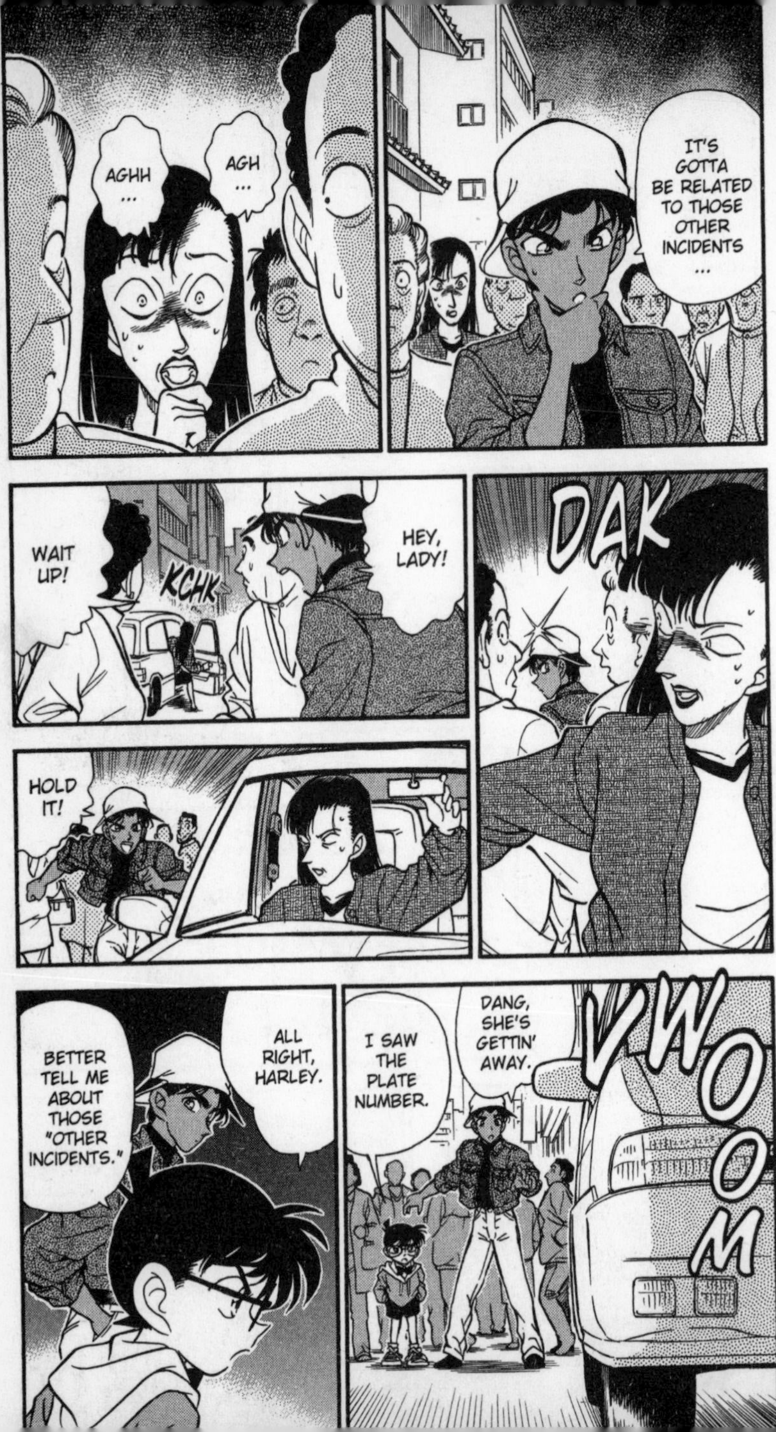
IT'S GOTTA BE RELATED TO THOSE OTHER INCIDENTS ...
AGH ...
AGHH ...
DAK
HEY, LADY!
WAIT UP!
KCHK
HOLD IT!
VWOOM
DANG, SHE'S GETTIN' AWAY.
I SAW THE PLATE NUMBER.
ALL RIGHT, HARLEY.
BETTER TELL ME ABOUT THOSE "OTHER INCIDENTS."

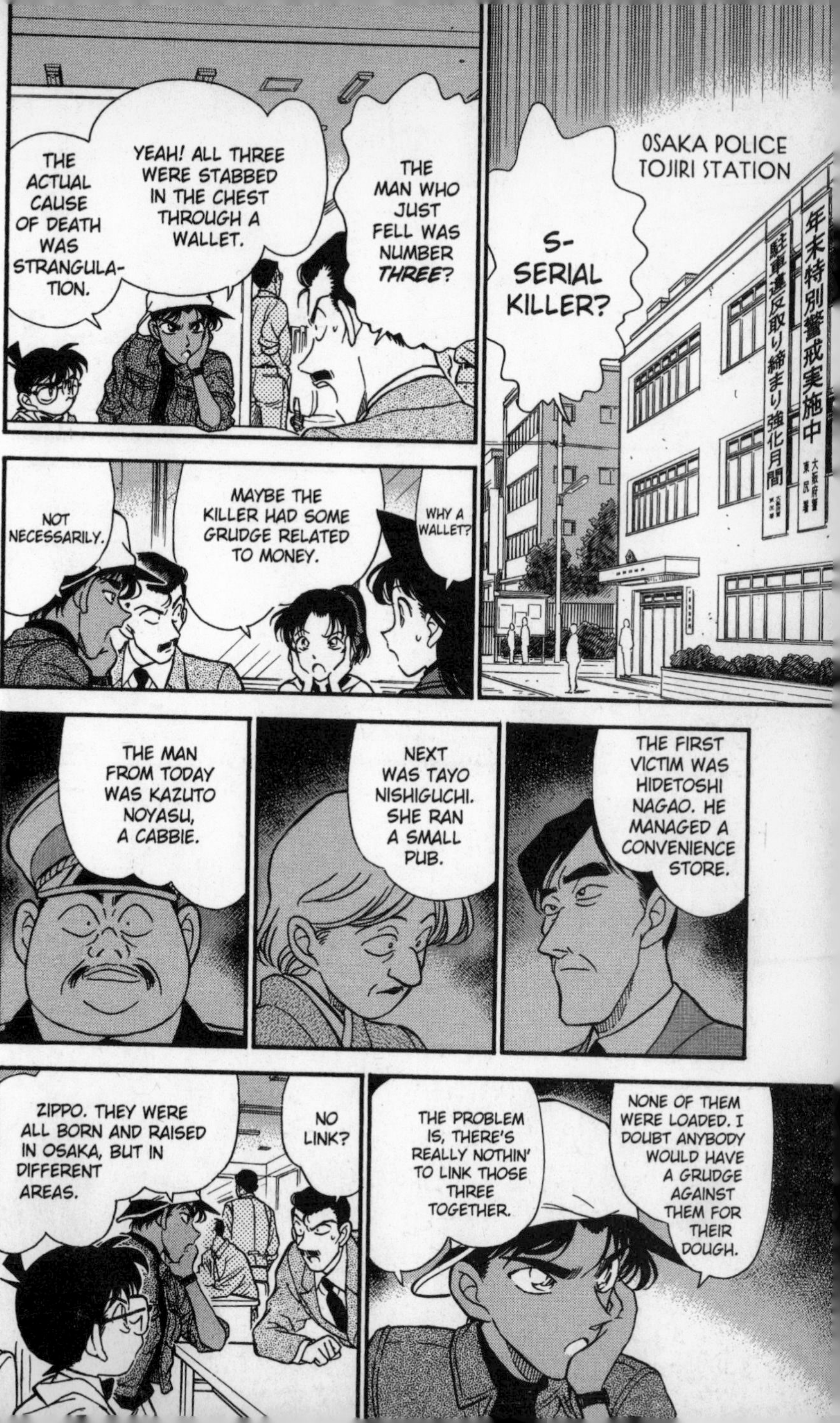
OSAKA POLICE TOJIRI STATION
年末特別警戒実施中
駐車違反取り締まり強化月間
S- SERIAL KILLER?
THE MAN WHO JUST FELL WAS NUMBER *THREE*?
YEAH! ALL THREE WERE STABBED IN THE CHEST THROUGH A WALLET.
THE ACTUAL CAUSE OF DEATH WAS STRANGULA- TION.
WHY A WALLET?
MAYBE THE KILLER HAD SOME GRUDGE RELATED TO MONEY.
NOT NECESSARILY.
THE FIRST VICTIM WAS HIDETOSHI NAGAO. HE MANAGED A CONVENIENCE STORE.
NEXT WAS TAYO NISHIGUCHI. SHE RAN A SMALL PUB.
THE MAN FROM TODAY WAS KAZUTO NOYASU, A CABBIE.
NONE OF THEM WERE LOADED. I DOUBT ANYBODY WOULD HAVE A GRUDGE AGAINST THEM FOR THEIR DOUGH.
THE PROBLEM IS, THERE'S REALLY NOTHIN' TO LINK THOSE THREE TOGETHER.
NO LINK?
ZIPPO. THEY WERE ALL BORN AND RAISED IN OSAKA, BUT IN DIFFERENT AREAS.

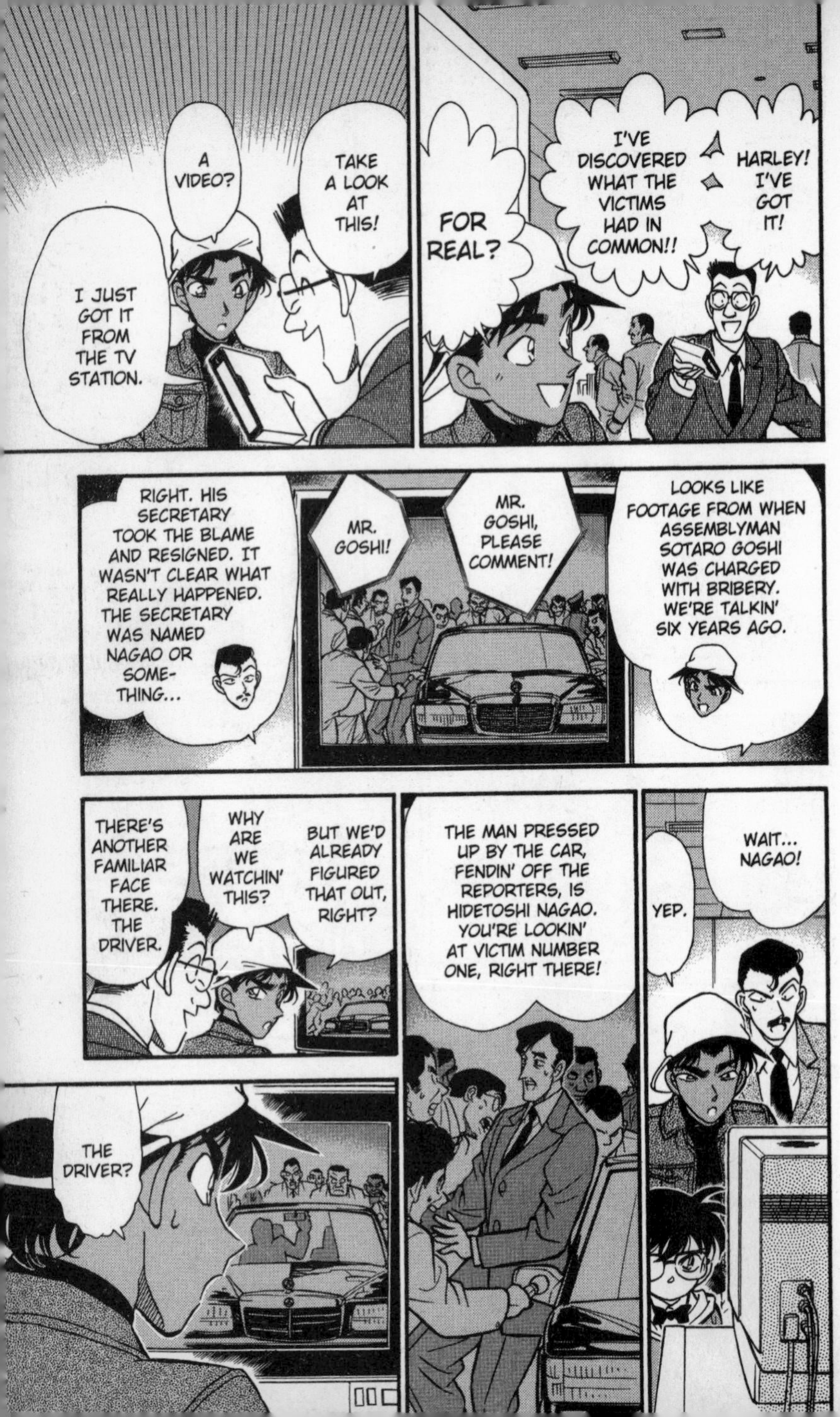
HARLEY! I'VE GOT IT!
I'VE DISCOVERED WHAT THE VICTIMS HAD IN COMMON!!
FOR REAL?
TAKE A LOOK AT THIS!
A VIDEO?
I JUST GOT IT FROM THE TV STATION.
LOOKS LIKE FOOTAGE FROM WHEN ASSEMBLYMAN SOTARO GOSHI WAS CHARGED WITH BRIBERY. WE'RE TALKIN' SIX YEARS AGO.
MR. GOSHI, PLEASE COMMENT!
MR. GOSHI!
RIGHT. HIS SECRETARY TOOK THE BLAME AND RESIGNED. IT WASN'T CLEAR WHAT REALLY HAPPENED. THE SECRETARY WAS NAMED NAGAO OR SOME-THING...
WAIT... NAGAO!
YEP.
THE MAN PRESSED UP BY THE CAR, FENDIN' OFF THE REPORTERS, IS HIDETOSHI NAGAO. YOU'RE LOOKIN' AT VICTIM NUMBER ONE, RIGHT THERE!
BUT WE'D ALREADY FIGURED THAT OUT, RIGHT?
WHY ARE WE WATCHIN' THIS?
THERE'S ANOTHER FAMILIAR FACE THERE. THE DRIVER.
THE DRIVER?

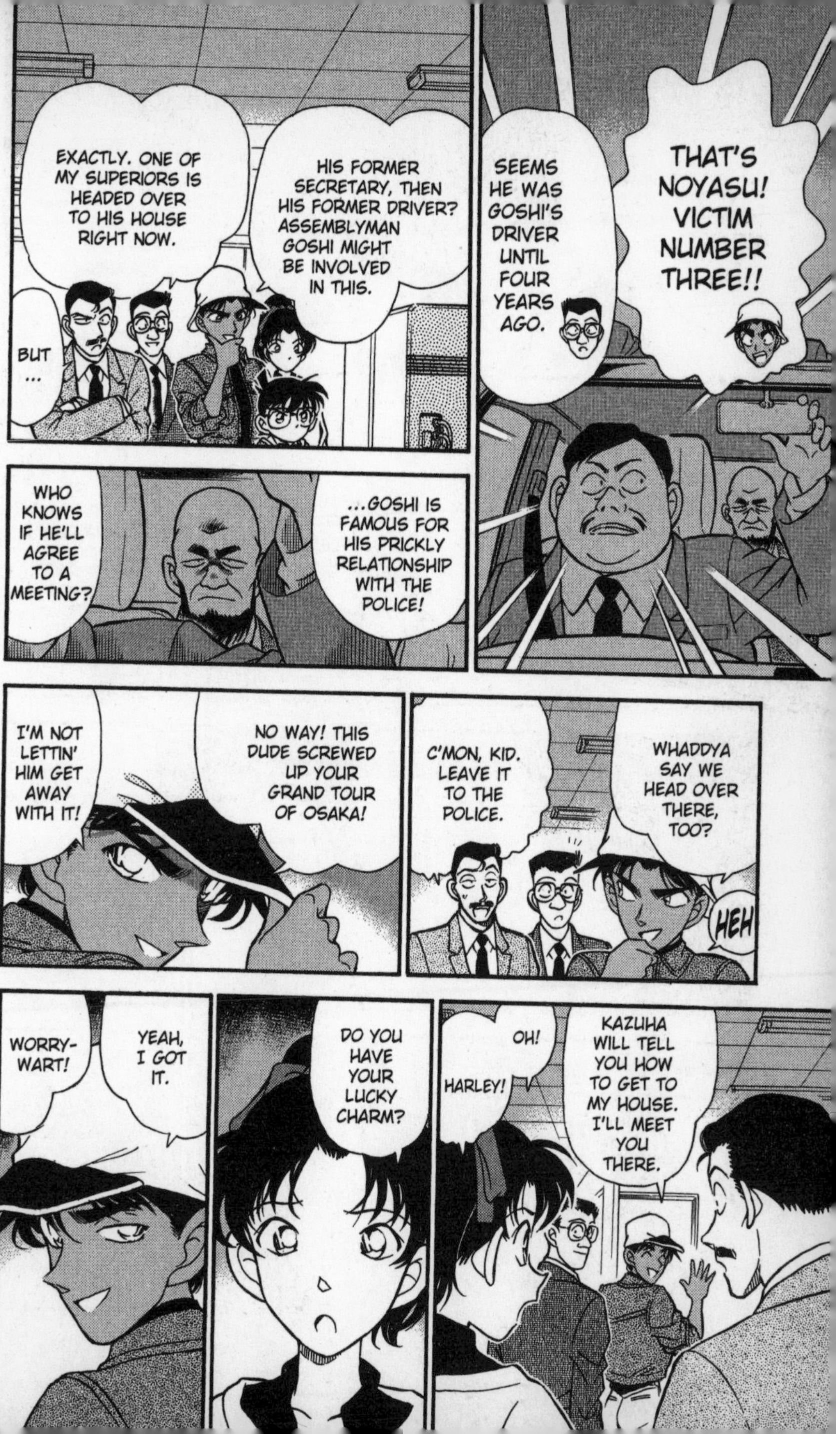
THAT'S NOYASU! VICTIM NUMBER THREE!!
SEEMS HE WAS GOSHI'S DRIVER UNTIL FOUR YEARS AGO.
HIS FORMER SECRETARY, THEN HIS FORMER DRIVER? ASSEMBLYMAN GOSHI MIGHT BE INVOLVED IN THIS.
EXACTLY. ONE OF MY SUPERIORS IS HEADED OVER TO HIS HOUSE RIGHT NOW.
BUT ...
...GOSHI IS FAMOUS FOR HIS PRICKLY RELATIONSHIP WITH THE POLICE!
WHO KNOWS IF HE'LL AGREE TO A MEETING?
WHADDYA SAY WE HEAD OVER THERE, TOO?
HEH
C'MON, KID. LEAVE IT TO THE POLICE.
NO WAY! THIS DUDE SCREWED UP YOUR GRAND TOUR OF OSAKA!
I'M NOT LETTIN' HIM GET AWAY WITH IT!
KAZUHA WILL TELL YOU HOW TO GET TO MY HOUSE. I'LL MEET YOU THERE.
OH!
HARLEY!
DO YOU HAVE YOUR LUCKY CHARM?
YEAH, I GOT IT.
WORRY-WART!

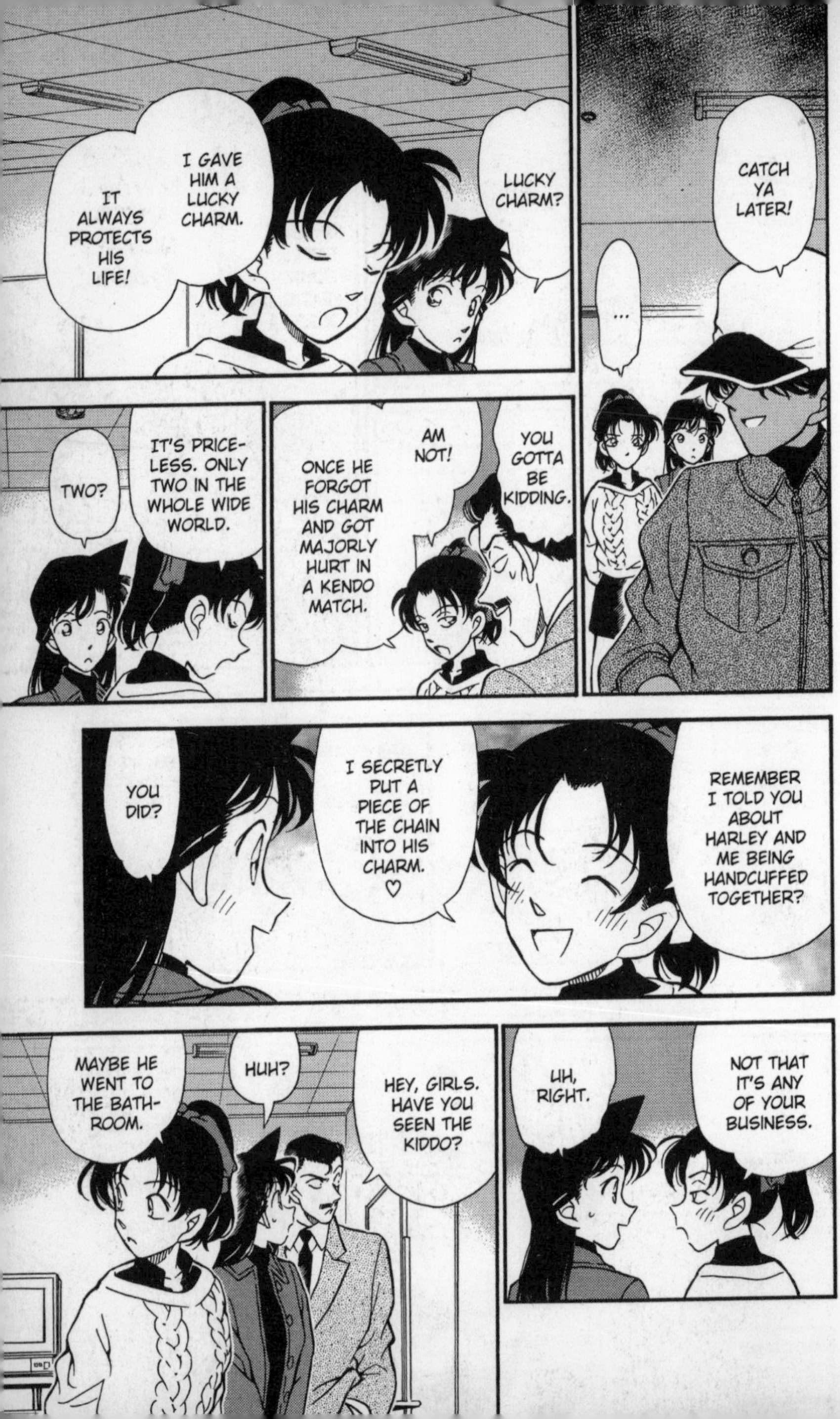
CATCH YA LATER!
...
LUCKY CHARM?
I GAVE HIM A LUCKY CHARM.
IT ALWAYS PROTECTS HIS LIFE!
YOU GOTTA BE KIDDING.
AM NOT!
ONCE HE FORGOT HIS CHARM AND GOT MAJORLY HURT IN A KENDO MATCH.
IT'S PRICELESS. ONLY TWO IN THE WHOLE WIDE WORLD.
TWO?
REMEMBER I TOLD YOU ABOUT HARLEY AND ME BEING HANDCUFFED TOGETHER?
I SECRETLY PUT A PIECE OF THE CHAIN INTO HIS CHARM. ♡
YOU DID?
NOT THAT IT'S ANY OF YOUR BUSINESS.
UH, RIGHT.
HEY, GIRLS. HAVE YOU SEEN THE KIDDO?
HUH?
MAYBE HE WENT TO THE BATHROOM.

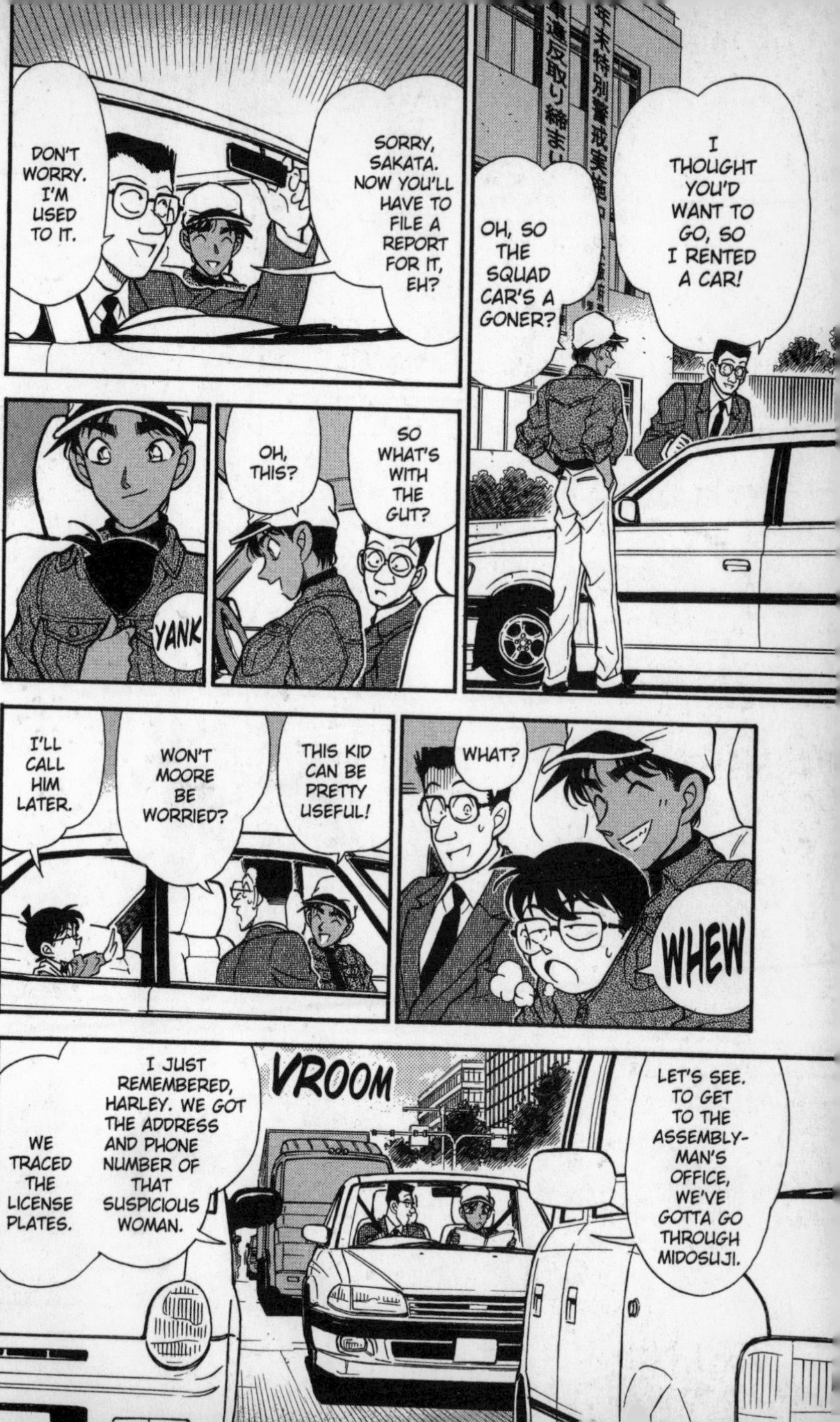
I THOUGHT YOU'D WANT TO GO, SO I RENTED A CAR!
OH, SO THE SQUAD CAR'S A GONER?
SORRY, SAKATA. NOW YOU'LL HAVE TO FILE A REPORT FOR IT, EH?
DON'T WORRY. I'M USED TO IT.
SO WHAT'S WITH THE GUT?
OH, THIS?
YANK
WHAT?
WHEW
THIS KID CAN BE PRETTY USEFUL!
WON'T MOORE BE WORRIED?
I'LL CALL HIM LATER.
LET'S SEE. TO GET TO THE ASSEMBLY-MAN'S OFFICE, WE'VE GOTTA GO THROUGH MIDOSUJI.
VROOM
I JUST REMEMBERED, HARLEY. WE GOT THE ADDRESS AND PHONE NUMBER OF THAT SUSPICIOUS WOMAN.
WE TRACED THE LICENSE PLATES.

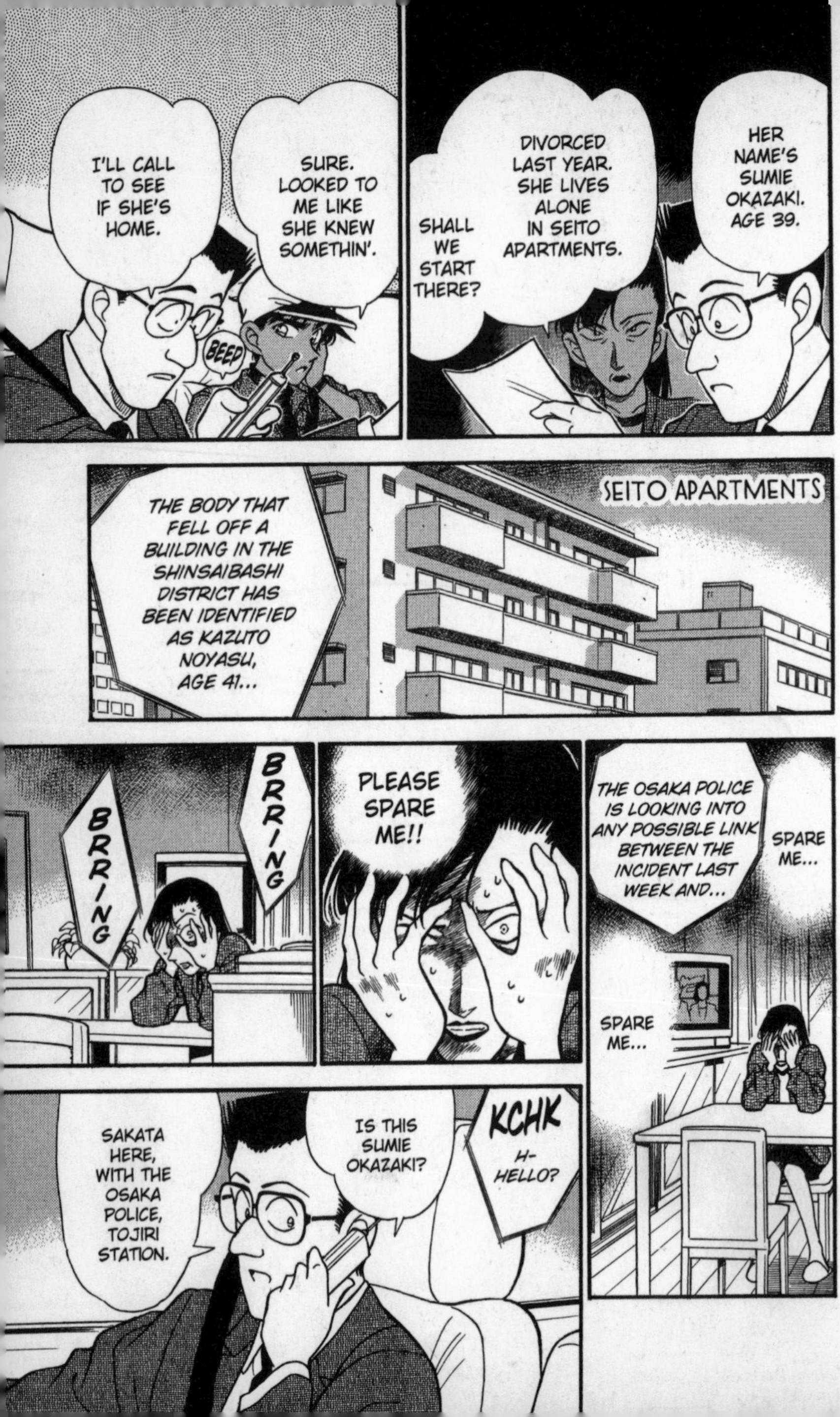
HER NAME'S SUMIE OKAZAKI. AGE 39.
DIVORCED LAST YEAR. SHE LIVES ALONE IN SEITO APARTMENTS.
SHALL WE START THERE?
SURE. LOOKED TO ME LIKE SHE KNEW SOMETHIN'.
BEEP
I'LL CALL TO SEE IF SHE'S HOME.
SEITO APARTMENTS
THE BODY THAT FELL OFF A BUILDING IN THE SHINSAIBASHI DISTRICT HAS BEEN IDENTIFIED AS KAZUTO NOYASU, AGE 41...
THE OSAKA POLICE IS LOOKING INTO ANY POSSIBLE LINK BETWEEN THE INCIDENT LAST WEEK AND...
SPARE ME...
SPARE ME...
PLEASE SPARE ME!!
BRRING
BRRING
KCHK
H-HELLO?
IS THIS SUMIE OKAZAKI?
SAKATA HERE, WITH THE OSAKA POLICE, TOJIRI STATION.

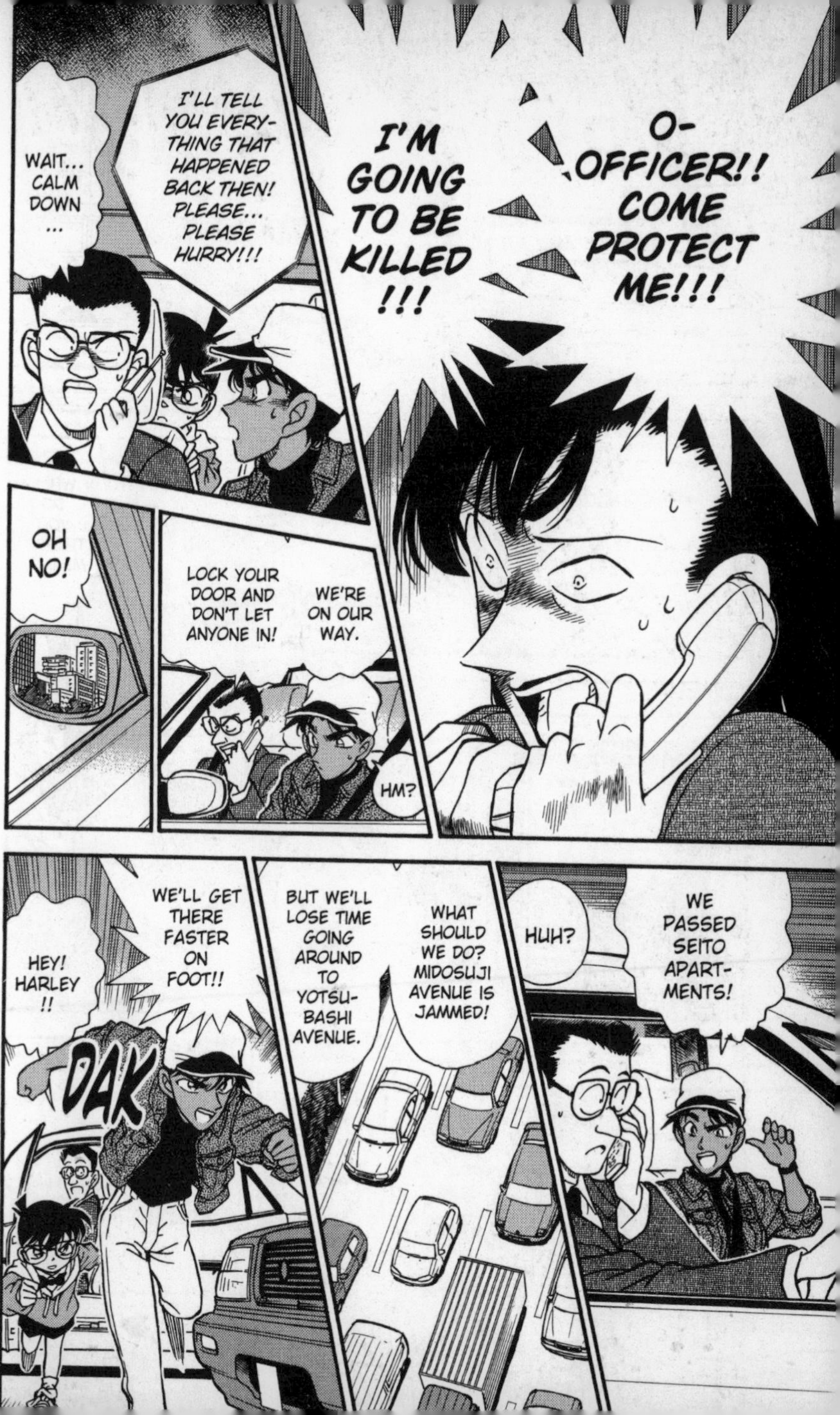
O-OFFICER!! COME PROTECT ME!!!
I'M GOING TO BE KILLED!!!
I'LL TELL YOU EVERYTHING THAT HAPPENED BACK THEN! PLEASE... PLEASE HURRY!!!
WAIT... CALM DOWN...
WE'RE ON OUR WAY.
LOCK YOUR DOOR AND DON'T LET ANYONE IN!
HM?
OH NO!
WE PASSED SEITO APARTMENTS!
HUH?
WHAT SHOULD WE DO? MIDOSUJI AVENUE IS JAMMED!
BUT WE'LL LOSE TIME GOING AROUND TO YOTSUBASHI AVENUE.
WE'LL GET THERE FASTER ON FOOT!!
DAK
HEY! HARLEY!!

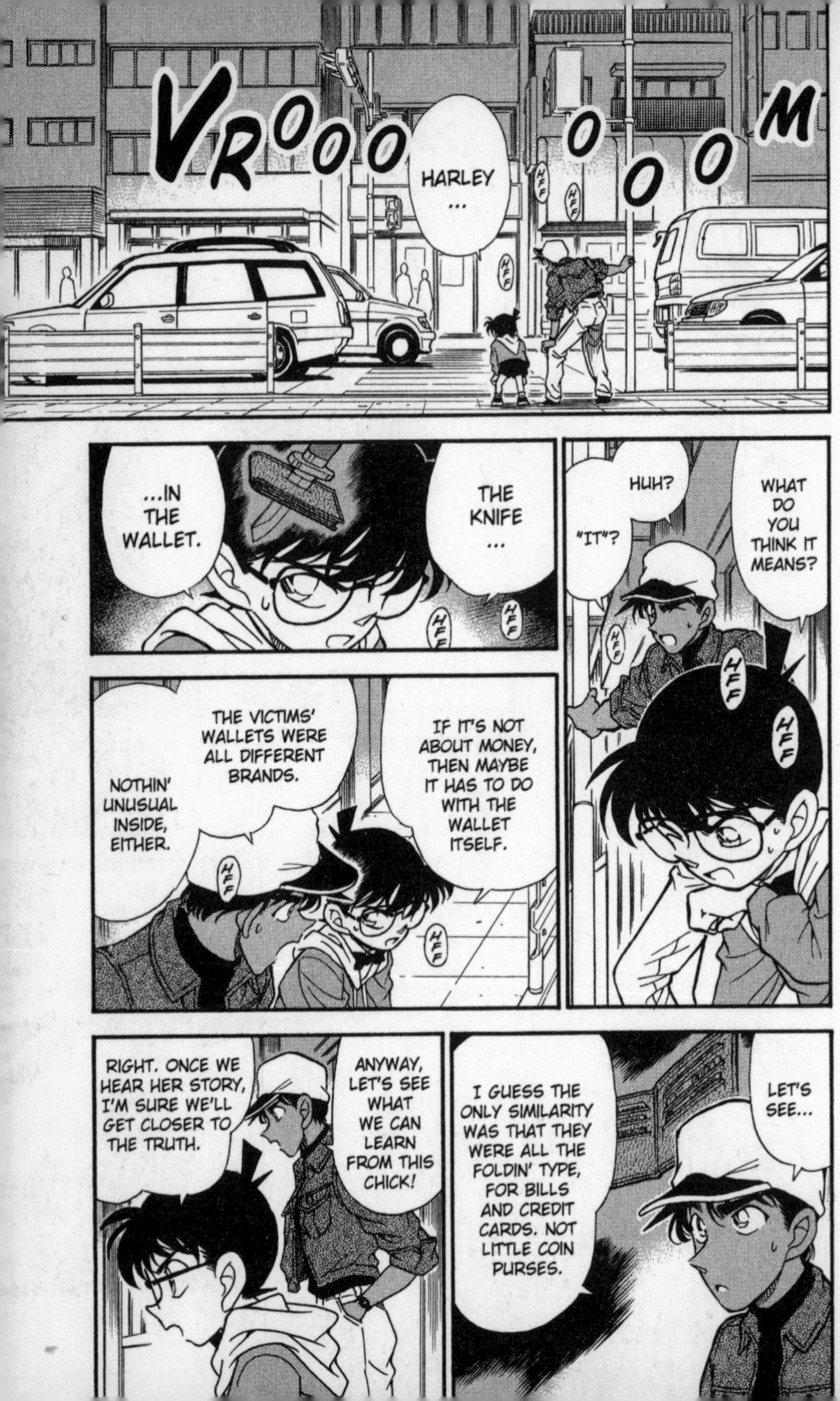
VROOOOOOOOM
HARLEY ...
HFF
HFF
HFF
WHAT DO YOU THINK IT MEANS?
HUH?
"IT"?
HFF
HFF
HFF
THE KNIFE ...
...IN THE WALLET.
HFF
IF IT'S NOT ABOUT MONEY, THEN MAYBE IT HAS TO DO WITH THE WALLET ITSELF.
THE VICTIMS' WALLETS WERE ALL DIFFERENT BRANDS.
NOTHIN' UNUSUAL INSIDE, EITHER.
HFF
HFF
LET'S SEE...
I GUESS THE ONLY SIMILARITY WAS THAT THEY WERE ALL THE FOLDIN' TYPE, FOR BILLS AND CREDIT CARDS. NOT LITTLE COIN PURSES.
ANYWAY, LET'S SEE WHAT WE CAN LEARN FROM THIS CHICK!
RIGHT. ONCE WE HEAR HER STORY, I'M SURE WE'LL GET CLOSER TO THE TRUTH.

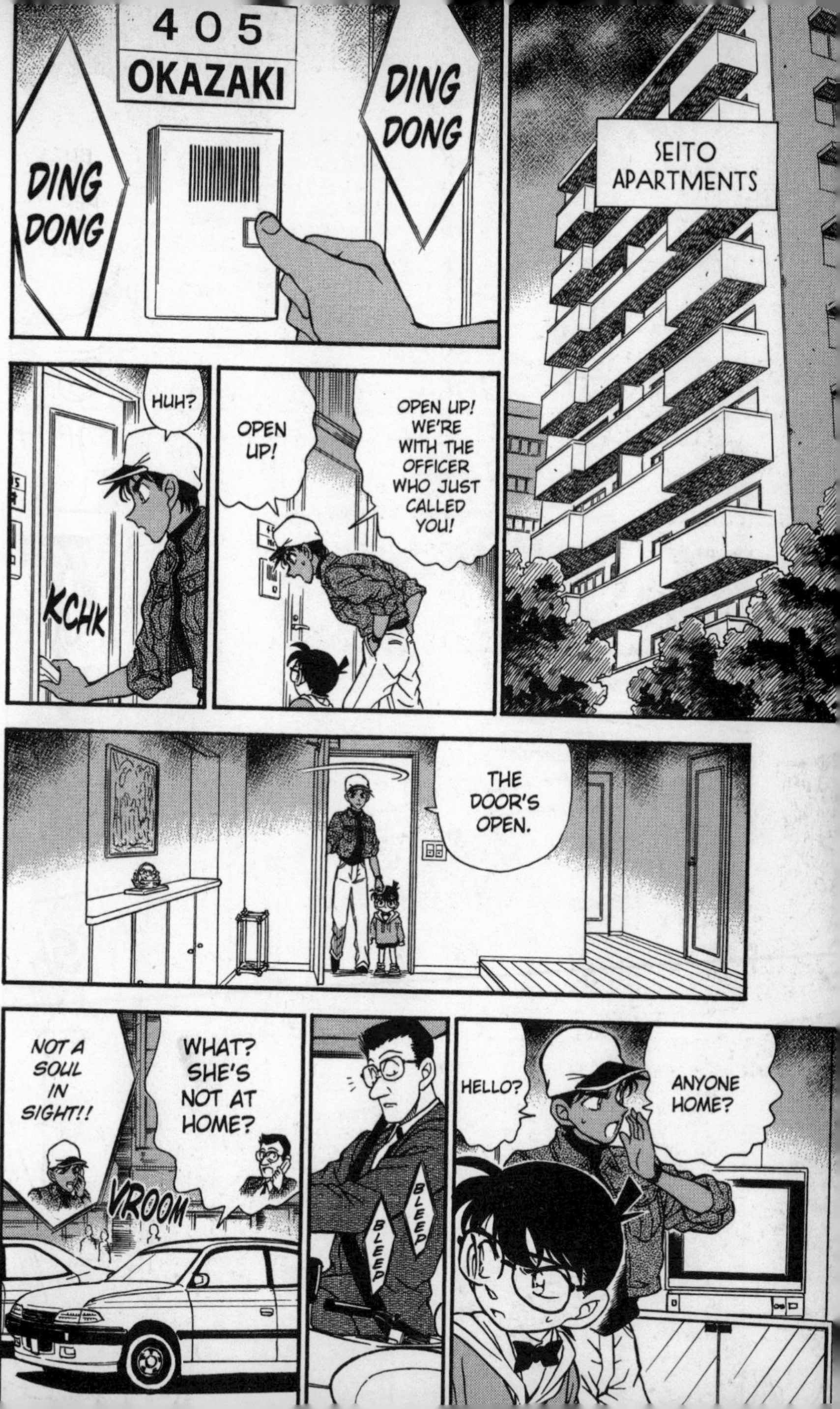

SEITO APARTMENTS
405 OKAZAKI
DING DONG
DING DONG
OPEN UP! WE'RE WITH THE OFFICER WHO JUST CALLED YOU!
OPEN UP!
HUH?
KCHK
THE DOOR'S OPEN.
ANYONE HOME?
HELLO?
BLEED
BLEED
WHAT? SHE'S NOT AT HOME?
NOT A SOUL IN SIGHT!!
VROOM

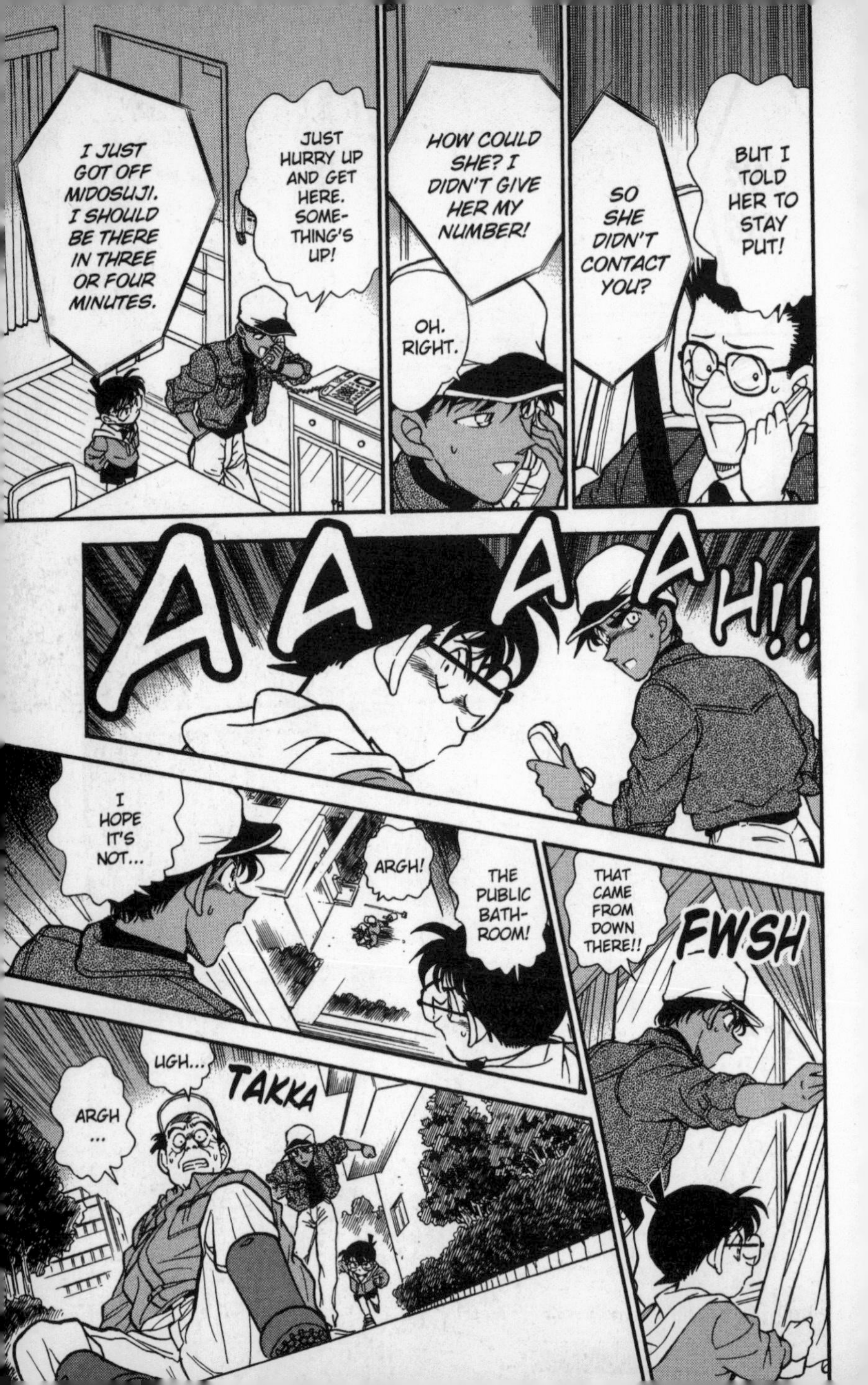

BUT I TOLD HER TO STAY PUT!
SO SHE DIDN'T CONTACT YOU?
HOW COULD SHE? I DIDN'T GIVE HER MY NUMBER!
OH. RIGHT.
JUST HURRY UP AND GET HERE. SOME-THING'S UP!
I JUST GOT OFF MIDOSUJI. I SHOULD BE THERE IN THREE OR FOUR MINUTES.
AAAAH!!
FWSH
THAT CAME FROM DOWN THERE!!
THE PUBLIC BATH-ROOM!
ARGH!
I HOPE IT'S NOT...
TAKKA
UGH...
ARGH ...

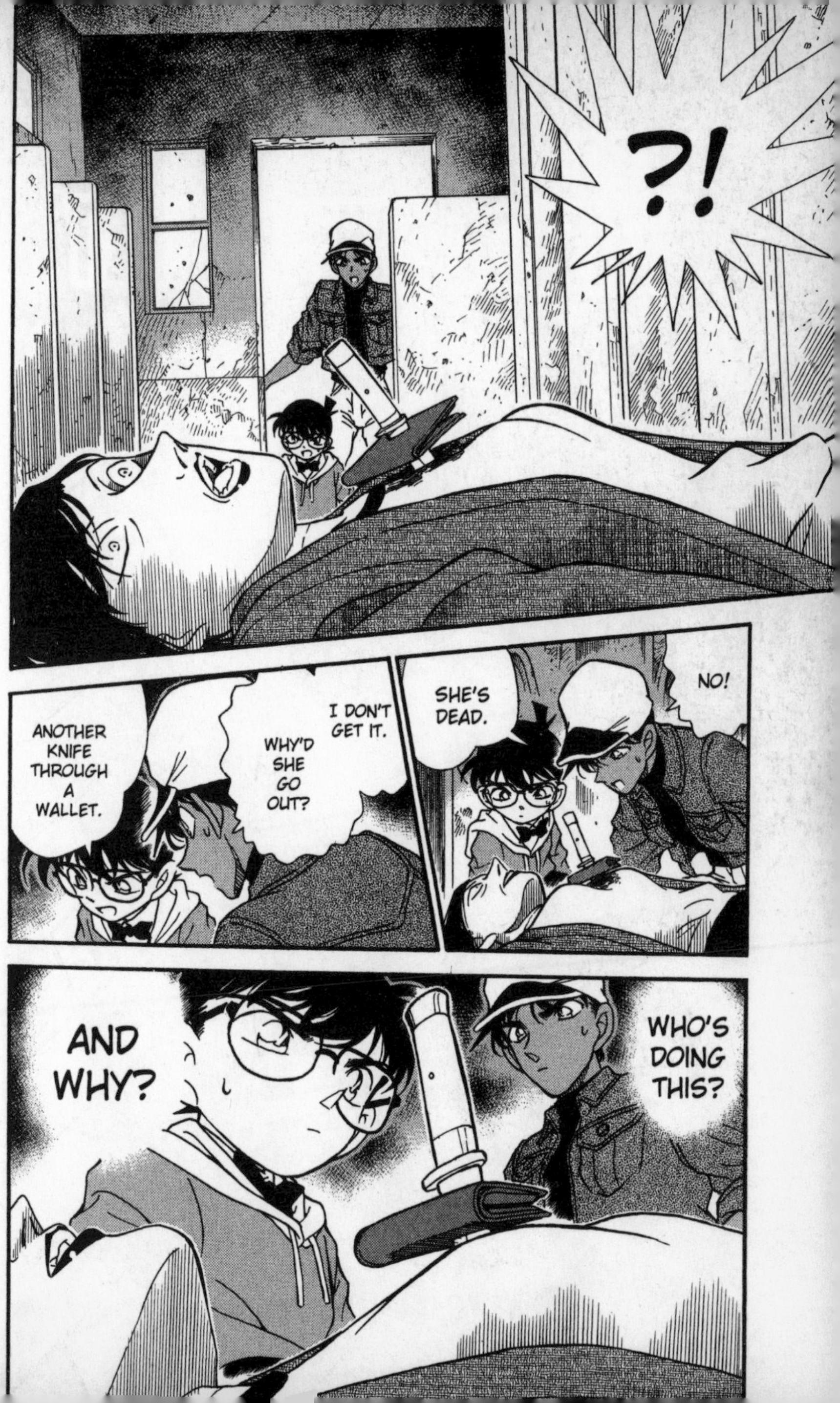
?!
NO!
SHE'S DEAD.
I DON'T GET IT.
WHY'D SHE GO OUT?
ANOTHER KNIFE THROUGH A WALLET.
WHO'S DOING THIS?
AND WHY?

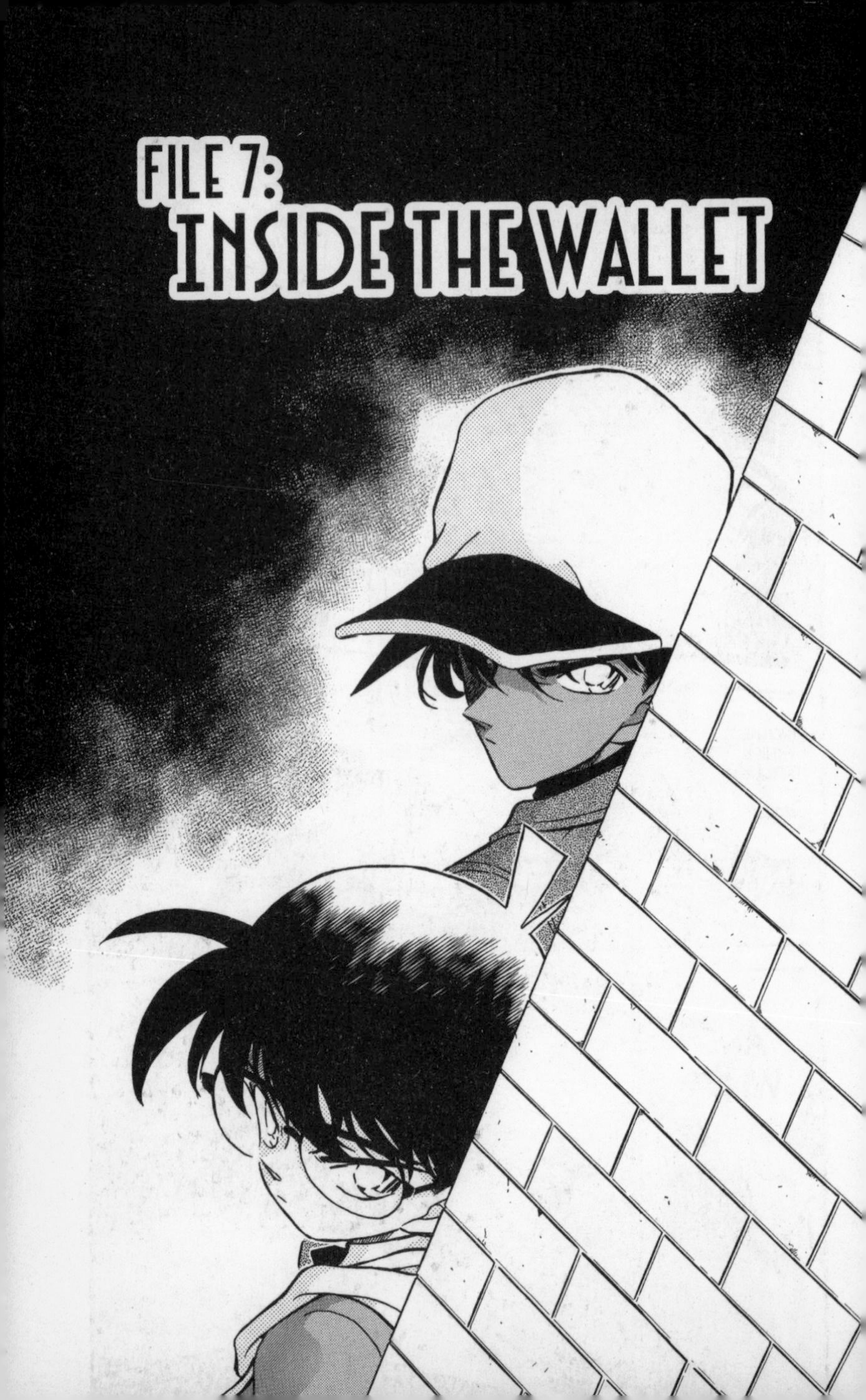
FILE 7:
INSIDE THE WALLET

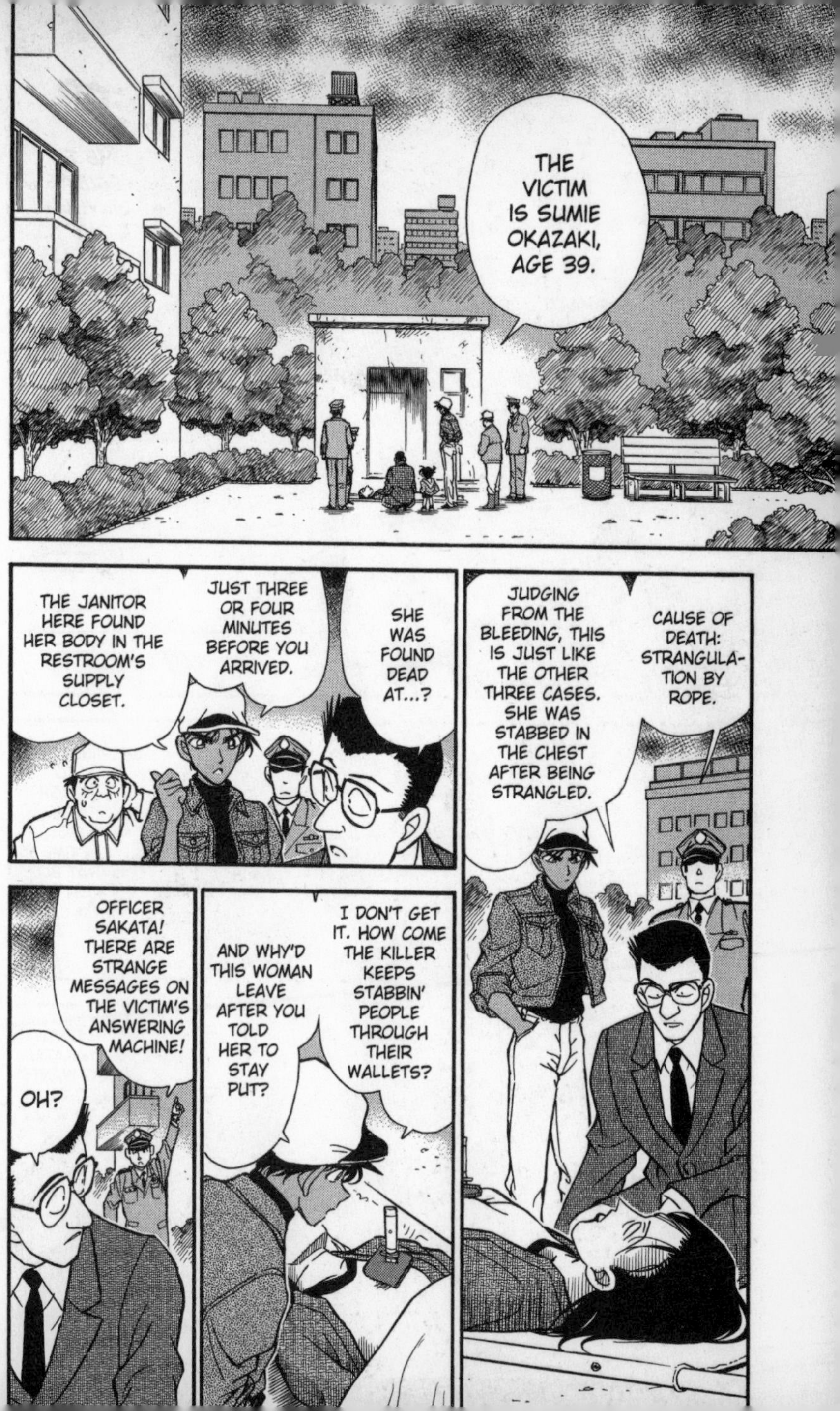
THE VICTIM IS SUMIE OKAZAKI, AGE 39.
CAUSE OF DEATH: STRANGULATION BY ROPE.
JUDGING FROM THE BLEEDING, THIS IS JUST LIKE THE OTHER THREE CASES. SHE WAS STABBED IN THE CHEST AFTER BEING STRANGLED.
SHE WAS FOUND DEAD AT...?
JUST THREE OR FOUR MINUTES BEFORE YOU ARRIVED.
THE JANITOR HERE FOUND HER BODY IN THE RESTROOM'S SUPPLY CLOSET.
I DON'T GET IT. HOW COME THE KILLER KEEPS STABBIN' PEOPLE THROUGH THEIR WALLETS?
AND WHY'D THIS WOMAN LEAVE AFTER YOU TOLD HER TO STAY PUT?
OFFICER SAKATA! THERE ARE STRANGE MESSAGES ON THE VICTIM'S ANSWERING MACHINE!
OH?

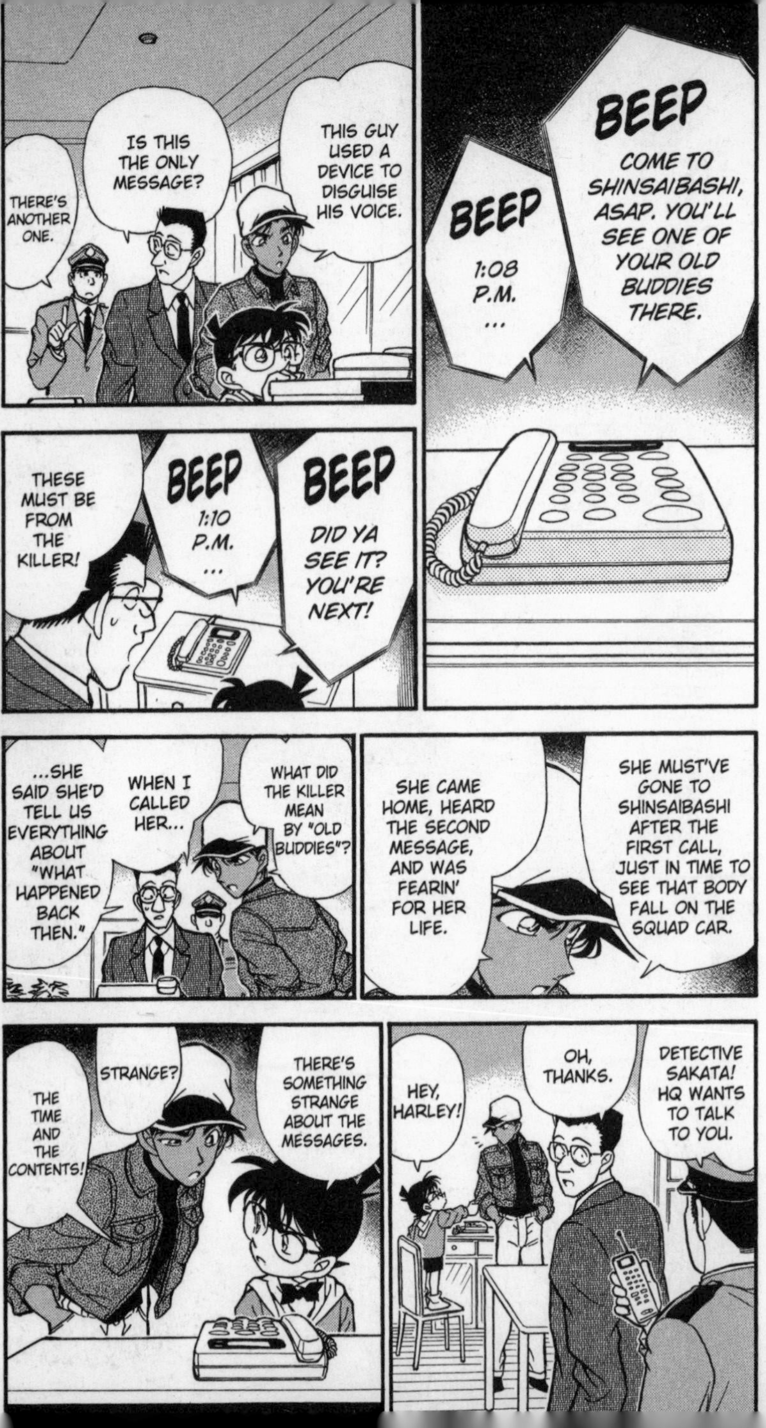
BEEP
COME TO SHINSAIBASHI, ASAP. YOU'LL SEE ONE OF YOUR OLD BUDDIES THERE.
BEEP
1:08 P.M. ...
THIS GUY USED A DEVICE TO DISGUISE HIS VOICE.
IS THIS THE ONLY MESSAGE?
THERE'S ANOTHER ONE.
BEEP
DID YA SEE IT? YOU'RE NEXT!
BEEP
1:10 P.M. ...
THESE MUST BE FROM THE KILLER!
SHE MUST'VE GONE TO SHINSAIBASHI AFTER THE FIRST CALL, JUST IN TIME TO SEE THAT BODY FALL ON THE SQUAD CAR.
SHE CAME HOME, HEARD THE SECOND MESSAGE, AND WAS FEARIN' FOR HER LIFE.
WHAT DID THE KILLER MEAN BY "OLD BUDDIES"?
WHEN I CALLED HER...
...SHE SAID SHE'D TELL US EVERYTHING ABOUT "WHAT HAPPENED BACK THEN."
DETECTIVE SAKATA! HQ WANTS TO TALK TO YOU.
OH, THANKS.
HEY, HARLEY!
THERE'S SOMETHING STRANGE ABOUT THE MESSAGES.
STRANGE?
THE TIME AND THE CONTENTS!

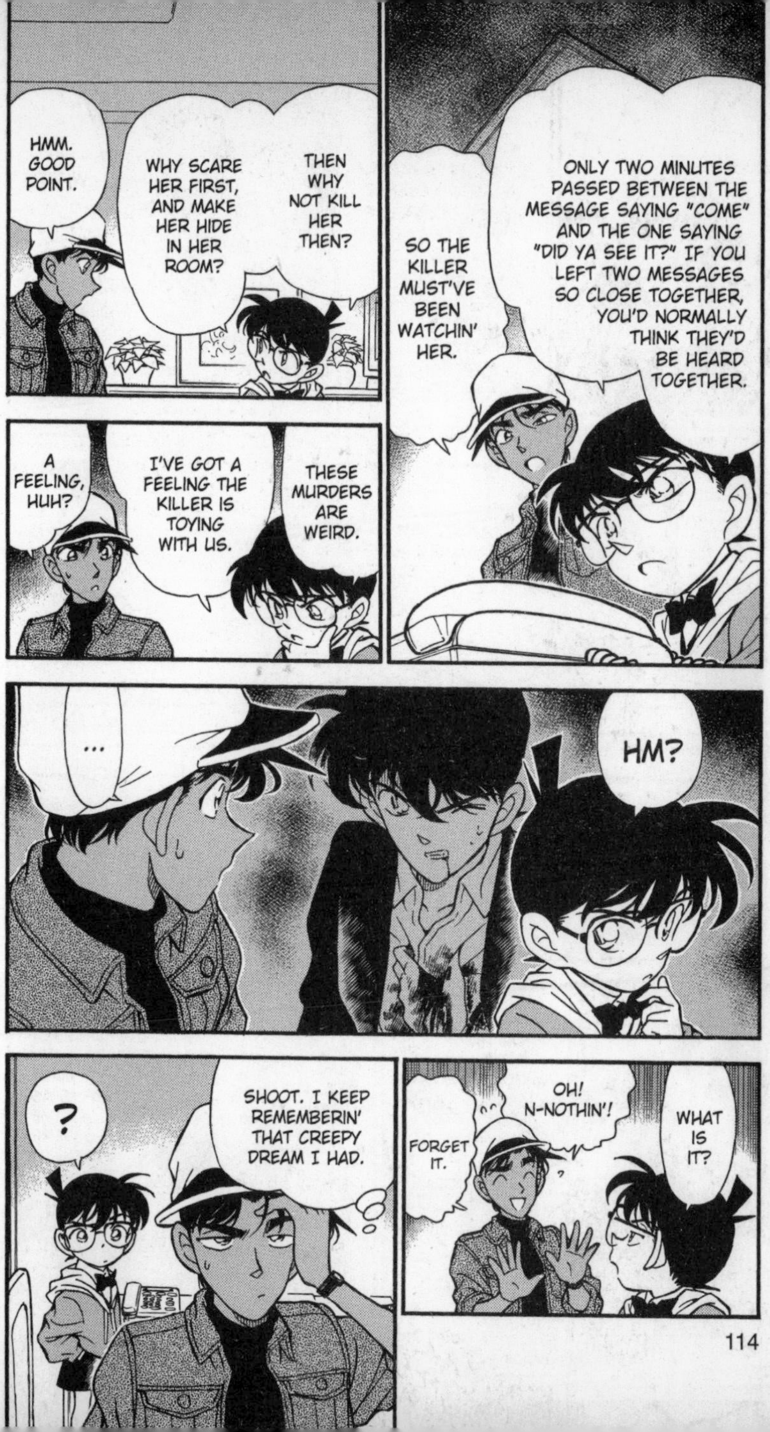
ONLY TWO MINUTES PASSED BETWEEN THE MESSAGE SAYING "COME" AND THE ONE SAYING "DID YA SEE IT?" IF YOU LEFT TWO MESSAGES SO CLOSE TOGETHER, YOU'D NORMALLY THINK THEY'D BE HEARD TOGETHER.
SO THE KILLER MUST'VE BEEN WATCHIN' HER.
THEN WHY NOT KILL HER THEN?
WHY SCARE HER FIRST, AND MAKE HER HIDE IN HER ROOM?
HMM. GOOD POINT.
THESE MURDERS ARE WEIRD.
I'VE GOT A FEELING THE KILLER IS TOYING WITH US.
A FEELING, HUH?
HM?
...
WHAT IS IT?
OH! N-NOTHIN'!
FORGET IT.
SHOOT. I KEEP REMEMBERIN' THAT CREEPY DREAM I HAD.
?

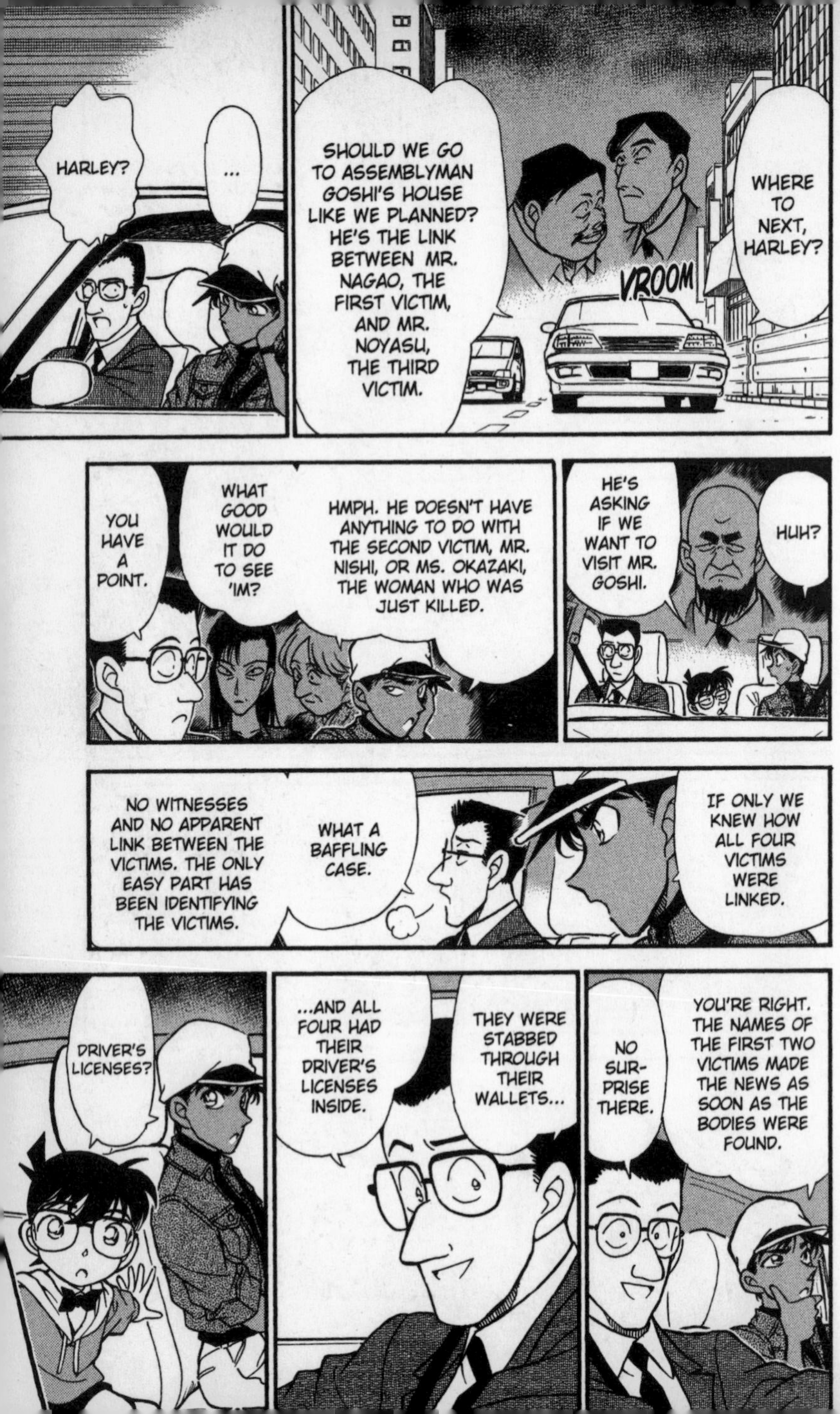
WHERE TO NEXT, HARLEY?
VROOM
SHOULD WE GO TO ASSEMBLYMAN GOSHI'S HOUSE LIKE WE PLANNED? HE'S THE LINK BETWEEN MR. NAGAO, THE FIRST VICTIM, AND MR. NOYASU, THE THIRD VICTIM.
...
HARLEY?
HUH?
HE'S ASKING IF WE WANT TO VISIT MR. GOSHI.
HMPH. HE DOESN'T HAVE ANYTHING TO DO WITH THE SECOND VICTIM, MR. NISHI, OR MS. OKAZAKI, THE WOMAN WHO WAS JUST KILLED.
WHAT GOOD WOULD IT DO TO SEE 'IM?
YOU HAVE A POINT.
IF ONLY WE KNEW HOW ALL FOUR VICTIMS WERE LINKED.
WHAT A BAFFLING CASE.
NO WITNESSES AND NO APPARENT LINK BETWEEN THE VICTIMS. THE ONLY EASY PART HAS BEEN IDENTIFYING THE VICTIMS.
YOU'RE RIGHT. THE NAMES OF THE FIRST TWO VICTIMS MADE THE NEWS AS SOON AS THE BODIES WERE FOUND.
NO SUR-PRISE THERE.
THEY WERE STABBED THROUGH THEIR WALLETS...
...AND ALL FOUR HAD THEIR DRIVER'S LICENSES INSIDE.
DRIVER'S LICENSES?

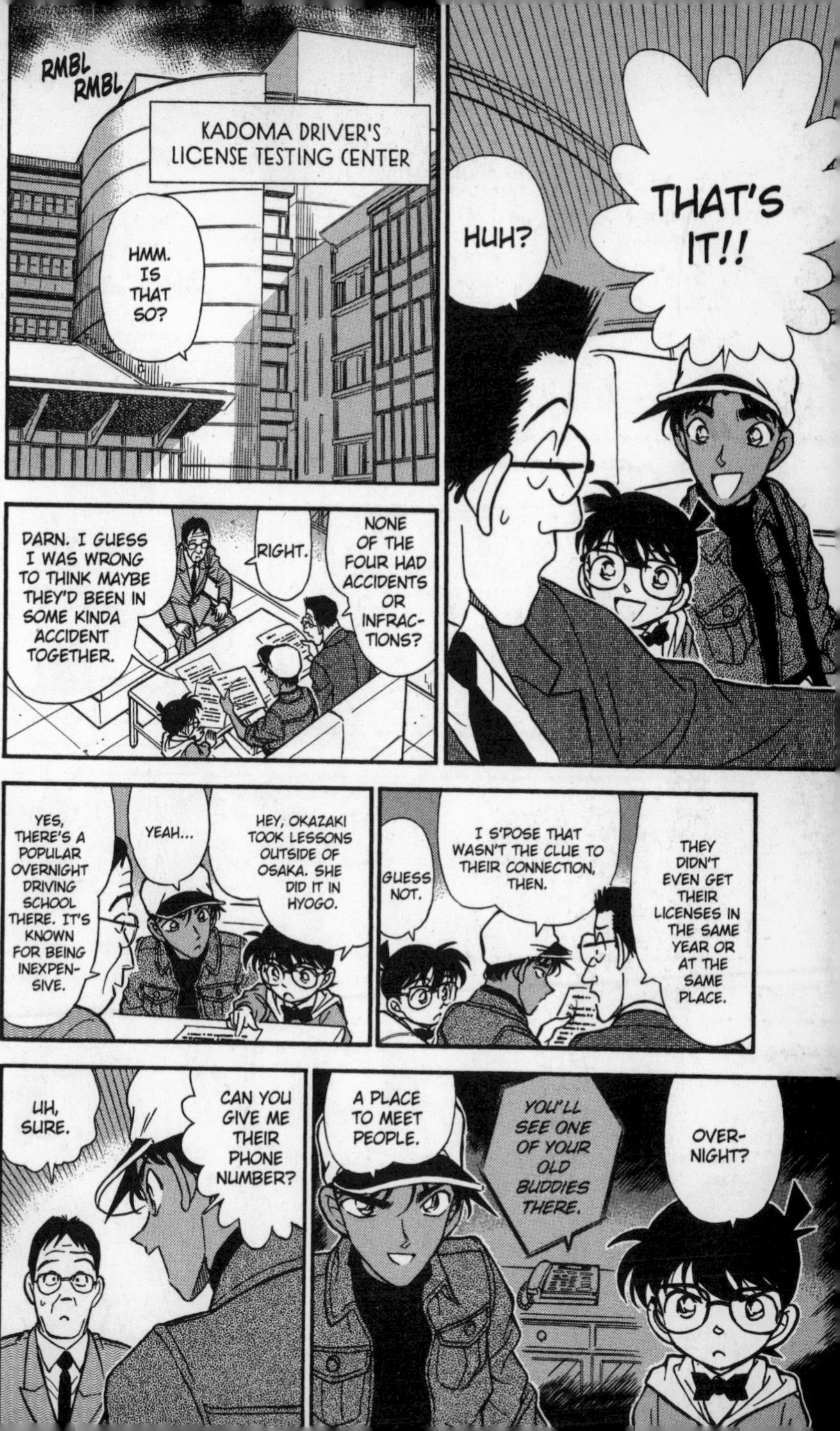
THAT'S IT!!
HUH?
RMBL RMBL
KADOMA DRIVER'S LICENSE TESTING CENTER
HMM. IS THAT SO?
NONE OF THE FOUR HAD ACCIDENTS OR INFRACTIONS?
RIGHT.
DARN. I GUESS I WAS WRONG TO THINK MAYBE THEY'D BEEN IN SOME KINDA ACCIDENT TOGETHER.
THEY DIDN'T EVEN GET THEIR LICENSES IN THE SAME YEAR OR AT THE SAME PLACE.
I S'POSE THAT WASN'T THE CLUE TO THEIR CONNECTION, THEN.
GUESS NOT.
HEY, OKAZAKI TOOK LESSONS OUTSIDE OF OSAKA. SHE DID IT IN HYOGO.
YEAH...
YES, THERE'S A POPULAR OVERNIGHT DRIVING SCHOOL THERE. IT'S KNOWN FOR BEING INEXPENSIVE.
OVER-NIGHT?
YOU'LL SEE ONE OF YOUR OLD BUDDIES THERE.
A PLACE TO MEET PEOPLE.
CAN YOU GIVE ME THEIR PHONE NUMBER?
UH, SURE.

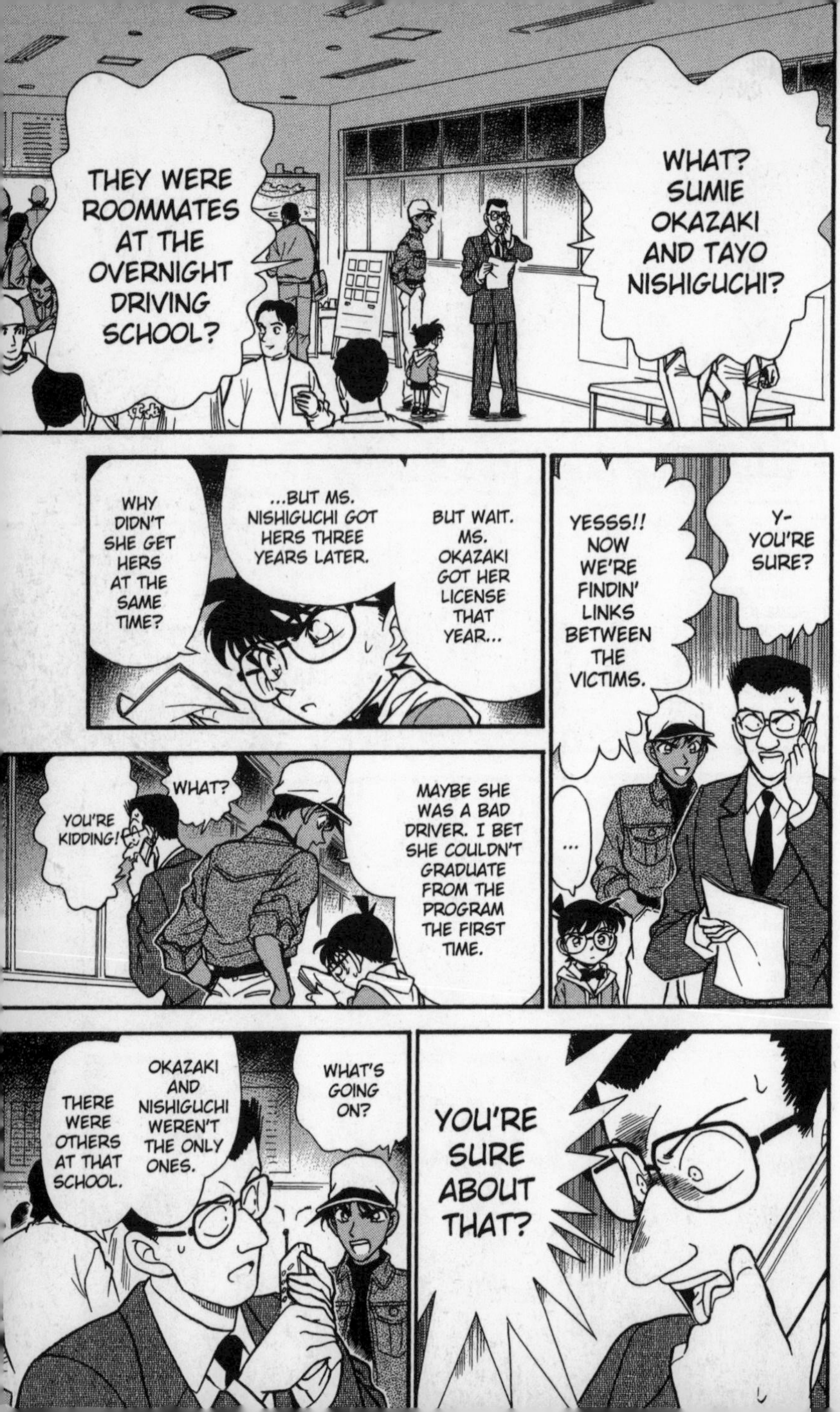
WHAT? SUMIE OKAZAKI AND TAYO NISHIGUCHI?
THEY WERE ROOMMATES AT THE OVERNIGHT DRIVING SCHOOL?
Y- YOU'RE SURE?
YESSS!! NOW WE'RE FINDIN' LINKS BETWEEN THE VICTIMS.
...
BUT WAIT. MS. OKAZAKI GOT HER LICENSE THAT YEAR...
...BUT MS. NISHIGUCHI GOT HERS THREE YEARS LATER.
WHY DIDN'T SHE GET HERS AT THE SAME TIME?
MAYBE SHE WAS A BAD DRIVER. I BET SHE COULDN'T GRADUATE FROM THE PROGRAM THE FIRST TIME.
WHAT?
YOU'RE KIDDING!
YOU'RE SURE ABOUT THAT?
WHAT'S GOING ON?
OKAZAKI AND NISHIGUCHI WEREN'T THE ONLY ONES.
THERE WERE OTHERS AT THAT SCHOOL.

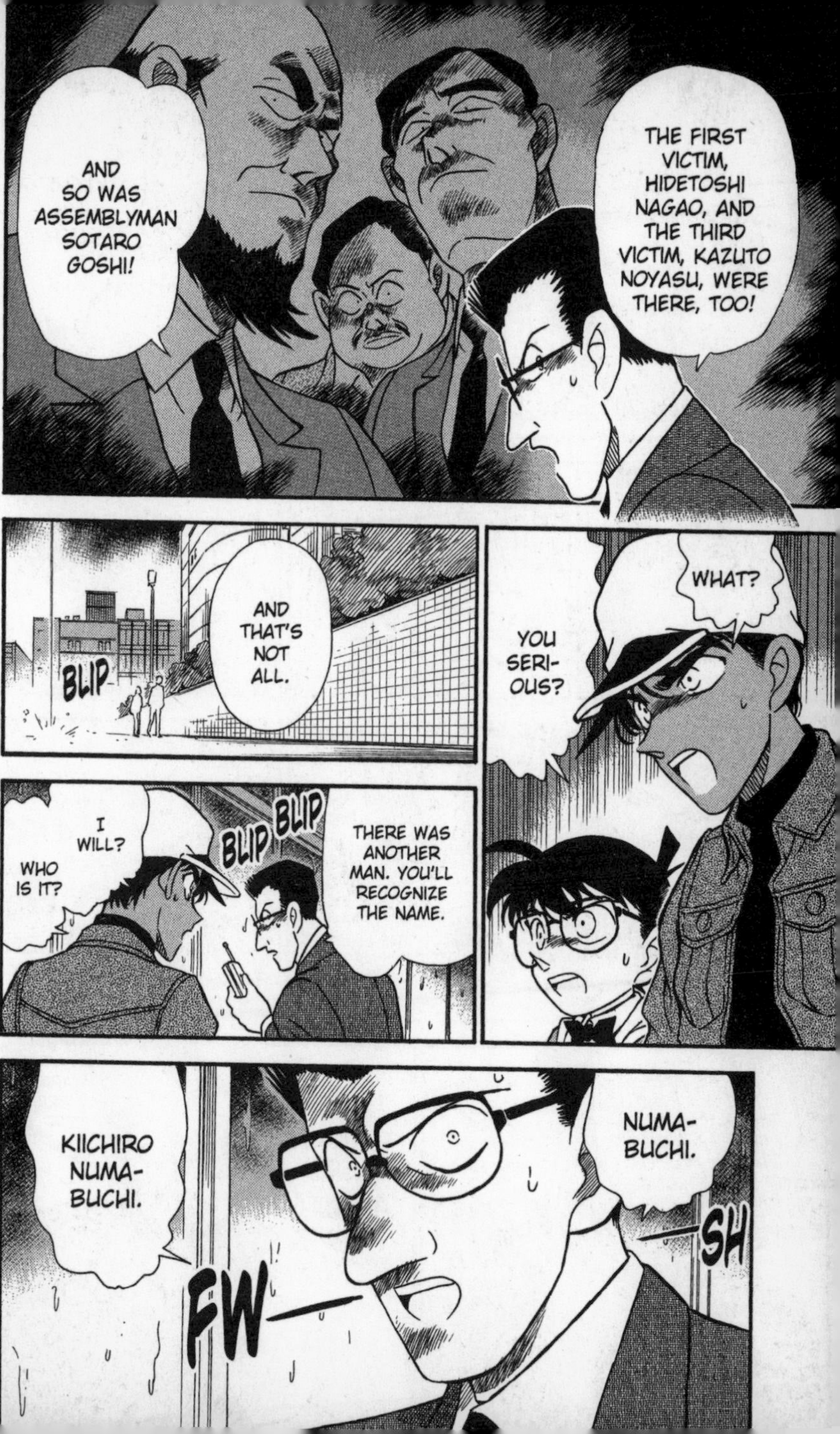
THE FIRST VICTIM, HIDETOSHI NAGAO, AND THE THIRD VICTIM, KAZUTO NOYASU, WERE THERE, TOO!
AND SO WAS ASSEMBLYMAN SOTARO GOSHI!
WHAT?
YOU SERI-OUS?
AND THAT'S NOT ALL.
BLIP
THERE WAS ANOTHER MAN. YOU'LL RECOGNIZE THE NAME.
BLIP BLIP
I WILL?
WHO IS IT?
NUMA-BUCHI.
KIICHIRO NUMA-BUCHI.
SH
FW

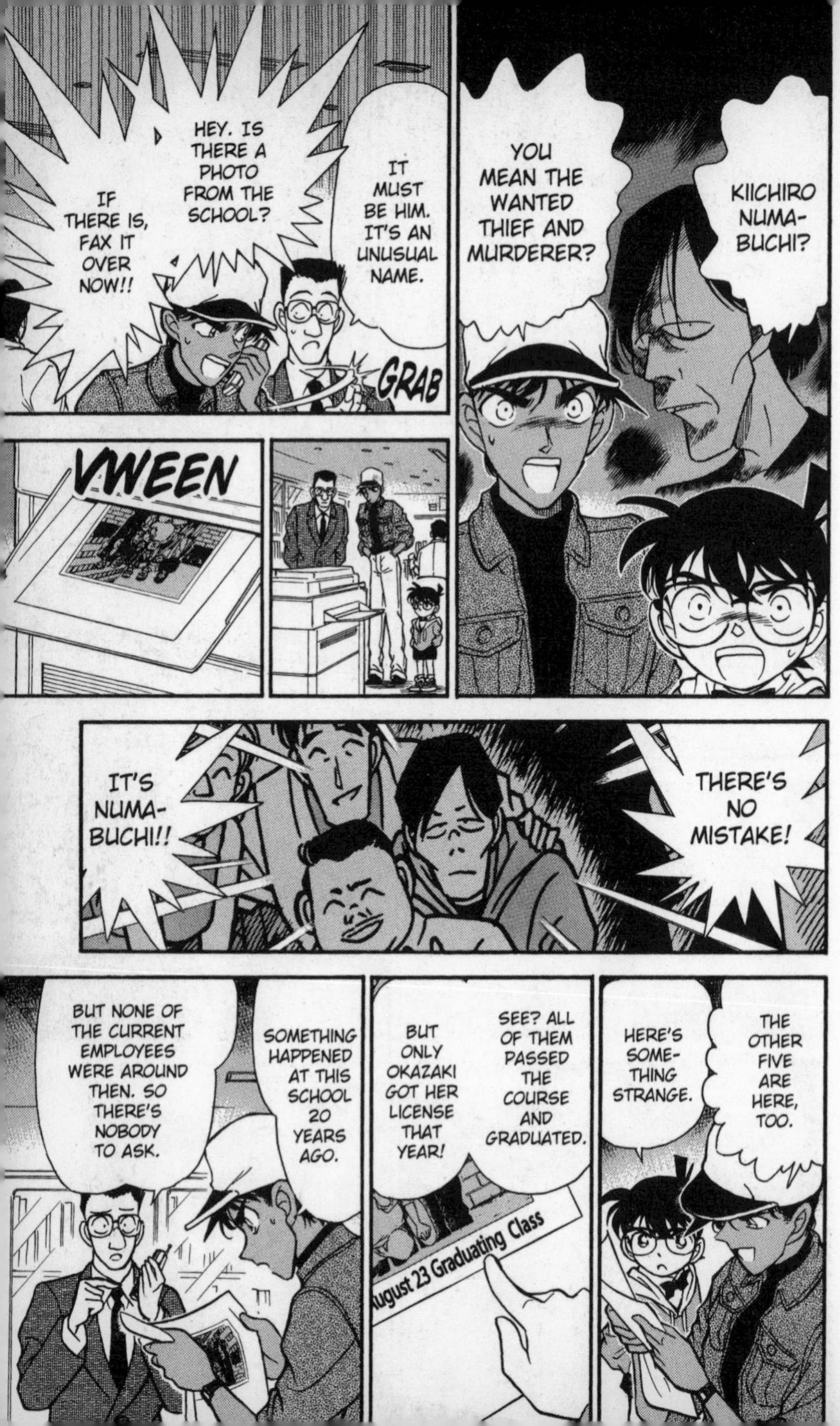
KIICHIRO NUMA-BUCHI?
YOU MEAN THE WANTED THIEF AND MURDERER?
IT MUST BE HIM. IT'S AN UNUSUAL NAME.
HEY. IS THERE A PHOTO FROM THE SCHOOL?
IF THERE IS, FAX IT OVER NOW!!
GRAB
VWEEN
THERE'S NO MISTAKE!
IT'S NUMA-BUCHI!!
THE OTHER FIVE ARE HERE, TOO.
HERE'S SOME-THING STRANGE.
SEE? ALL OF THEM PASSED THE COURSE AND GRADUATED.
BUT ONLY OKAZAKI GOT HER LICENSE THAT YEAR!
ugust 23 Graduating Class
SOMETHING HAPPENED AT THIS SCHOOL 20 YEARS AGO.
BUT NONE OF THE CURRENT EMPLOYEES WERE AROUND THEN. SO THERE'S NOBODY TO ASK.

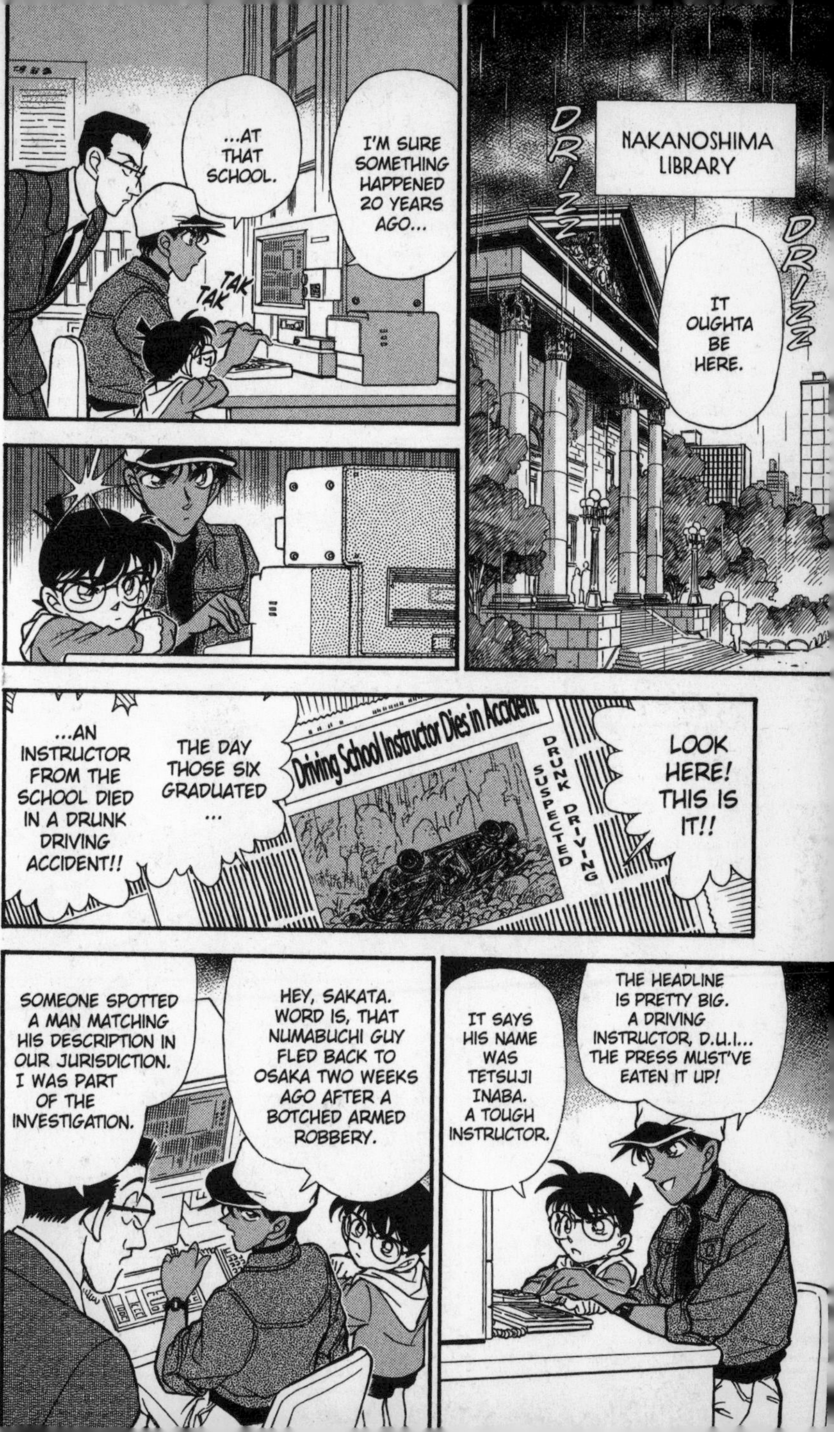
NAKANOSHIMA LIBRARY
DRIZZ
DRIZZ
IT OUGHTA BE HERE.
I'M SURE SOMETHING HAPPENED 20 YEARS AGO...
...AT THAT SCHOOL.
TAK TAK
LOOK HERE! THIS IS IT!!
Driving School Instructor Dies in Accident
DRUNK DRIVING SUSPECTED
THE DAY THOSE SIX GRADUATED ...
...AN INSTRUCTOR FROM THE SCHOOL DIED IN A DRUNK DRIVING ACCIDENT!!
THE HEADLINE IS PRETTY BIG. A DRIVING INSTRUCTOR, D.U.I... THE PRESS MUST'VE EATEN IT UP!
IT SAYS HIS NAME WAS TETSUJI INABA. A TOUGH INSTRUCTOR.
HEY, SAKATA. WORD IS, THAT NUMABUCHI GUY FLED BACK TO OSAKA TWO WEEKS AGO AFTER A BOTCHED ARMED ROBBERY.
SOMEONE SPOTTED A MAN MATCHING HIS DESCRIPTION IN OUR JURISDICTION. I WAS PART OF THE INVESTIGATION.

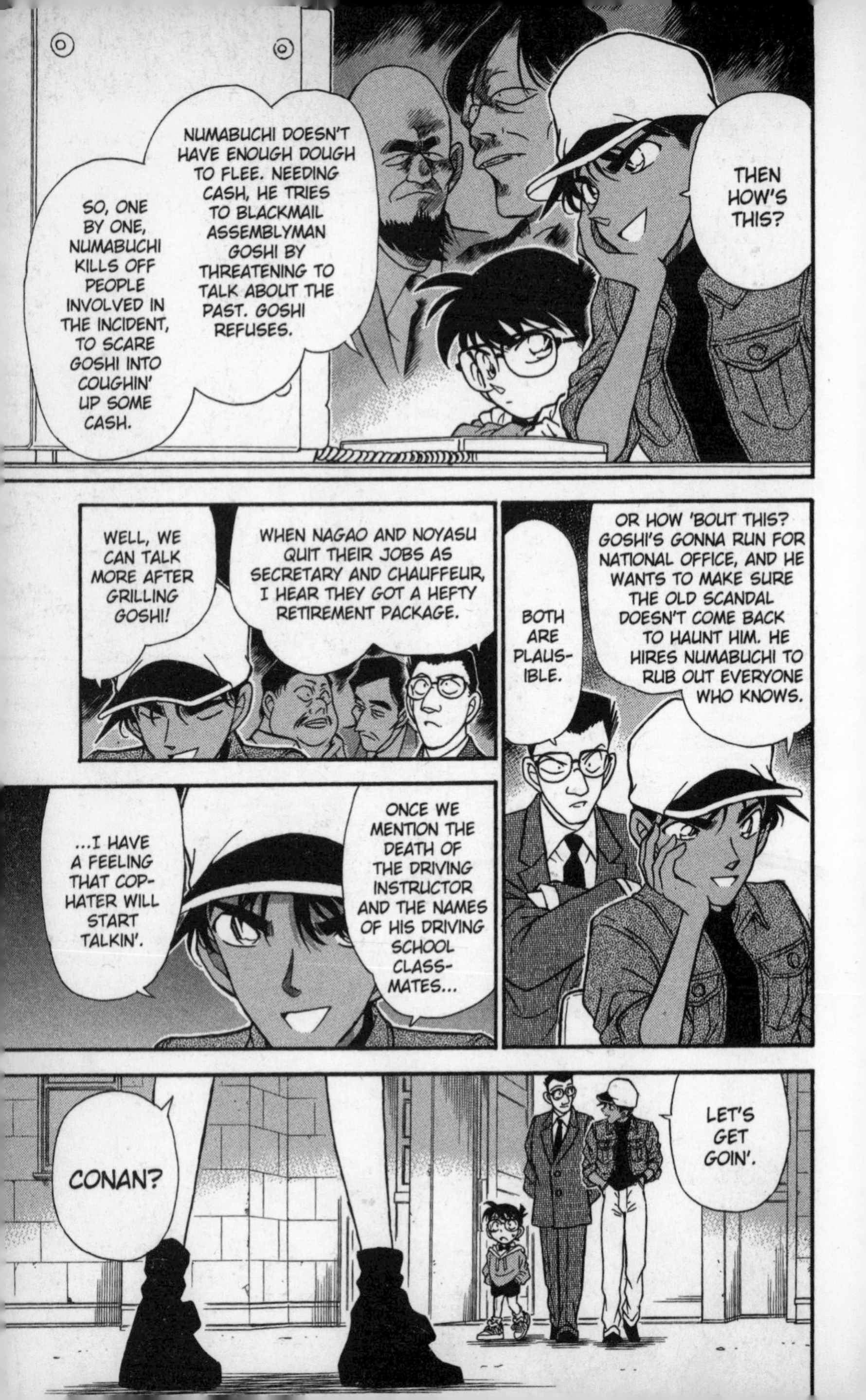
THEN HOW'S THIS?
NUMABUCHI DOESN'T HAVE ENOUGH DOUGH TO FLEE. NEEDING CASH, HE TRIES TO BLACKMAIL ASSEMBLYMAN GOSHI BY THREATENING TO TALK ABOUT THE PAST. GOSHI REFUSES.
SO, ONE BY ONE, NUMABUCHI KILLS OFF PEOPLE INVOLVED IN THE INCIDENT, TO SCARE GOSHI INTO COUGHIN' UP SOME CASH.
OR HOW 'BOUT THIS? GOSHI'S GONNA RUN FOR NATIONAL OFFICE, AND HE WANTS TO MAKE SURE THE OLD SCANDAL DOESN'T COME BACK TO HAUNT HIM. HE HIRES NUMABUCHI TO RUB OUT EVERYONE WHO KNOWS.
BOTH ARE PLAUS-IBLE.
WHEN NAGAO AND NOYASU QUIT THEIR JOBS AS SECRETARY AND CHAUFFEUR, I HEAR THEY GOT A HEFTY RETIREMENT PACKAGE.
WELL, WE CAN TALK MORE AFTER GRILLING GOSHI!
ONCE WE MENTION THE DEATH OF THE DRIVING INSTRUCTOR AND THE NAMES OF HIS DRIVING SCHOOL CLASS-MATES...
...I HAVE A FEELING THAT COP-HATER WILL START TALKIN'.
LET'S GET GOIN'.
CONAN?

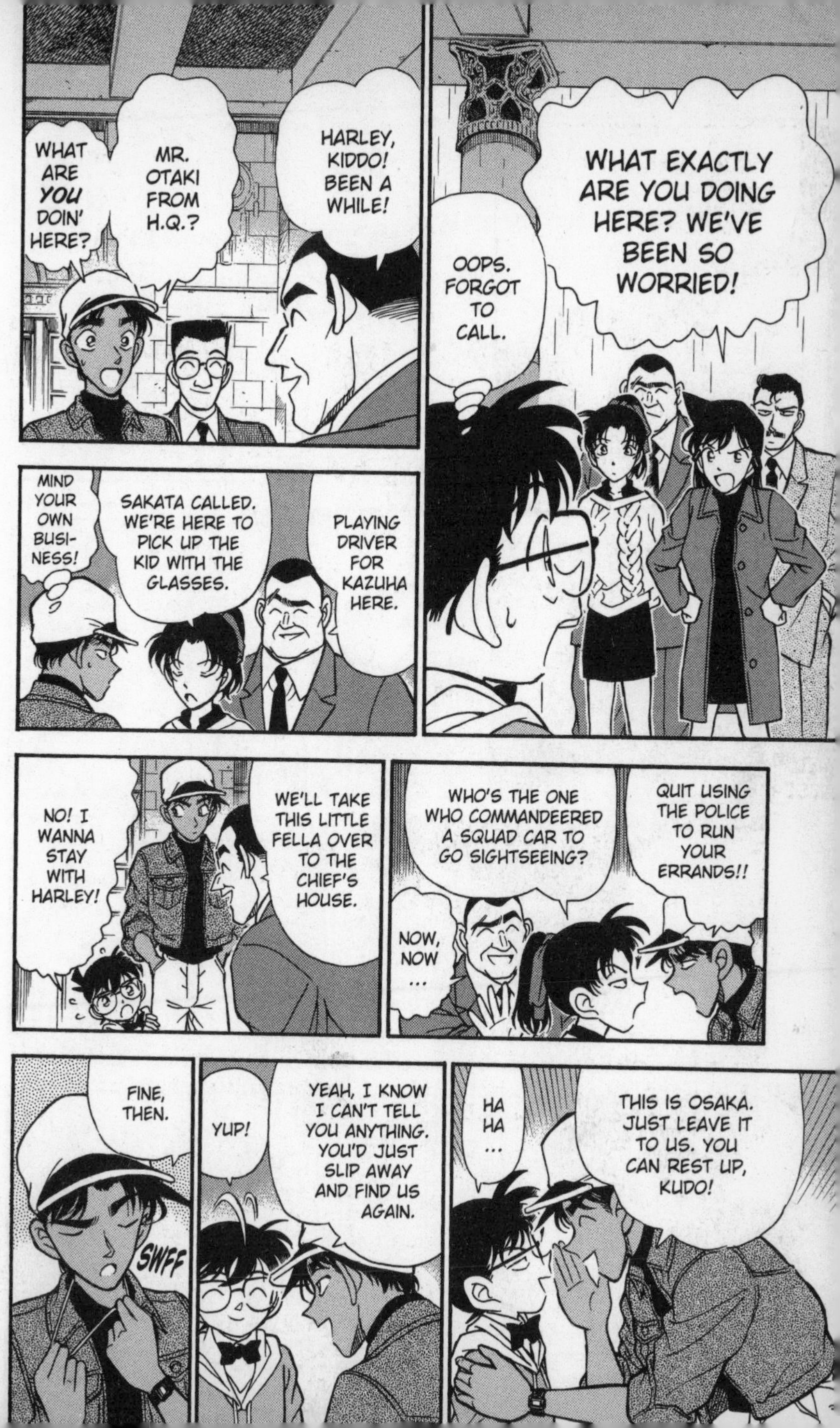
WHAT EXACTLY ARE YOU DOING HERE? WE'VE BEEN SO WORRIED!
OOPS. FORGOT TO CALL.
HARLEY, KIDDO! BEEN A WHILE!
MR. OTAKI FROM H.Q.?
WHAT ARE YOU DOIN' HERE?
PLAYING DRIVER FOR KAZUHA HERE.
SAKATA CALLED. WE'RE HERE TO PICK UP THE KID WITH THE GLASSES.
MIND YOUR OWN BUSINESS!
QUIT USING THE POLICE TO RUN YOUR ERRANDS!!
WHO'S THE ONE WHO COMMANDEERED A SQUAD CAR TO GO SIGHTSEEING?
NOW, NOW ...
WE'LL TAKE THIS LITTLE FELLA OVER TO THE CHIEF'S HOUSE.
NO! I WANNA STAY WITH HARLEY!
THIS IS OSAKA. JUST LEAVE IT TO US. YOU CAN REST UP, KUDO!
HA HA ...
YEAH, I KNOW I CAN'T TELL YOU ANYTHING. YOU'D JUST SLIP AWAY AND FIND US AGAIN.
YUP!
FINE, THEN.
SWFF

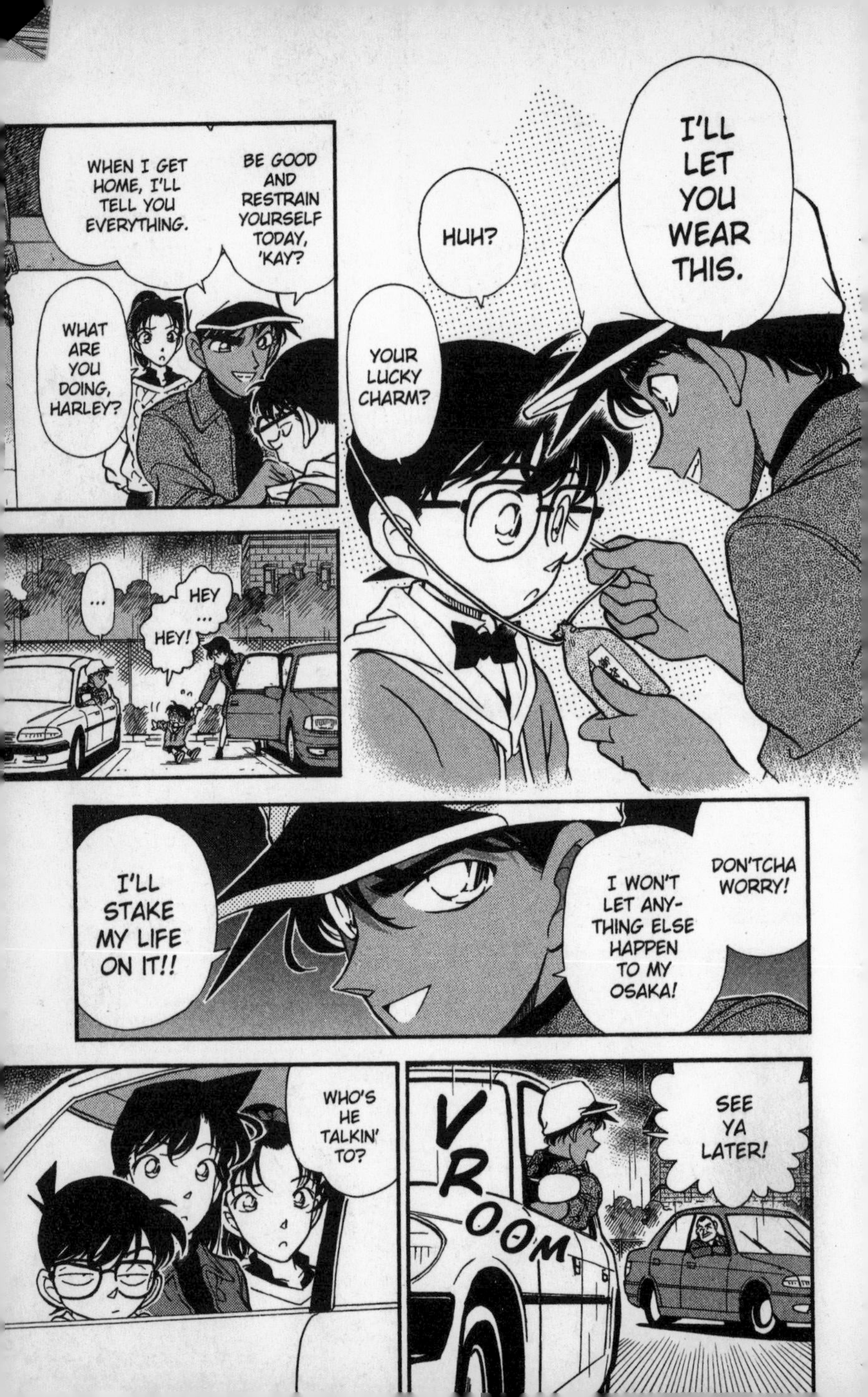
I'LL LET YOU WEAR THIS.
HUH?
YOUR LUCKY CHARM?
BE GOOD AND RESTRAIN YOURSELF TODAY, 'KAY?
WHEN I GET HOME, I'LL TELL YOU EVERYTHING.
WHAT ARE YOU DOING, HARLEY?
HEY ... HEY!
...
DON'TCHA WORRY!
I WON'T LET ANY-THING ELSE HAPPEN TO MY OSAKA!
I'LL STAKE MY LIFE ON IT!!
SEE YA LATER!
VROOM
WHO'S HE TALKIN' TO?

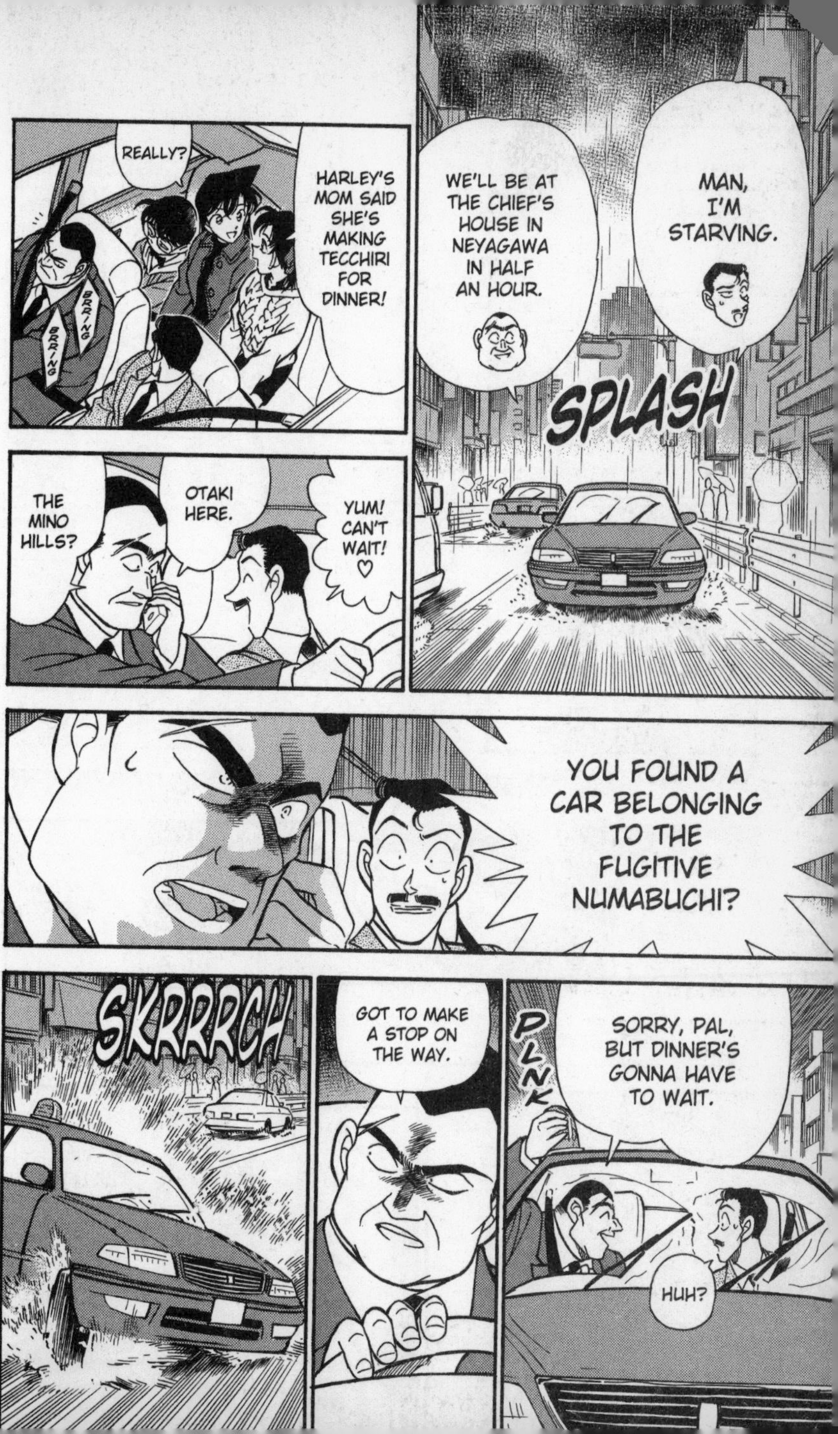
MAN, I'M STARVING.
WE'LL BE AT THE CHIEF'S HOUSE IN NEYAGAWA IN HALF AN HOUR.
SPLASH
HARLEY'S MOM SAID SHE'S MAKING TECCHIRI FOR DINNER!
REALLY?
BRRING
BRRING
YUM! CAN'T WAIT! ♡
OTAKI HERE.
THE MINO HILLS?
YOU FOUND A CAR BELONGING TO THE FUGITIVE NUMABUCHI?
SORRY, PAL, BUT DINNER'S GONNA HAVE TO WAIT.
PLNK
HUH?
GOT TO MAKE A STOP ON THE WAY.
SKRRRCH

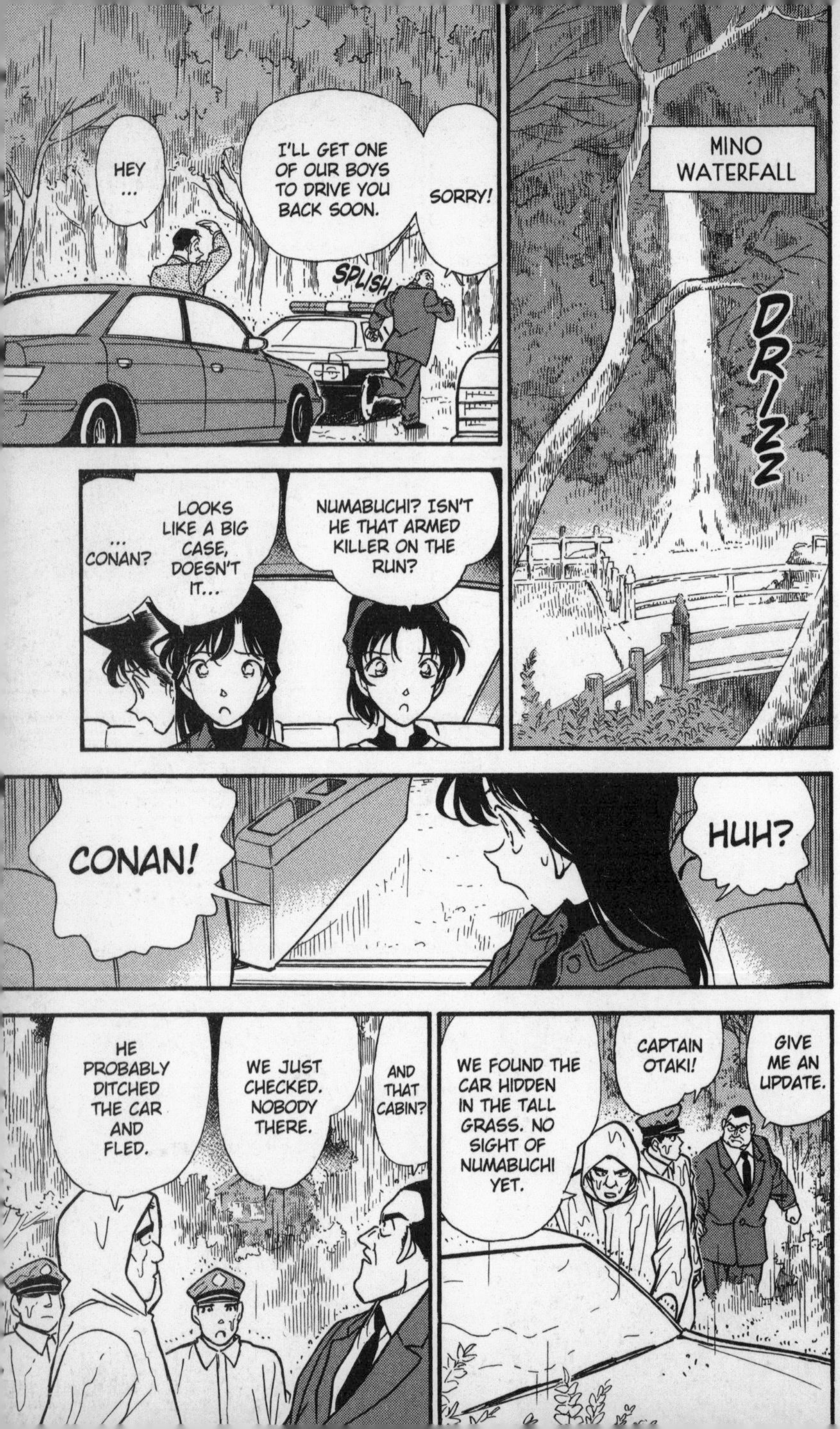
MINO WATERFALL
DRIZZ
SORRY!
I'LL GET ONE OF OUR BOYS TO DRIVE YOU BACK SOON.
SPLISH
HEY ...
NUMABUCHI? ISN'T HE THAT ARMED KILLER ON THE RUN?
LOOKS LIKE A BIG CASE, DOESN'T IT...
... CONAN?
HUH?
CONAN!
GIVE ME AN UPDATE.
CAPTAIN OTAKI!
WE FOUND THE CAR HIDDEN IN THE TALL GRASS. NO SIGHT OF NUMABUCHI YET.
AND THAT CABIN?
WE JUST CHECKED. NOBODY THERE.
HE PROBABLY DITCHED THE CAR AND FLED.

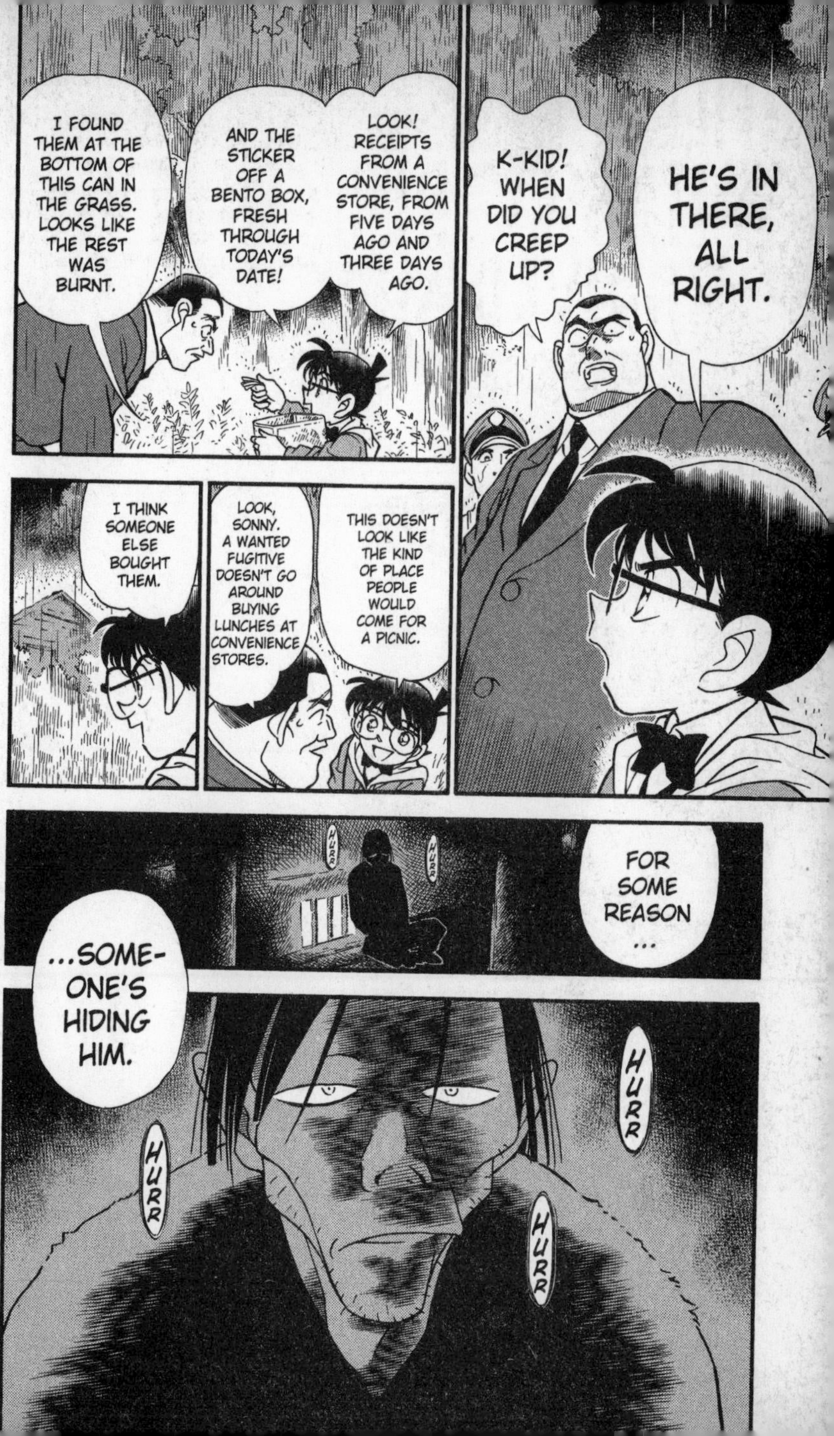
HE'S IN THERE, ALL RIGHT.
K-KID! WHEN DID YOU CREEP UP?
LOOK! RECEIPTS FROM A CONVENIENCE STORE, FROM FIVE DAYS AGO AND THREE DAYS AGO.
AND THE STICKER OFF A BENTO BOX, FRESH THROUGH TODAY'S DATE!
I FOUND THEM AT THE BOTTOM OF THIS CAN IN THE GRASS. LOOKS LIKE THE REST WAS BURNT.
THIS DOESN'T LOOK LIKE THE KIND OF PLACE PEOPLE WOULD COME FOR A PICNIC.
LOOK, SONNY. A WANTED FUGITIVE DOESN'T GO AROUND BUYING LUNCHES AT CONVENIENCE STORES.
I THINK SOMEONE ELSE BOUGHT THEM.
FOR SOME REASON...
HURR
HURR
...SOMEONE'S HIDING HIM.
HURR
HURR
HURR

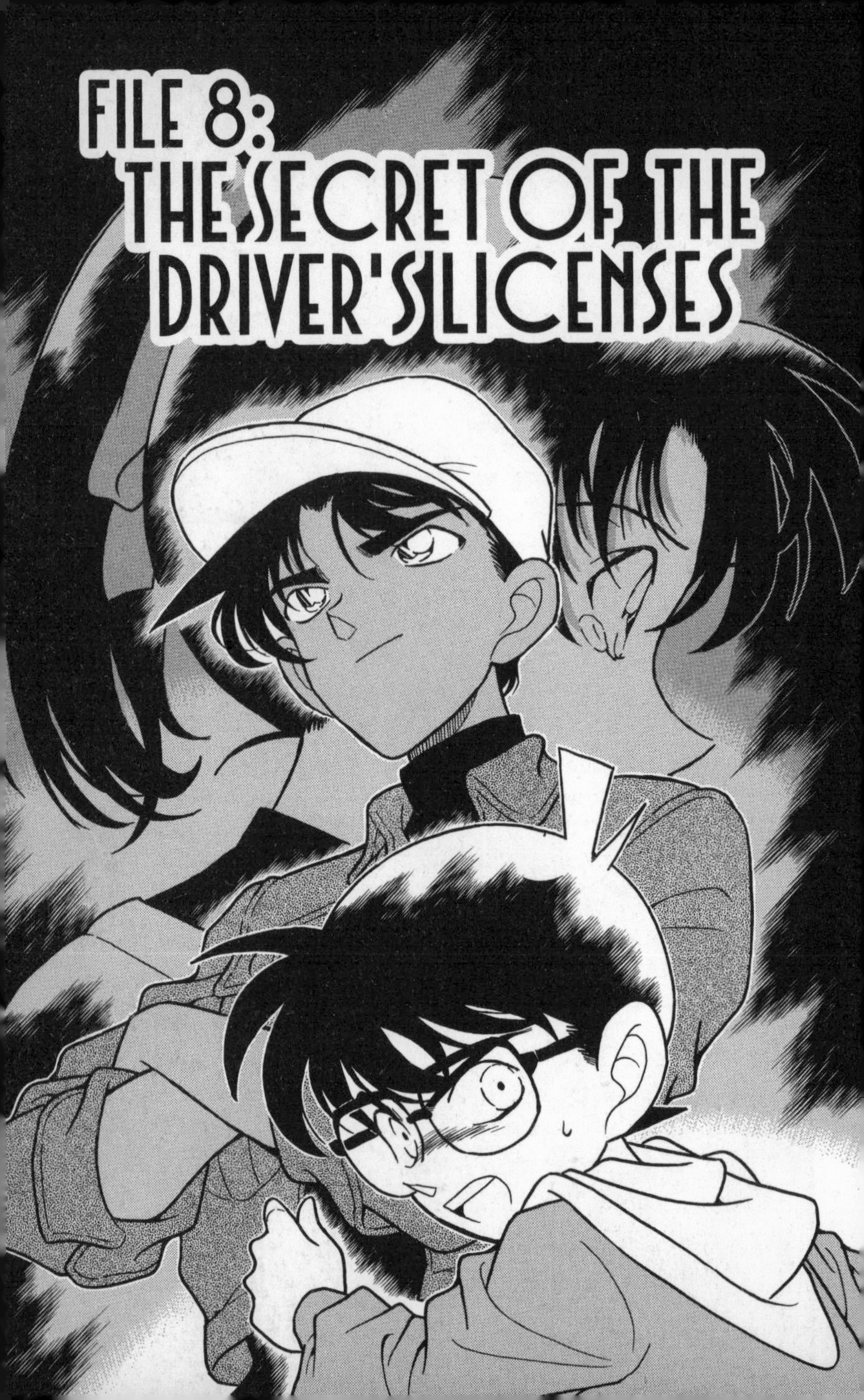
FILE 8:
THE SECRET OF THE DRIVER'S LICENSES

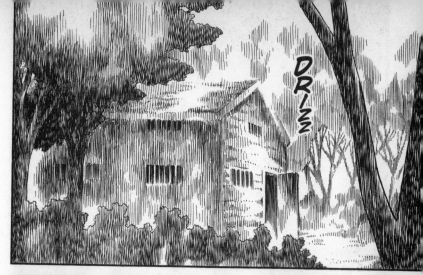

DRIZZ

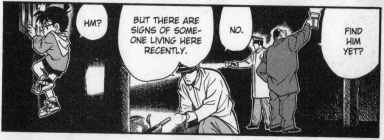

HM?

BUT THERE ARE SIGNS OF SOME- ONE LIVING HERE RECENTLY.

NO.

FIND HIM YET?

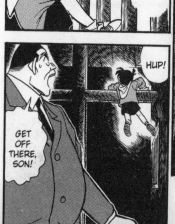

IF YOU STEP ONTO THE SILL...

HUP!

GET OFF THERE, SON!

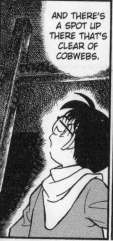

AND THERE'S A SPOT UP THERE THAT'S CLEAR OF COBWEBS.

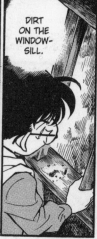

DIRT ON THE WINDOW- SILL.

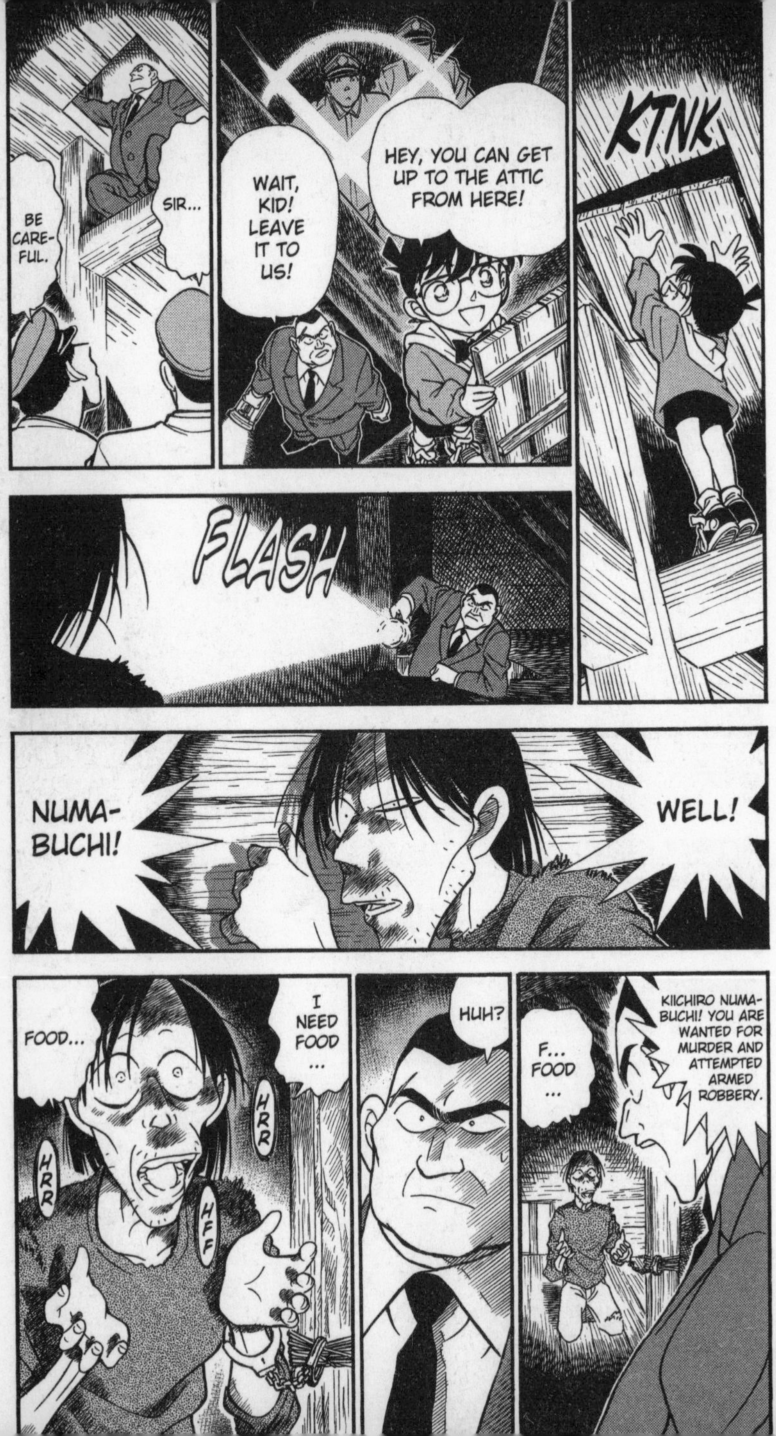
KTNK
HEY, YOU CAN GET UP TO THE ATTIC FROM HERE!
WAIT, KID! LEAVE IT TO US!
SIR...
BE CARE-FUL.
FLASH
WELL!
NUMA-BUCHI!
KIICHIRO NUMA-BUCHI! YOU ARE WANTED FOR MURDER AND ATTEMPTED ARMED ROBBERY.
F... FOOD ...
HUH?
I NEED FOOD ...
HRR
FOOD...
HFF
HRR

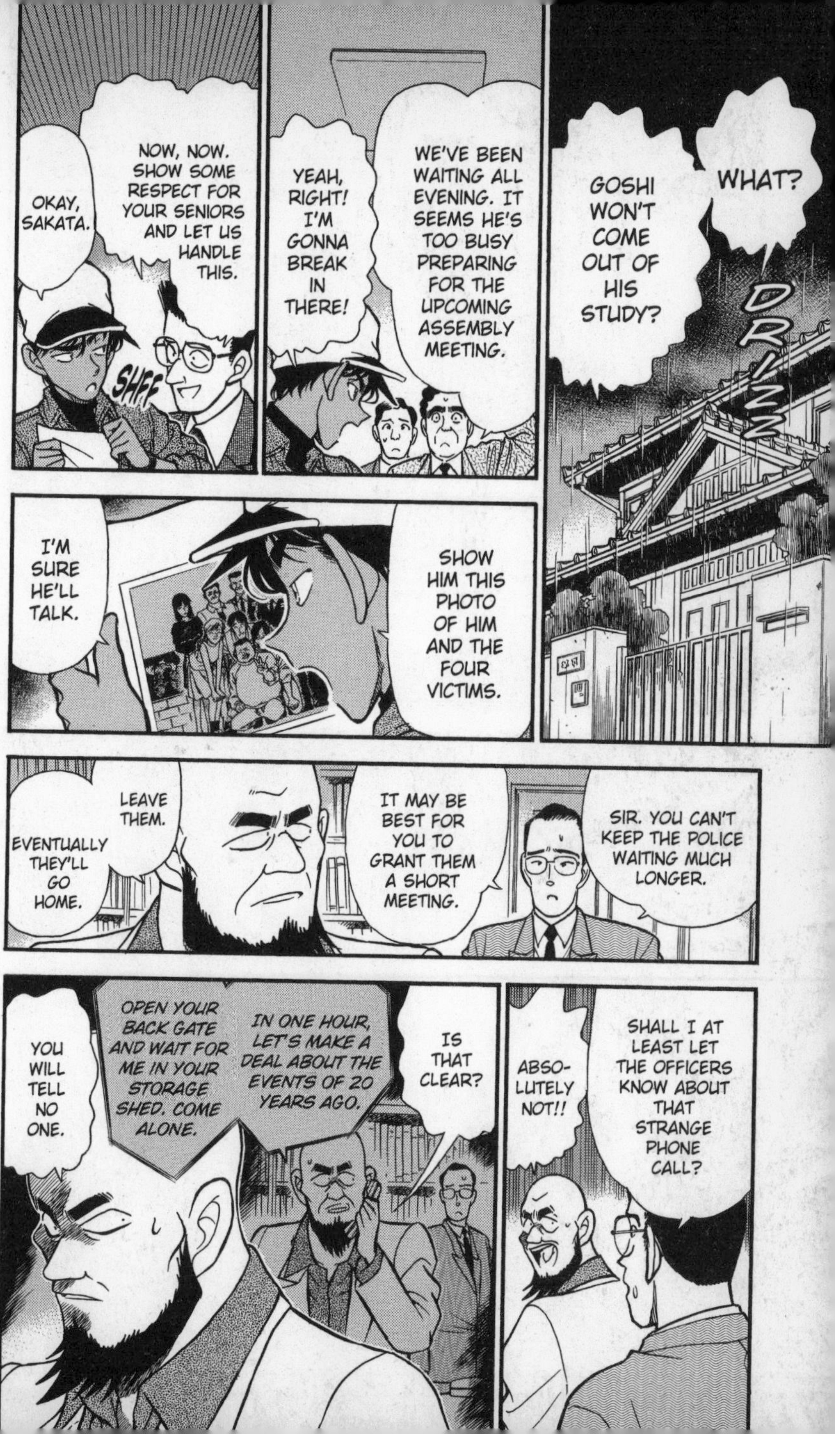
WHAT?
GOSHI WON'T COME OUT OF HIS STUDY?
DRIZZ
WE'VE BEEN WAITING ALL EVENING. IT SEEMS HE'S TOO BUSY PREPARING FOR THE UPCOMING ASSEMBLY MEETING.
YEAH, RIGHT! I'M GONNA BREAK IN THERE!
NOW, NOW. SHOW SOME RESPECT FOR YOUR SENIORS AND LET US HANDLE THIS.
OKAY, SAKATA.
SHFF
SHOW HIM THIS PHOTO OF HIM AND THE FOUR VICTIMS.
I'M SURE HE'LL TALK.
SIR. YOU CAN'T KEEP THE POLICE WAITING MUCH LONGER.
IT MAY BE BEST FOR YOU TO GRANT THEM A SHORT MEETING.
LEAVE THEM.
EVENTUALLY THEY'LL GO HOME.
SHALL I AT LEAST LET THE OFFICERS KNOW ABOUT THAT STRANGE PHONE CALL?
ABSO-LUTELY NOT!!
IS THAT CLEAR?
IN ONE HOUR, LET'S MAKE A DEAL ABOUT THE EVENTS OF 20 YEARS AGO.
OPEN YOUR BACK GATE AND WAIT FOR ME IN YOUR STORAGE SHED. COME ALONE.
YOU WILL TELL NO ONE.

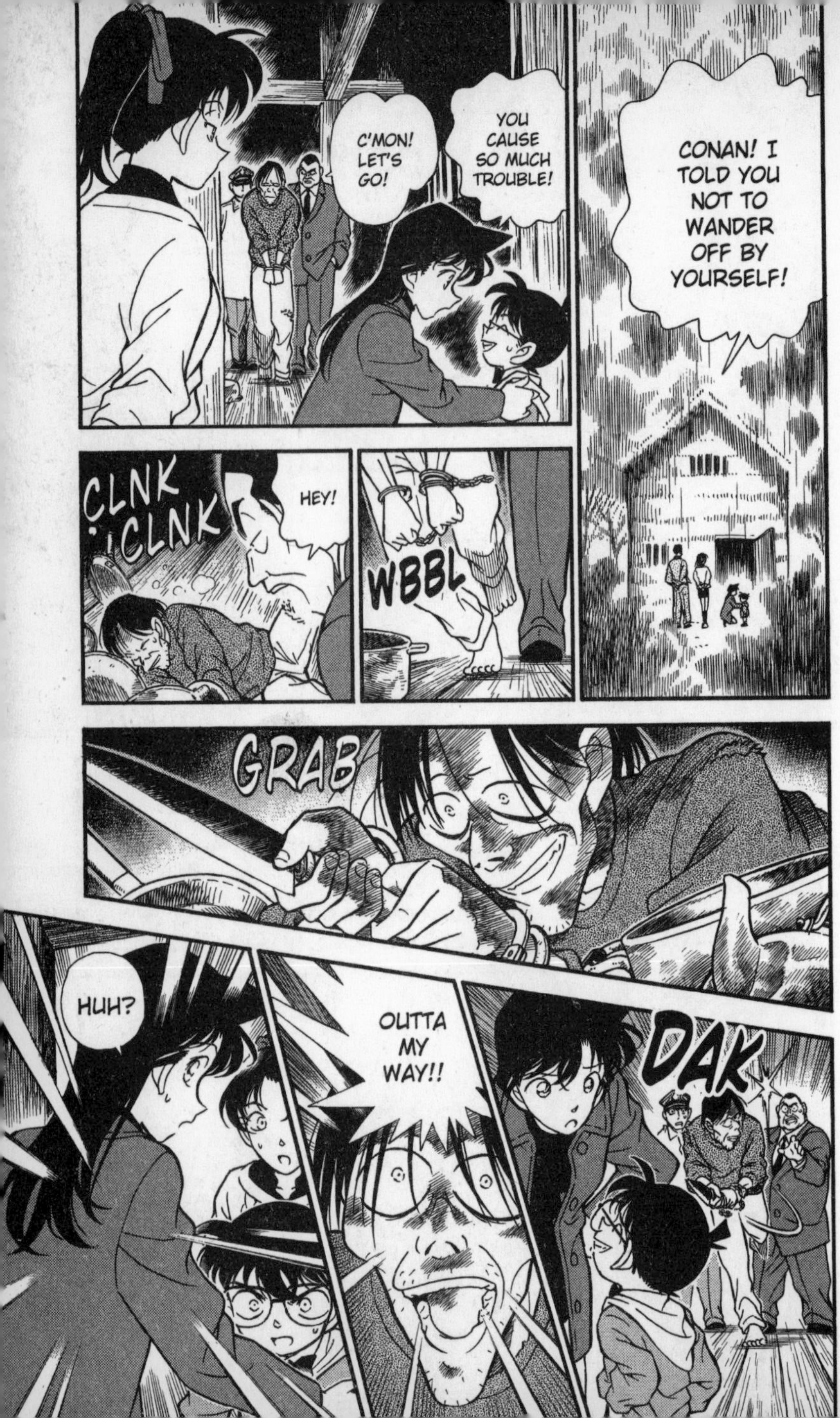
CONAN! I TOLD YOU NOT TO WANDER OFF BY YOURSELF!
YOU CAUSE SO MUCH TROUBLE!
C'MON! LET'S GO!
WBBL
CLNK CLNK
HEY!
GRAB
DAK
OUTTA MY WAY!!
HUH?

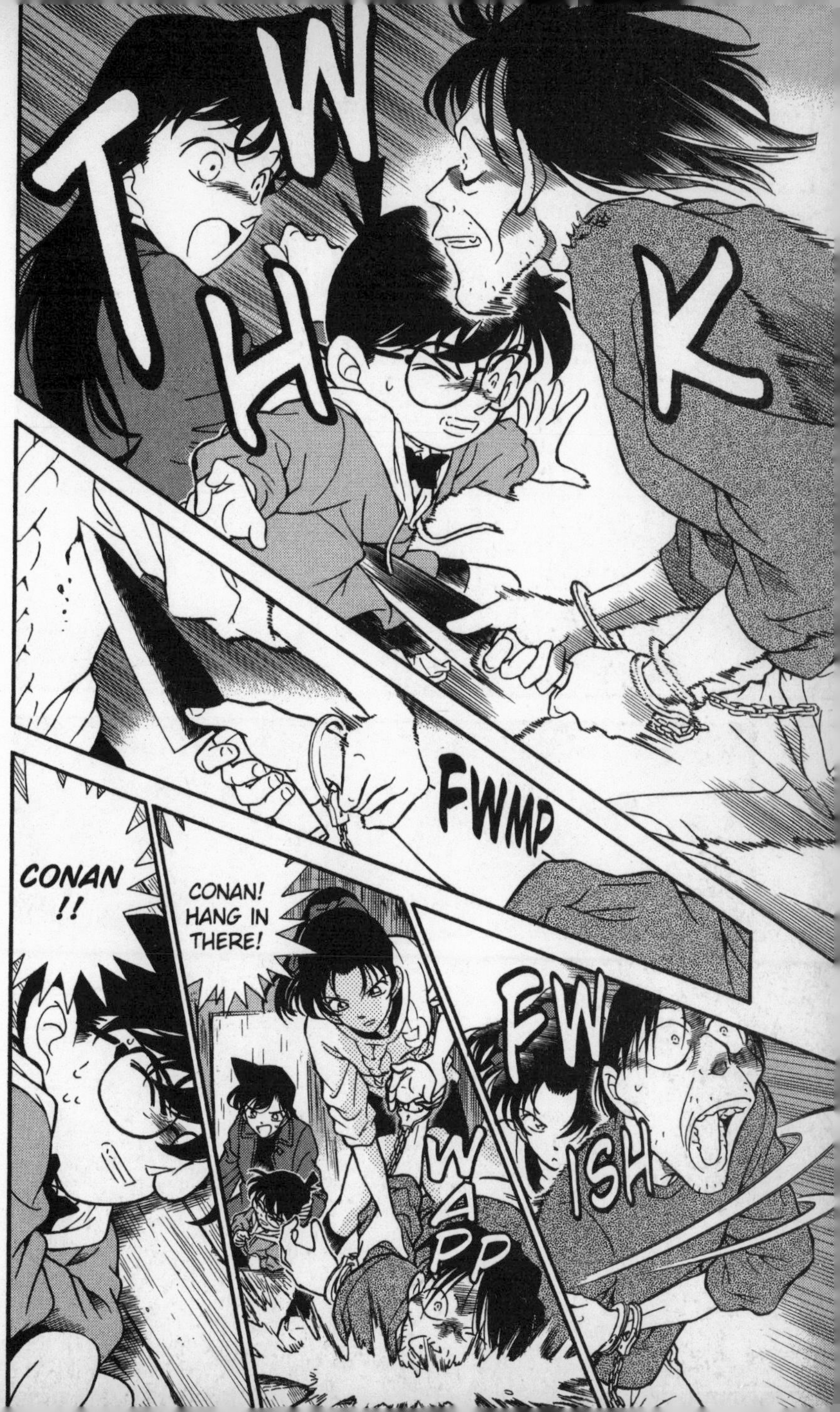
THWK
FWMP
FWISH
WAPP
CONAN! HANG IN THERE!
CONAN !!

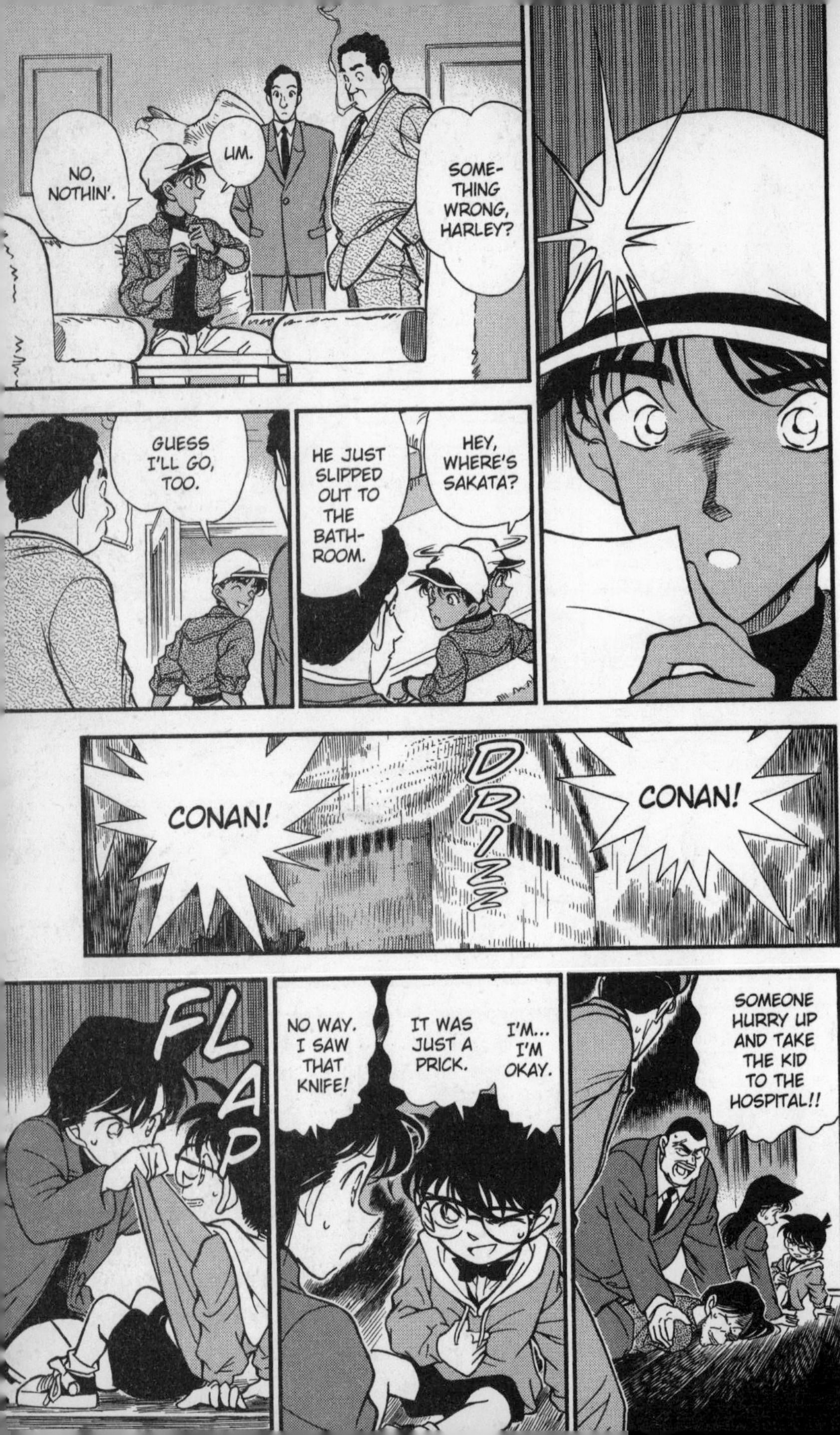
SOMETHING WRONG, HARLEY?
UM.
NO, NOTHIN'.
HEY, WHERE'S SAKATA?
HE JUST SLIPPED OUT TO THE BATHROOM.
GUESS I'LL GO, TOO.
CONAN!
DRIZZ
CONAN!
SOMEONE HURRY UP AND TAKE THE KID TO THE HOSPITAL!!
I'M... I'M OKAY.
IT WAS JUST A PRICK.
NO WAY. I SAW THAT KNIFE!
FLAP

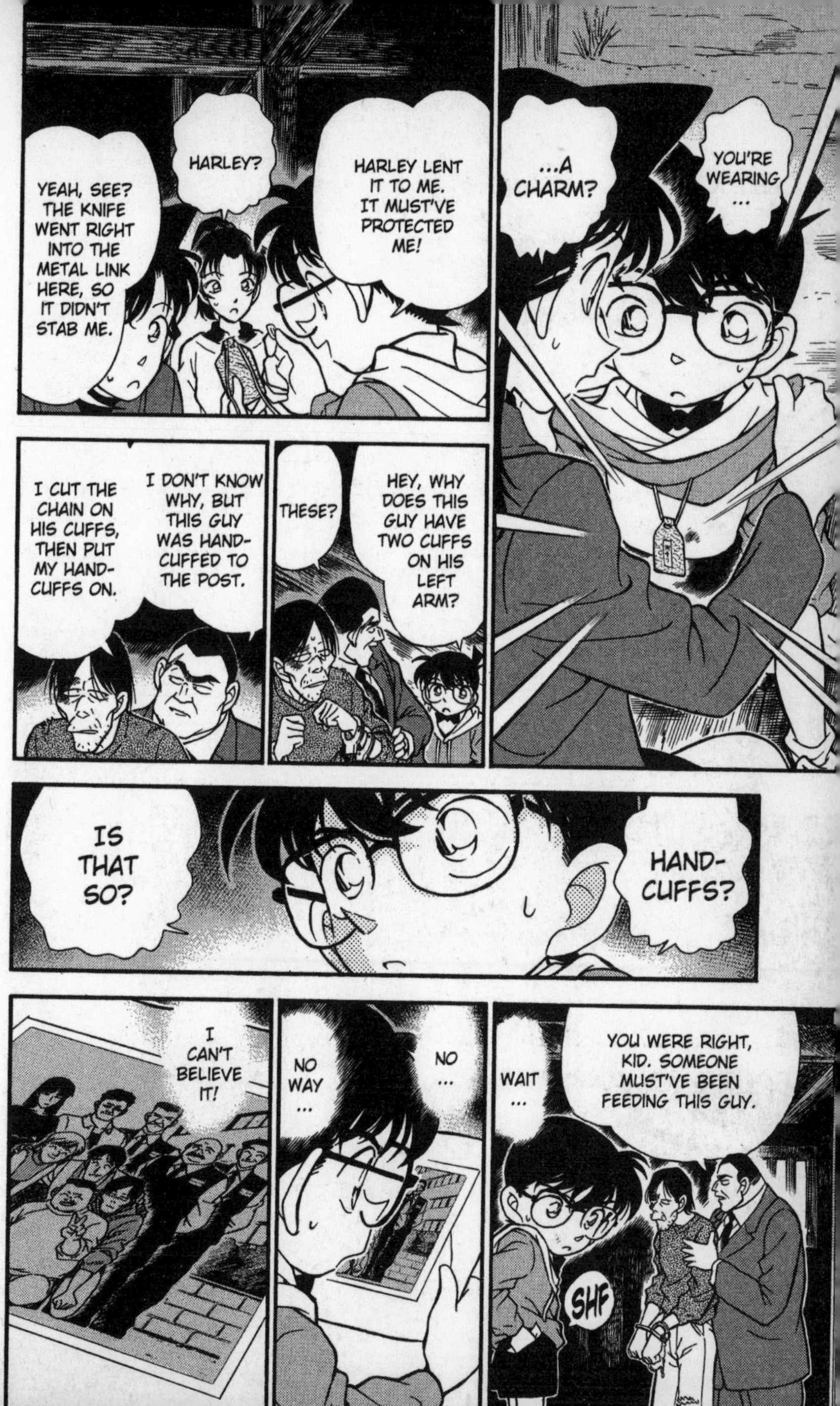
YOU'RE WEARING ...
...A CHARM?
HARLEY LENT IT TO ME. IT MUST'VE PROTECTED ME!
HARLEY?
YEAH, SEE? THE KNIFE WENT RIGHT INTO THE METAL LINK HERE, SO IT DIDN'T STAB ME.
HEY, WHY DOES THIS GUY HAVE TWO CUFFS ON HIS LEFT ARM?
THESE?
I DON'T KNOW WHY, BUT THIS GUY WAS HAND-CUFFED TO THE POST.
I CUT THE CHAIN ON HIS CUFFS, THEN PUT MY HAND-CUFFS ON.
HAND-CUFFS?
IS THAT SO?
YOU WERE RIGHT, KID. SOMEONE MUST'VE BEEN FEEDING THIS GUY.
WAIT ...
SHF
NO ...
NO WAY ...
I CAN'T BELIEVE IT!

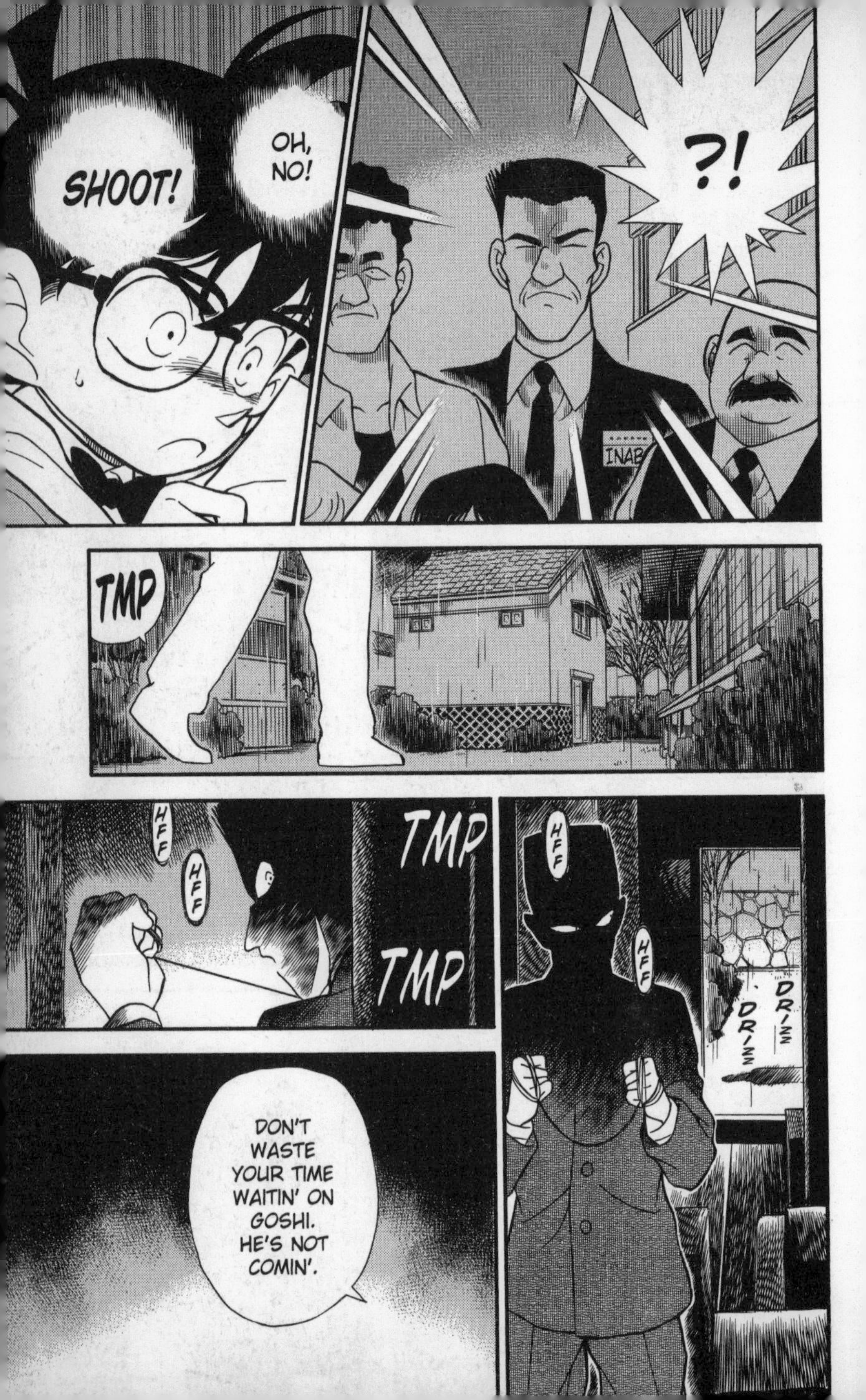
?!
OH, NO!
SHOOT!
TMP
HFF
DRIZZ
DRIZZ
TMP
TMP
HFF
HFF
DON'T WASTE YOUR TIME WAITIN' ON GOSHI. HE'S NOT COMIN'.

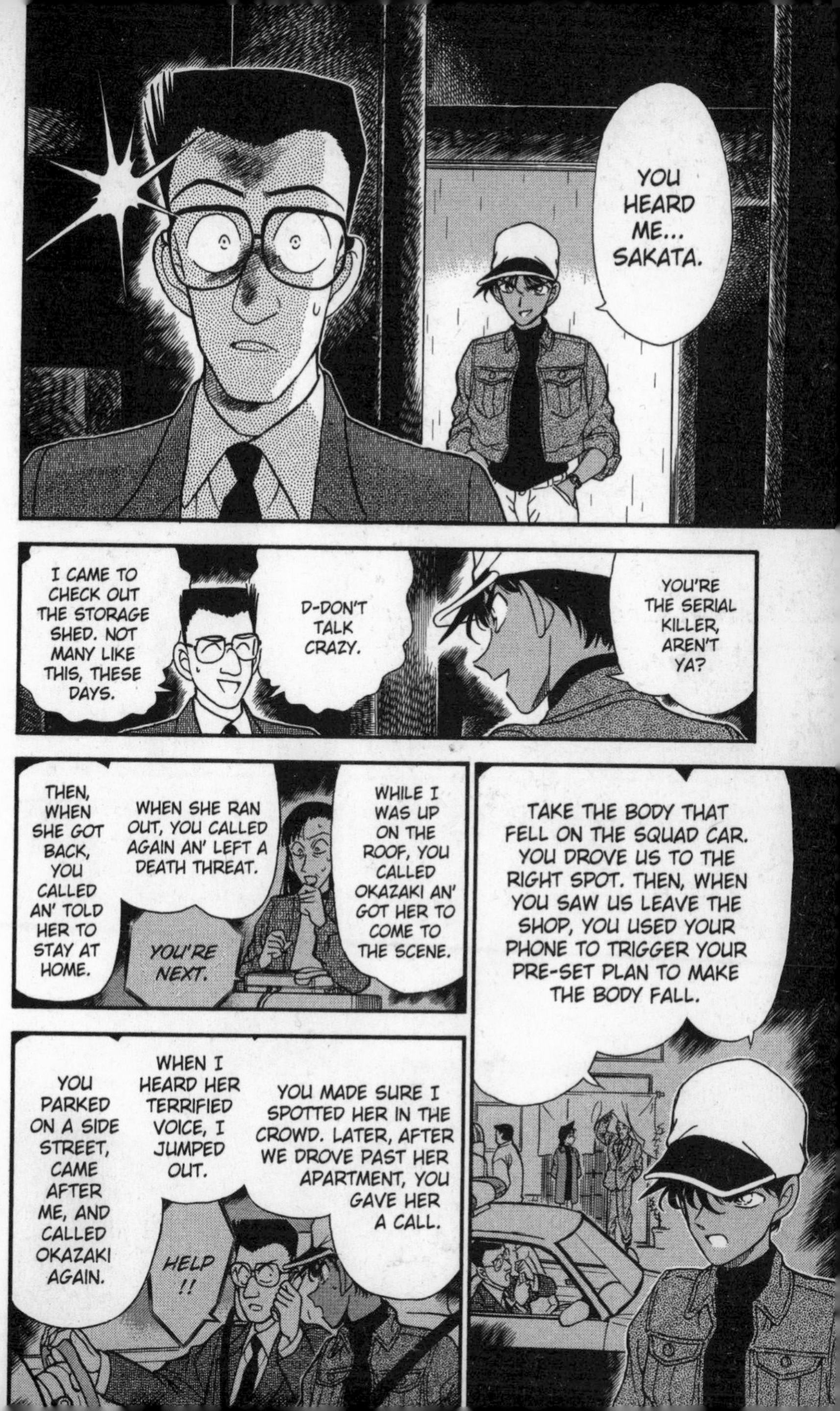
YOU HEARD ME... SAKATA.
YOU'RE THE SERIAL KILLER, AREN'T YA?
D-DON'T TALK CRAZY.
I CAME TO CHECK OUT THE STORAGE SHED. NOT MANY LIKE THIS, THESE DAYS.
TAKE THE BODY THAT FELL ON THE SQUAD CAR. YOU DROVE US TO THE RIGHT SPOT. THEN, WHEN YOU SAW US LEAVE THE SHOP, YOU USED YOUR PHONE TO TRIGGER YOUR PRE-SET PLAN TO MAKE THE BODY FALL.
WHILE I WAS UP ON THE ROOF, YOU CALLED OKAZAKI AN' GOT HER TO COME TO THE SCENE.
WHEN SHE RAN OUT, YOU CALLED AGAIN AN' LEFT A DEATH THREAT.
YOU'RE NEXT.
THEN, WHEN SHE GOT BACK, YOU CALLED AN' TOLD HER TO STAY AT HOME.
YOU MADE SURE I SPOTTED HER IN THE CROWD. LATER, AFTER WE DROVE PAST HER APARTMENT, YOU GAVE HER A CALL.
WHEN I HEARD HER TERRIFIED VOICE, I JUMPED OUT.
YOU PARKED ON A SIDE STREET, CAME AFTER ME, AND CALLED OKAZAKI AGAIN.
HELP !!

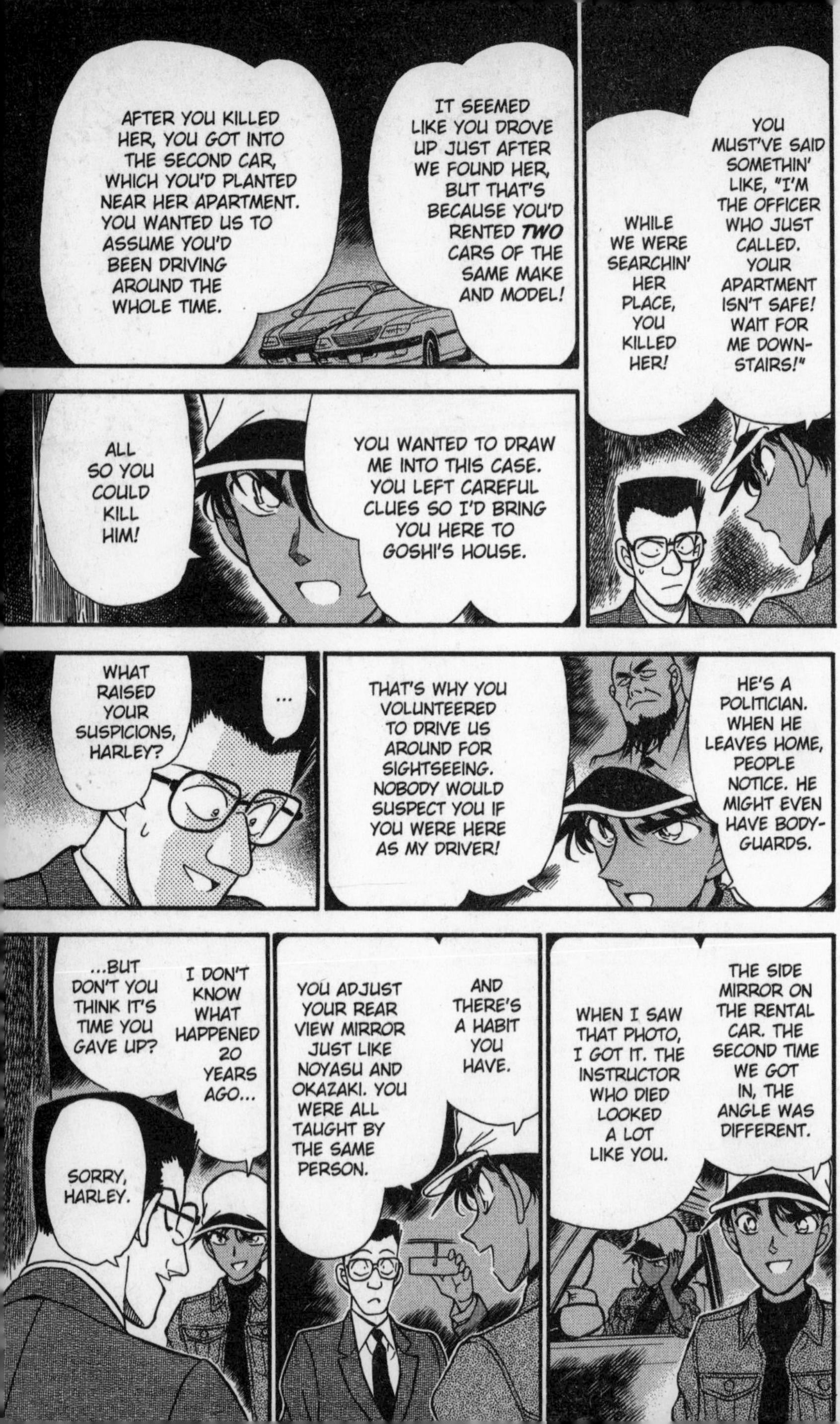

YOU MUST'VE SAID SOMETHIN' LIKE, "I'M THE OFFICER WHO JUST CALLED. YOUR APARTMENT ISN'T SAFE! WAIT FOR ME DOWN-STAIRS!"
WHILE WE WERE SEARCHIN' HER PLACE, YOU KILLED HER!
IT SEEMED LIKE YOU DROVE UP JUST AFTER WE FOUND HER, BUT THAT'S BECAUSE YOU'D RENTED ***TWO*** CARS OF THE SAME MAKE AND MODEL!
AFTER YOU KILLED HER, YOU GOT INTO THE SECOND CAR, WHICH YOU'D PLANTED NEAR HER APARTMENT. YOU WANTED US TO ASSUME YOU'D BEEN DRIVING AROUND THE WHOLE TIME.
YOU WANTED TO DRAW ME INTO THIS CASE. YOU LEFT CAREFUL CLUES SO I'D BRING YOU HERE TO GOSHI'S HOUSE.
ALL SO YOU COULD KILL HIM!
HE'S A POLITICIAN. WHEN HE LEAVES HOME, PEOPLE NOTICE. HE MIGHT EVEN HAVE BODY-GUARDS.
THAT'S WHY YOU VOLUNTEERED TO DRIVE US AROUND FOR SIGHTSEEING. NOBODY WOULD SUSPECT YOU IF YOU WERE HERE AS MY DRIVER!
...
WHAT RAISED YOUR SUSPICIONS, HARLEY?
THE SIDE MIRROR ON THE RENTAL CAR. THE SECOND TIME WE GOT IN, THE ANGLE WAS DIFFERENT.
WHEN I SAW THAT PHOTO, I GOT IT. THE INSTRUCTOR WHO DIED LOOKED A LOT LIKE YOU.
AND THERE'S A HABIT YOU HAVE.
YOU ADJUST YOUR REAR VIEW MIRROR JUST LIKE NOYASU AND OKAZAKI. YOU WERE ALL TAUGHT BY THE SAME PERSON.
I DON'T KNOW WHAT HAPPENED 20 YEARS AGO...
...BUT DON'T YOU THINK IT'S TIME YOU GAVE UP?
SORRY, HARLEY.

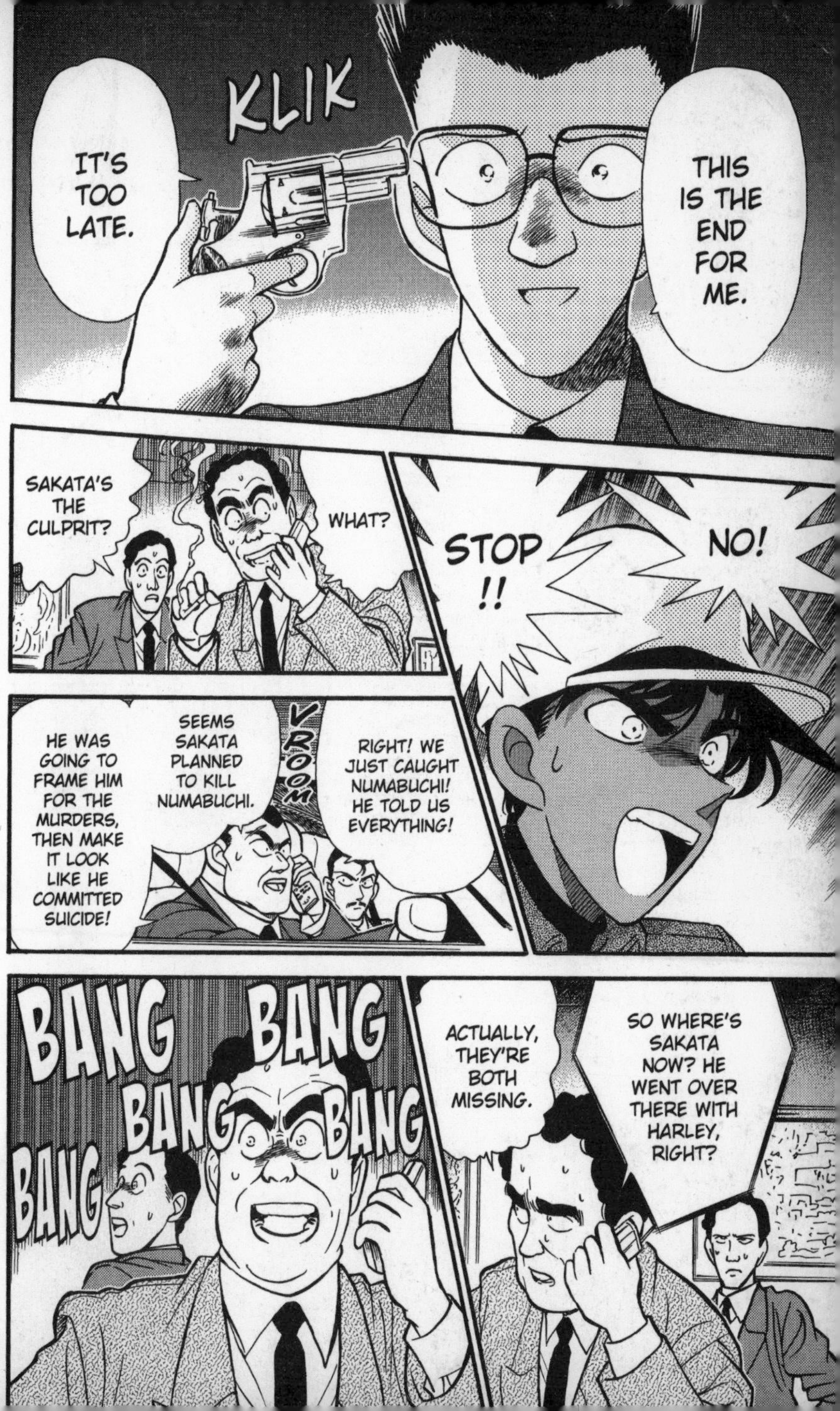
THIS IS THE END FOR ME.
KLIK
IT'S TOO LATE.
NO!
STOP !!
WHAT?
SAKATA'S THE CULPRIT?
RIGHT! WE JUST CAUGHT NUMABUCHI! HE TOLD US EVERYTHING!
VROOM
SEEMS SAKATA PLANNED TO KILL NUMABUCHI.
HE WAS GOING TO FRAME HIM FOR THE MURDERS, THEN MAKE IT LOOK LIKE HE COMMITTED SUICIDE!
SO WHERE'S SAKATA NOW? HE WENT OVER THERE WITH HARLEY, RIGHT?
ACTUALLY, THEY'RE BOTH MISSING.
BANG BANG BANG BANG BANG

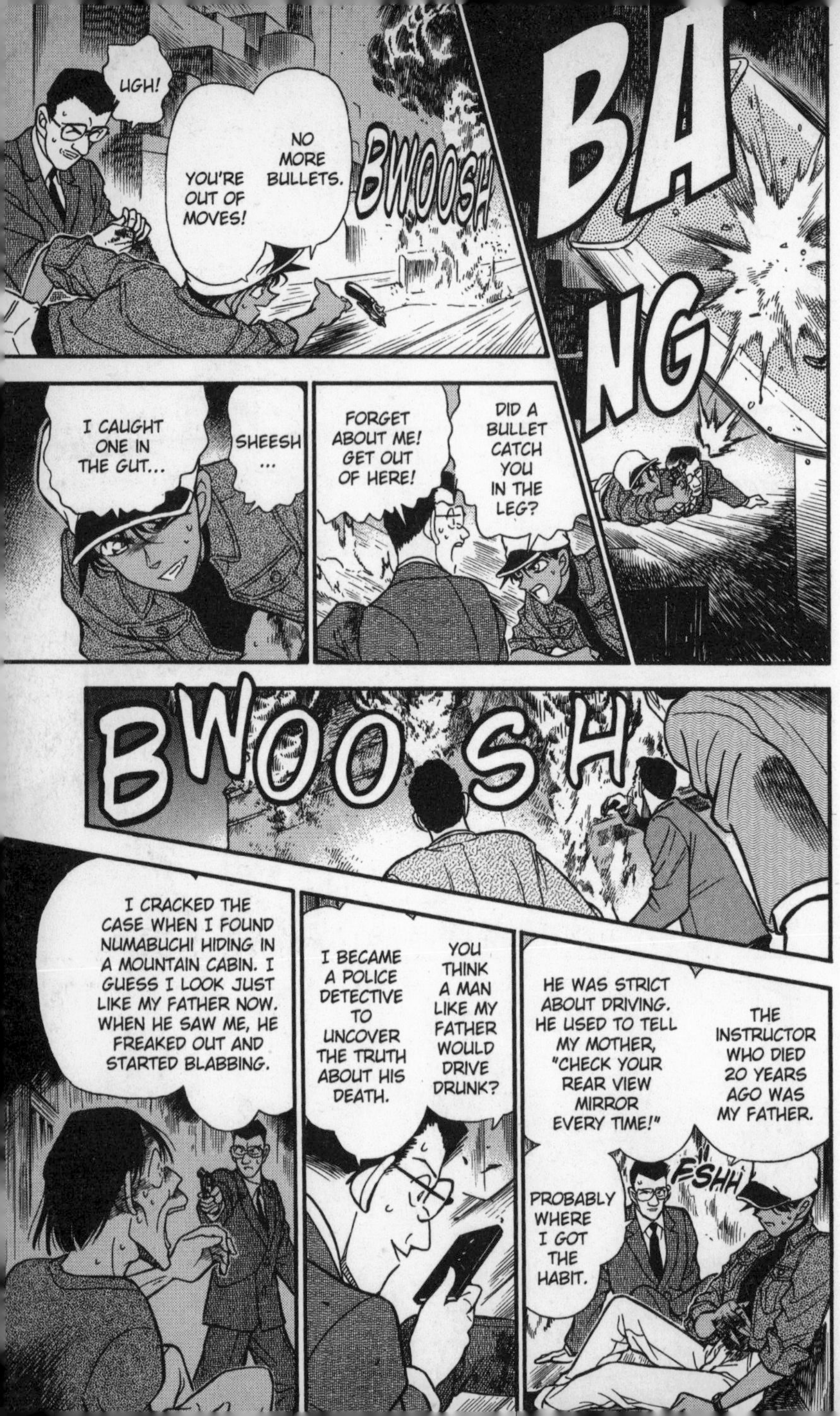
BANG
BWOOSH
NO MORE BULLETS.
YOU'RE OUT OF MOVES!
UGH!
DID A BULLET CATCH YOU IN THE LEG?
FORGET ABOUT ME! GET OUT OF HERE!
SHEESH...
I CAUGHT ONE IN THE GUT...
BWOOSH
THE INSTRUCTOR WHO DIED 20 YEARS AGO WAS MY FATHER.
HE WAS STRICT ABOUT DRIVING. HE USED TO TELL MY MOTHER, "CHECK YOUR REAR VIEW MIRROR EVERY TIME!"
FSHH
PROBABLY WHERE I GOT THE HABIT.
YOU THINK A MAN LIKE MY FATHER WOULD DRIVE DRUNK?
I BECAME A POLICE DETECTIVE TO UNCOVER THE TRUTH ABOUT HIS DEATH.
I CRACKED THE CASE WHEN I FOUND NUMABUCHI HIDING IN A MOUNTAIN CABIN. I GUESS I LOOK JUST LIKE MY FATHER NOW. WHEN HE SAW ME, HE FREAKED OUT AND STARTED BLABBING.

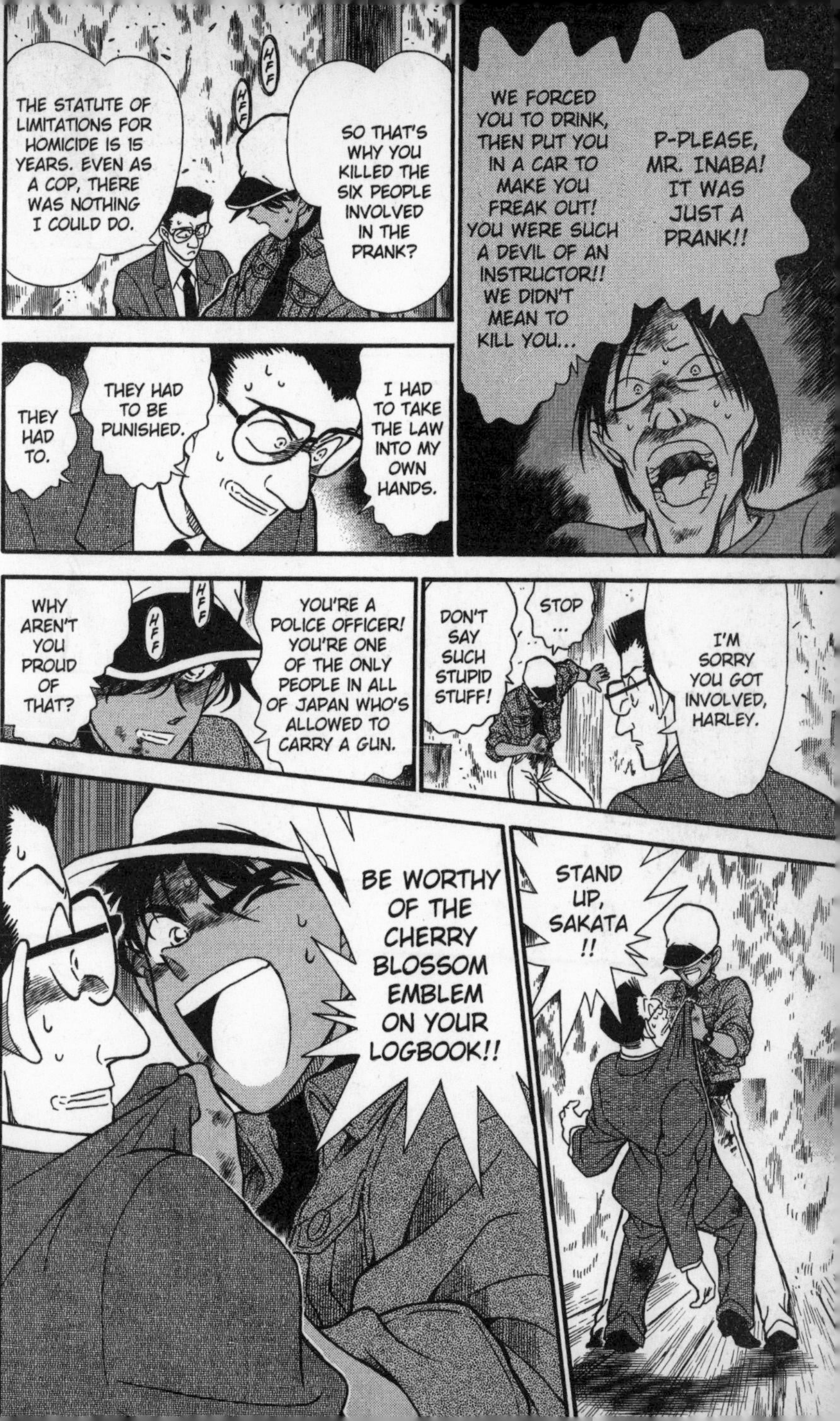
P-PLEASE, MR. INABA! IT WAS JUST A PRANK!!
WE FORCED YOU TO DRINK, THEN PUT YOU IN A CAR TO MAKE YOU FREAK OUT! YOU WERE SUCH A DEVIL OF AN INSTRUCTOR!! WE DIDN'T MEAN TO KILL YOU...
HFF
HFF
SO THAT'S WHY YOU KILLED THE SIX PEOPLE INVOLVED IN THE PRANK?
THE STATUTE OF LIMITATIONS FOR HOMICIDE IS 15 YEARS. EVEN AS A COP, THERE WAS NOTHING I COULD DO.
I HAD TO TAKE THE LAW INTO MY OWN HANDS.
THEY HAD TO BE PUNISHED.
THEY HAD TO.
I'M SORRY YOU GOT INVOLVED, HARLEY.
STOP ...
DON'T SAY SUCH STUPID STUFF!
HFF
HFF
YOU'RE A POLICE OFFICER! YOU'RE ONE OF THE ONLY PEOPLE IN ALL OF JAPAN WHO'S ALLOWED TO CARRY A GUN.
WHY AREN'T YOU PROUD OF THAT?
STAND UP, SAKATA !!
BE WORTHY OF THE CHERRY BLOSSOM EMBLEM ON YOUR LOGBOOK!!

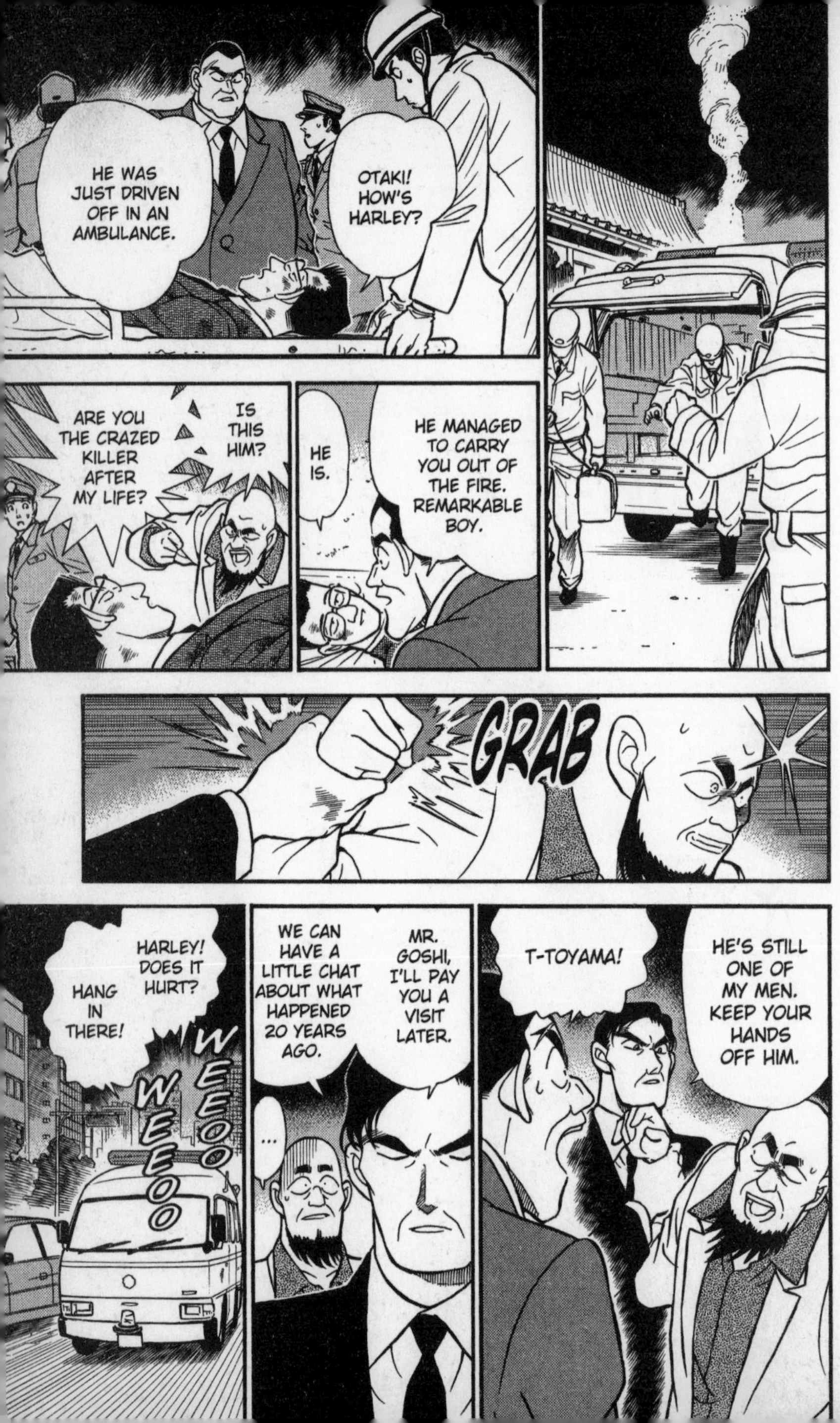
OTAKI! HOW'S HARLEY?
HE WAS JUST DRIVEN OFF IN AN AMBULANCE.
HE MANAGED TO CARRY YOU OUT OF THE FIRE. REMARKABLE BOY.
HE IS.
IS THIS HIM?
ARE YOU THE CRAZED KILLER AFTER MY LIFE?
GRAB
HE'S STILL ONE OF MY MEN. KEEP YOUR HANDS OFF HIM.
T-TOYAMA!
MR. GOSHI, I'LL PAY YOU A VISIT LATER.
WE CAN HAVE A LITTLE CHAT ABOUT WHAT HAPPENED 20 YEARS AGO.
...
HARLEY! DOES IT HURT?
HANG IN THERE!
WEEOO
WEEOO

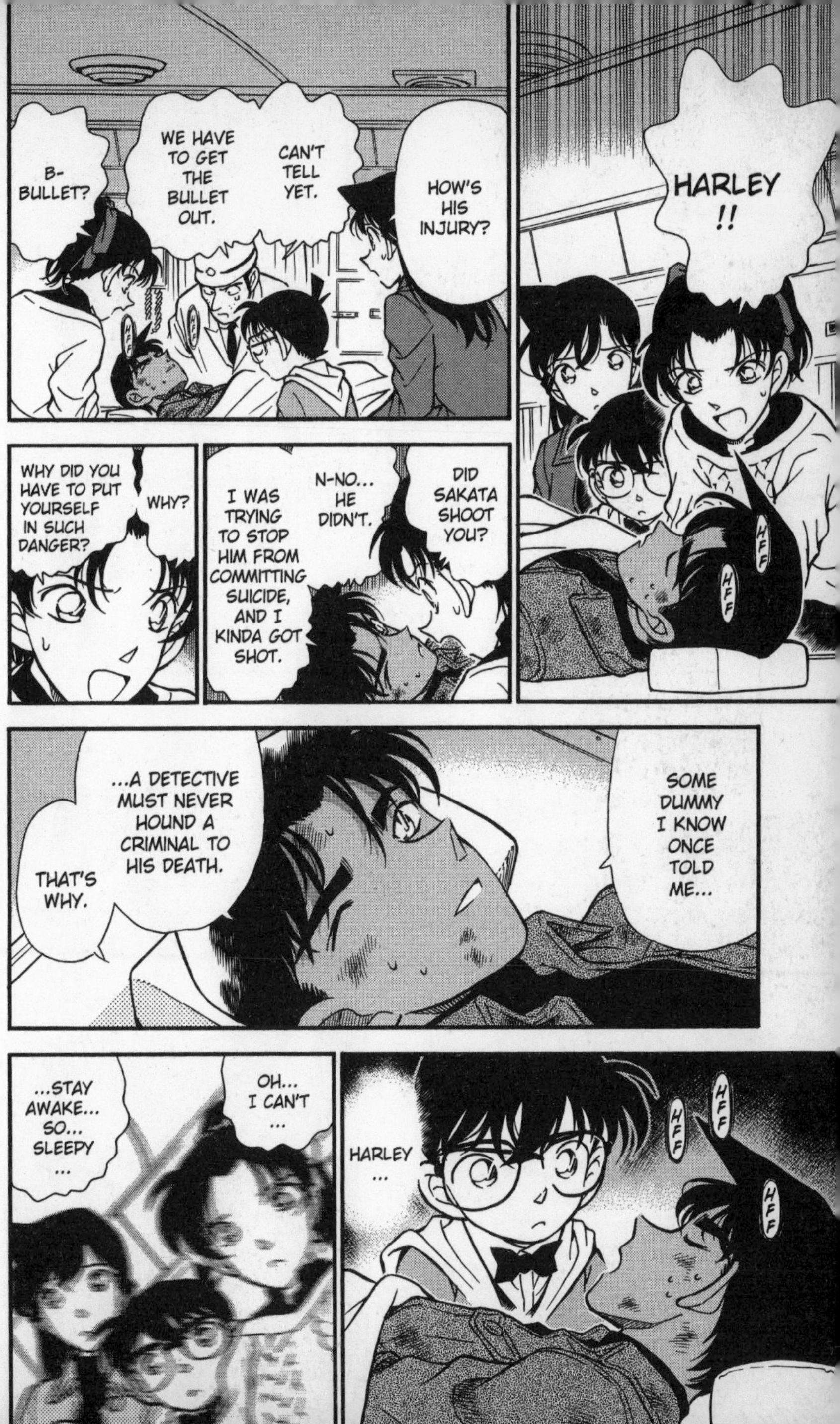
HARLEY !!
HFF
HFF
HOW'S HIS INJURY?
CAN'T TELL YET.
WE HAVE TO GET THE BULLET OUT.
B-BULLET?
HFF
HFF
DID SAKATA SHOOT YOU?
N-NO... HE DIDN'T.
I WAS TRYING TO STOP HIM FROM COMMITTING SUICIDE, AND I KINDA GOT SHOT.
WHY?
WHY DID YOU HAVE TO PUT YOURSELF IN SUCH DANGER?
SOME DUMMY I KNOW ONCE TOLD ME...
...A DETECTIVE MUST NEVER HOUND A CRIMINAL TO HIS DEATH.
THAT'S WHY.
HFF
HFF
HFF
HARLEY ...
OH... I CAN'T ...
...STAY AWAKE... SO... SLEEPY ...

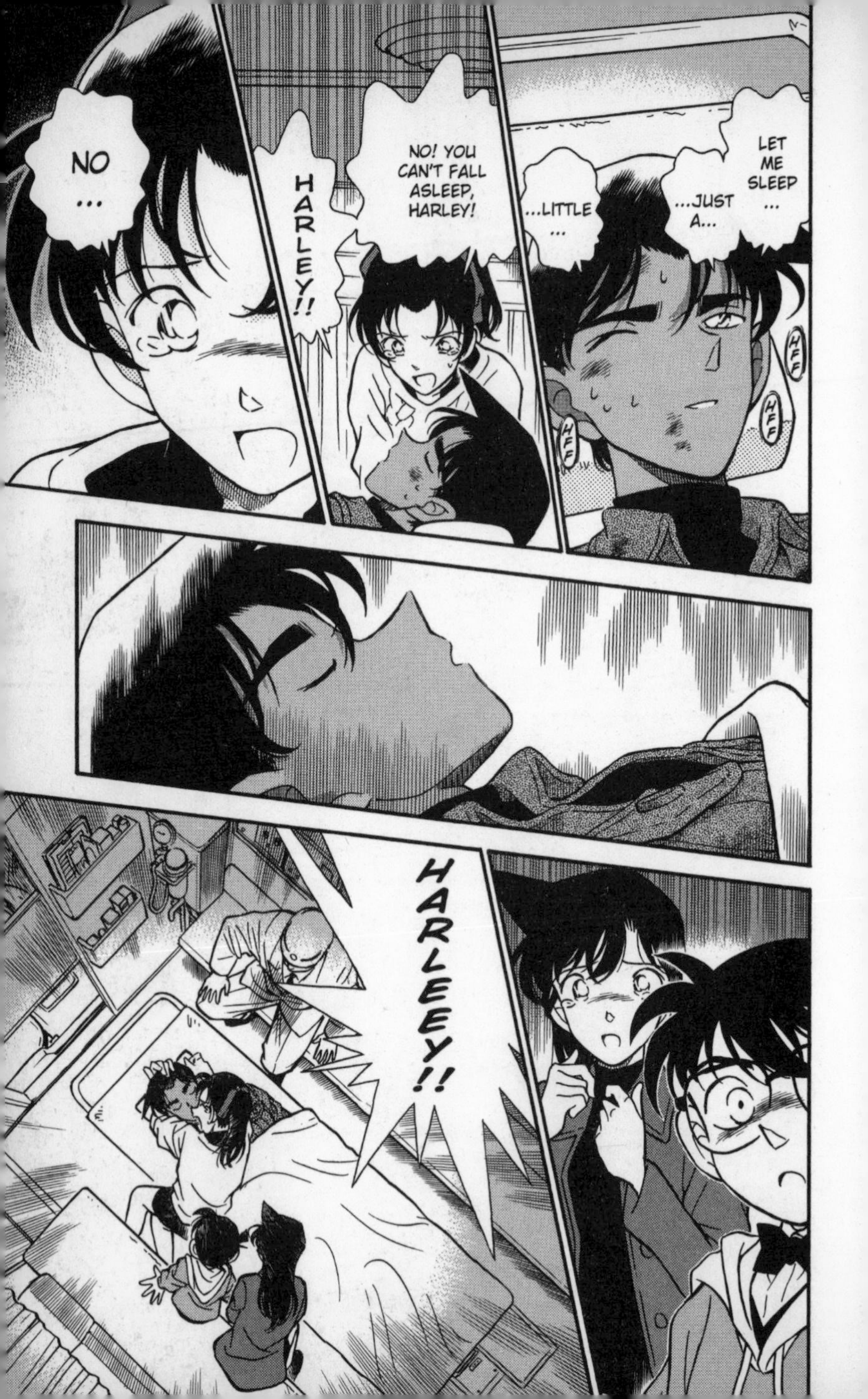
LET ME SLEEP ...
...JUST A...
...LITTLE ...
HFF
HFF
HFF
NO! YOU CAN'T FALL ASLEEP, HARLEY!
HARLEY!!
NO ...
HARLEEY!!

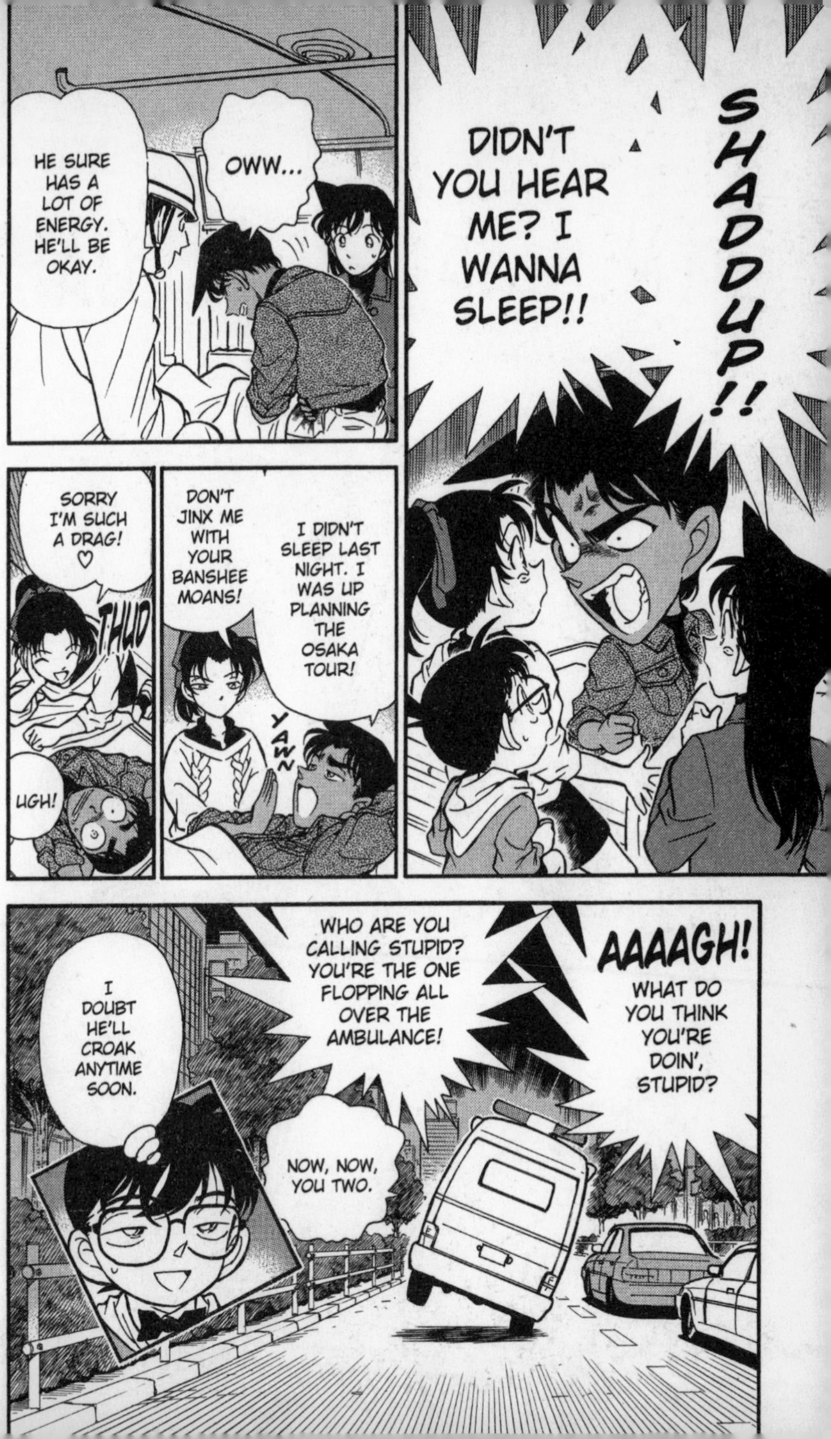
SHADDUP!!
DIDN'T YOU HEAR ME? I WANNA SLEEP!!
OWW...
HE SURE HAS A LOT OF ENERGY. HE'LL BE OKAY.
DON'T JINX ME WITH YOUR BANSHEE MOANS!
I DIDN'T SLEEP LAST NIGHT. I WAS UP PLANNING THE OSAKA TOUR!
YAWN
SORRY I'M SUCH A DRAG! ♡
THUD
UGH!
AAAAGH!
WHAT DO YOU THINK YOU'RE DOIN', STUPID?
WHO ARE YOU CALLING STUPID? YOU'RE THE ONE FLOPPING ALL OVER THE AMBULANCE!
NOW, NOW, YOU TWO.
I DOUBT HE'LL CROAK ANYTIME SOON.

FILE 9: THE TARGETED BALL

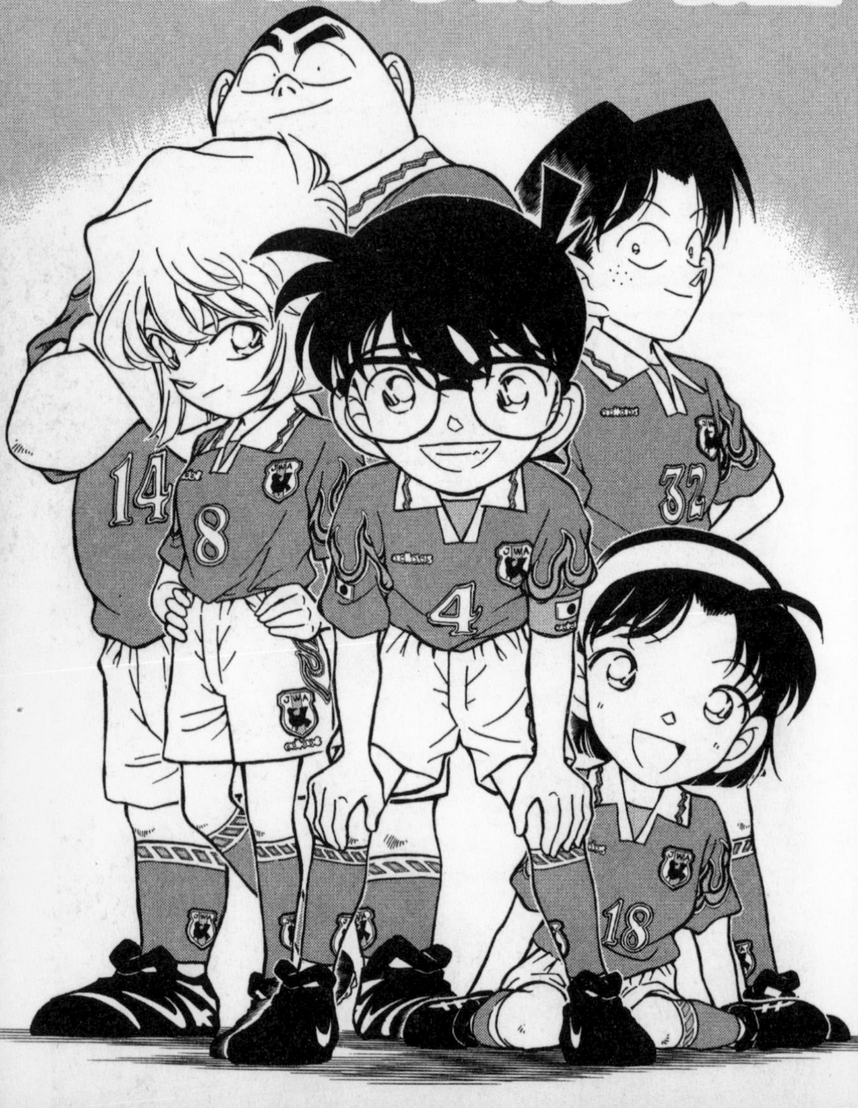

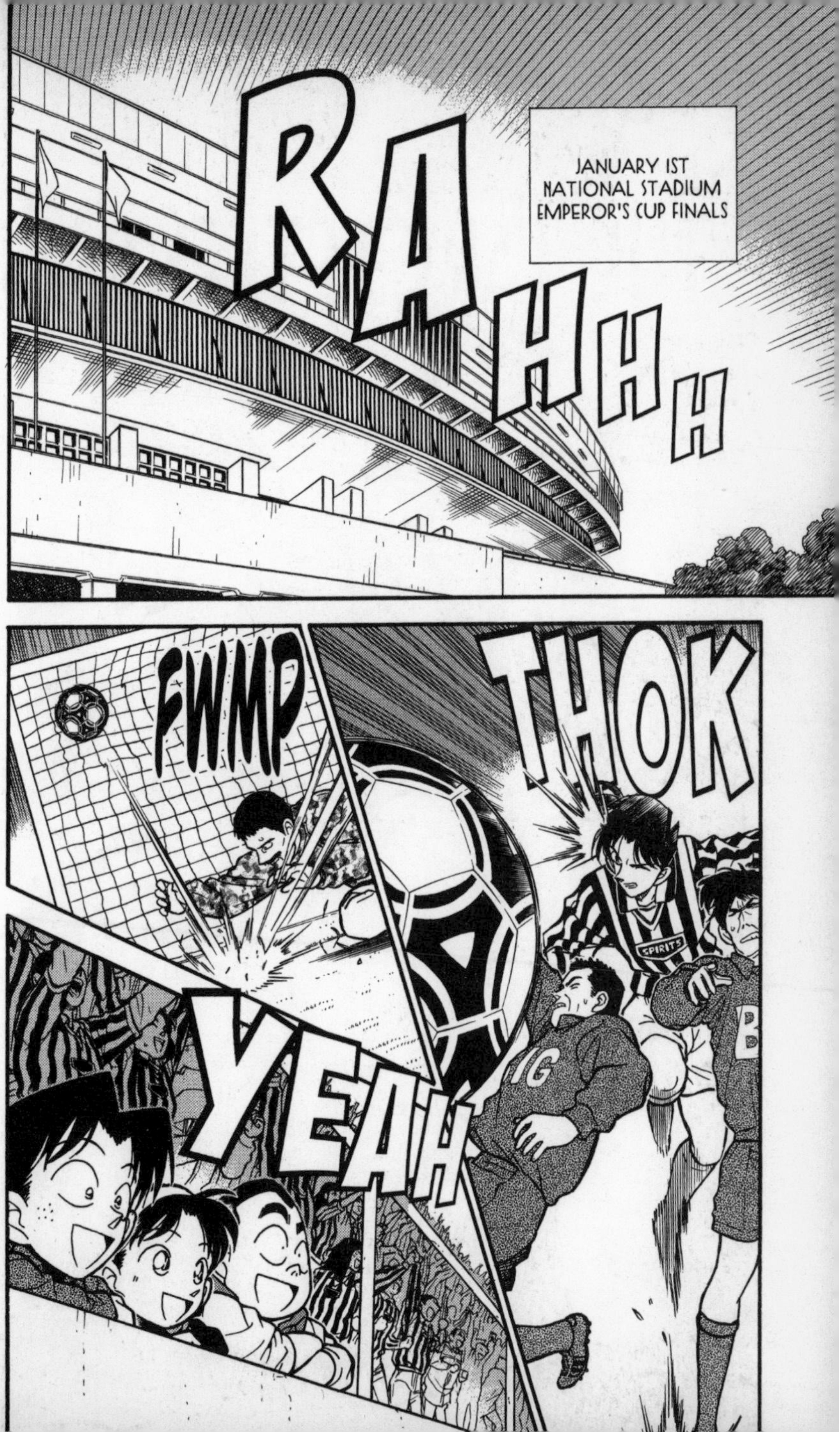
JANUARY 1ST
NATIONAL STADIUM
EMPEROR'S CUP FINALS
RAHHHH
THOK
FWMP
YEAH

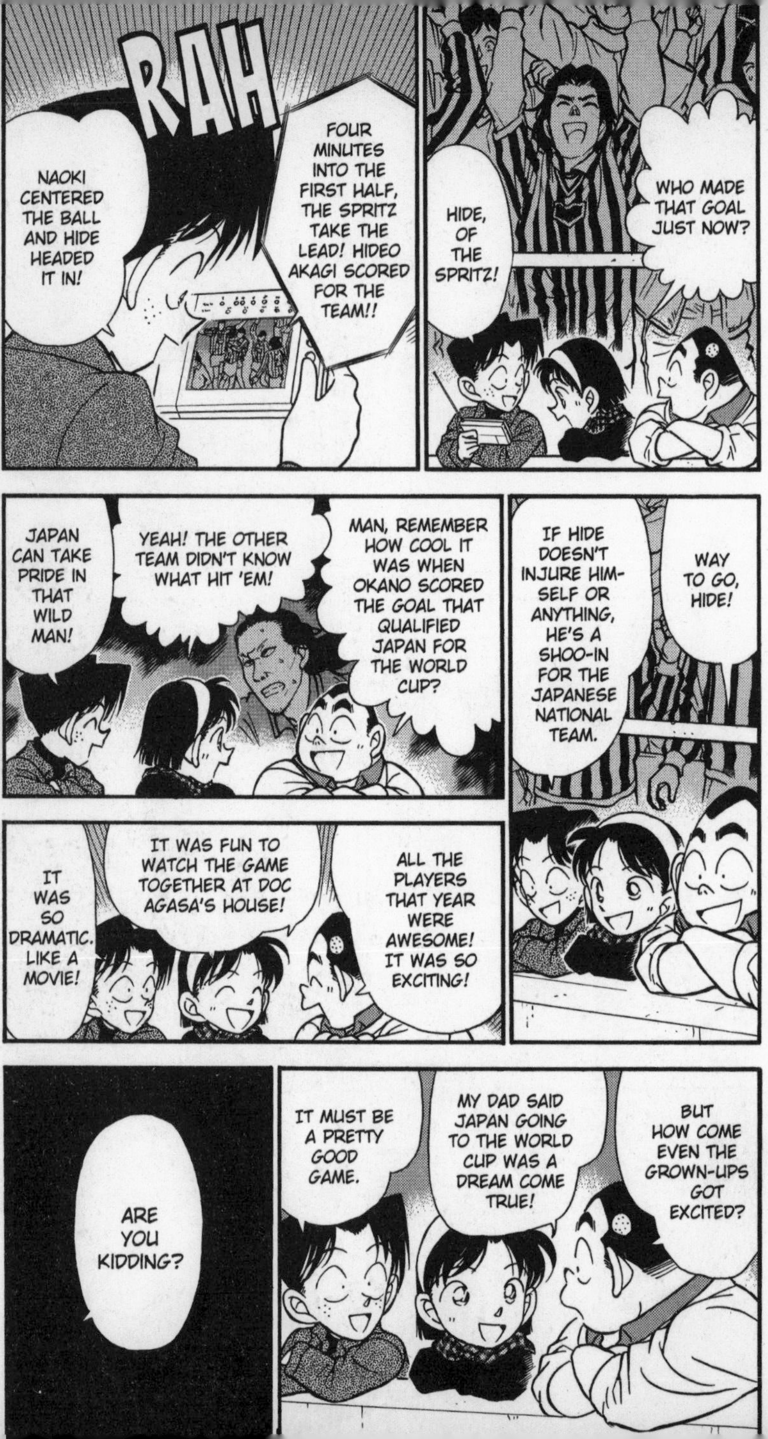
WHO MADE THAT GOAL JUST NOW?
HIDE, OF THE SPRITZ!
RAH
FOUR MINUTES INTO THE FIRST HALF, THE SPRITZ TAKE THE LEAD! HIDEO AKAGI SCORED FOR THE TEAM!!
NAOKI CENTERED THE BALL AND HIDE HEADED IT IN!
WAY TO GO, HIDE!
IF HIDE DOESN'T INJURE HIM-SELF OR ANYTHING, HE'S A SHOO-IN FOR THE JAPANESE NATIONAL TEAM.
MAN, REMEMBER HOW COOL IT WAS WHEN OKANO SCORED THE GOAL THAT QUALIFIED JAPAN FOR THE WORLD CUP?
YEAH! THE OTHER TEAM DIDN'T KNOW WHAT HIT 'EM!
JAPAN CAN TAKE PRIDE IN THAT WILD MAN!
ALL THE PLAYERS THAT YEAR WERE AWESOME! IT WAS SO EXCITING!
IT WAS FUN TO WATCH THE GAME TOGETHER AT DOC AGASA'S HOUSE!
IT WAS SO DRAMATIC. LIKE A MOVIE!
BUT HOW COME EVEN THE GROWN-UPS GOT EXCITED?
MY DAD SAID JAPAN GOING TO THE WORLD CUP WAS A DREAM COME TRUE!
IT MUST BE A PRETTY GOOD GAME.
ARE YOU KIDDING?

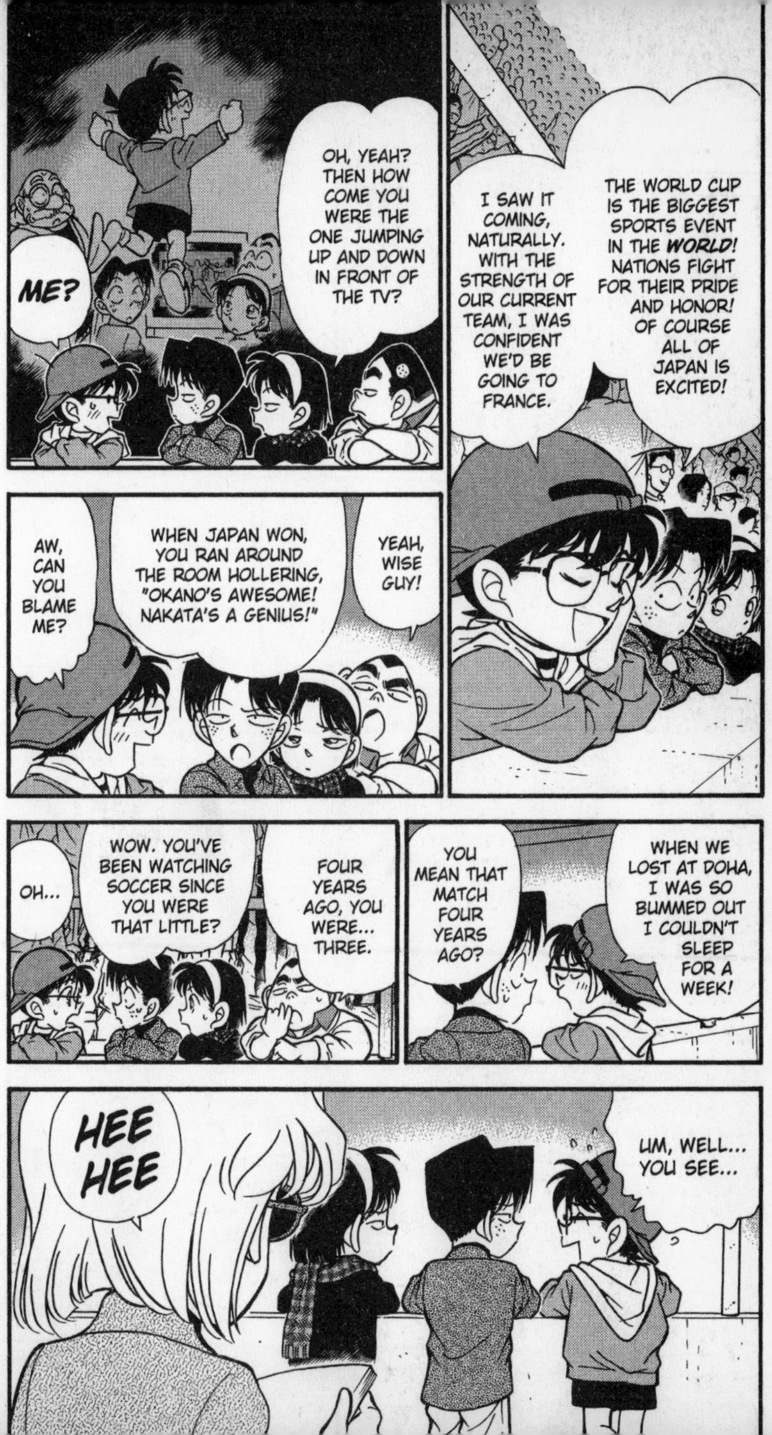
THE WORLD CUP IS THE BIGGEST SPORTS EVENT IN THE ***WORLD***! NATIONS FIGHT FOR THEIR PRIDE AND HONOR! OF COURSE ALL OF JAPAN IS EXCITED!
I SAW IT COMING, NATURALLY. WITH THE STRENGTH OF OUR CURRENT TEAM, I WAS CONFIDENT WE'D BE GOING TO FRANCE.
OH, YEAH? THEN HOW COME YOU WERE THE ONE JUMPING UP AND DOWN IN FRONT OF THE TV?
ME?
YEAH, WISE GUY!
WHEN JAPAN WON, YOU RAN AROUND THE ROOM HOLLERING, "OKANO'S AWESOME! NAKATA'S A GENIUS!"
AW, CAN YOU BLAME ME?
WHEN WE LOST AT DOHA, I WAS SO BUMMED OUT I COULDN'T SLEEP FOR A WEEK!
YOU MEAN THAT MATCH FOUR YEARS AGO?
FOUR YEARS AGO, YOU WERE... THREE.
WOW. YOU'VE BEEN WATCHING SOCCER SINCE YOU WERE THAT LITTLE?
OH...
UM, WELL... YOU SEE...
HEE HEE

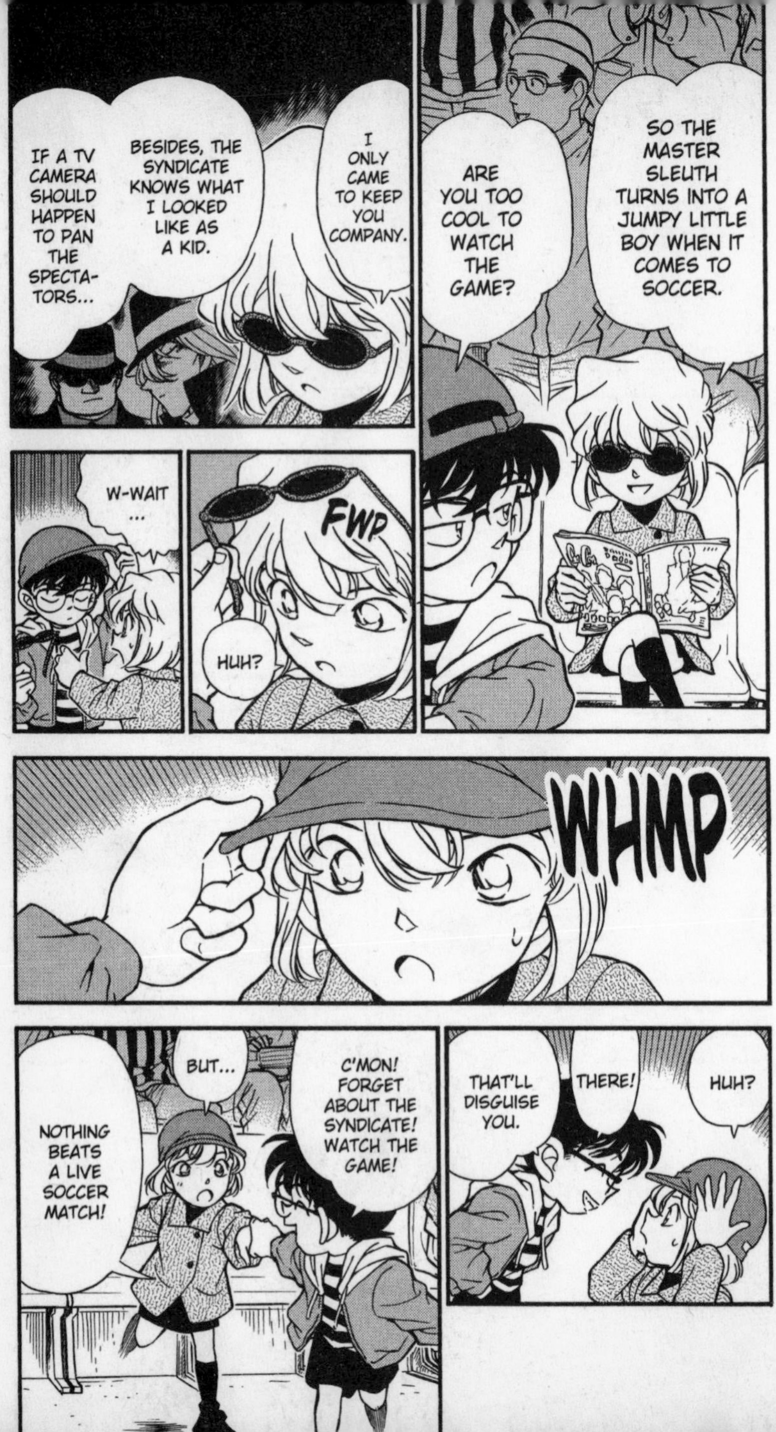
SO THE MASTER SLEUTH TURNS INTO A JUMPY LITTLE BOY WHEN IT COMES TO SOCCER.
ARE YOU TOO COOL TO WATCH THE GAME?
I ONLY CAME TO KEEP YOU COMPANY.
BESIDES, THE SYNDICATE KNOWS WHAT I LOOKED LIKE AS A KID.
IF A TV CAMERA SHOULD HAPPEN TO PAN THE SPECTATORS...
FWP
HUH?
W-WAIT ...
WHMP
HUH?
THERE!
THAT'LL DISGUISE YOU.
C'MON! FORGET ABOUT THE SYNDICATE! WATCH THE GAME!
BUT...
NOTHING BEATS A LIVE SOCCER MATCH!

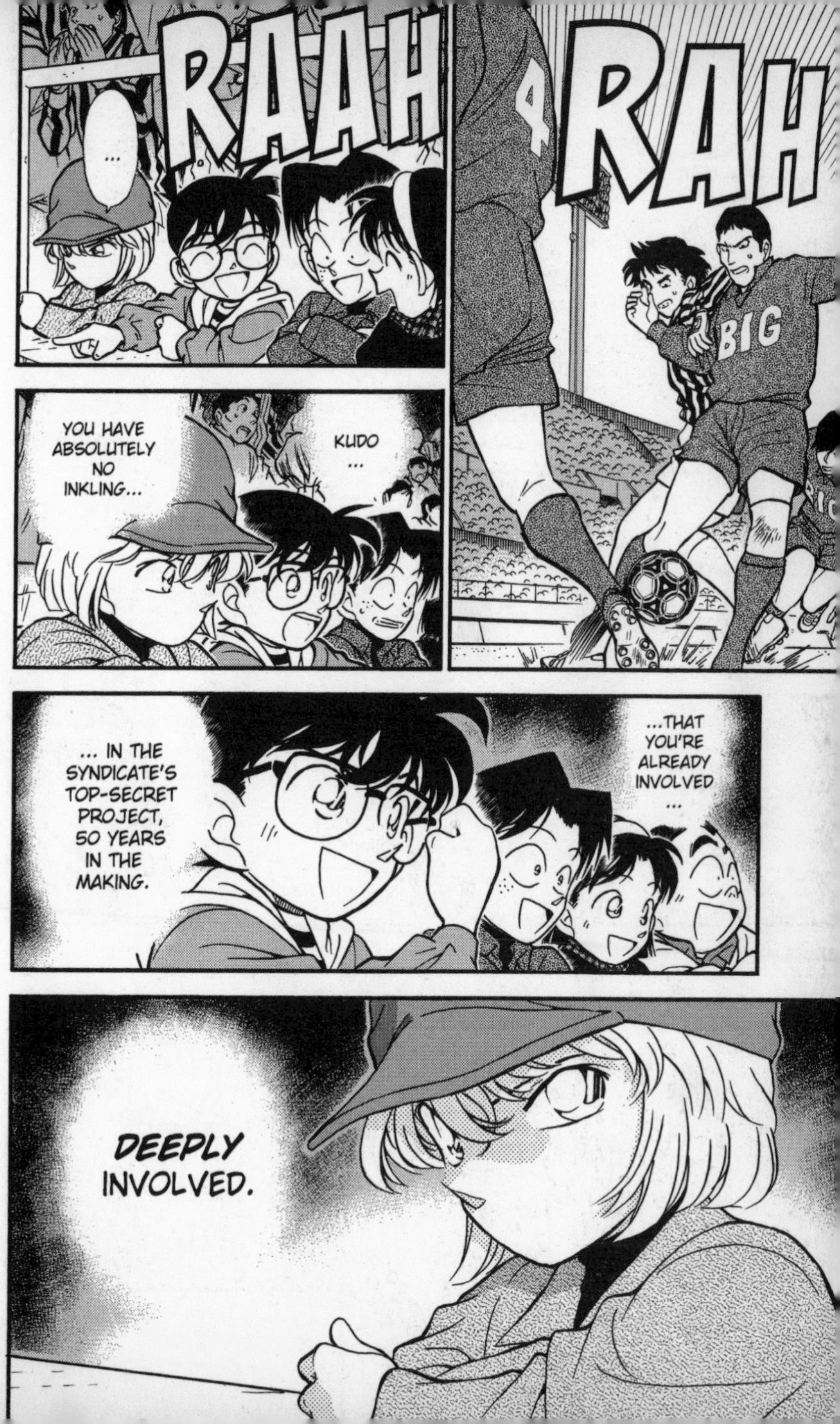
RAH
RAAH
...
KUDO ...
YOU HAVE ABSOLUTELY NO INKLING...
...THAT YOU'RE ALREADY INVOLVED ...
... IN THE SYNDICATE'S TOP-SECRET PROJECT, 50 YEARS IN THE MAKING.
DEEPLY INVOLVED.

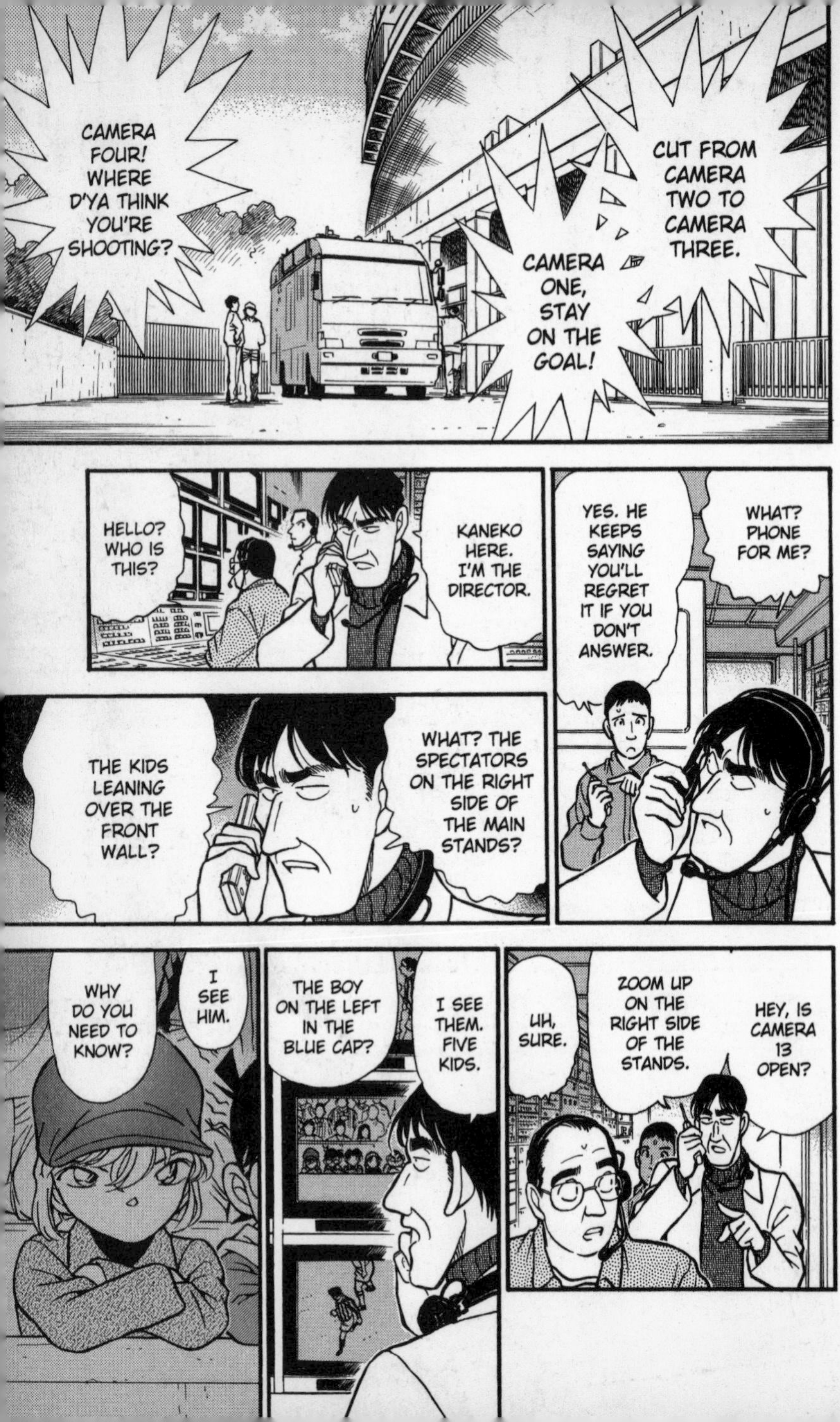
CUT FROM CAMERA TWO TO CAMERA THREE.
CAMERA ONE, STAY ON THE GOAL!
CAMERA FOUR! WHERE D'YA THINK YOU'RE SHOOTING?
WHAT? PHONE FOR ME?
YES. HE KEEPS SAYING YOU'LL REGRET IT IF YOU DON'T ANSWER.
KANEKO HERE. I'M THE DIRECTOR.
HELLO? WHO IS THIS?
WHAT? THE SPECTATORS ON THE RIGHT SIDE OF THE MAIN STANDS?
THE KIDS LEANING OVER THE FRONT WALL?
HEY, IS CAMERA 13 OPEN?
ZOOM UP ON THE RIGHT SIDE OF THE STANDS.
UH, SURE.
I SEE THEM. FIVE KIDS.
THE BOY ON THE LEFT IN THE BLUE CAP?
I SEE HIM.
WHY DO YOU NEED TO KNOW?

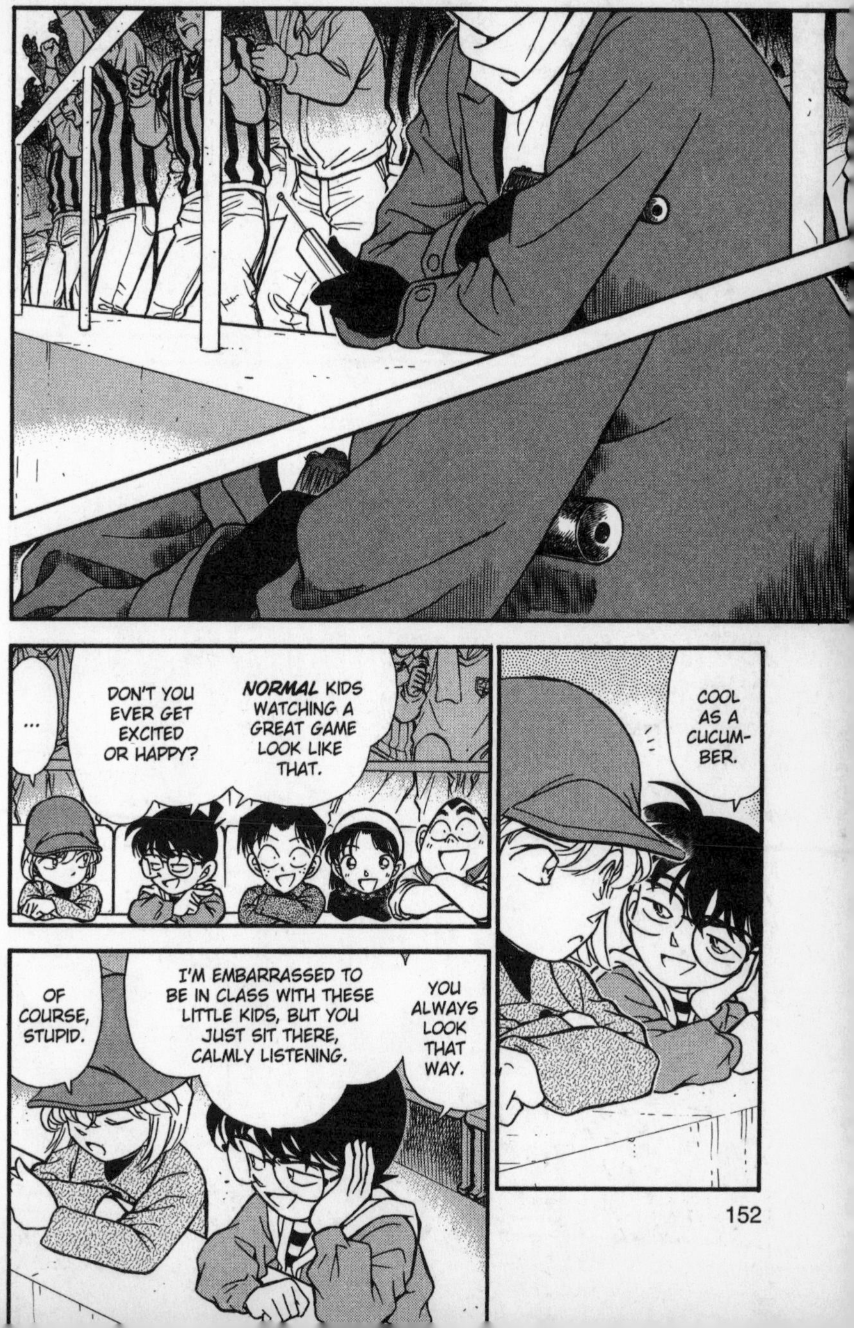
COOL AS A CUCUMBER.
NORMAL KIDS WATCHING A GREAT GAME LOOK LIKE THAT.
DON'T YOU EVER GET EXCITED OR HAPPY?
...
YOU ALWAYS LOOK THAT WAY.
I'M EMBARRASSED TO BE IN CLASS WITH THESE LITTLE KIDS, BUT YOU JUST SIT THERE, CALMLY LISTENING.
OF COURSE, STUPID.

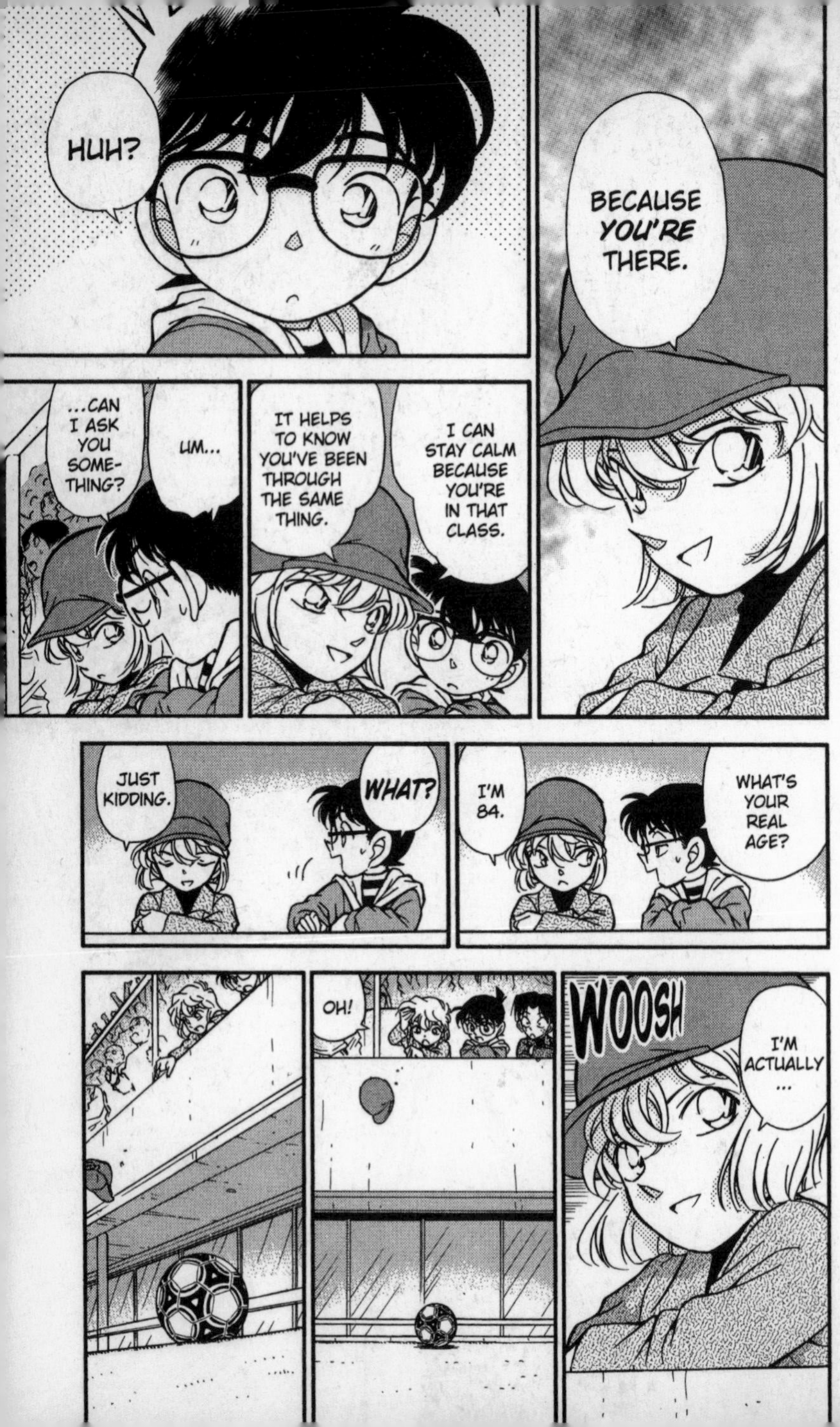
BECAUSE *YOU'RE* THERE.
HUH?
I CAN STAY CALM BECAUSE YOU'RE IN THAT CLASS.
IT HELPS TO KNOW YOU'VE BEEN THROUGH THE SAME THING.
UM...
...CAN I ASK YOU SOME-THING?
WHAT'S YOUR REAL AGE?
I'M 84.
WHAT?
JUST KIDDING.
WOOSH
I'M ACTUALLY ...
OH!

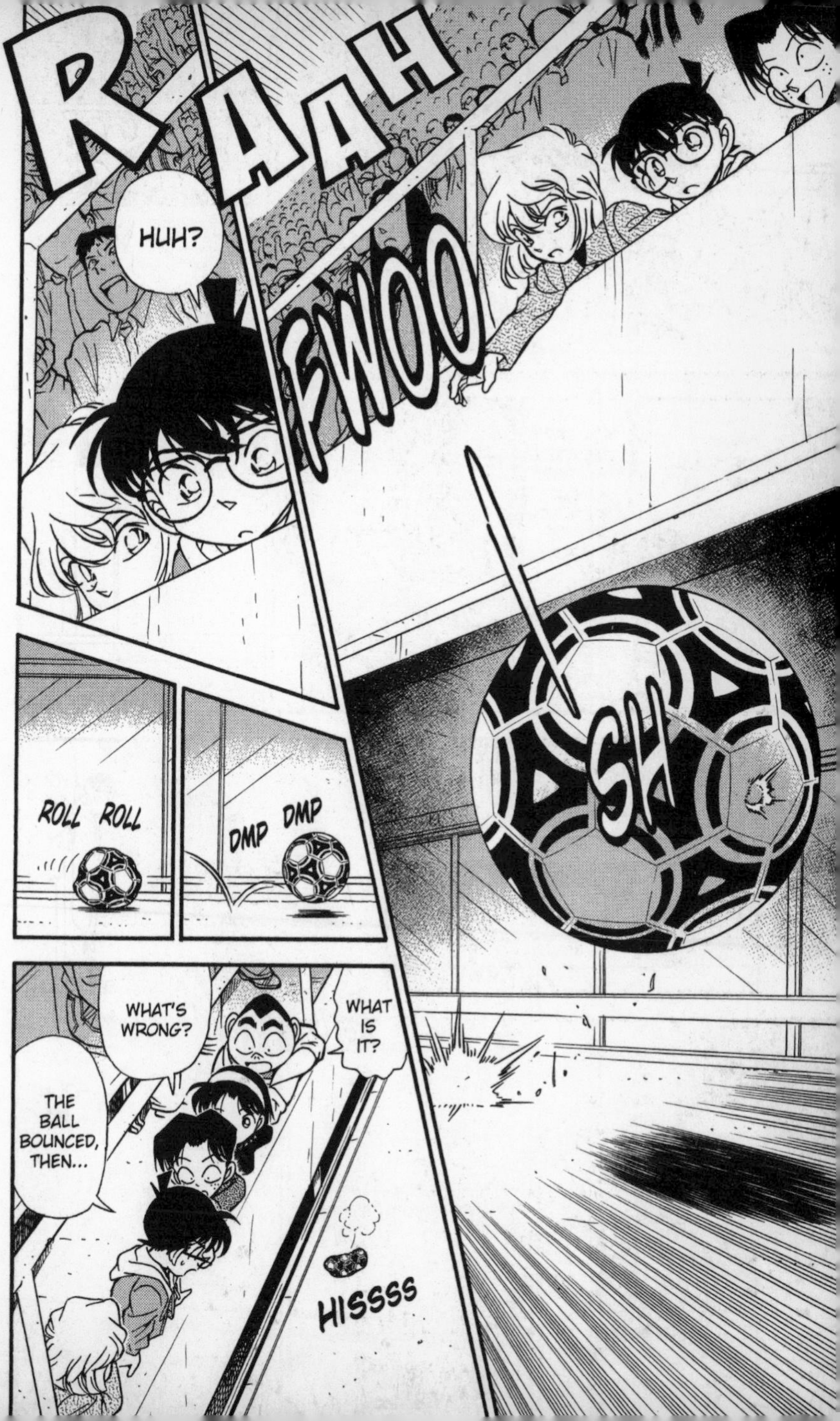
RAAH
HUH?
FWOO
SH
DMP DMP
ROLL ROLL
WHAT IS IT?
WHAT'S WRONG?
THE BALL BOUNCED, THEN...
HISSSS

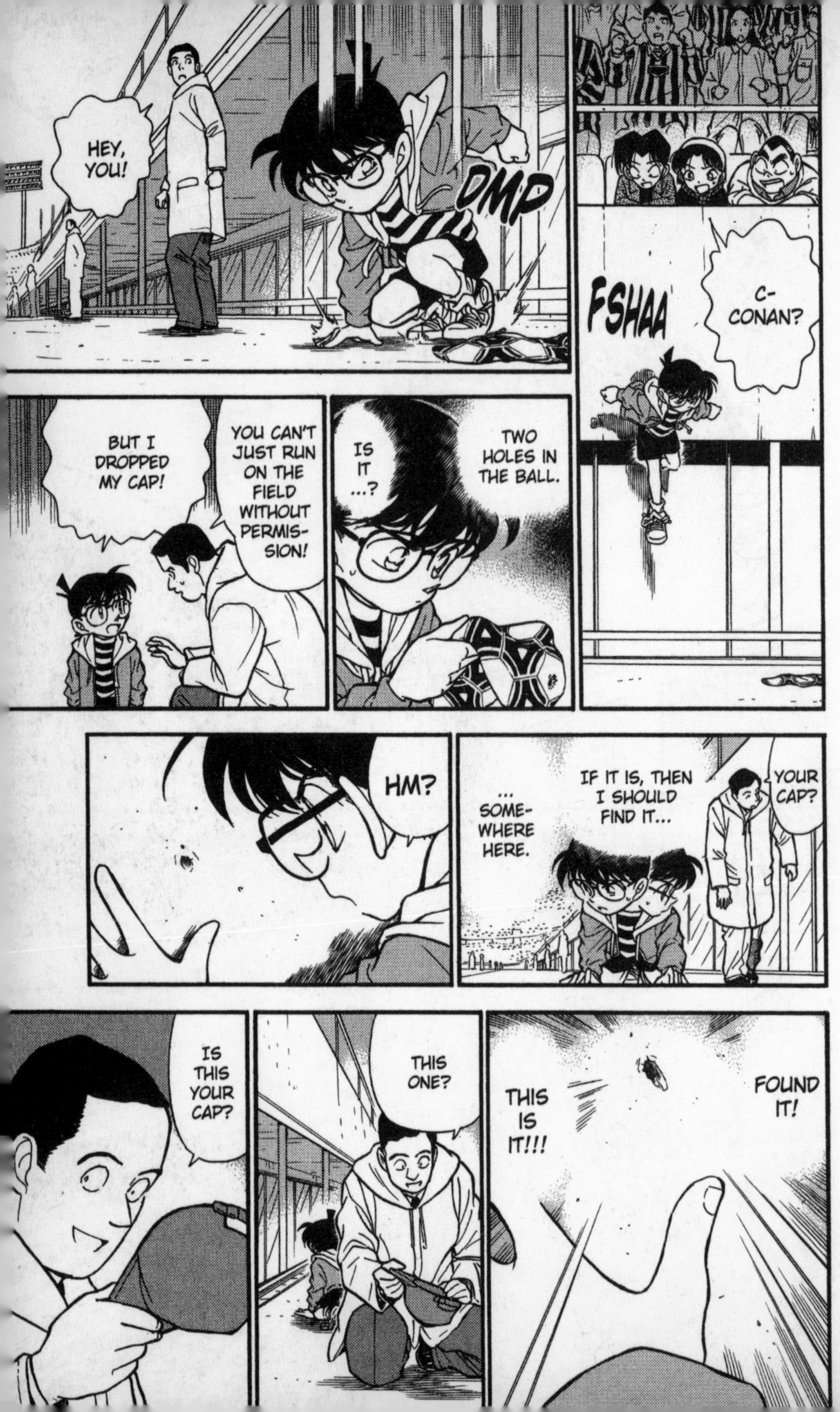
C-CONAN?
FSHAA
DMP
HEY, YOU!
TWO HOLES IN THE BALL.
IS IT ...?
YOU CAN'T JUST RUN ON THE FIELD WITHOUT PERMISSION!
BUT I DROPPED MY CAP!
YOUR CAP?
IF IT IS, THEN I SHOULD FIND IT...
... SOMEWHERE HERE.
HM?
FOUND IT!
THIS IS IT!!!
THIS ONE?
IS THIS YOUR CAP?

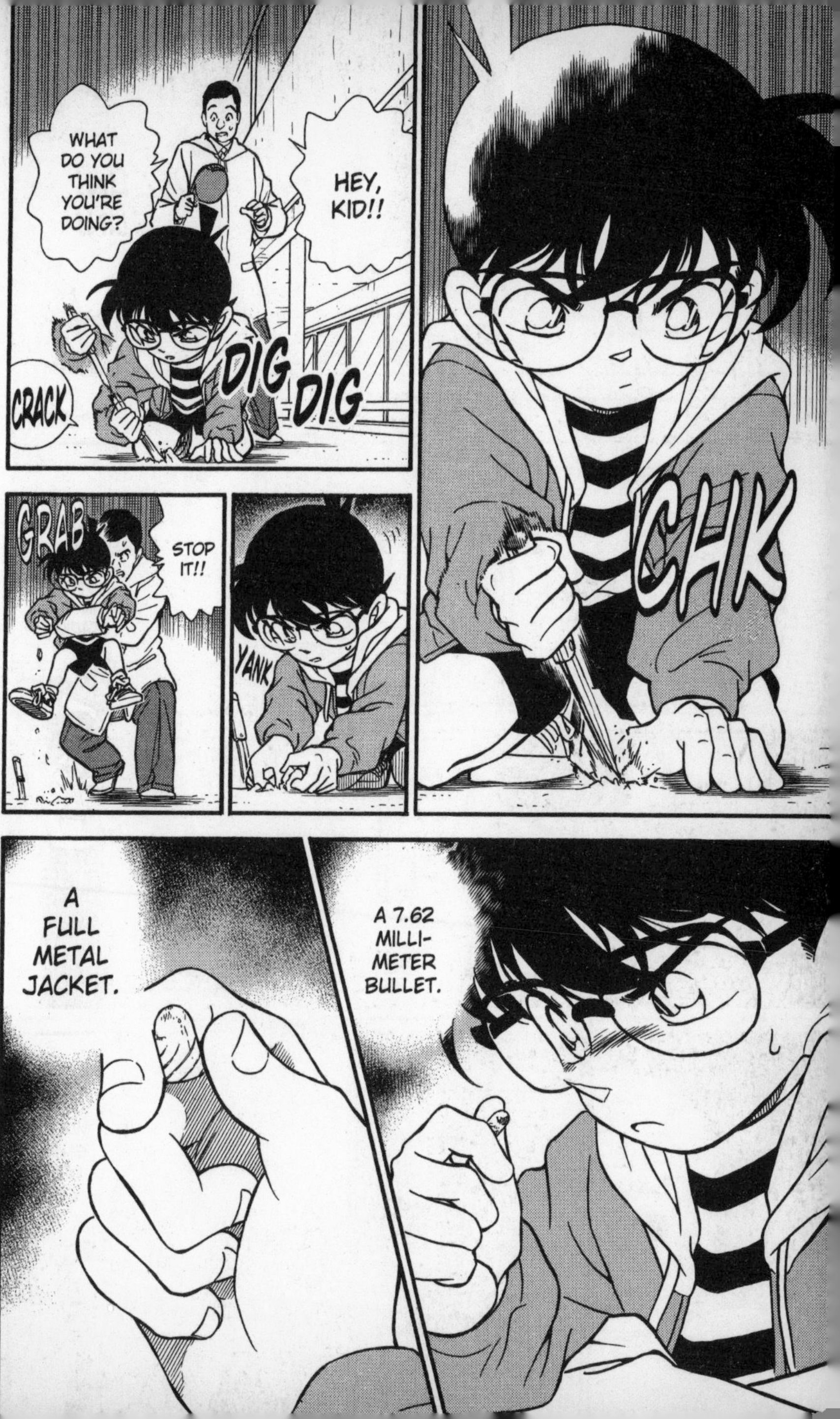
CHK
HEY, KID!!
WHAT DO YOU THINK YOU'RE DOING?
DIG DIG
CRACK
YANK
STOP IT!!
GRAB
A 7.62 MILLI-METER BULLET.
A FULL METAL JACKET.

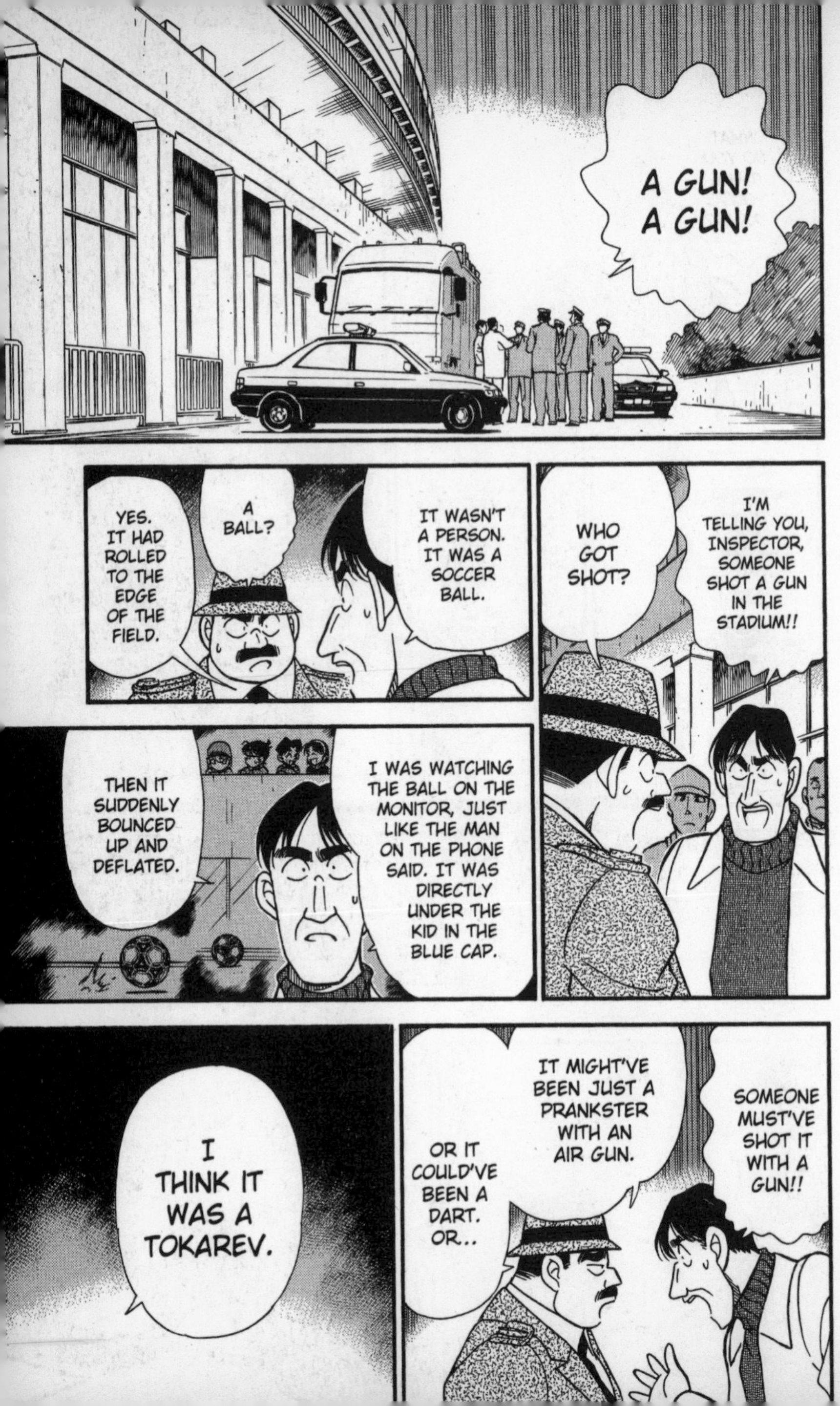
A GUN! A GUN!
I'M TELLING YOU, INSPECTOR, SOMEONE SHOT A GUN IN THE STADIUM!!
WHO GOT SHOT?
IT WASN'T A PERSON. IT WAS A SOCCER BALL.
A BALL?
YES. IT HAD ROLLED TO THE EDGE OF THE FIELD.
I WAS WATCHING THE BALL ON THE MONITOR, JUST LIKE THE MAN ON THE PHONE SAID. IT WAS DIRECTLY UNDER THE KID IN THE BLUE CAP.
THEN IT SUDDENLY BOUNCED UP AND DEFLATED.
SOMEONE MUST'VE SHOT IT WITH A GUN!!
IT MIGHT'VE BEEN JUST A PRANKSTER WITH AN AIR GUN.
OR IT COULD'VE BEEN A DART. OR...
I THINK IT WAS A TOKAREV.

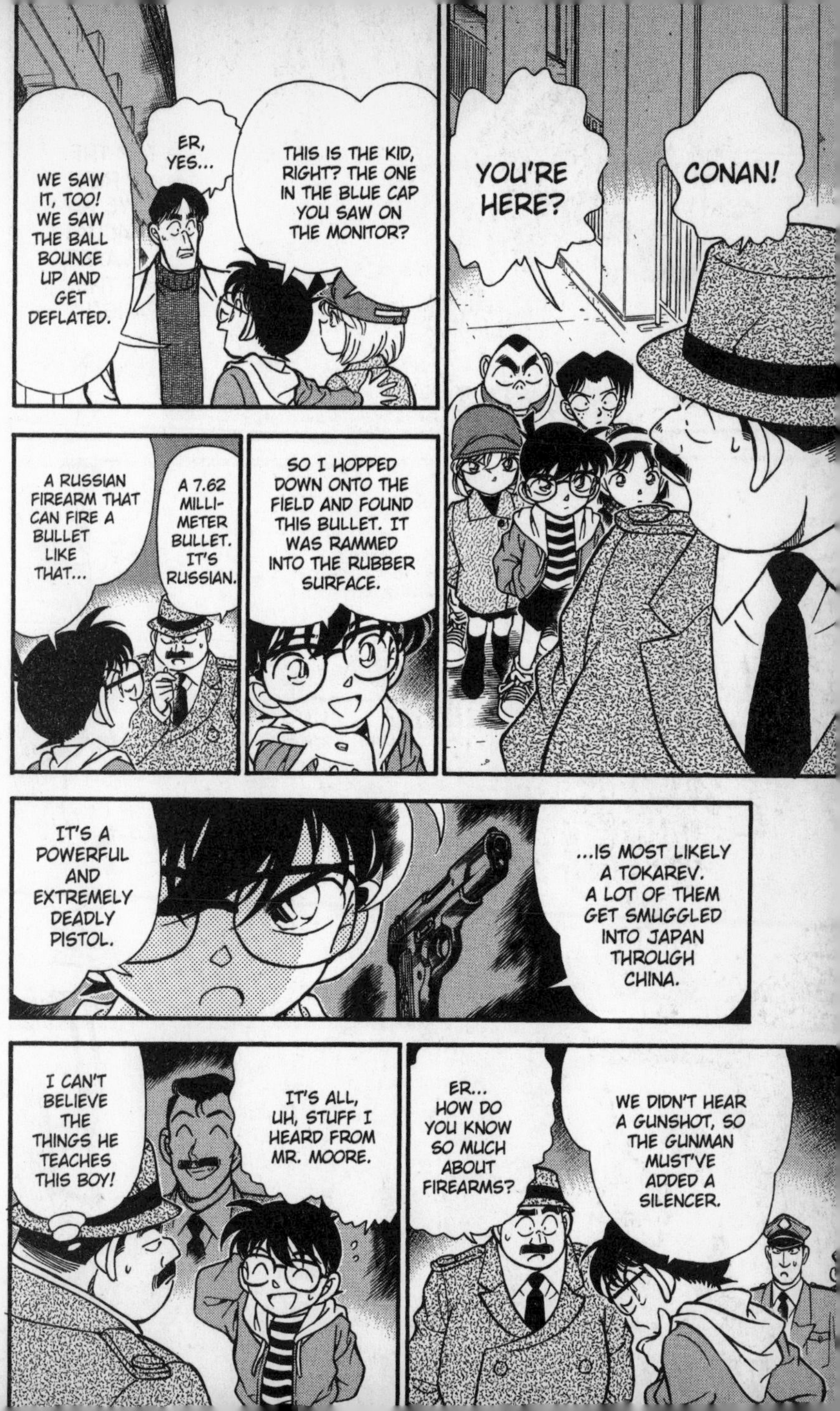
CONAN!
YOU'RE HERE?
THIS IS THE KID, RIGHT? THE ONE IN THE BLUE CAP YOU SAW ON THE MONITOR?
ER, YES...
WE SAW IT, TOO! WE SAW THE BALL BOUNCE UP AND GET DEFLATED.
SO I HOPPED DOWN ONTO THE FIELD AND FOUND THIS BULLET. IT WAS RAMMED INTO THE RUBBER SURFACE.
A 7.62 MILLI-METER BULLET. IT'S RUSSIAN.
A RUSSIAN FIREARM THAT CAN FIRE A BULLET LIKE THAT...
...IS MOST LIKELY A TOKAREV. A LOT OF THEM GET SMUGGLED INTO JAPAN THROUGH CHINA.
IT'S A POWERFUL AND EXTREMELY DEADLY PISTOL.
WE DIDN'T HEAR A GUNSHOT, SO THE GUNMAN MUST'VE ADDED A SILENCER.
ER... HOW DO YOU KNOW SO MUCH ABOUT FIREARMS?
IT'S ALL, UH, STUFF I HEARD FROM MR. MOORE.
I CAN'T BELIEVE THE THINGS HE TEACHES THIS BOY!

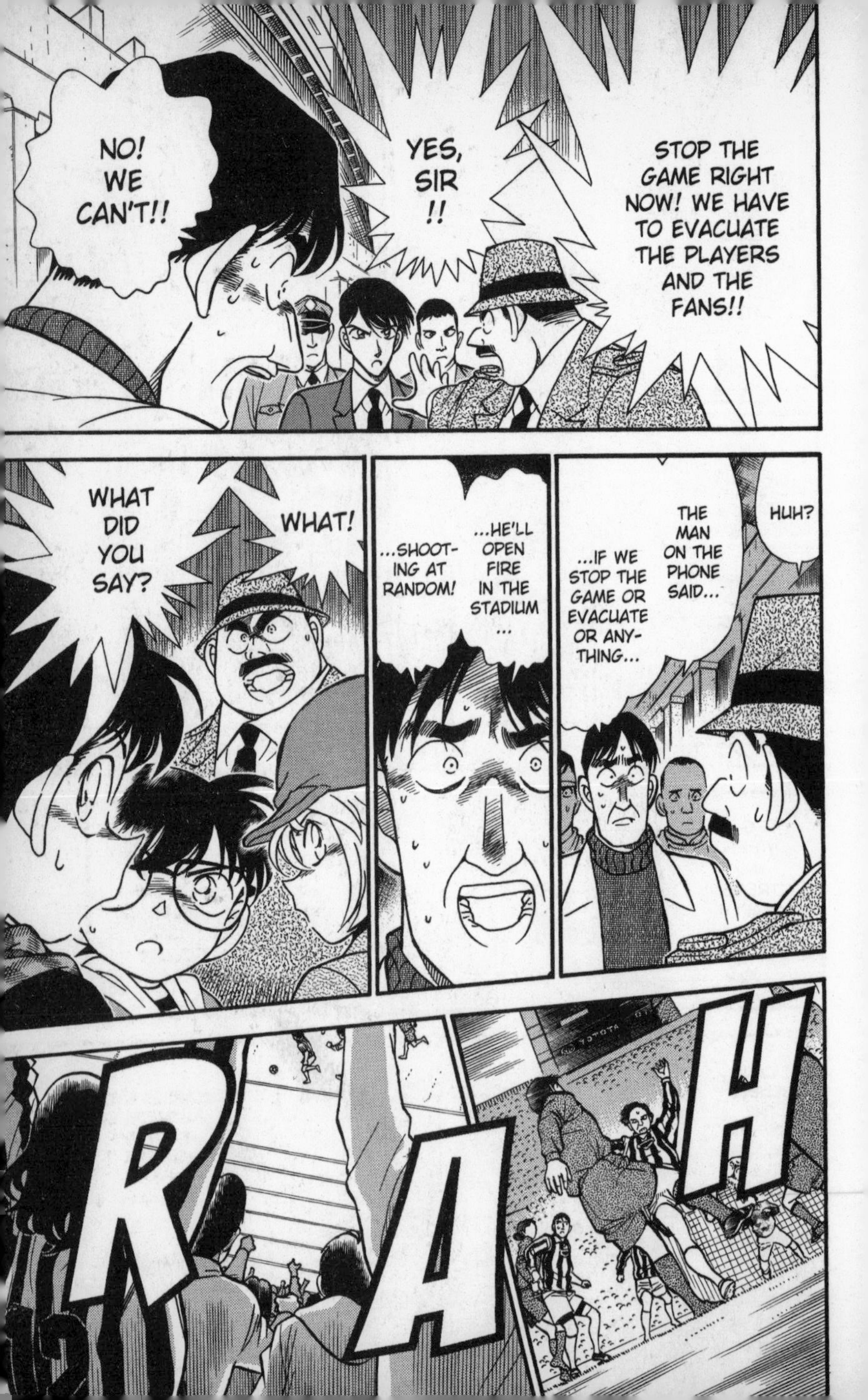
STOP THE GAME RIGHT NOW! WE HAVE TO EVACUATE THE PLAYERS AND THE FANS!!
YES, SIR !!
NO! WE CAN'T!!
HUH?
THE MAN ON THE PHONE SAID...
...IF WE STOP THE GAME OR EVACUATE OR ANY-THING...
...HE'LL OPEN FIRE IN THE STADIUM ...
...SHOOT-ING AT RANDOM!
WHAT!
WHAT DID YOU SAY?
RAH

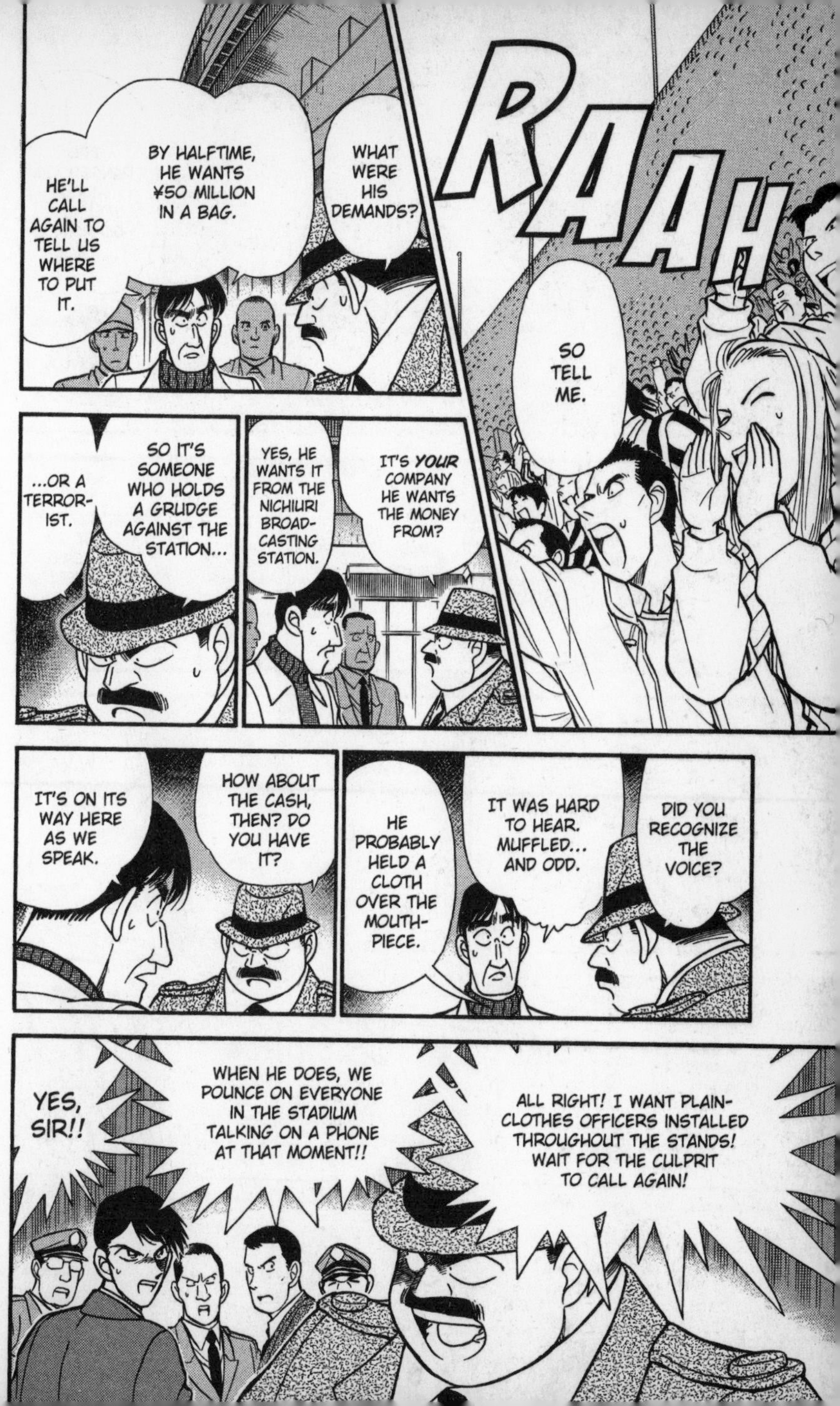
RAAH
SO TELL ME.
WHAT WERE HIS DEMANDS?
BY HALFTIME, HE WANTS ¥50 MILLION IN A BAG.
HE'LL CALL AGAIN TO TELL US WHERE TO PUT IT.
IT'S *YOUR* COMPANY HE WANTS THE MONEY FROM?
YES, HE WANTS IT FROM THE NICHIURI BROAD-CASTING STATION.
SO IT'S SOMEONE WHO HOLDS A GRUDGE AGAINST THE STATION...
...OR A TERROR-IST.
DID YOU RECOGNIZE THE VOICE?
IT WAS HARD TO HEAR. MUFFLED... AND ODD.
HE PROBABLY HELD A CLOTH OVER THE MOUTH-PIECE.
HOW ABOUT THE CASH, THEN? DO YOU HAVE IT?
IT'S ON ITS WAY HERE AS WE SPEAK.
ALL RIGHT! I WANT PLAIN-CLOTHES OFFICERS INSTALLED THROUGHOUT THE STANDS! WAIT FOR THE CULPRIT TO CALL AGAIN!
WHEN HE DOES, WE POUNCE ON EVERYONE IN THE STADIUM TALKING ON A PHONE AT THAT MOMENT!!
YES, SIR!!

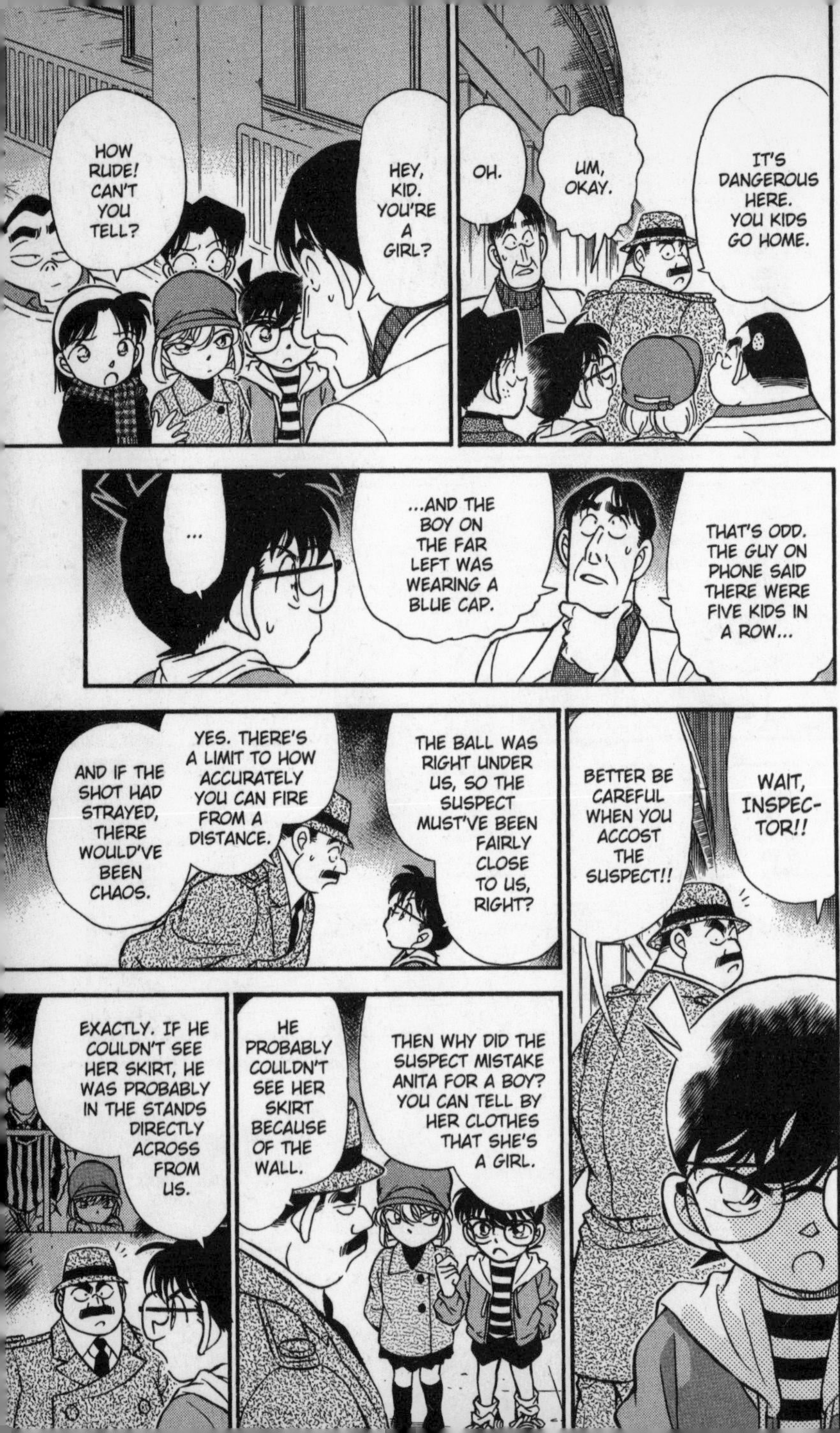
IT'S DANGEROUS HERE. YOU KIDS GO HOME.
UM, OKAY.
OH.
HEY, KID. YOU'RE A GIRL?
HOW RUDE! CAN'T YOU TELL?
THAT'S ODD. THE GUY ON PHONE SAID THERE WERE FIVE KIDS IN A ROW...
...AND THE BOY ON THE FAR LEFT WAS WEARING A BLUE CAP.
...
WAIT, INSPECTOR!!
BETTER BE CAREFUL WHEN YOU ACCOST THE SUSPECT!!
THE BALL WAS RIGHT UNDER US, SO THE SUSPECT MUST'VE BEEN FAIRLY CLOSE TO US, RIGHT?
YES. THERE'S A LIMIT TO HOW ACCURATELY YOU CAN FIRE FROM A DISTANCE.
AND IF THE SHOT HAD STRAYED, THERE WOULD'VE BEEN CHAOS.
THEN WHY DID THE SUSPECT MISTAKE ANITA FOR A BOY? YOU CAN TELL BY HER CLOTHES THAT SHE'S A GIRL.
HE PROBABLY COULDN'T SEE HER SKIRT BECAUSE OF THE WALL.
EXACTLY. IF HE COULDN'T SEE HER SKIRT, HE WAS PROBABLY IN THE STANDS DIRECTLY ACROSS FROM US.

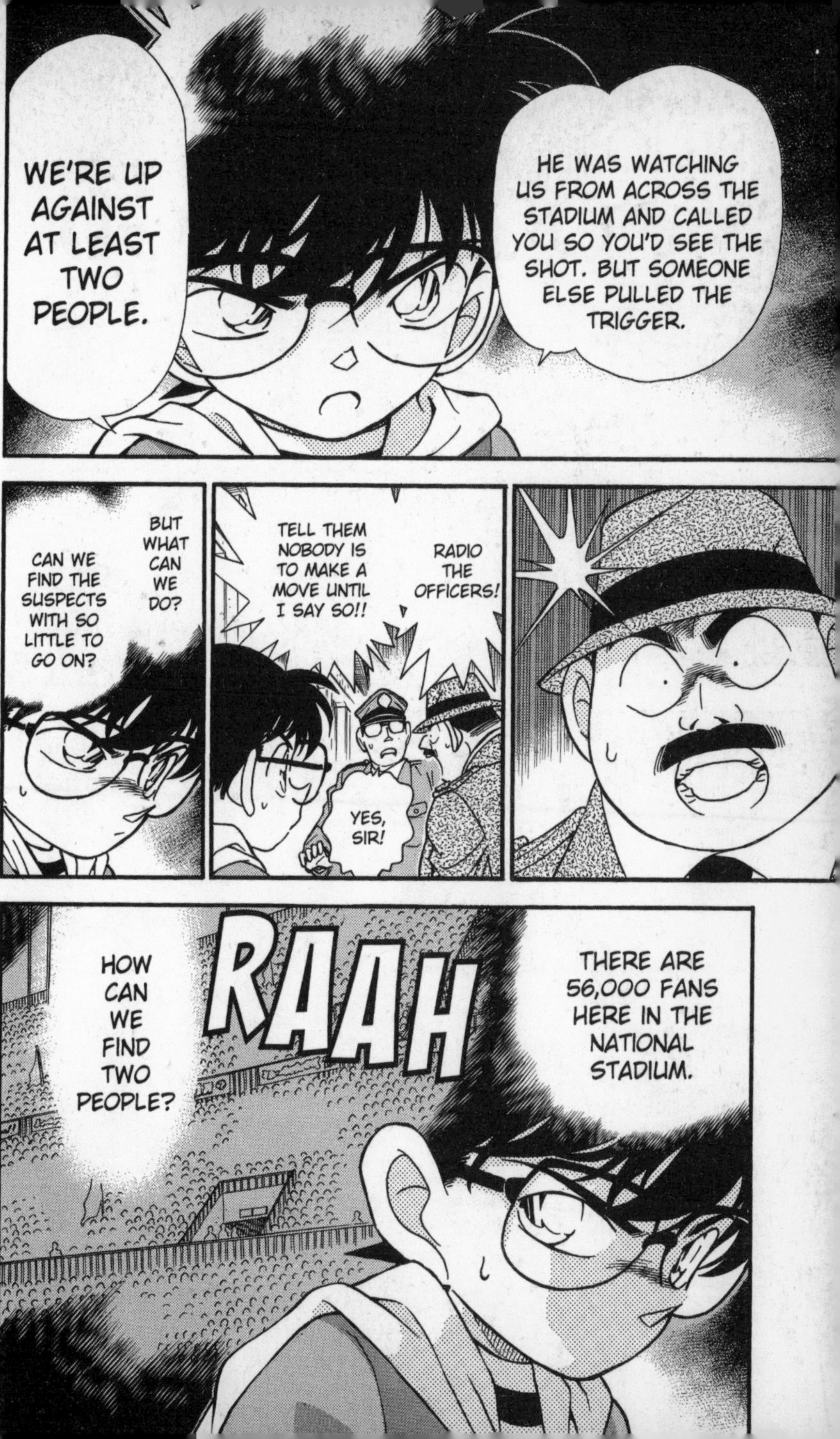
HE WAS WATCHING US FROM ACROSS THE STADIUM AND CALLED YOU SO YOU'D SEE THE SHOT. BUT SOMEONE ELSE PULLED THE TRIGGER.
WE'RE UP AGAINST AT LEAST TWO PEOPLE.
RADIO THE OFFICERS!
TELL THEM NOBODY IS TO MAKE A MOVE UNTIL I SAY SO!!
YES, SIR!
BUT WHAT CAN WE DO?
CAN WE FIND THE SUSPECTS WITH SO LITTLE TO GO ON?
THERE ARE 56,000 FANS HERE IN THE NATIONAL STADIUM.
RAAH
HOW CAN WE FIND TWO PEOPLE?

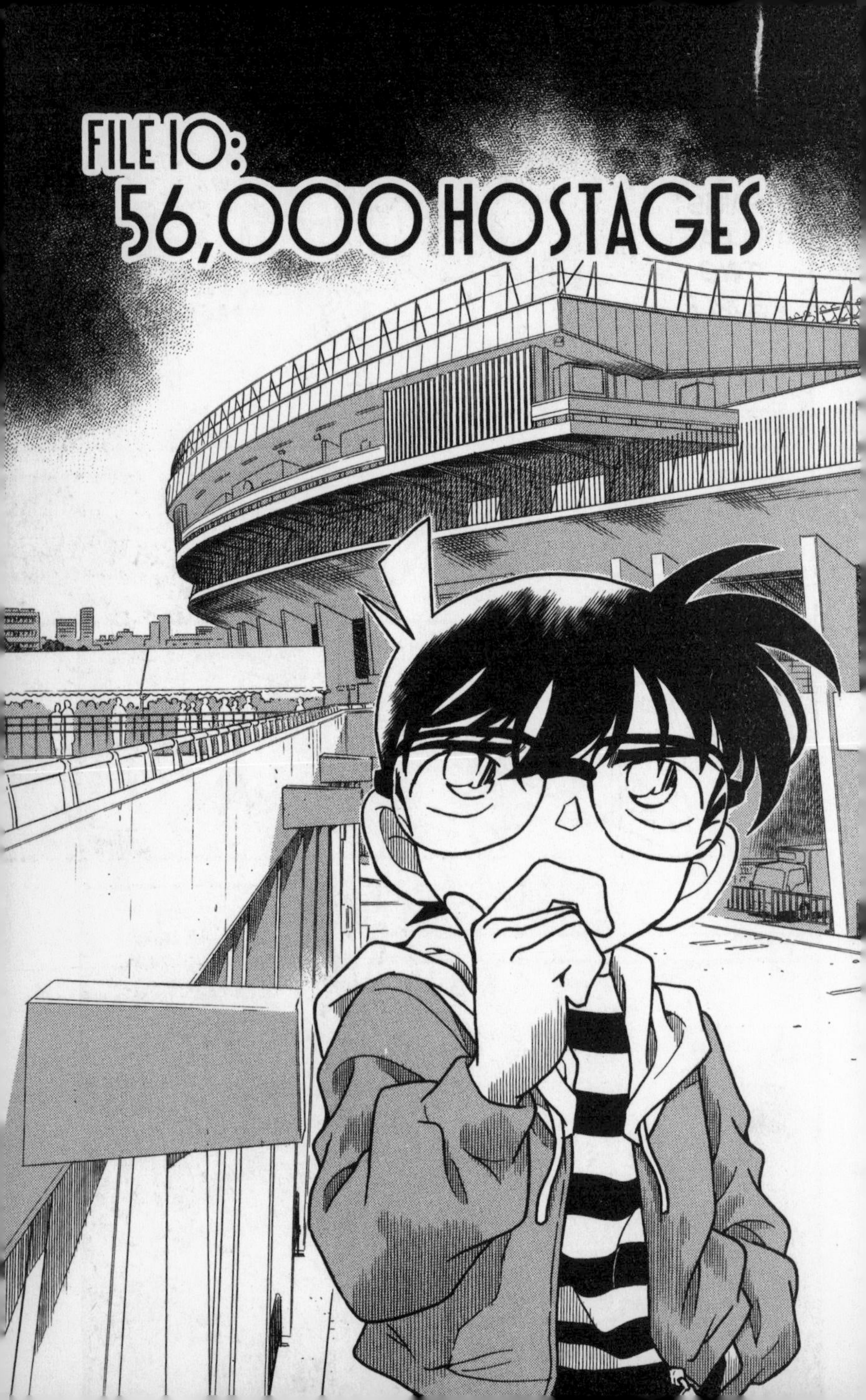
FILE 10:
56,000 HOSTAGES

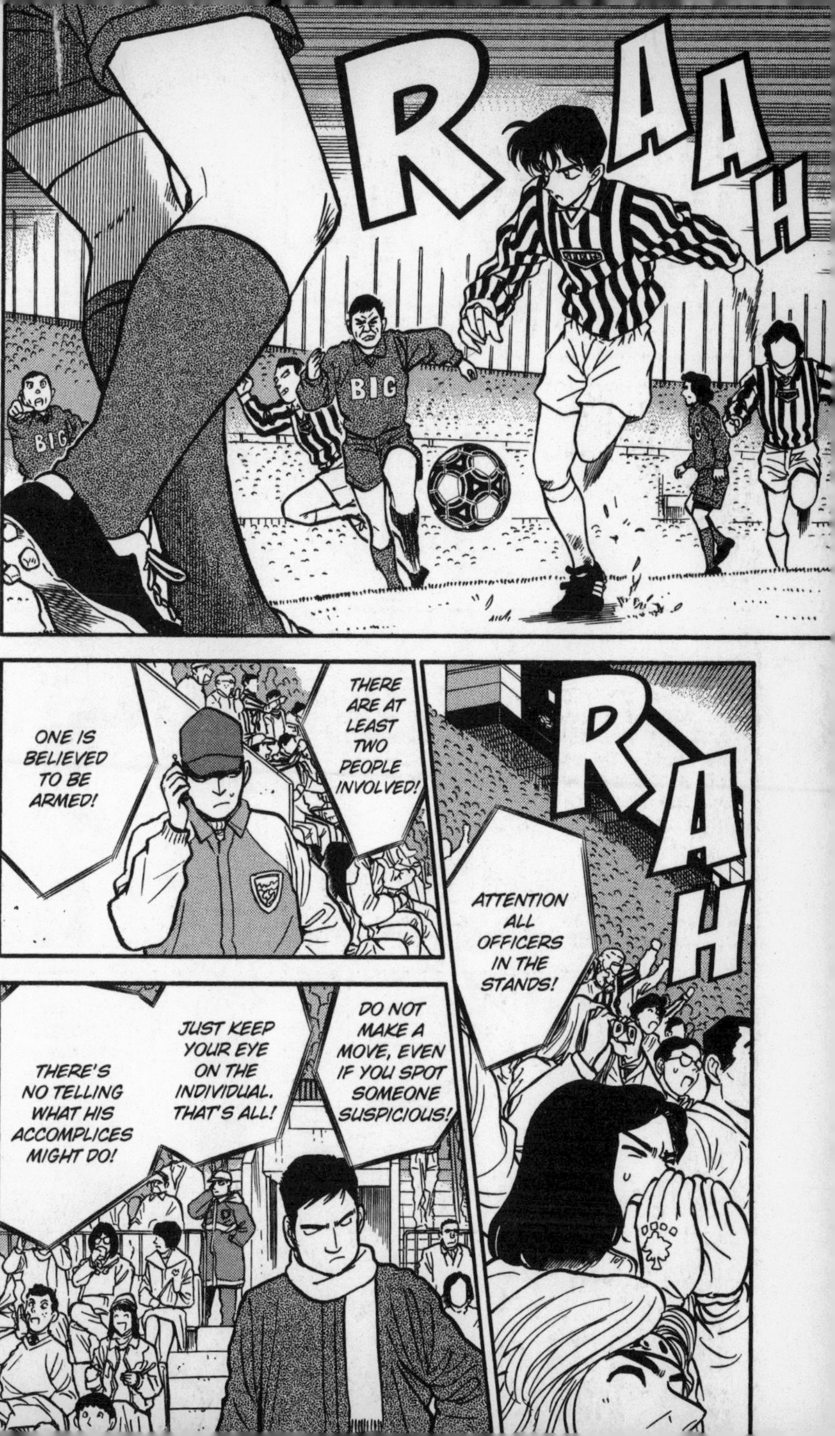
RAAAH
RAAH
ATTENTION ALL OFFICERS IN THE STANDS!
THERE ARE AT LEAST TWO PEOPLE INVOLVED!
ONE IS BELIEVED TO BE ARMED!
DO NOT MAKE A MOVE, EVEN IF YOU SPOT SOMEONE SUSPICIOUS!
JUST KEEP YOUR EYE ON THE INDIVIDUAL. THAT'S ALL!
THERE'S NO TELLING WHAT HIS ACCOMPLICES MIGHT DO!

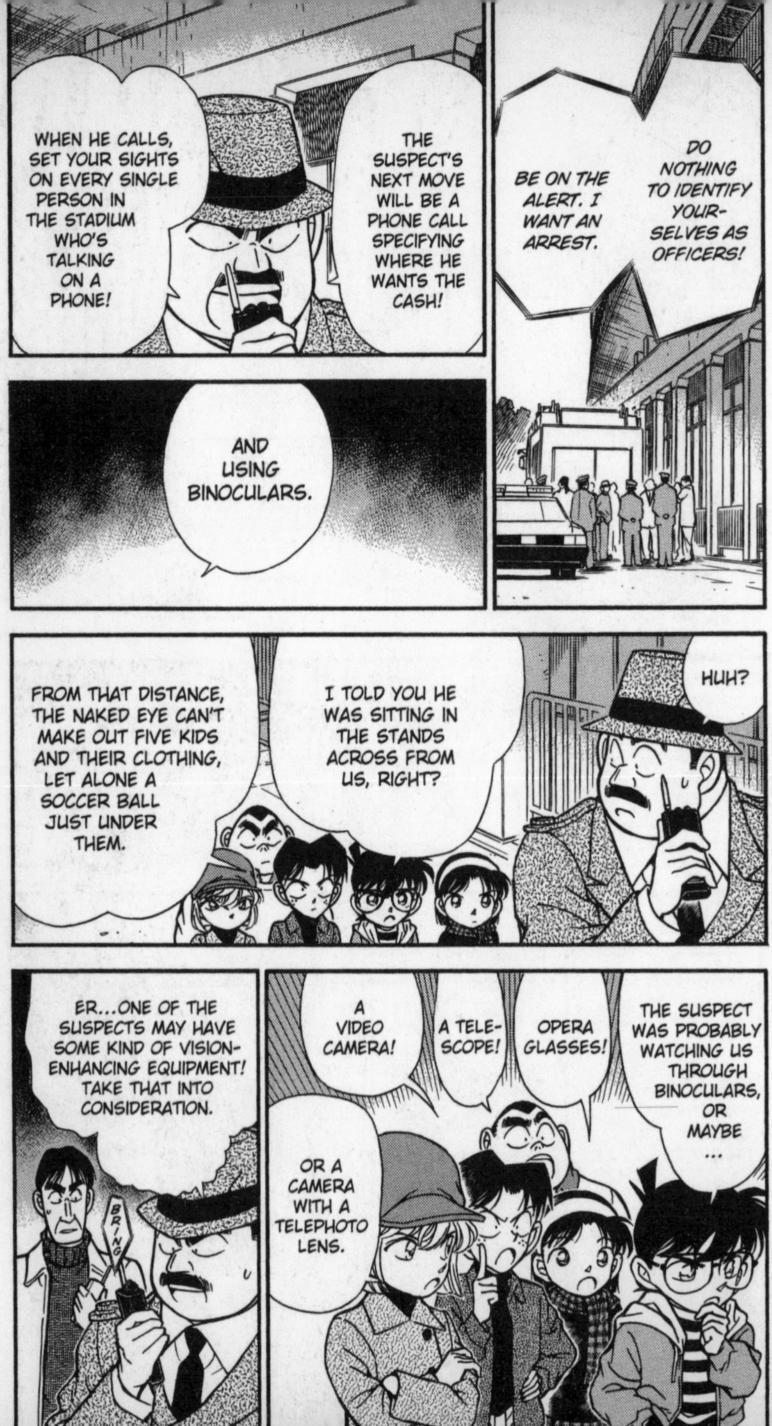
DO NOTHING TO IDENTIFY YOUR-SELVES AS OFFICERS!
BE ON THE ALERT. I WANT AN ARREST.
THE SUSPECT'S NEXT MOVE WILL BE A PHONE CALL SPECIFYING WHERE HE WANTS THE CASH!
WHEN HE CALLS, SET YOUR SIGHTS ON EVERY SINGLE PERSON IN THE STADIUM WHO'S TALKING ON A PHONE!
AND USING BINOCULARS.
HUH?
I TOLD YOU HE WAS SITTING IN THE STANDS ACROSS FROM US, RIGHT?
FROM THAT DISTANCE, THE NAKED EYE CAN'T MAKE OUT FIVE KIDS AND THEIR CLOTHING, LET ALONE A SOCCER BALL JUST UNDER THEM.
THE SUSPECT WAS PROBABLY WATCHING US THROUGH BINOCULARS, OR MAYBE...
OPERA GLASSES!
A TELE-SCOPE!
A VIDEO CAMERA!
OR A CAMERA WITH A TELEPHOTO LENS.
ER...ONE OF THE SUSPECTS MAY HAVE SOME KIND OF VISION-ENHANCING EQUIPMENT! TAKE THAT INTO CONSIDERATION.
BRING

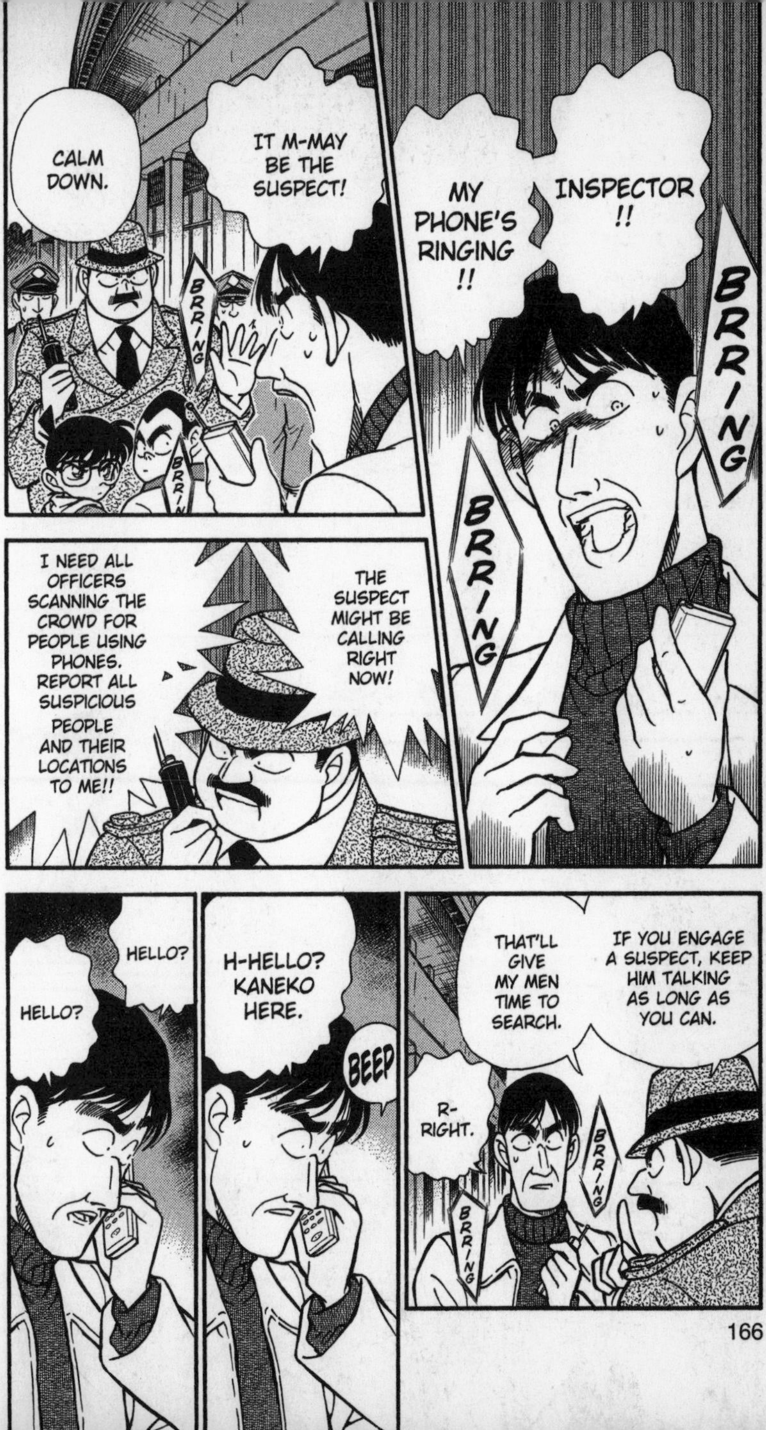
INSPECTOR!!
MY PHONE'S RINGING!!
BRRING
BRRING
IT M-MAY BE THE SUSPECT!
CALM DOWN.
BRRING
BRRIN
THE SUSPECT MIGHT BE CALLING RIGHT NOW!
I NEED ALL OFFICERS SCANNING THE CROWD FOR PEOPLE USING PHONES. REPORT ALL SUSPICIOUS PEOPLE AND THEIR LOCATIONS TO ME!!
IF YOU ENGAGE A SUSPECT, KEEP HIM TALKING AS LONG AS YOU CAN.
THAT'LL GIVE MY MEN TIME TO SEARCH.
R-RIGHT.
BRRING
BRRING
BEEP
H-HELLO? KANEKO HERE.
HELLO?
HELLO?

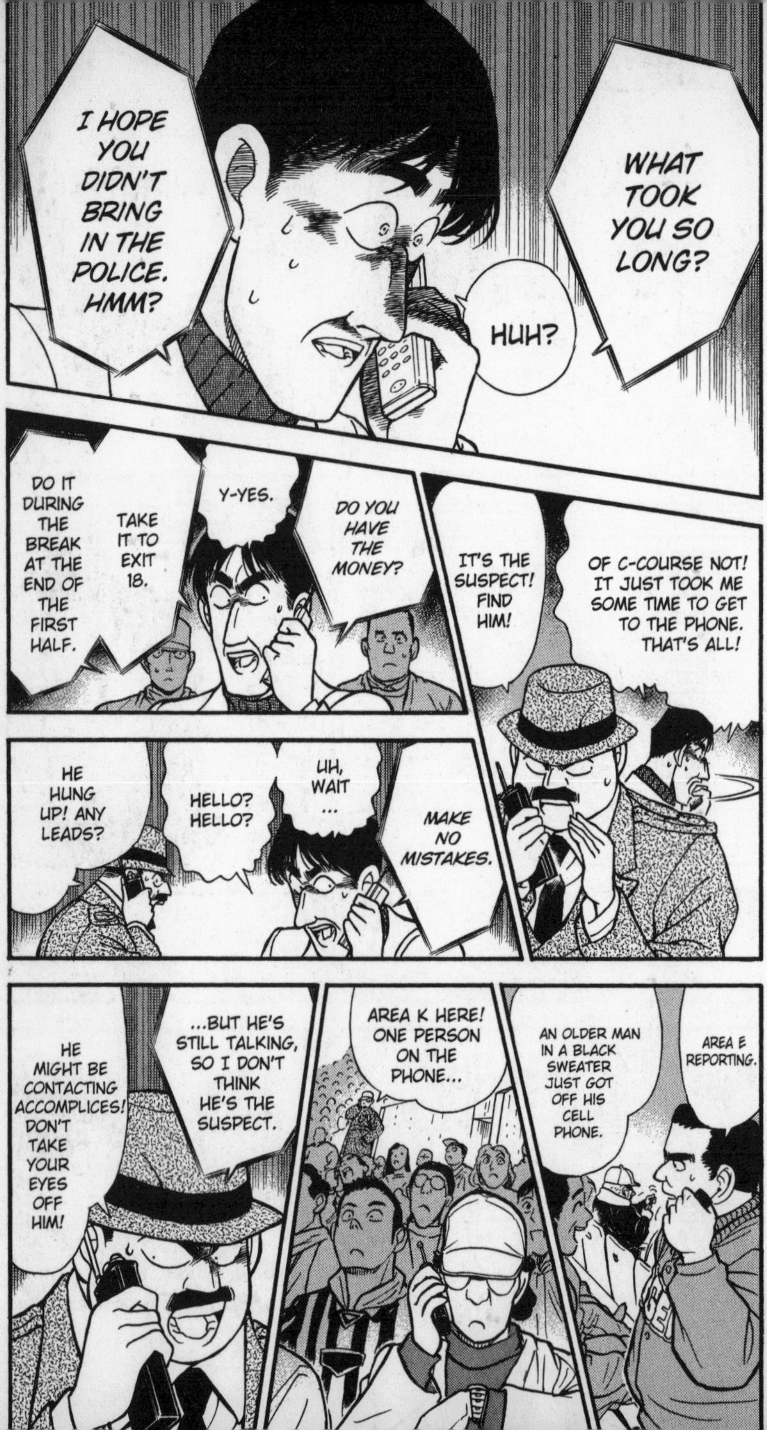
WHAT TOOK YOU SO LONG?
HUH?
I HOPE YOU DIDN'T BRING IN THE POLICE. HMM?
OF C-COURSE NOT! IT JUST TOOK ME SOME TIME TO GET TO THE PHONE. THAT'S ALL!
IT'S THE SUSPECT! FIND HIM!
DO YOU HAVE THE MONEY?
Y-YES.
TAKE IT TO EXIT 18.
DO IT DURING THE BREAK AT THE END OF THE FIRST HALF.
MAKE NO MISTAKES.
UH, WAIT ...
HELLO? HELLO?
HE HUNG UP! ANY LEADS?
AREA E REPORTING.
AN OLDER MAN IN A BLACK SWEATER JUST GOT OFF HIS CELL PHONE.
AREA K HERE! ONE PERSON ON THE PHONE...
...BUT HE'S STILL TALKING, SO I DON'T THINK HE'S THE SUSPECT.
HE MIGHT BE CONTACTING ACCOMPLICES! DON'T TAKE YOUR EYES OFF HIM!

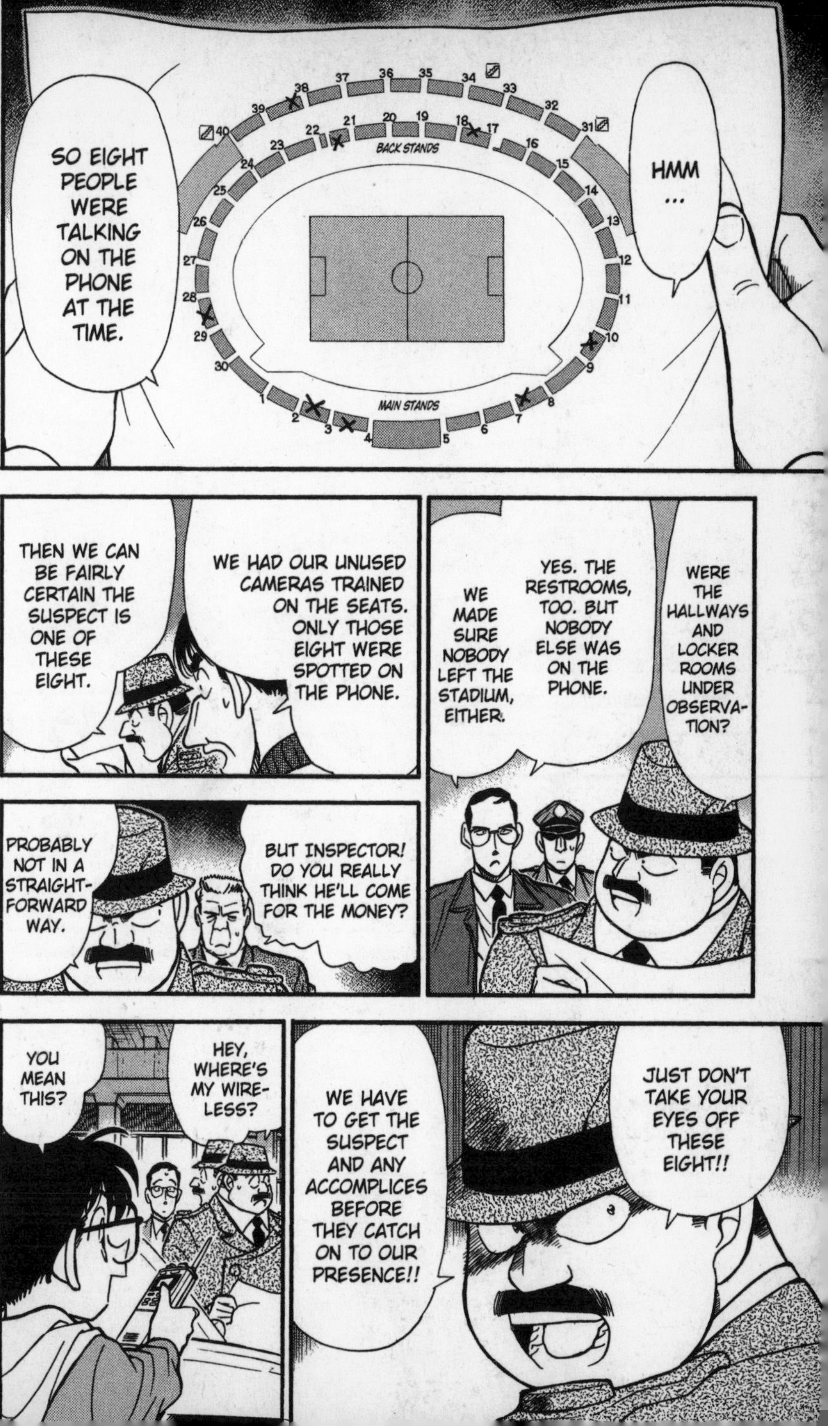
HMM ...
SO EIGHT PEOPLE WERE TALKING ON THE PHONE AT THE TIME.
BACK STANDS
MAIN STANDS
WERE THE HALLWAYS AND LOCKER ROOMS UNDER OBSERVATION?
YES. THE RESTROOMS, TOO. BUT NOBODY ELSE WAS ON THE PHONE.
WE MADE SURE NOBODY LEFT THE STADIUM, EITHER.
WE HAD OUR UNUSED CAMERAS TRAINED ON THE SEATS. ONLY THOSE EIGHT WERE SPOTTED ON THE PHONE.
THEN WE CAN BE FAIRLY CERTAIN THE SUSPECT IS ONE OF THESE EIGHT.
BUT INSPECTOR! DO YOU REALLY THINK HE'LL COME FOR THE MONEY?
PROBABLY NOT IN A STRAIGHT-FORWARD WAY.
JUST DON'T TAKE YOUR EYES OFF THESE EIGHT!!
WE HAVE TO GET THE SUSPECT AND ANY ACCOMPLICES BEFORE THEY CATCH ON TO OUR PRESENCE!!
HEY, WHERE'S MY WIRE-LESS?
YOU MEAN THIS?

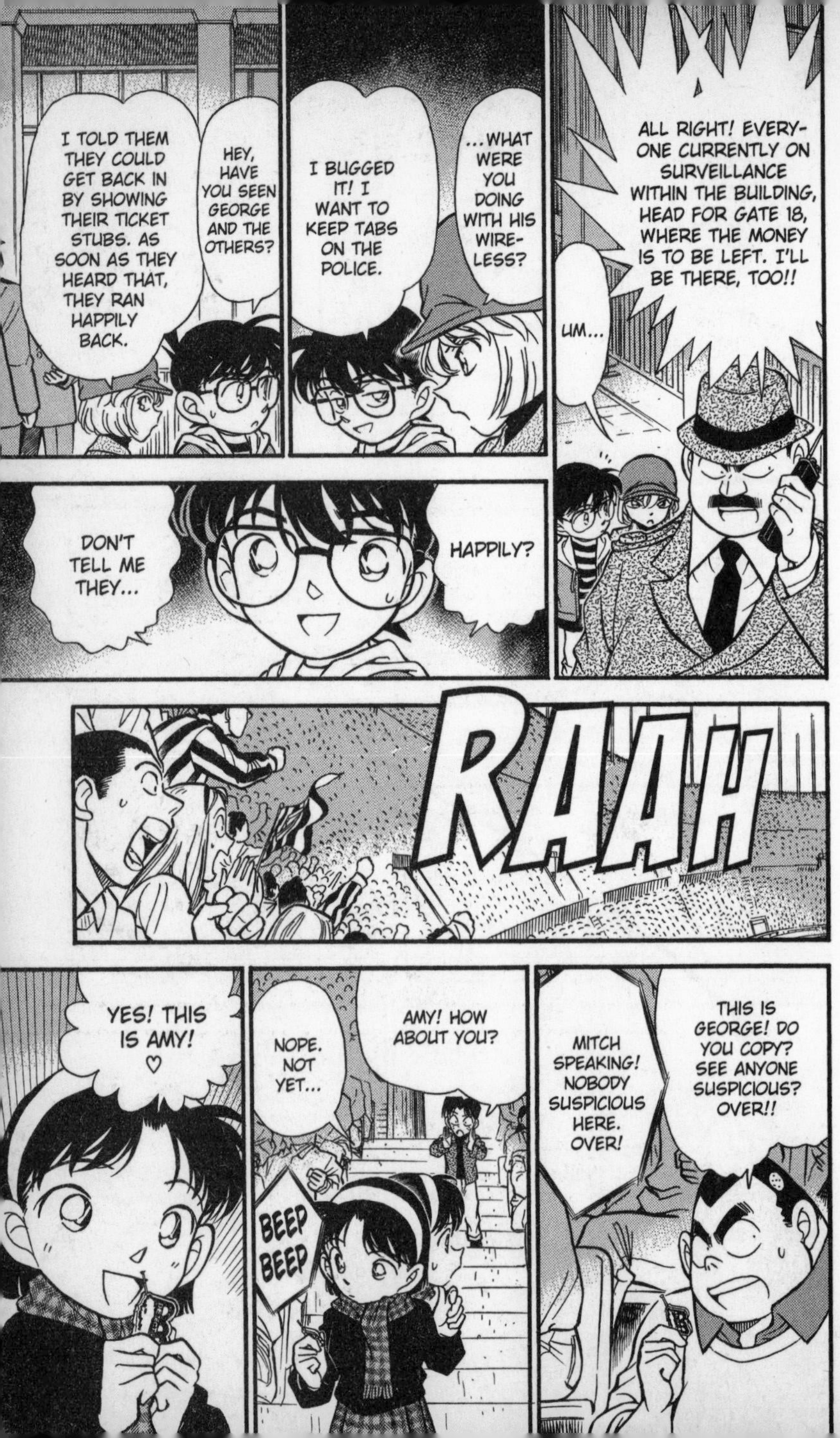
ALL RIGHT! EVERYONE CURRENTLY ON SURVEILLANCE WITHIN THE BUILDING, HEAD FOR GATE 18, WHERE THE MONEY IS TO BE LEFT. I'LL BE THERE, TOO!!
UM...
...WHAT WERE YOU DOING WITH HIS WIRELESS?
I BUGGED IT! I WANT TO KEEP TABS ON THE POLICE.
HEY, HAVE YOU SEEN GEORGE AND THE OTHERS?
I TOLD THEM THEY COULD GET BACK IN BY SHOWING THEIR TICKET STUBS. AS SOON AS THEY HEARD THAT, THEY RAN HAPPILY BACK.
HAPPILY?
DON'T TELL ME THEY...
RAAH
THIS IS GEORGE! DO YOU COPY? SEE ANYONE SUSPICIOUS? OVER!!
MITCH SPEAKING! NOBODY SUSPICIOUS HERE. OVER!
AMY! HOW ABOUT YOU?
NOPE. NOT YET...
BEEP BEEP
YES! THIS IS AMY! ♡

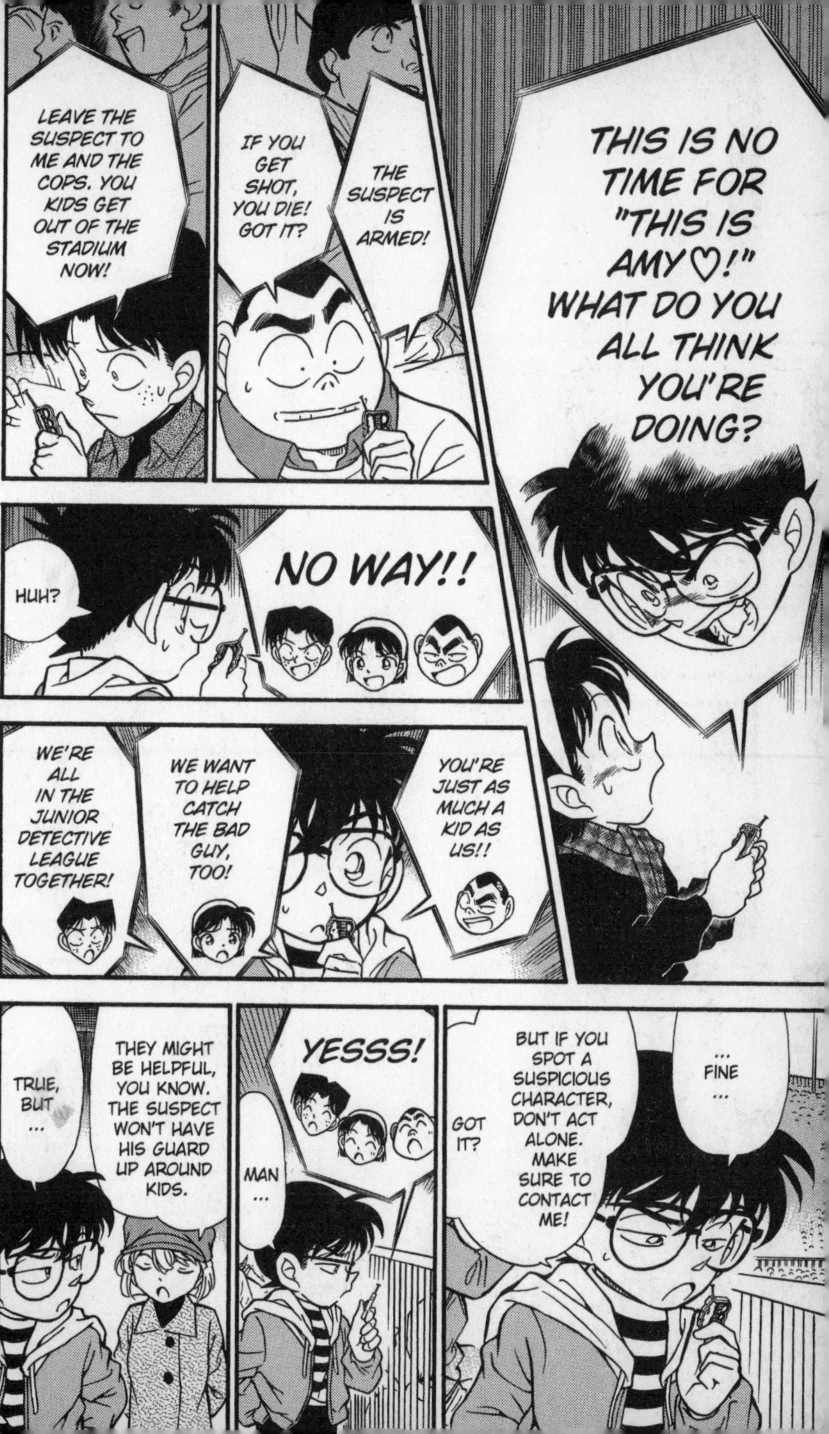
THIS IS NO TIME FOR "THIS IS AMY♡!" WHAT DO YOU ALL THINK YOU'RE DOING?
THE SUSPECT IS ARMED!
IF YOU GET SHOT, YOU DIE! GOT IT?
LEAVE THE SUSPECT TO ME AND THE COPS. YOU KIDS GET OUT OF THE STADIUM NOW!
NO WAY!!
HUH?
YOU'RE JUST AS MUCH A KID AS US!!
WE WANT TO HELP CATCH THE BAD GUY, TOO!
WE'RE ALL IN THE JUNIOR DETECTIVE LEAGUE TOGETHER!
... FINE ...
BUT IF YOU SPOT A SUSPICIOUS CHARACTER, DON'T ACT ALONE. MAKE SURE TO CONTACT ME!
GOT IT?
YESSS!
MAN ...
THEY MIGHT BE HELPFUL, YOU KNOW. THE SUSPECT WON'T HAVE HIS GUARD UP AROUND KIDS.
TRUE, BUT ...

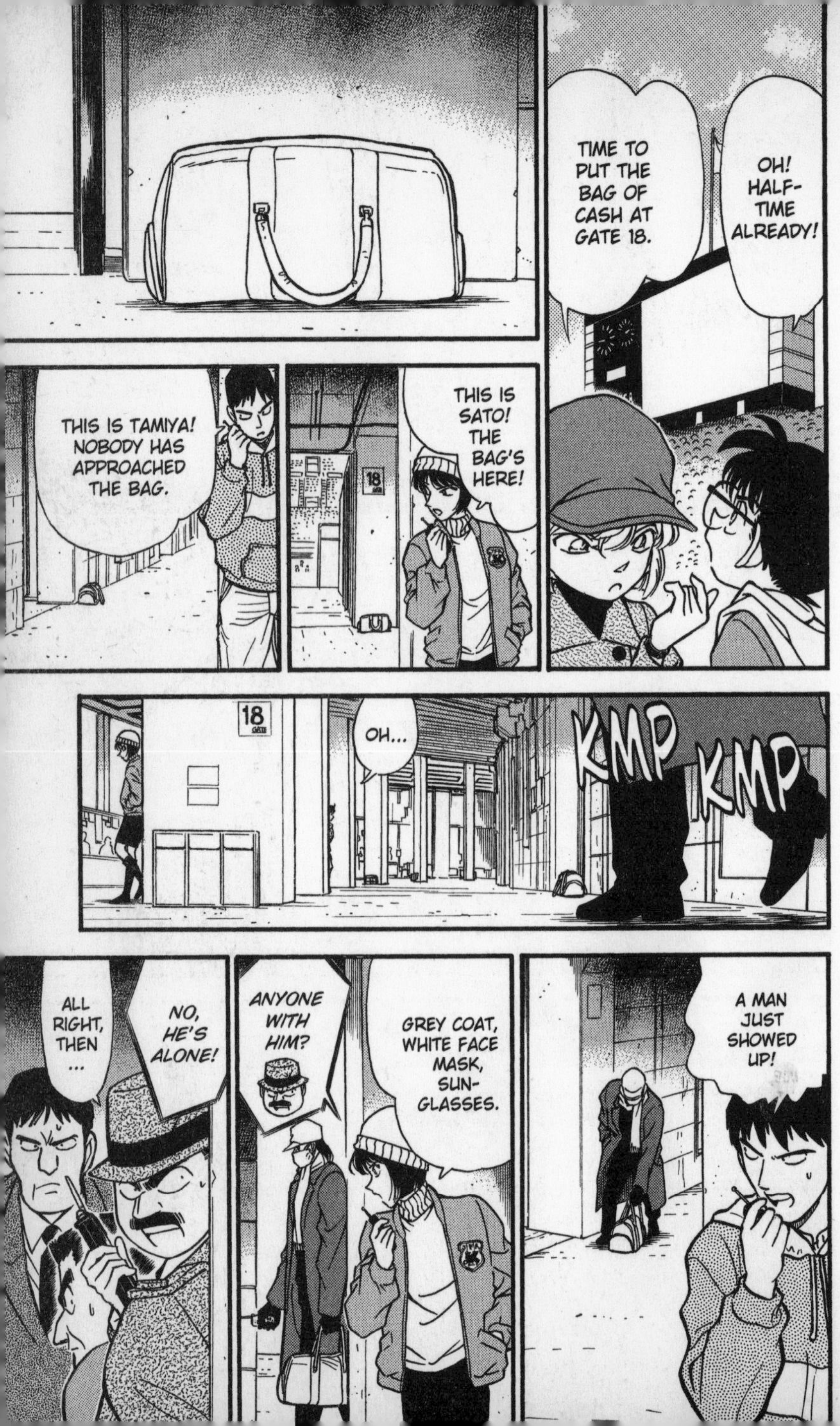
OH! HALF-TIME ALREADY!
TIME TO PUT THE BAG OF CASH AT GATE 18.
THIS IS SATO! THE BAG'S HERE!
18
THIS IS TAMIYA! NOBODY HAS APPROACHED THE BAG.
KMP KMP
OH...
18 GATE
A MAN JUST SHOWED UP!
GREY COAT, WHITE FACE MASK, SUN-GLASSES.
ANYONE WITH HIM?
NO, HE'S ALONE!
ALL RIGHT, THEN ...

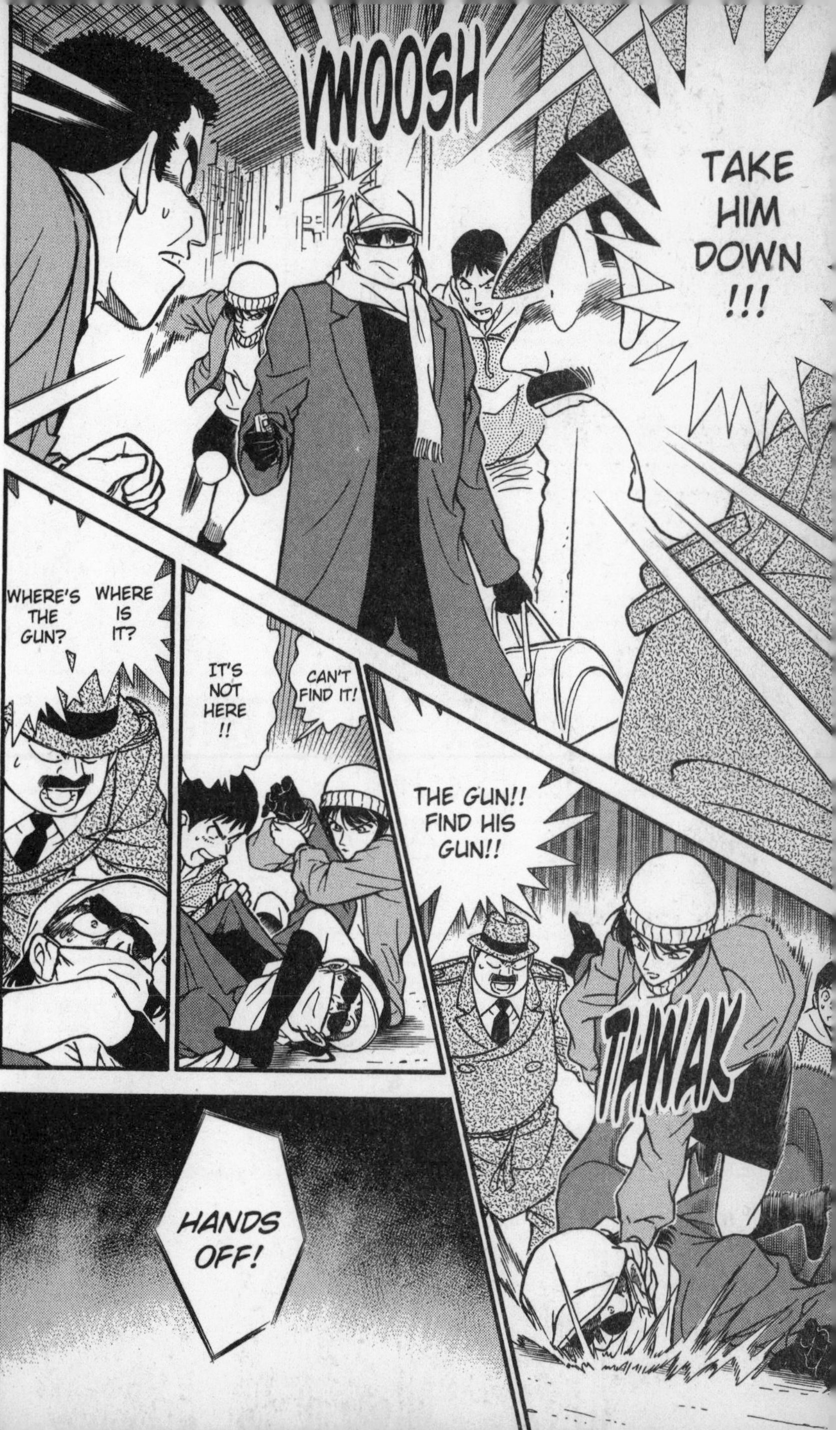
VWOOSH
TAKE HIM DOWN!!!
THE GUN!! FIND HIS GUN!!
THWAK
CAN'T FIND IT!
IT'S NOT HERE!!
WHERE IS IT?
WHERE'S THE GUN?
HANDS OFF!

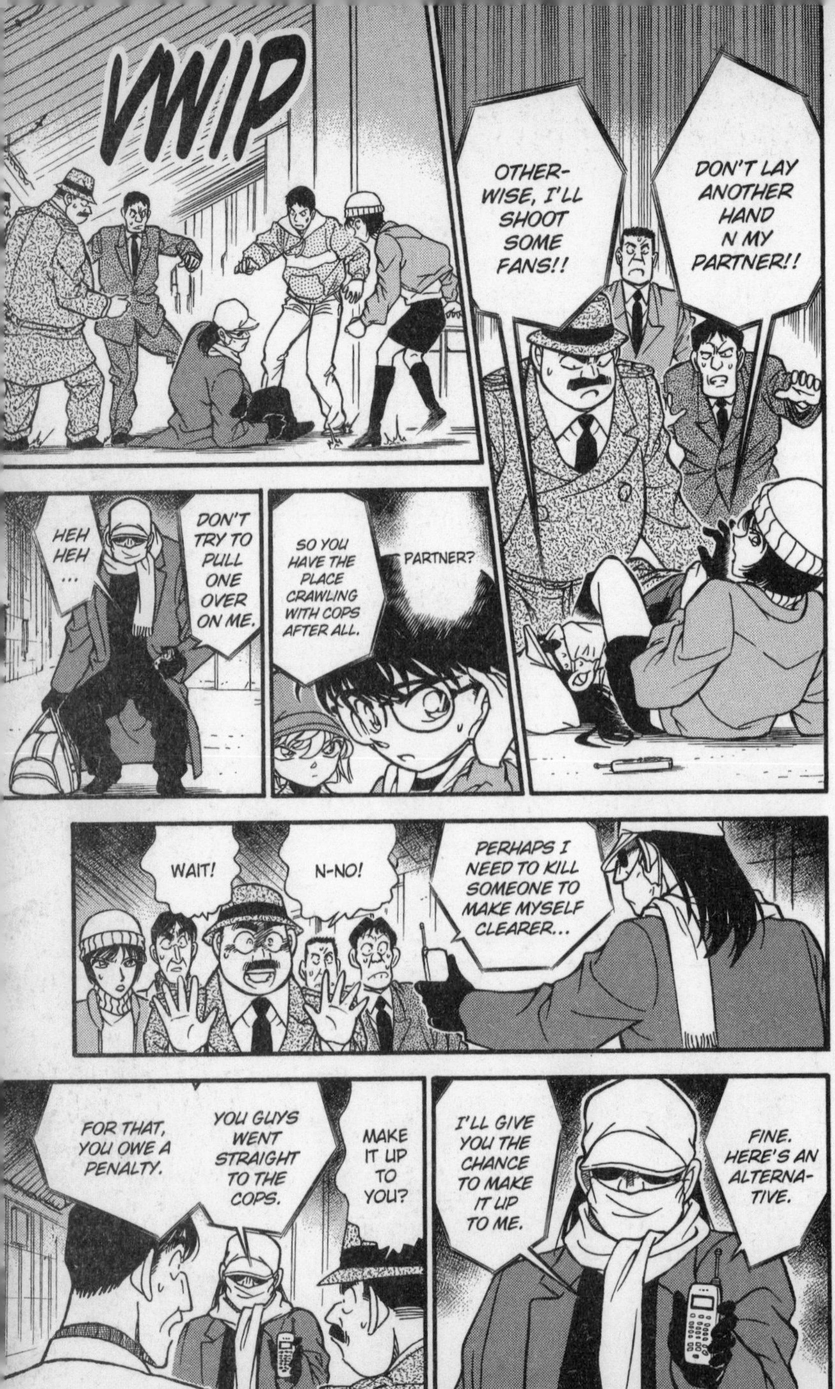
DON'T LAY ANOTHER HAND N MY PARTNER!!
OTHER-WISE, I'LL SHOOT SOME FANS!!
VWIP
PARTNER?
SO YOU HAVE THE PLACE CRAWLING WITH COPS AFTER ALL.
DON'T TRY TO PULL ONE OVER ON ME.
HEH HEH ...
PERHAPS I NEED TO KILL SOMEONE TO MAKE MYSELF CLEARER...
N-NO!
WAIT!
FINE. HERE'S AN ALTERNA-TIVE.
I'LL GIVE YOU THE CHANCE TO MAKE IT UP TO ME.
MAKE IT UP TO YOU?
YOU GUYS WENT STRAIGHT TO THE COPS.
FOR THAT, YOU OWE A PENALTY.

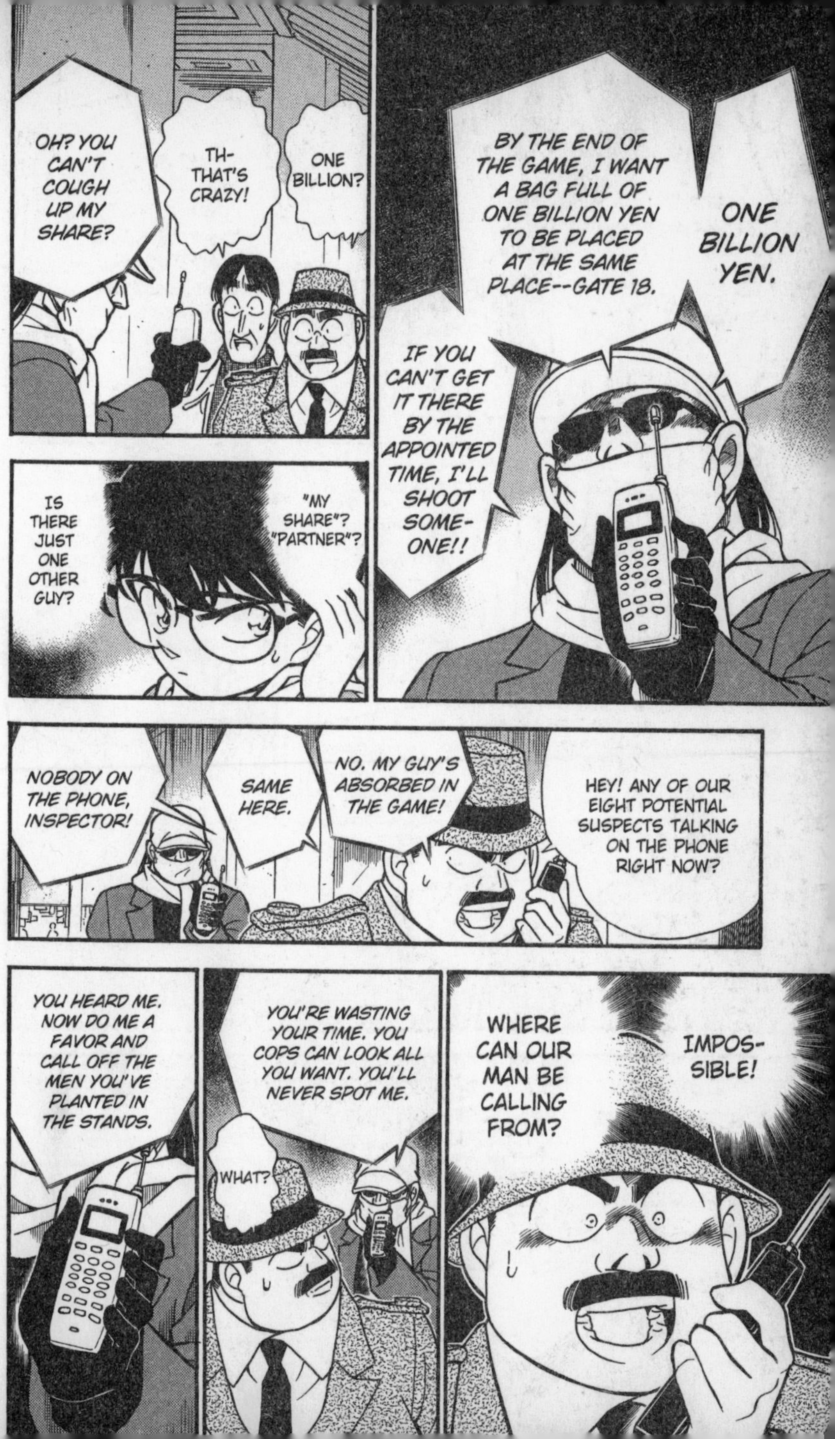
BY THE END OF THE GAME, I WANT A BAG FULL OF ONE BILLION YEN TO BE PLACED AT THE SAME PLACE--GATE 18.
ONE BILLION YEN.
IF YOU CAN'T GET IT THERE BY THE APPOINTED TIME, I'LL SHOOT SOME-ONE!!
ONE BILLION?
TH- THAT'S CRAZY!
OH? YOU CAN'T COUGH UP MY SHARE?
"MY SHARE"? "PARTNER"?
IS THERE JUST ONE OTHER GUY?
HEY! ANY OF OUR EIGHT POTENTIAL SUSPECTS TALKING ON THE PHONE RIGHT NOW?
NO. MY GUY'S ABSORBED IN THE GAME!
SAME HERE.
NOBODY ON THE PHONE, INSPECTOR!
IMPOS-SIBLE!
WHERE CAN OUR MAN BE CALLING FROM?
YOU'RE WASTING YOUR TIME. YOU COPS CAN LOOK ALL YOU WANT. YOU'LL NEVER SPOT ME.
WHAT?
YOU HEARD ME. NOW DO ME A FAVOR AND CALL OFF THE MEN YOU'VE PLANTED IN THE STANDS.

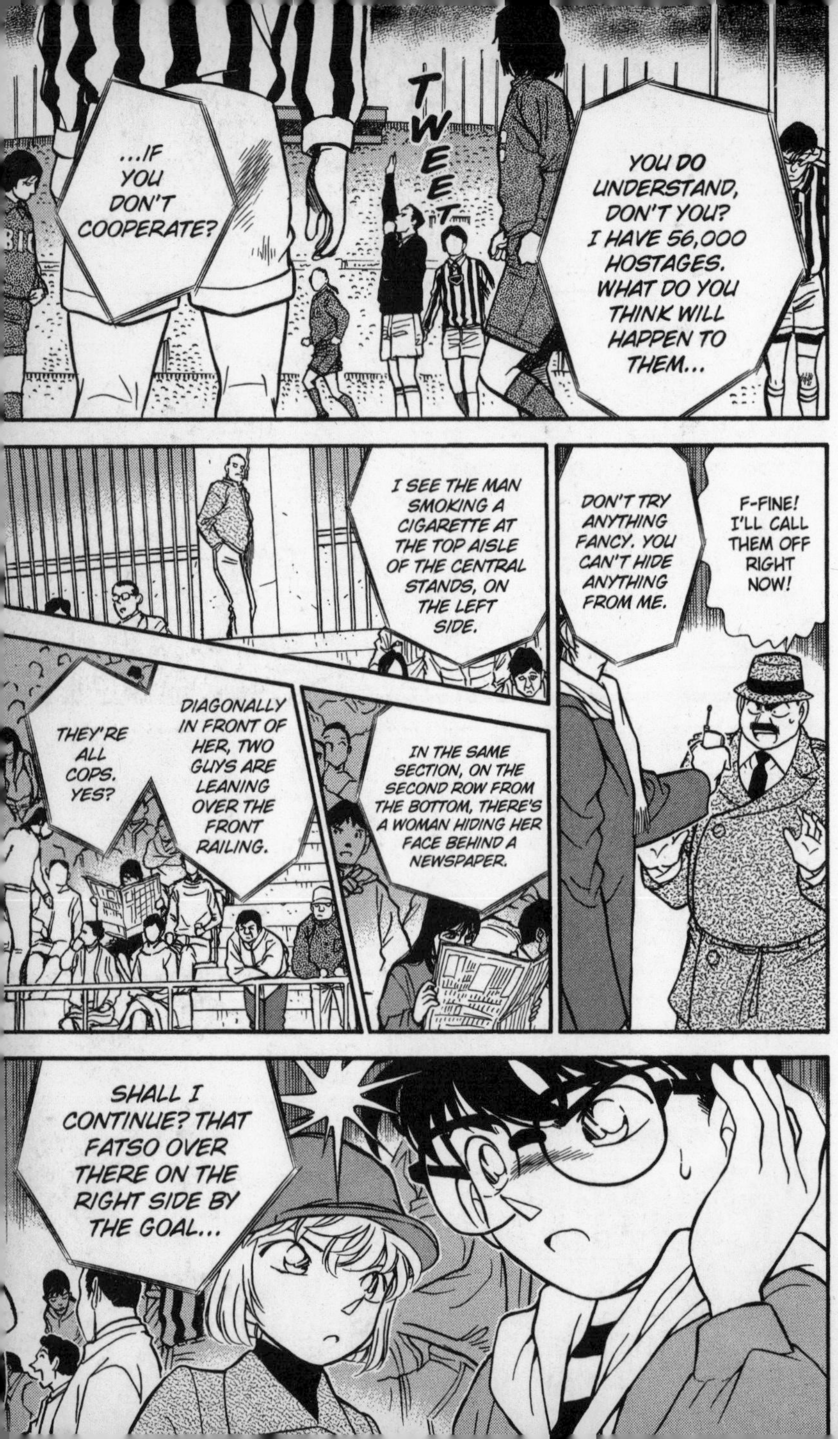

YOU DO UNDERSTAND, DON'T YOU? I HAVE 56,000 HOSTAGES. WHAT DO YOU THINK WILL HAPPEN TO THEM...
TWEET
...IF YOU DON'T COOPERATE?
F-FINE! I'LL CALL THEM OFF RIGHT NOW!
DON'T TRY ANYTHING FANCY. YOU CAN'T HIDE ANYTHING FROM ME.
I SEE THE MAN SMOKING A CIGARETTE AT THE TOP AISLE OF THE CENTRAL STANDS, ON THE LEFT SIDE.
IN THE SAME SECTION, ON THE SECOND ROW FROM THE BOTTOM, THERE'S A WOMAN HIDING HER FACE BEHIND A NEWSPAPER.
DIAGONALLY IN FRONT OF HER, TWO GUYS ARE LEANING OVER THE FRONT RAILING.
THEY'RE ALL COPS. YES?
SHALL I CONTINUE? THAT FATSO OVER THERE ON THE RIGHT SIDE BY THE GOAL...

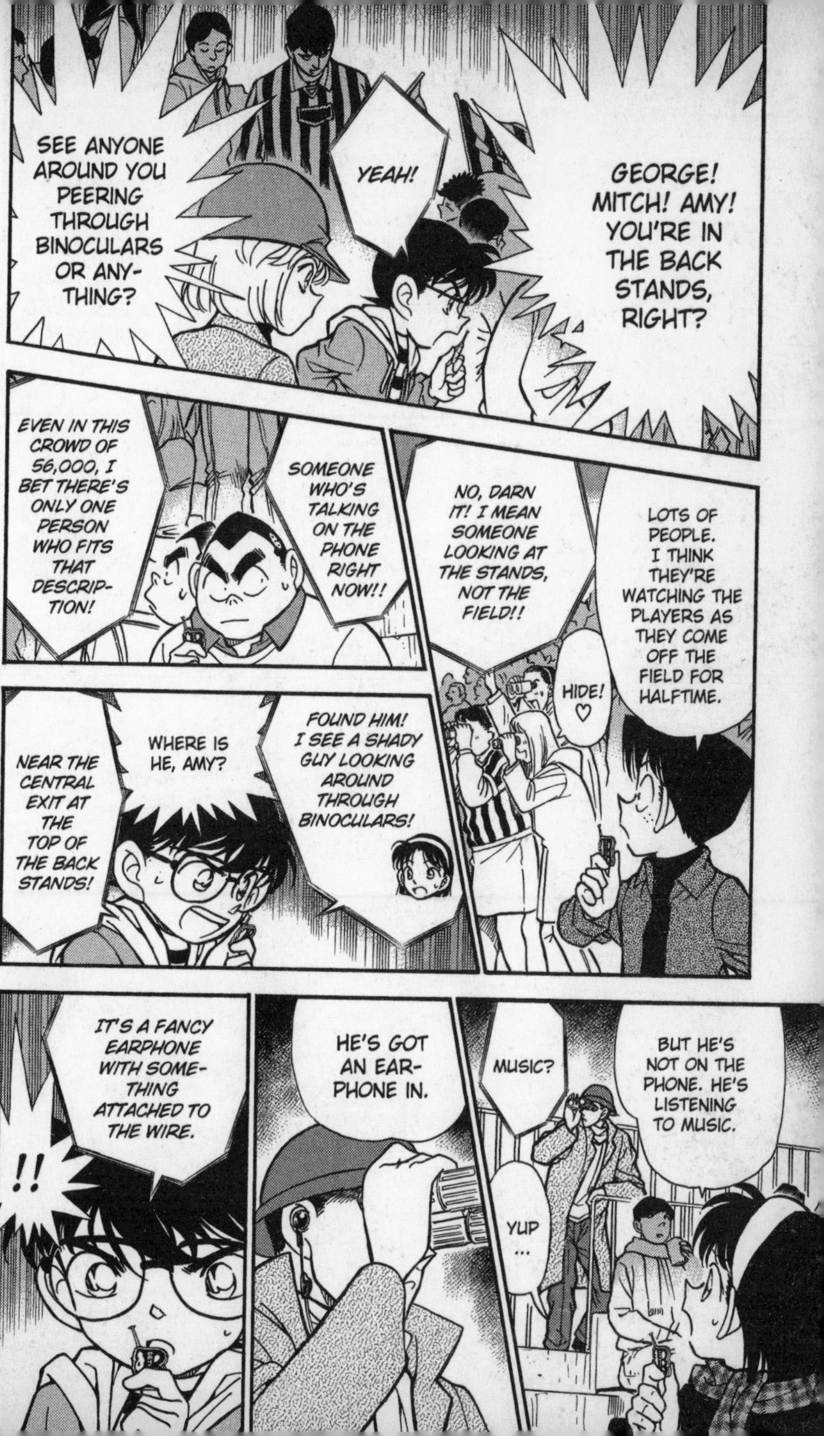
GEORGE! MITCH! AMY! YOU'RE IN THE BACK STANDS, RIGHT?
YEAH!
SEE ANYONE AROUND YOU PEERING THROUGH BINOCULARS OR ANY-THING?
LOTS OF PEOPLE. I THINK THEY'RE WATCHING THE PLAYERS AS THEY COME OFF THE FIELD FOR HALFTIME.
NO, DARN IT! I MEAN SOMEONE LOOKING AT THE STANDS, NOT THE FIELD!!
HIDE! ♡
SOMEONE WHO'S TALKING ON THE PHONE RIGHT NOW!!
EVEN IN THIS CROWD OF 56,000, I BET THERE'S ONLY ONE PERSON WHO FITS THAT DESCRIP-TION!
FOUND HIM! I SEE A SHADY GUY LOOKING AROUND THROUGH BINOCULARS!
WHERE IS HE, AMY?
NEAR THE CENTRAL EXIT AT THE TOP OF THE BACK STANDS!
BUT HE'S NOT ON THE PHONE. HE'S LISTENING TO MUSIC.
MUSIC?
YUP ...
HE'S GOT AN EAR-PHONE IN.
IT'S A FANCY EARPHONE WITH SOME-THING ATTACHED TO THE WIRE.
!!

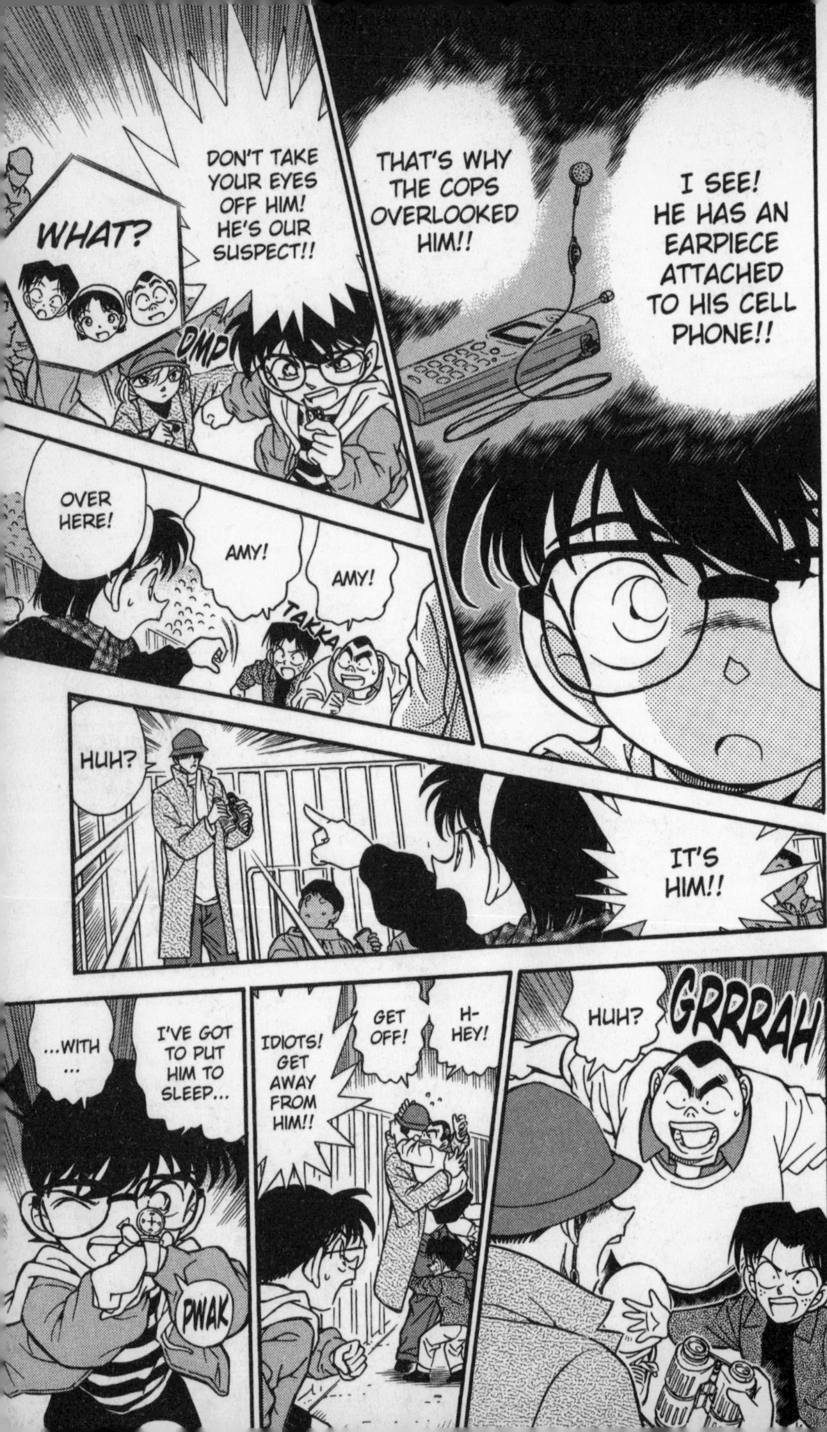
I SEE! HE HAS AN EARPIECE ATTACHED TO HIS CELL PHONE!!
THAT'S WHY THE COPS OVERLOOKED HIM!!
DON'T TAKE YOUR EYES OFF HIM! HE'S OUR SUSPECT!!
WHAT?
DMP
AMY!
AMY!
TAKKA
OVER HERE!
IT'S HIM!!
HUH?
GRRRAH
HUH?
H- HEY!
GET OFF!
IDIOTS! GET AWAY FROM HIM!!
I'VE GOT TO PUT HIM TO SLEEP...
...WITH ...
PWAK

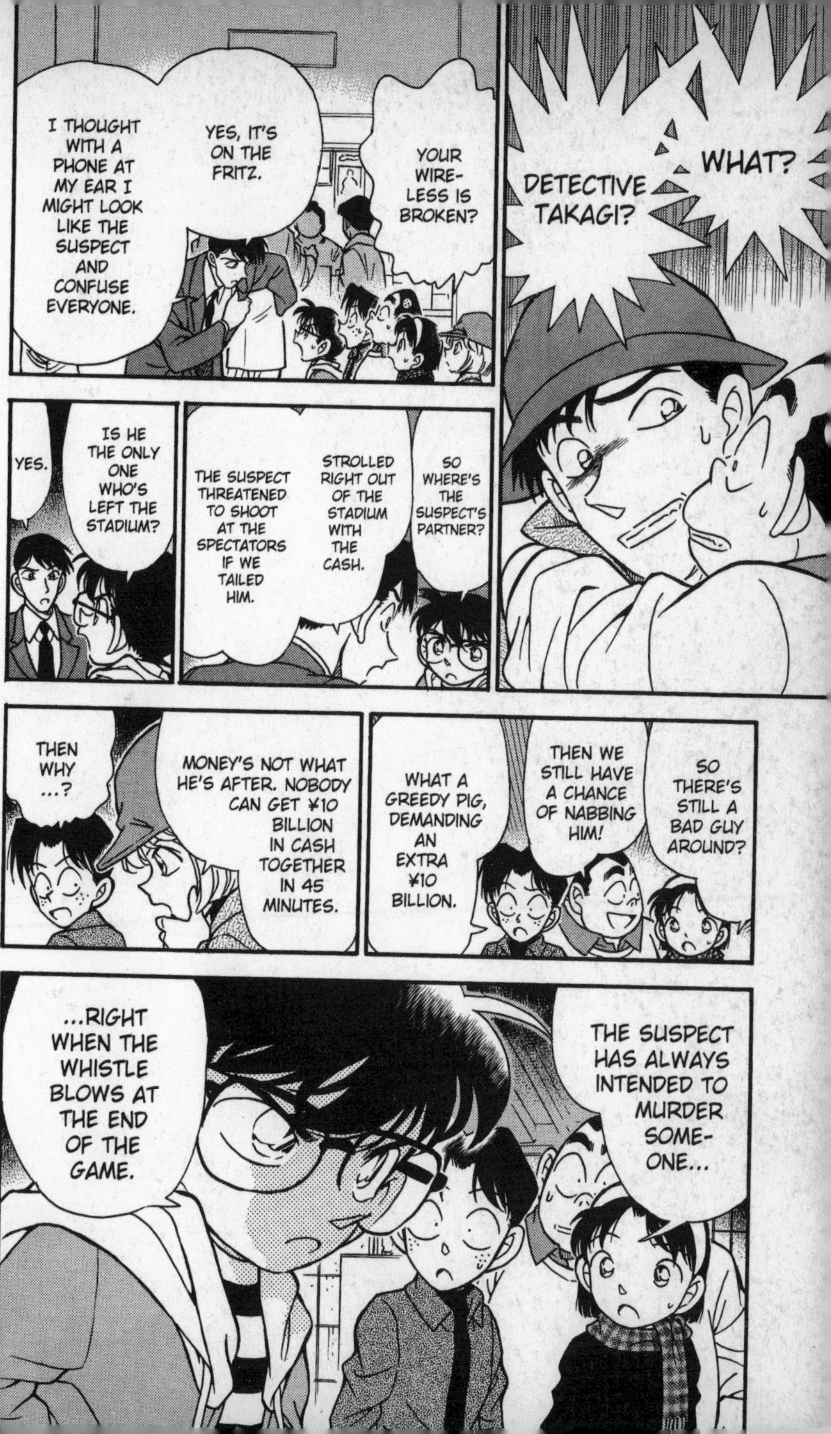
WHAT?
DETECTIVE TAKAGI?
YOUR WIRELESS IS BROKEN?
YES, IT'S ON THE FRITZ.
I THOUGHT WITH A PHONE AT MY EAR I MIGHT LOOK LIKE THE SUSPECT AND CONFUSE EVERYONE.
SO WHERE'S THE SUSPECT'S PARTNER?
STROLLED RIGHT OUT OF THE STADIUM WITH THE CASH.
THE SUSPECT THREATENED TO SHOOT AT THE SPECTATORS IF WE TAILED HIM.
IS HE THE ONLY ONE WHO'S LEFT THE STADIUM?
YES.
SO THERE'S STILL A BAD GUY AROUND?
THEN WE STILL HAVE A CHANCE OF NABBING HIM!
WHAT A GREEDY PIG, DEMANDING AN EXTRA ¥10 BILLION.
MONEY'S NOT WHAT HE'S AFTER. NOBODY CAN GET ¥10 BILLION IN CASH TOGETHER IN 45 MINUTES.
THEN WHY ...?
THE SUSPECT HAS ALWAYS INTENDED TO MURDER SOME-ONE...
...RIGHT WHEN THE WHISTLE BLOWS AT THE END OF THE GAME.

Hello, Aoyama here.

It's here! The eagerly (?) awaited Osaka volume! Conan and friends are eating their way across Osaka! Why couldn't I have gone there to do research? *(Sob.)*

Udon, takoyaki, okonomiyaki, blowfish hot pot...Pork buns from Horai, pork tonpeiyaki omelettes, curry from Jiyuken...And the omelette-rice at Meijiken...And the red bean soup at Meoto Zenzai...

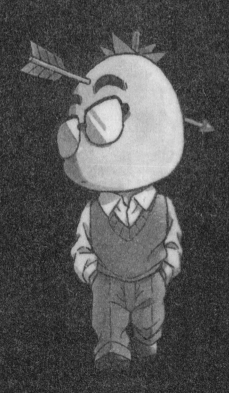

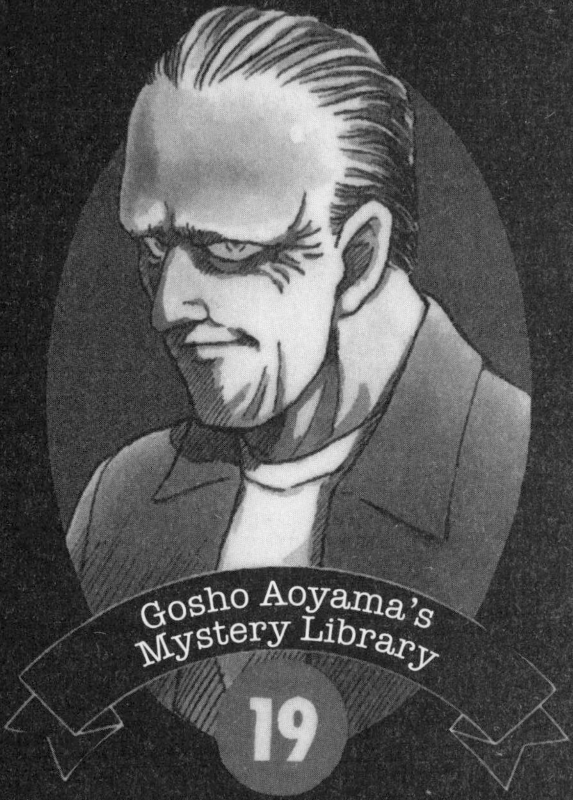
Gosho Aoyama's
Mystery Library
19

HANNIBAL LECTER

Not all great detectives are on the side of justice. Allow me to introduce Dr. Hannibal Lecter. He's a criminal genius, known in Japan as "Holmes in Prison," created by author Thomas Harris. He was originally a psychiatrist, but is now confined to a maximum-security facility for criminals. His attitude is always quiet and gentlemanly. He's knowledgeable in a wide variety of subjects and appreciates the arts. At first glance, he seems like a trustworthy character. In fact, he gives clues to fledgling FBI investigator Clarice Starling, helping her solve a big case. But don't be fooled. He's a psychopathic killer, nicknamed "Hannibal the Cannibal," who has murdered nine people! He can be your most dependable ally, but anyone wanting advice from him had better be prepared to pay a price. I recommend *Silence of the Lambs*.

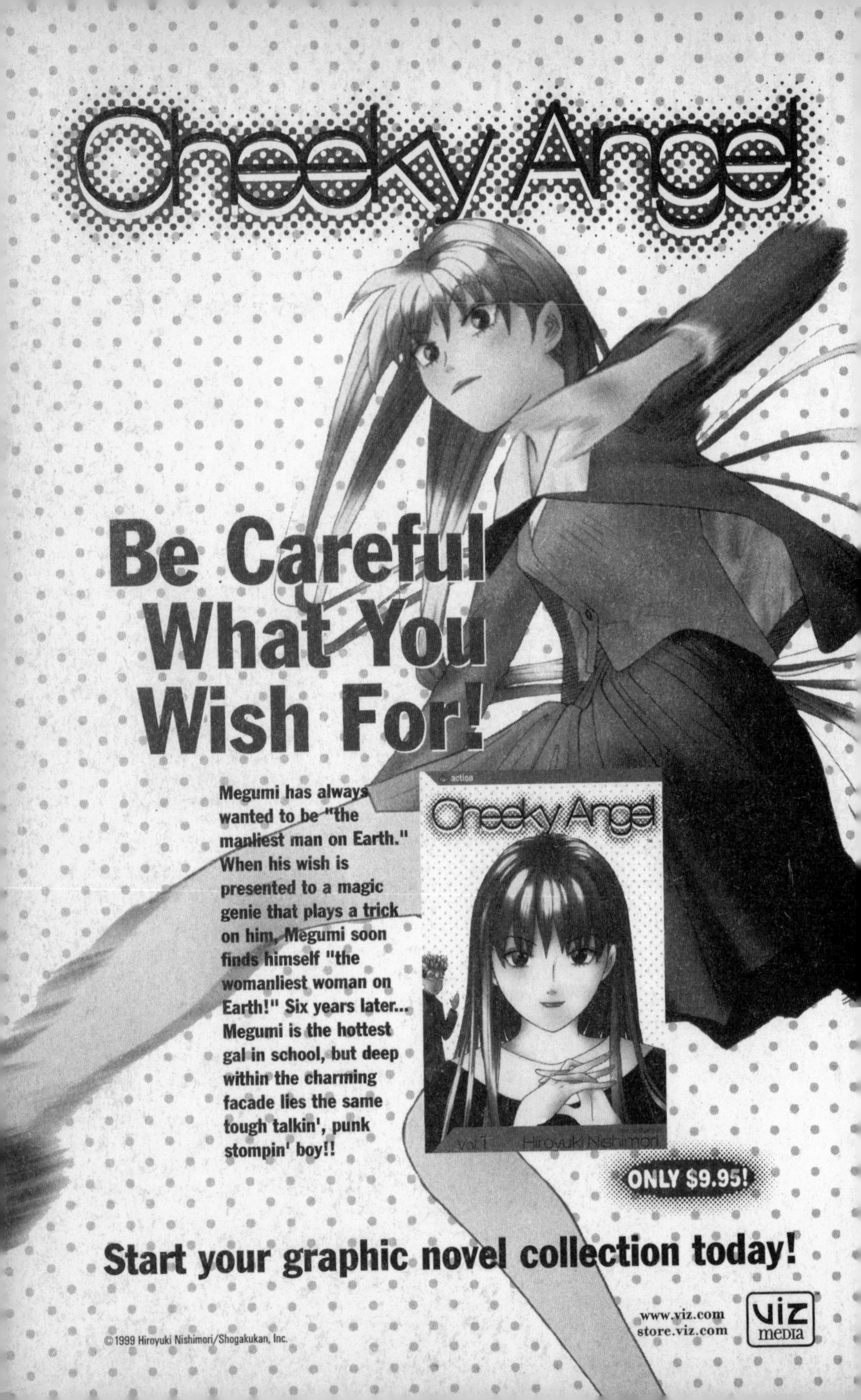
Cheeky Angel
Be Careful What You Wish For!
Megumi has always wanted to be "the manliest man on Earth." When his wish is presented to a magic genie that plays a trick on him, Megumi soon finds himself "the womanliest woman on Earth!" Six years later... Megumi is the hottest gal in school, but deep within the charming facade lies the same tough talkin', punk stompin' boy!!
action
Cheeky Angel
Vol.1
Hiroyuki Nishimori
ONLY $9.95!
Start your graphic novel collection today!
www.viz.com
store.viz.com
VIZ media
©1999 Hiroyuki Nishimori/Shogakukan, Inc.

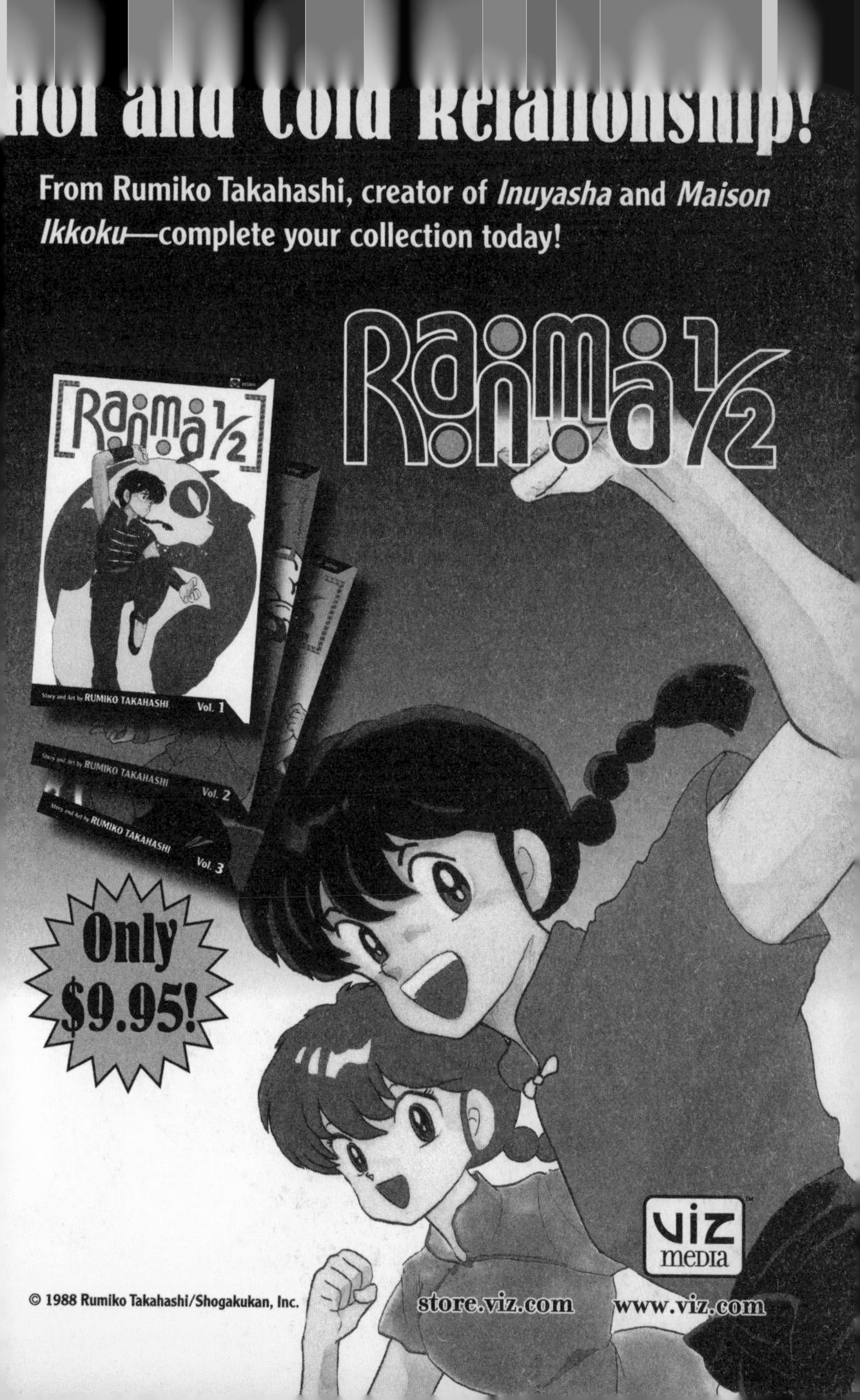
ot and Cold Relationship!
From Rumiko Takahashi, creator of *Inuyasha* and *Maison Ikkoku*—complete your collection today!
Ranma 1/2
Ranma 1/2
Story and Art by RUMIKO TAKAHASHI Vol. 1
Story and Art by RUMIKO TAKAHASHI Vol. 2
Story and Art by RUMIKO TAKAHASHI Vol. 3
Only $9.95!
VIZ MEDIA
© 1988 Rumiko Takahashi/Shogakukan, Inc.
store.viz.com
www.viz.com

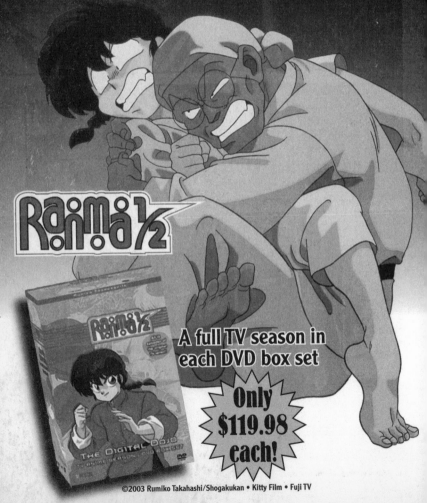

LOVE MANGA?
LET US

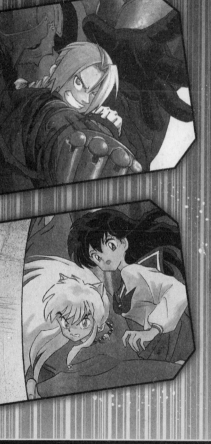

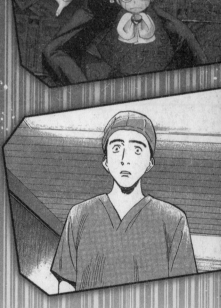

HELP US MAKE THE MANGA
YOU LOVE BETTER!

VIZ
media